STUDIES IN EARLY MODERN CULTURAL,
POLITICAL AND SOCIAL HISTORY

Volume 13

GOD, DUTY AND COMMUNITY IN ENGLISH ECONOMIC LIFE, 1660–1720

Studies in Early Modern Cultural, Political and Social History

ISSN: 1476–9107

Previously published titles in the series
are listed at the back of this volume

GOD, DUTY AND COMMUNITY IN ENGLISH ECONOMIC LIFE, 1660–1720

Brodie Waddell

THE BOYDELL PRESS

First published 2012
The Boydell Press, Woodbridge

ISBN 978–1–84383–779–4

The Boydell Press is an imprint of Boydell & Brewer Ltd
PO Box 9, Woodbridge, Suffolk IP12 3DF, UK
and of Boydell & Brewer Inc.
668 Mt Hope Avenue, Rochester, NY 14620–2731, USA
website: www.boydellandbrewer.com

A catalogue record for this book is available
from the British Library

The publisher has no responsibility for the continued existence or
accuracy of URLs for external or third-party internet websites referred
to in this book, and does not guarantee that any content on
such websites is, or will remain, accurate or appropriate.

Papers used by Boydell & Brewer Ltd are natural,
recyclable products made from wood grown in sustainable forests

Printed and bound in Great Britain by
CPI Group (UK) Ltd, Croydon, CR0 4YY

To Danielle and Ben

Contents

Illustrations

Acknowledgements

A brief note buried in the front matter of a lengthy academic tome is an extraordinarily insufficient response to years of help and support. I can only hope that the preachers of the seventeenth century were right, in which case those mentioned here will be providentially rewarded with 'blessings upon their Souls, Bodies, Estates, Names, [and] Posterity'. My greatest academic gratitude is due to Steve Hindle. Attempting to list his contributions would put me well over my word limit. Thanks also to Bernard Capp, Peter Marshall, Andrea McKenzie, Alexandra Walsham, Phil Withington and Andy Wood for their suggestions and guidance, as well as to my examiners – Mark Knights and Adam Fox – for their invaluably thorough appraisals. To Mark Hailwood, for both scholarly insights and alehouse sociability. To the other students and faculty at Warwick, for making those three years such a rewarding experience, and to my collegues at York and Cambridge for welcoming me into their worlds. To more than a dozen different conference audiences (and the bodies that funded my ability to be there), for helping me refine my arguments. To the University of Warwick, the late Rena Fenteman and her trustees, the Borthwick Institute for Archives, the University of York, the Leverhulme Trust, the Isaac Newton Trust, and the University of Cambridge for supplying financial and institutional support. To Malcolm Chase, for providing me with a digital copy of one of the volumes of the Bufton notebooks. To the staff of the archives and libraries for their patience and efficiency. Finally, I owe an immeasurable debt to my mother and father, who have helped and encouraged me throughout my academic adventurers. And to Danielle, for everything, including even an inexplicable willingness to move from the Canadian West Coast to the English West Midlands for the sake of my studies.

An early version of some material in Chapter 3 has been published in 'Neighbours and Strangers: The Locality in Later Stuart Economic Culture', in Fiona Williamson (ed.), *Locating Agency: Space, Power and Popular Politics, c. 1500–1900* (Cambridge: Cambridge Scholars Publishing, 2010), and is published with the permission of Cambridge Scholars Publishing. I am grateful to the publishers for permitting it to be republished here.

Conventions

When quoting primary sources, the original spelling and punctuation has been retained, with the following exceptions: common abbreviations have been silently expanded; proper names have been capitalized; and italicisation has been ignored when it is not used for emphasis. When quoting scripture, the Authorized Version of 1611 has been used for all scriptural quotations. Dates are given in the modern style, with the year commencing on 1 January rather than on 25 March. Shortened titles have been used for most printed primary sources as the full titles are often several lines long. Broadside ballads are cited principally by collection: their titles and approximate dates of publication are included in footnotes for ease of reference, but only the collections are listed in the bibliography. In the case of archival documents that have not been numbered at the item level (e.g. West Riding quarter sessions rolls after 1681), additional information has been included in parentheses after the reference.

Abbreviations

BIA	Borthwick Institute for Archives
BL	British Library
CA	Cambridgeshire Archives
Carlisle Muni. Recs	*Some Municipal Records of the City of Carlisle*, R. S. Ferguson and W. Nanson eds (Carlisle and London, 1887)
CHC	Coventry History Centre
CSPD	*Calendar of State Papers Domestic*
CSPV	*Calendar of State Papers, Venice*
CTB	*Calendar of Treasury Books*
CUA	Cambridge University Archives
DA	Doncaster Archives
DRO	Devon Record Office
EB	'The Euing Ballads', facsimile edition published online at <http://ebba.english.ucsb.edu/> (English Broadside Ballad Archive, University of California – Santa Barbara)
ERO	Essex Record Office
HA	Hertfordshire Archives
HMC	Historical Manuscripts Commission
Homilies	*Certain Sermons or Homilies, Appointed to be Read in Churches* (2 vols; London, 1673)
JHC	*Journals of the House of Commons*
JHL	*Journals of the House of Lords*
Leic. Boro. Recs	*Records of the Borough of Leicester*, M. Bateson et al. eds (7 vols, Leicester, 1899–1974)
LMA	London Metropolitan Archives
NLS	National Library of Scotland
Northam. Boro. Recs	*Records of the Borough of Northampton*, C. A. Markham and J. C. Cox eds (2 vols, Northampton, 1898)
Northants. RO	Northamptonshire Record Office
Nott.Boro. Recs	*Records of the Borough of Nottingham*, W. H. Stevenson et al. eds (9 vols, London, 1882–1951)
NRO	Norfolk Record Office
NYCRO	North Yorkshire County Record Office
ODNB	*Oxford Dictionary of National Biography* (online edition, last revised in 2004)

OED	*Oxford English Dictionary* (online edition, last revised in 2007)
PB	*The Pepys Ballads*, W. G. Gay, ed. (5 vols, Cambridge, 1987), facsimile edition published online at <http://ebba.english.ucsb.edu/> (English Broadside Ballad Archive, University of California – Santa Barbara)
RB	'The Roxburghe Ballads', facsimile edition published online at <http://ebba.english.ucsb.edu/> (English Broadside Ballad Archive, University of California – Santa Barbara)
RyB	'The Rosebery Ballads', facsimiles published online at <http://digital.nls.uk/broadsides/> (The Word on the Street, NLS)
St Albans Corp. Recs	*The Corporation Records of St Albans*, A. E. Gibbs ed. (St Albans, 1890)
SRO–BSE	Suffolk Record Office at Bury St Edmunds
SRO–I	Suffolk Record Office at Ipswich
Statutes of the Realm	*The Statutes of the Realm*, John Raithby et al. eds (9 vols, London, 1816–28)
Tilley, *Proverbs*	Morris Tilley, A *Dictionary of Proverbs in England in the Sixteenth and Seventeenth Centuries* (Ann Arbor, 1950)
TNA	The National Archives
VCH	*Victoria County History*
WB	'The Wood Ballads', facsimiles published online at <http://www.bodley.ox.ac.uk/ballads/> (Bodleian Library Broadside Ballads database, University of Oxford)
WYAS–W	West Yorkshire Archive Service at Wakefield
YCA	York City Archives
YMA	York Minster Archives

Introduction

> But must I needs want solidness, because
> By metaphors I speak?
>
> John Bunyan, The Pilgrim's Progress (1678)

The 'solidness' of what John Bunyan called 'types, shadows and metaphors' is too rarely contemplated by scholars attempting to understand the
history of economic life.[1] This is especially true of historians studying the
early modern period, a time when everyone, irrespective of status or locale,
was surrounded by moralised representations of work, markets, wealth, and
other worldly affairs. These images and ideas circulated in a variety of forms,
including daily conversation, written correspondence, cheap printed works,
religious instruction, state proclamation, or any number of equally widespread 'texts'.[2] But whatever their shape, they framed the way in which men
and women made sense of their world and thus structured much social interaction. So, if we hope to understand how most people, especially 'the poorer
sort', dealt with the hard material realities of the early modern economy, we
must explore the culture which gave these realities meaning. We need, in
other words, a history of the material impact of immaterial 'parables' and
'metaphors'.

Bunyan's best-selling allegorical narrative, *The Pilgrim's Progress*, provides
an apt starting point as it exemplifies the degree to which later Stuart culture
was suffused with direct and indirect commentary on social and economic
relations. The text, which ran through dozens of editions during this period,
was peopled with ungodly characters such as the hypocrite Talkative, who
gladly defrauded his neighbours but refused to help widows and orphans,
and Mr Money-love, who studiously practised 'the art of getting, either by
violence, cozenage, flattery, lying or putting on a guise of religion'.[3] However,
the pilgrim also encountered virtuous individuals such as Charity, a member
of the household of the Lord on the Hill, who welcomed poor travellers into

---

[1]   John Bunyan, *The Pilgrim's Progress*, Roger Sharrock, ed. (1678; Harmondsworth,
1965), p. 34.
[2]   Here and elsewhere, the term 'text' is intended to be taken in its widest possible
sense, meaning '(a unit of) connected discourse whose function is communicative and
which forms the object of analysis and description', therefore including spoken words
and ritualised actions as well as more conventional written works: *OED*, s.v. 'text'.
[3]   Bunyan, *Pilgrim's Progress*, pp. 114–15, 138.

the nobleman's stately mansion and feasted them with generous hospitality.[4] Bunyan's second parable, *Mr. Badman*, included still more discussion of the necessity of dealing justly with one's neighbours. In it, the titular anti-hero and other 'Vermin of the Common-wealth' were condemned for cheating customers with false weights and measures, hoarding corn to raise the price of the poor's provisions, taking usurious interest for pawned goods, and swindling lawful creditors through false declarations of bankruptcy.[5] Bunyan may not have been a typical early modern author – in fact, he was an itinerant dissenting preacher who spent over a decade in gaol. Yet, as will be seen, he was entirely conventional in seeing ethics and economics as irreversibly intertwined.

These moralised understandings of economic life are the focal point of this book. Or, to use E. P. Thompson's famous expression, this is a study of 'the moral economy' in later Stuart England.[6] Indeed, in spite of the many flaws in Thompson's concept, his formulation serves as a useful shorthand for the knot of issues that binds this project together: cultural norms, economic relations, social protest, and much else besides. Rather than trying to study each of these topics comprehensively, my aim is to trace the underlying relationships between them. This book is, in essence, an attempt to engage with the very idea of 'economic morality' by investigating its contours in a particular place and time. While there are obvious limitations inherent to such a project, I believe that the result both illuminates several facets of life in an important and relatively neglected period in English history and contributes something to the much more fundamental task of historicising the way we think about economic behaviour.

Problems and Possibilities

For those of us interested in the symbiotic relationship between material life and social morality, there exists an intimidating array of previous scholarship. The giants upon whose shoulders we stand – Marx, Weber, Tawney, Hill, Thompson – are some of the most colossal figures on the academic landscape. Moreover, recent generations of historians have refined and remoulded the narratives of their predecessors, expanding the parameters of the discussion with new evidence and new angles of analysis. This is

---

[4] Ibid., pp. 78–89. For further discussion of the moral implications of merchandise, trade, riches, and charity see ibid., pp. 125, 128–9, 144–6, 247–8, 318, 325–6, 344, 361–2.

[5] John Bunyan, *The Life and Death of Mr. Badman* (1680), pp. 164–232.

[6] E. P. Thompson, 'The Moral Economy of the English Crowd in the Eighteenth Century', *Past & Present*, 50 (1971), pp. 76–136, reprinted in his *Customs in Common: Studies in Traditional Popular Culture* (New York, 1993), ch. 4. All subsequent references to this essay will cite the latter.

the wellspring from which I draw my inspiration, and I rely heavily on the growing breadth of this research and the lively debates it engenders. However, as will be seen, I have also come to realise that the depth of its coverage is decidedly shallow in places.

Historians have, since Max Weber's analysis of the 'Protestant Ethic' if not before, added immeasurably to our understanding of the 'immaterial' aspects of economic life in early modern England.[7] Richard Tawney laid the foundation for much of what followed with his passionate account of the moral debates that accompanied agrarian change and commercial development in the sixteenth and early seventeenth centuries.[8] Then, in the postwar decades, Christopher Hill and E. P. Thompson offered their own magisterial contributions to this historiography, culminating in the latter formulating the idea of 'the moral economy'.[9] This approach, sometimes called 'culturalist', was both ambitious and extremely influential. More recently, historians of early modern England have produced a wealth of studies investigating the economic impact of specific ideals and beliefs.[10] We are now very aware, thanks to their efforts, of the importance of 'custom',[11] 'trust' and 'credit',[12] 'hospitality' and gift-giving,[13] local 'communities' and 'neighbourhoods',[14] 'improvement' and 'industriousness',[15] urban

---

[7]   Max Weber, *The Protestant Ethic and the "Spirit" of Capitalism, and Other Writings*, T. B. Bottomore and Maxilien Rubel eds (New York, 2002).

[8]   R. H. Tawney, *The Agrarian Problem in the Sixteenth Century* (London, 1912), esp. pp. 347–51; idem, *Religion and the Rise of Capitalism* (1926; London, 1948).

[9]   Christopher Hill, *Society and Puritanism in Pre-Revolutionary England* (London, 1964); idem, *The World Turned Upside Down: Radical Ideas During the English Revolution* (1972; London and New York, 1991); E. P. Thompson, *The Making of the English Working Class* (1963; London, 1991); idem, *Customs in Common*, ch. 4.

[10] The notes that follow cite only the most prominent and chronologically relevant examples from a vast and growing scholarship.

[11] Thompson, *Customs in Common*; Andy Wood, *The Politics of Social Conflict: The Peak Country, 1520–1770* (Cambridge, 1999); Jeanette Neeson, *Commoners: Common Right, Enclosure and Social Change in England, 1700–1820* (Cambridge, 1993).

[12] Craig Muldrew, *The Economy of Obligation: The Culture of Credit and Social Relation in Early Modern England* (Basingstoke, 1998).

[13] Felicity Heal, *Hospitality in Early Modern England* (Oxford, 1990); Ilana Krausman Ben-Amos, *The Culture of Giving: Informal Support and Gift-Exchange in Early Modern England* (Cambridge, 2008).

[14] Steve Hindle, *On the Parish? The Micro-Politics of Poor Relief in Rural England, c. 1550– 1750* (Oxford, 2004); Keith Snell, *Parish and Belonging: Community, Identity, and Welfare in England and Wales, 1700–1950* (Cambridge, 2006); Naomi Tadmor, *The Social Universe of the English Bible: Scripture, Society, and Culture in Early Modern England* (Cambridge, 2010), ch. 1; Keith Wrightson, 'The "Decline of Neighbourliness" Revisited', in Norman Jones and Daniel Woolf (eds), *Local Identities in Late Medieval and Early Modern England* (Basingstoke, 2007), pp. 19–49.

[15] Paul Slack, *From Reformation to Improvement: Public Welfare in Early Modern England: The Ford Lectures* (Oxford, 1999); Craig Muldrew, *Food, Energy and the Creation of*

'civic' identities,[16] and other powerful ideals. Although E. P. Thompson would almost certainly disapprove, all of these examples might be loosely grouped under the term 'moral economy'.[17]

There has also been a considerable amount of energy devoted to examining the supposed inverse of these ideals. This scholarship has roots in the 'culturalist' approach as well, but it has focused on 'the spirit of capitalism' rather than on 'the moral economy'. Weber, Tawney, Hill, and Thompson all discussed this 'ethic' at length, and it has featured regularly in scholarly work right to the present day. C. B. Macpherson offered an early elucidation of the intellectual development of 'possessive individualism', but it was only when Alan Macfarlane published his polemical essay on the long history of 'English individualism' in 1978 that this ideal came to be seen as a potentially popular early modern worldview.[18] Since then, scholarship on 'capitalist' attitudes during this period has become less explicit. Yet, much of the extensive research into 'the middling sorts' conducted over the past two decades has highlighted their apparent propensity to value profits and commercial gain.[19] Furthermore, the 'acquisitive' principles associated with profit-making may also have been linked to attitudes towards consumption. Although much of the vast literature on the (variously dated) 'consumer revolution' has consisted of 'the historical equivalent of window-shopping', this research has convincingly shown that the desire for non-essential commodities greatly influenced economic behaviour in the seventeenth and eighteenth centuries.[20] More importantly, the pursuit of 'fashion', 'taste',

---

Industriousness: Work and Material Culture in Agrarian England, 1550–1780 (Cambridge, 2011), ch. 7.

[16] Jonathan Barry, 'Bourgeois Collectivism? Urban Association and the Middling Sort', in Jonathan Barry and Christopher Brooks (eds), *The Middling Sort of People: Culture, Society and Politics in England, 1550–1800* (Basingstoke, 1994), pp. 84–112; Phil Withington, *The Politics of Commonwealth: Citizens and Freemen in Early Modern England* (Cambridge, 2005), ch. 6; Joseph Ward, *Metropolitan Communities: Trade Guilds, Identity and Change in Early Modern London* (Stanford, CA, 1997).

[17] For his insistence on a narrow definition of 'moral economy' see Thompson, *Customs in Common*, pp. 338–40.

[18] C. B. Macpherson, *The Political Theory of Possessive Individualism: Hobbes to Locke* (Oxford, 1962); Alan Macfarlane, *The Origins of English Individualism: The Family, Property and Social Transition* (Oxford, 1978).

[19] Keith Wrightson, *English Society, 1580–1680* (2nd edn; London, 2003), pp. 142–4, 234; Peter Earle, *The Making of the English Middle Class: Business, Society and Family Life in London, 1660–1730* (Berkeley, 1989), pp. 77–80, 130, 332; Margaret Hunt, *The Middling Sort: Commerce, Gender, and the Family in England, 1680–1780* (Berkeley, 1996), p. 182. For a caution against this tendency see Henry French, *The Middle Sort of People in Provincial England, 1600–1750* (Oxford, 2007), pp. 262–3.

[20] Lorna Weatherill, *Consumer Behaviour and Material Culture in Britain, 1660–1760* (2nd edn, London, 1996); Carole Shammas, *The Pre-Industrial Consumer in England and America* (Oxford, 1990); John Brewer and Roy Porter (eds), *Consumption and the World of Goods* (London, 1993); Maxine Berg, *Luxury and Pleasure in Eighteenth-Century*

and 'luxury' was enabled, at least in part, by the same proprietary notions of personal ownership that encouraged other 'capitalist' values.

So, the economic culture of early modern England has spawned an incredible range of research. But much of this scholarship suffers from noticeable deficiencies, some of them grave. On the most practical level, the later Stuart period constitutes an obvious gap in this historiography. Rather, scholarship on this period has been dominated by rather different concerns, with politics foremost amongst them. Historians have, in fact, produced a range of studies examining the Restoration regime, partisan struggles in Parliament, the rise of the 'fiscal–military state', 'politics out-of-doors', and the 'politics of the public sphere'.[21] In many cases, this work has directly or, more often, indirectly touched on issues that are central to this book, but it has remained primarily focused elsewhere.[22] Moreover, the relatively few examples of substantial research into later Stuart economic culture have included almost no discussion of the beliefs and behaviour of the humble majority – instead, their objects of study have been limited to the wealthy minority. Recent monographs by Natasha Glaisyer and Perry Gauci, for instance, have offered valuable insights into the minds of mercantile elites, but have almost nothing to say about those who spent their days labouring in fields and workshops.[23] Likewise, since J. G. A. Pocock's 1975 essay on 'Neo-Machiavellian Political Economy' and Joyce Appleby's 1978 study of

---

Britain (Oxford, 2005); Mark Overton, Jane Whittle, Darron Dean, and Andrew Hann, *Production and Consumption in English Households, 1600–1750* (London, 2004), esp. ch. 5; Linda Peck, *Consuming Splendor: Society and Culture in Seventeenth-Century England* (Cambridge, 2005). For a critique of the 'window-shopping' tendency in this historiography see Sara Pennell, 'Consumption and Consumerism in Early Modern England', *Historical Journal*, 42 (1999), pp. 549–64.

[21] Major recent examples include Tim Harris, *Restoration: Charles II and His Kingdoms, 1660–1685* (London and New York, 2005); idem, *Revolution: The Great Crisis of the British Monarchy, 1685–1720* (London and New York, 2006); Gary De Kray, *Restoration and Revolution in Britain: A Political History of the Era of Charles II and the Glorious Revolution* (Basingstoke, 2007); Mark Knights, *Representation and Misrepresentation in Later Stuart Britain: Partisanship and Political Culture* (Oxford, 2005); John Miller, *Cities Divided: Politics and Religion in English Provincial Towns, 1660–1722* (Oxford, 2007); Peter Lake and Steven Pincus (eds), *The Politics of the Public Sphere in Early Modern England* (Manchester, 2007), ch. 9–11; Steven Pincus, *1688: The First Modern Revolution* (Newhaven, 2009). For the classic studies of 'the fiscal-military state' and of 'politics out-of-doors' see John Brewer, *The Sinews of Power: War, Money and the English State, 1688–1783* (London, 1989); Tim Harris, *London Crowds in the Reign of Charles II: Propaganda and Politics from the Restoration until the Exclusion Crisis* (Cambridge, 1987).

[22] Especially relevant studies include Steven Pincus's work on 'Political Economy' such as Pincus, *1688*, ch. 12; idem, 'From Holy Cause to Economic Interest: The Study of Population and the Intervention of the State', in Alan Houston and Steven Pincus (eds), *A Nation Transformed: England after the Restoration* (Cambridge, 2001), pp. 272–98; and Tim Harris on 'The Economics of Crowd Politics', in *London Crowds*, ch. 8.

[23] Natasha Glaisyer, *The Culture of Commerce in England, 1660–1720* (Woodbridge,

Economic Thought and Ideology in Seventeenth-Century England, historians have produced a great deal of excellent work on this aspect of early modern intellectual history, much of which has concentrated on the later Stuart period.[24] Yet, here too 'the lower orders' are notably absent.

Instead, scholars interested in the 'moral economies' of less wealthy groups – and social historians more generally – have largely neglected the later Stuart era in favour of earlier or later periods. They have usually either avoided this era entirely or subsumed it within an analysis with a much longer chronology. For example, Keith Wrightson's most influential work focused on the late sixteenth and early seventeenth centuries, while Thompson's research concentrated on the Georgian period.[25] Moreover, many of their students and successors have done the same. This is especially true in the case of scholarship on social protest, but broader studies of economic culture and social relations often suffer from the same problem.[26] Obviously, those scholars who have adopted a long-term perspective have produced

2006); Perry Gauci, *The Politics of Trade: The Overseas Merchant in State and Society, 1660–1720* (Oxford, 2001).

[24] J. G. A. Pocock, *The Machiavellian Moment: Florentine Political Thought and the Atlantic Republican Tradition* (Princeton, 1975), ch. 3; Joyce Appleby, *Economic Thought and Ideology in Seventeenth-Century England* (Princeton, 1978). For more recent work see Pincus, 'From Holy Cause'; Andrea Finkelstein, *Harmony and the Balance: An Intellectual History of Seventeenth-Century English Economic Thought* (Ann Arbor, 2000). ch. 6–14; Paul Slack, 'The Politics of Consumption and England's Happiness in the Later Seventeenth Century', *English Historical Review*, 122:497 (2007), pp. 609–31; idem, 'Material Progress and the Challenge of Affluence in Seventeenth-Century England' Economic History Review, 62:3 (2009), pp. 576–603; Julian Hoppit, 'The Contexts and Contours of British Economic Literature, 1660–1760', *Historical Journal*, 49:1 (2006), pp. 79–110.

[25] Wrightson, *English Society*; Thompson, *Making of the English Working Class*; and, to a lesser extent, his *Customs in Common*, esp. ch. 4–6.

[26] The last scholar to undertake systematic primary research on the 'popular disturbances' of this period was Max Beloff in his *Public Order and Popular Disturbances, 1660–1714* (London, 1938). Surveys that have followed have continued to rely heavily on Beloff for these years: Andrew Charlesworth, *An Atlas of Rural Protest in Britain, 1548–1900* (London, 1983), ch. 2.11, 3.3; John Bohstedt, *The Politics of Provisions: Food Riots, Moral Economy, and Market Transition in England, c. 1550–1850* (Farnham, 2010), ch. 3. Several historians have discussed particular incidents, but even these accounts are few and far between. Examples include Harris, *London Crowds*, ch. 8; Malcolm Wanklyn, 'The Bridgnorth Food Riots of 1693/4', *Transactions of the Shropshire Archaeological and Historical Society*, 68 (1993), pp. 99–102; Molly McClain, 'The Wentwood Forest Riot: Property Rights and Political Culture in Restoration England', in Susan Amussen and Mark Kishlansky (eds), *Political Culture and Cultural Politics in Early Modern England* (Manchester, 1995), pp. 112–32; Kevin Burley, 'A Note on a Labour Dispute in Early Eighteenth-Century Colchester', *Bulletin of the Institute of Historical Research*, 29 (1956), pp. 220–30; R. M. Dunn, 'The London Weavers' Riot of 1675', *Guildhall Studies in London History*, 1:1 (1973), pp. 13–23.

studies that are more immediately useful.[27] Yet, on occasion, they too have neglected the unique attributes of later Stuart economic culture. Sometimes this is because they have offered a largely synchronic analysis of the early modern period as a whole; in other cases, they have merely emphasised the differences between, say, the sixteenth and eighteenth centuries, with little attention paid to more short-term phenomena. As a result of these various historiographical trends there exists a profound lacuna in our knowledge of English economic culture, a mostly uncharted territory stretching over half a century of historical terrain.[28] Moreover, the practical issues of periodisation are compounded by much deeper problems, both methodological and substantive.

The importance of changing ideas and social norms in the history of economic life is obvious, yet at least two streams of scholarship rely on analytical models that fail to fully account for this reality. These are the 'economistic' and 'instrumentalist' approaches – the first focused entirely on quantifiable facts and figures, the second acknowledging the role of the 'cultural' but demoting it to a mere adjunct of underlying economic structures. However, one must begin with a rudimentary survey of the point of origin of these two streams. This can be found in the writings of nineteenth-century theorists and social scientists, whose emphasis on materiality continues to shape perceptions of economic history. One of these deterministic models, inspired by Adam Smith's discussion of 'self-love', was proposed by J. S. Mill in 1836 when he suggested that a student of 'political economy' should employ

> an arbitrary definition of man, as a being who inevitably does that by which he may obtain the greatest amount of necessaries, conveniences, and luxuries, with the smallest quantity of labour and physical self-denial with which they can be obtained.[29]

---

[27] Keith Wrightson and David Levine, *Poverty and Piety in an English Village: Terling, 1525–1700* (2nd edn, Oxford, 1995); David Levine and Keith Wrightson, *The Making of an Industrial Society: Whickham, 1560–1765* (Oxford, 1991); Keith Wrightson, *Earthly Necessities: Economic Lives in Early Modern Britain, 1470–1750* (London, 2002); Muldrew, *Economy of Obligation*; Ben-Amos, *Culture of Giving*; Wood, *Politics of Social Conflict*; Hindle, *On the Parish*; Paul Slack, *Poverty and Policy in Tudor and Stuart England* (London, 1988); idem, *From Reformation*.

[28] Wrightson noted this chronological gap in his critique of 'The Enclosure of English Social History', in Adrian Wilson (ed.), *Rethinking Social History: English Society, 1570–1920 and Its Interpretation* (Manchester, 1993), p. 62.

[29] Adam Smith, *An Inquiry into the Nature and Causes of the Wealth of Nations* (London, 1776), bk. I, ch. 2; J. S. Mill, *Essays on Some Unsettled Questions of Political Economy* (London, 1844), p. 144. For discussions of the usefulness (and limits) of this model see Joseph Persky, 'Retrospectives: The Ethology of *Homo Economicus*', *Journal of Economic Perspectives*, 9:2 (1995), pp. 221–31. For the genealogy of 'economic man', including both Mill's predecessors (especially Adam Smith) and his successors, see Mary S. Morgan,

This became a foundational premise in neoclassical economics, a discipline that has proved to be highly influential. Indeed, Mill's self-consciously 'arbitrary' methodology became, through a process of vulgarisation, a supposedly accurate description of reality. Social relations were, according to this simplistic version of the neoclassical model, conducted exclusively by rational agents pursuing their own material 'interests', concerned not with 'morality' but with 'utility'. Paradoxically, a similar premise has been shared by many scholars who regarded themselves as opponents of neoclassical theory. After all, the most naïve variants of Marx's 'materialist conception of history' simply replaced the struggle between self-interested individuals with the struggle between self-interested classes:

> The history of all hitherto existing society is the history of class struggles. Freeman and slave, patrician and plebeian, lord and serf, guild-master and journeyman, in a word, oppressor and oppressed, stood in constant opposition to one another, carried on an uninterrupted, now hidden, now open fight.[30]

Transformed from a snippet in a partisan tract into a principle of academic analysis, this formulation popularised the notion that 'class interest' could provide a universal explanation for social behaviour. As a result, numerous scholars – both on the 'left' and on the 'right' – have shared a belief in the omnipresence of *homo economicus vulgaris*, though for some he is an individual while for others he is a collective.[31]

This widely held supposition has manifested itself in many different accounts of English economic life in the seventeenth and eighteenth centuries. The most explicitly materialist methodology can be found in 'economistic' histories, which have tended to neglect the influence of social and cultural norms altogether. Max Beloff, for example, in his survey of 'popular disturbances' in later Stuart England, often used crudely mechanistic explanations when describing the motives and behaviour of food rioters.[32] Amazingly, despite the fact that the book became the object of E. P. Thompson's very first attack on the 'spasmodic view' of social protest, this exemplar of 'crass economic reductionism' remains the most substantive work on this topic for the later Stuart period.[33] Such overtly materialist depictions of food riots became rare in the wake of Thompson's assault. Nonetheless, as

'Economic Man as Model Man: Ideal Types, Idealization and Caricatures', *Journal of the History of Economic Thought*, 28:1 (2006), pp. 1–27; Albert O. Hirschman, *The Passions and the Interests: Political Arguments for Capitalism Before Its Triumph* (Princeton, 1977).
[30] Karl Marx and Fredrick Engels, *The Communist Manifesto* (Harmondsworth, 1967), p. 79.
[31] It must be emphasised that this is not intended as a critique of Mill and Marx. Rather, these assumptions are bastardised forms of sophisticated and often insightful theories.
[32] Beloff, *Public Order*, ch. 3, esp. p. 75.
[33] Thompson, *Customs in Common*, pp. 185–7.

will be seen, the problematic legacy of this reductionism has continued to influence even the most sophisticated research into economic relations.

Moreover, much of the subsequent work on late seventeenth- and early eighteenth-century economic issues has been quantitative. For example, systematic excavation of population figures, wage rates, agricultural prices, and consumption patterns have revealed the long-term trends in vitally important metrics.[34] By collecting long series of data and representing them in wonderfully unambiguous graphs, this scholarship appears to provide sturdy explanatory tools for historians seeking to understand past economic relations. Yet, although this methodology has provided invaluable context for other types of research, the relative absence of attempts to explore the 'immaterial' aspects of later Stuart economic life has meant that statistical data has sometimes weighed too heavily on the historiography. Indeed, it has sometimes been seen as a skeleton key, capable of unlocking any interpretive problem. As this book shows, such 'economistic' approaches profoundly underestimate the impact of cultural factors. Hence, it is misguided to try to explain the behaviour of men and women simply through references to, for example, gradual improvements in real wages and expansions in the availability of parish relief. Neither workers nor paupers were merely utility-maximising automatons.

A more subtle form of economic reductionism has inflected many of the discussions of the interaction between 'the rich' and 'the poor' that have appeared since Thompson's powerful intervention in 1971. Here, too, material 'interest' has occasionally been regarded as the sole motivating factor, which has led to 'instrumentalist' interpretations of social relations wherein morality apparently plays no part. Thompson himself contributed to this tendency through his influential remarks about patrician 'theatre' and plebeian 'countertheatre', for he claimed that 'just as the rulers asserted their hegemony by a studied theatrical style, so the plebs asserted their presence by a theatre of threat and sedition'.[35] The gentry, according to Thompson, disingenuously projected 'the illusion of paternalism' and the poor responded with 'simulated deference' or 'symbolic' protest.[36] In the

---

[34] Prominent examples include E. A. Wrigley and R. S. Schofield, *The Population History of England, 1541–1871* (2nd edn, Cambridge, 1989); P. J. Bowden, 'Agricultural Prices, Wages, Farm Profits, and Rents', in Joan Thirsk (ed.), *The Agrarian History of England and Wales, Vol. V: 1640–1750* (2 parts, Cambridge, 1985), pt. 2, pp. 1–118; Shammas, *Pre-Industrial Consumer*; Overton et al., *Production and Consumption*.

[35] Thompson, *Customs in Common*, p. 67.

[36] Ibid., pp. 46, 66, 78. Thompson was far from consistent on this. For instance, elsewhere he acknowledged the existence of 'genuine' paternalism (p. 83 n. 1) and in his 'moral economy' essays he emphasised the moral convictions of the crowd (ch. 4–5), but his work on 'patricians and plebs' mostly stressed that both sides were performing 'theatre', 'often without the least illusion' (p. 85), and even his argument for a 'moral economy' included repeated assertions that riots were 'usually a rational response' (p. 265) to material deprivation. For another example of this approach emphasising the

early modern period, it seems, people were apparently far too clever to believe their own rhetoric. Thompson's interpretation has received explicit theoretical support from the anthropologist James C. Scott. In Scott's model, 'rulers' and 'subalterns' wore 'masks' behind which they hid 'their real intentions', publicly genuflecting to 'the hegemony of dominant values' while privately acting according to their 'class position'.[37] The morality of the established order was apparently little more than a veil that each side cynically used as a cover for their own interests.

The influence of these instrumentalist perspectives can be seen in some of the research on social protest that has published in the wake of Thompson and Scott. John Bohstedt, for example, has argued that 'food riots were measures of emergency collective self-defence rather than eruptions of an alternative moral-economic order' – the actions and rhetoric of the crowd were simply 'a collection of pragmatic tactics' used to counter the immediate threat of starvation.[38] Drawing directly on Scott's concept of 'public transcripts', John Walter has offered a similar account of economic relations. At one pole, 'the elites' sought 'to secure ideological hegemony and hence legitimation' for their material power; at the other pole, 'the people' sought to win 'the struggle over subsistence' by 'manipulating the public transcript'. Thus, according to Walter, the 'moralization of economic relationships' was 'a resource to be drawn upon' by both the strong and the weak, a 'rhetorical strategy' employed to defend each group's inter-

---

poor's 'conscious exploitation' of official rhetoric and policy see John Walter and Keith Wrightson, 'Dearth and the Social Order in Early Modern England', *Past & Present*, 71 (1976), pp. 32–4.

[37] Throughout this analysis he routinely uses a terminology which splits 'real' interests from calculated 'public' assertions (e.g. 'acting', 'euphemize', 'dissimulation', 'manipulation', 'facade', etc.): James C. Scott, *Domination and the Arts of Resistance: Hidden Transcripts* (New Haven, 1990), pp. 4, 8, and passim. He earlier devoted considerable attention to 'ideology' as a 'rationalizing' tool, specifically arguing that economic inequality led the rich and the poor to offer 'two social constructions of the facts, each designed and employed to promote the interests of a different class'; idem, *Weapons of the Weak: Everyday Forms of Peasant Resistance* (New Haven, 1985), ch. 6 (quote at p. 204). Earlier still, he argued that the peasantry asserted 'a right to subsistence' as 'a moral principle', but that this 'subsistence ethic' was essentially superstructural – i.e. it 'grew out of the needs of cultivators – out of peasant economics': idem, *The Moral Economy of the Peasant: Rebellion and Subsistence in Southeast Asia* (New Haven, 1977), pp. 4–7.

[38] John Bohstedt, 'The Moral Economy and the Discipline of Historical Context', *Journal of Social History*, 26 (1992), pp. 269, 274; idem, *Politics of Provisions*, pp. 50–51, 117–18, 265–6. For an earlier argument that consumers 'rioted within the context of the marketing system', motivated by 'problems of self-sufficiency' rather than morality, see Dale Williams, 'Morals, Markets and the English Crowd in 1766', *Past & Present*, 104 (1984), pp. 70–71. For discussion of food riots that ignored the 'moral' dimension almost entirely and focused on 'material' causes see John Stevenson, *Popular Disturbances in England, 1700–1832* (2nd edn, London, 1992), ch. 5.

ests.[39] Other scholars, such as Keith Wrightson and Andy Wood, have sometimes relied on the same model. They have stressed, for instance, that labouring people carefully worked to 'exploit' notions of paternalism and reciprocity in their efforts to secure access to 'earthly necessities', 'moved more by tactics than deference'.[40] Underlying all of these portraits of early modern economic relations is an explanatory framework in which morality serves as a 'public transcript' to be shrewdly manipulated by essentially self-serving actors. Indeed, even instances of cooperation between apparently opposing groups can be interpreted as rational calculations. Hence, Steve Hindle has argued that seventeenth-century conflicts over enclosure varied according to 'different configurations of economic and social *interests*'. In economic disputes, these localised coalitions were what 'really matter[ed] on the ground', because elite groups could temporarily unite with subordinate groups 'when their interests ran in similar directions'.[41] This analysis, like the others mentioned above, presents its subjects as unimpeachably rational and self-interested.

The implication is that disputes involving issues normally considered central to the 'moral economy' – such as food prices, poor relief, and common rights – were not particularly 'moral' after all. Instead, these conflicts were apparently driven by material 'interests' (or, at times of crisis, by 'subsistence') which then motivated people to 'exploit' morality as a 'rhetorical strategy' to achieve their 'real' aims. This approach is, I believe, misguided. Of course, the scholarship reviewed above is still invaluable. It must be noted, for example, that none of these historians have applied the instrumentalist model universally or absolutely – it is more a case of emphasis than of dogma.[42] Moreover, the 'public transcript' approach has contributed

---

[39] John Walter, 'Public Transcripts, Popular Agency and the Politics of Subsistence in Early Modern England', in Michael Braddick and John Walter (eds), *Negotiating Power in Early Modern Society: Order, Hierarchy and Subordination in Britain and Ireland* (Cambridge, 2001), pp. 132, 137–9, 148. He also argued that 'calculated deference … could itself be a tactic to extract aid' (p. 131). For a more general discussion of applying Scott's model to early modern England, in which the authors argued that 'behind the public transcript of compliance and deference lies a more knowing and manipulating consciousness' as manifested in 'the tactics by which the relatively powerless seek to defend their interests', see Michael Braddick and John Walter, 'Grids of Power: Order, Hierarchy and Subordination in Early Modern Society', in Braddick and Walter, *Negotiating Power*, pp. 5–10 (quotes at pp. 5, 7).

[40] Wrightson, *Earthly Necessities*, p. 326; Wood, *Politics of Social Conflict*, p. 22. Likewise, Wrightson claimed that the notion of 'the utility of poverty' was 'a new spin on the age-old need to justify, and thereby strengthen, an existing structure of inequality and subordination' (pp. 320–21); and that 'authoritarian paternalism' was a 'conventional strategy' for 'rendering labouring people more industrious and compliant' (p. 325).

[41] Steve Hindle, 'Persuasion and Protest in the Caddington Common Enclosure Dispute, 1635–1639', *Past & Present*, 158 (1998), p. 75 (emphasis in original).

[42] For example, Hindle did not ignore the claims of 'custom' that 'legitimated' protesters and he also noted that 'leading commoners' showed a 'combination of paternalism and

to our understanding of economic relations by directly examining contemporary evocations of morality – even if only as 'pragmatic tactics' – which had been often ignored entirely by historians prior to Thompson. Yet, for all that, there are clearly weaknesses inherent in this model. It ultimately reduces the 'moral economy' to a superstructural façade supported by the 'real' economy. Beliefs and values become strategic poses; 'types, shadows and metaphors' become cultural resources to be exploited and appropriated. Such a perspective may allow the historian to see many aspects of the past that were invisible to those who saw the actions of the poor as 'spasmodic' and 'irrational', but much of the intricacy of economic culture has remained obscured, hidden from view by the assumed primacy of 'interests'. Even the most sophisticated versions of this methodology fail to do justice to the power of ideals and beliefs as motivating factors in English economic relations, as they ultimately rely on 'an abbreviated view of economic man'.[43]

So, if we hope to understand the history of economic life, we must move beyond the materialism inherent in much quantitative research and even beyond the more sophisticated, thoughtful instrumentalist approaches. This book shows, I hope, the potential value of this endeavour. As such, it draws on a critical tradition that stretches back almost to the birth of classical economics. As early as 1860, for example, John Ruskin provided an emotive critique of the supposedly scientific basis of classical economics. He saw *homo economicus* as a being who was 'all skeleton' and no flesh, arguing that any theory based on this assumption required the 'negation of a soul'.[44] A generation later, in rather less elegant idioms, Max Weber showed that particular economic relations could be studied as manifestations of larger social and cultural systems. Instead of following Mill or Marx in ascribing causation to an individual's 'interest' or a material 'base', his work described how culture could assert a powerful influence on the economy.[45] A distaste for 'crass economic reductionism' is also obvious in Thompson's seminal 1971 essay, especially in his emphasis on 'moral assumptions', 'social norms', and 'the complexities of motive, behaviour, and function'.[46] Although his work was overly materialist and instrumentalist on more than one occasion,

self-interest', but the vast majority of the article focused on the coalitions of 'interest' which, he asserted, were 'crucial': ibid., pp. 56, 72–3, 75. Such exceptions to the rule can be seen even in Scott's theoretical work. In one instance, he argues that 'submission and stupidity are often no more than a pose – a necessary tactic', and that the goals of rioters 'are often quite rational indeed'; but he then recognises, in a footnote, that George Rudé 'has gone too far in turning rioters into sober, domesticated, bourgeois political actors': Scott, *Weapons of the Weak*, p. 37.

43 Thompson, *Customs in Common*, p. 187.

44 Ruskin, 'Unto this Last' (1862) in *Unto This Last, and Other Writings*, Clive Wilmer ed. (Harmondsworth, 1985), p. 168.

45 Weber, *Protestant Ethic*; idem, *Economy and Society: An Outline of Interpretative Sociology*, Guenther Roth and Claus Wittich eds (3 vols, New York, 1968).

46 Thompson, *Customs in Common*, pp. 187–8. Thompson's idea of 'a complex' (p. 207)

the very concept of a 'moral economy' significantly advanced our under-standing of economic culture. More recently, numerous scholars – including several of those criticised above – have devoted at least some of their atten-tion to the role of morality and belief in worldly affairs. One of the most consistent has been Craig Muldrew, who has argued that much historiog-raphy 'has presented a very reductionist, instrumental account of "rational" self-interested behaviour, and this has been an obstacle to a more compre-hensive treatment of market relations'.[47] Even economists themselves have shown increasing interest in the economic consequences of ethics, morality, rhetoric, and other apparently 'irrational' influences.[48]

In sum, then, it is clear that historians must still be on their guard against 'crass economic reductionism', and even against its more sophisticated cousins. We must study not only 'hard facts' but also culture, and we cannot rationalise this culture – it cannot be demoted to the derivative 'superstruc-ture' of a particular 'base' or reduced to utilitarian 'tactics' protecting an underlying 'interest'. We must regard it not as an epiphenomenon but as a powerful entity in its own right. Only then will we begin to understand the ways in which cultural presumptions and moral values inflected every single economic interaction in early modern England.

The second fundamental fact that must be acknowledged is the vibrant diversity of later Stuart economic culture. This is a recurrent theme in the chapters that follow, which highlight the multitude of different ways of thinking that could influence social relations during this period and empha-sise the variety of ways that cultural presumptions changed over time. In contrast, much of the previous historiography has described these issues using stark dichotomies. Thompson provided perhaps the most concise encapsula-tion of this view when he claimed that the eighteenth century, and perhaps the whole 'great arch' of English history, had witnessed 'a succession of confrontations between an innovative market economy and the customary moral economy of the plebs', a long war in which morality was ultimately conquered by the market.[49] This dichromatic portrait of economic culture contains several notable features. The 'confrontations' at the centre of the

of different motive forces matches my own approach, discussed further in the Conclusion below.

[47] Craig Muldrew, 'Interpreting the Market: The Ethics of Credit and Community Relations in Early Modern England', *Social History*, 18:2 (1993), p. 164.

[48] Especially helpful are Amartya Sen, *On Ethics and Economics* (Oxford, 1987), ch. 1; Donald McCloskey, *The Rhetoric of Economics* (Brighton, 1985); Arjo Klamer, Donald McCloskey and Robert Solow (eds), *The Consequences of Economic Rhetoric* (Cambridge, 1988). See also the recent interest in 'behavioural economics' as exemplified in two recent popular discussions of the subject: Dan Ariely, *Predictably Irrational: The Hidden Forces that Shape Our Decisions* (New York, 2008); George A. Akerlof and Robert J. Shiller, *Animal Spirits: How Human Psychology Drives the Economy, and Why It Matters for Global Capitalism* (Princeton, 2009).

[49] Thompson, *Customs in Common*, p. 12.

image show that it is a battle scene rather than some mundane pastoral landscape. Also, there are just two principal figures – the 'moral economy' and the 'market economy' – rather than a host of different characters all thronging and milling about together. Lastly, the arms brandished by each side – one wielding 'innovation', the other holding only 'custom' – gives the viewer an unmistakable indication of the course of this war over the long term, and hints at the eventual victor. These three features – the focus on conflict, the apparent unity of each 'economy', and the underlying teleology – are interdependent, but I will address them in turn, concentrating especially on the last.

Since the 1960s, historians inspired by Marxian ideas of 'class conflict' and seeking to 'rescue' the authentic voice of the poor from 'the enormous condescension of posterity' have often concentrated on one of the few places where such struggles are overt and where the poor are agents in the historical record: the riot. This is evident even in the title of Thompson's foundational article, for here it is 'the crowd' rather than 'the consumer' that gets top billing. In the years that followed the use of moments of spectacular conflict as the primary evidence for 'the moral economy' became nearly universal. In fact, Thompson's attention to other aspects of this topic – issues such as marketing practices, regulatory policies, intellectual debates, and so forth – compared favourably with much of the subsequent historiography.[50] There is now a huge number of studies that have discussed 'the moral economy' while focusing mostly or entirely on riots.[51] Even the most

---

[50] See, for example, ibid., pp. 189–212.

[51] For examples of this reliance on 'riot' in work on 'the moral economy' see chapters by Adrian Randall, Andrew Charlesworth, John Rule, Buchanan Sharp, and John Bohstedt in Adrian Randall and Andrew Charlesworth (eds), *Moral Economy and Popular Protest: Crowds, Conflict and Authority* (London, 2000); chapters by Randall, Charlesworth, Richard Sheldon, David Walsh, Wendy Thwaites, and Roger Wells in Adrian Randall and Andrew Charlesworth (eds), *Markets, Market Culture and Popular Protest in Eighteenth-Century Britain and Ireland* (Liverpool, 1996); Williams, 'Morals'; John Walter, 'Faces in the Crowd: Gender and Age in the Early Modern Crowd', in Helen Berry and Elizabeth Foyster (eds), *The Family in Early Modern England* (Cambridge, 2007), pp. 96–125; John Walter, 'Grain Riots and Popular Attitudes to the Law: Maldon and the Crisis of 1629' and Robert Malcolmson, '"A set of ungovernable people": The Kingswood Colliers in Eighteenth in the Eighteenth Century', both in John Brewer and John Styles (eds), *An Ungovernable People? The English and Their Law in the Seventeenth and Eighteenth Centuries* (London, 1980), pp. 47–84, 85–127. This bias also helps to account for the extensive use of the 'moral economy' model in more general surveys of social protest: Charlesworth (ed.), *Atlas*; Stevenson, *Popular Disturbances*, ch. 3, 5–6; Ian Gilmour, *Riot, Rising and Revolution: Governance and Violence in Eighteenth Century England* (London, 1992), ch. 11–12; H. T. Dickinson, *The Politics of the People in Eighteenth-Century Britain* (Basingstoke, 1995), ch. 4; Andy Wood, *Riot, Rebellion and Popular Politics in Early Modern England* (Houndsmills, 2002), esp. ch. 3. Note, however, that the bias toward 'riot' seems most pronounced among those studying the eighteenth century and it must also be added that hints of a critique of this focus on crowd actions can be found in Thompson's own

recent addition to this literature, John Bohstedt's long-term survey of 'the politics of provisions' in England, centres on protesting crowds.[52] By examining so closely these exceptionally antagonistic situations while largely neglecting the economic culture of everyday life, these studies have tended to depict 'the moral economy' as a defensive response to crisis. This has left little space for cooperation, collaboration or even benign coexistence, all of which were essential parts of the mundane economic relations inherent in work and commerce in early modern England.

The popularity of viewing this issue through the lens of 'riot' is related to the second problem with this historiography: dualism. When seen only in the peculiar context of overt conflict, the complex diversity of economic culture often appeared to coalesce into two opposing ideologies. Thompson's sweeping image of the battlefield, even after detailed additions from many later scholars, shows this stark contrast clearly.[53] On one side stood 'the market economy', an entity that was 'disinfested of intrusive moral imperatives', hostile to 'the meddlesome interference of the State and of popular prejudice', and deferential only to the pursuit of profit and to the defence of private property. Its supporters were a motley crew whose membership varied considerably depending on the perspective of the observer. Hence it received encouragement from such luminaries as John Locke, Nicholas Barbon, and other early economic thinkers, while being forcibly implemented by improving landowners, wealthy manufacturers, substantial farmers, corn factors, entrepreneurial millers, and many similarly 'vigorous capitalist classes'.[54] On the other side stood 'the moral economy', an amalgam that seemed to include every 'non-market' belief or concept expressed during this period, especially ideals associated with 'common rights', 'customary consciousness', and 'old paternalist market regulation'. It had a similarly wide-ranging collection of adherents. The poor, the gentry,

---

writings, among others: Thompson, *Customs in Common*, pp. 115, 120–21, 189, 241–6; Walter and Wrightson, 'Dearth', pp. 32–3, 41–2; Andy Wood, 'Subordination, Solidarity and the Limits of Popular Agency in a Yorkshire Valley c.1596–1615', *Past & Present*, 193 (2006), pp. 45–6.

[52] Bohstedt, *Politics of Provisions*. Interestingly, even some recent attempts to focus on 'deference' rather than 'defiance' have been predicated on the assumption that a lack of conflict resulted from class-based repression just as conflict resulted from class-based exploitation: Wood, 'Subordination'; idem, 'Fear, Hatred and the Hidden Injuries of Class in Early Modern England', *Journal of Social History*, 39:3 (2006), pp. 803–26.

[53] Although the summary that follows is based on 'the moral economy' historiography as a whole, the quotations can be found in Thompson, *Customs in Common*, pp. 179–81, 189–90, 201–3. I have included references only for elements that cannot be found in ibid., ch. 1–6.

[54] For Locke and Barbon see Macpherson, *Political Theory*, ch. 5; Andrea Finkelstein, 'Nicholas Barbon and the Quality of Infinity', *History of Political Economy*, 32:1 (2000), pp. 83–102. For substantial farmers (sometimes labelled 'the yeomanry', 'village notables', 'rural middling sort') see Wrightson, *English Society*, pp. 142–4, 234.

and even 'the middling sort' can be found espousing 'the moral economy', though apparently its most committed defenders were 'plebeians'.[55] These two mutually exclusive 'economies' have served as the analytical foundation for much of the scholarship that followed.

Not every historian of early modern economic culture has used the terminology of 'moral' and 'market', but nearly all have at least implicitly relied on the same duality. The influential article on 'Dearth and the Social Order' by John Walter and Keith Wrightson, for example, presented a tidy split between the vast majority of both 'government and governed' who 'subscribed to a common consensus' about 'the ideal ordering of economic transactions' and 'a significant element in local society' who prioritised 'individual profit' over 'obligations of neighbourliness'.[56] Another scholar of seventeenth-century social relations, David Underdown, has described how 'rioters and petitioners were inspired by the values of a vaguely sensed "moral economy"', in contrast to the values of the market economy now being adopted by increasing numbers of the middling sort'.[57] The same dichotomy has structured many analyses that focus on the eighteenth century. Robert Malcolmson, for example, has portrayed Georgian England as a society divided between 'men of property and privilege' who 'favoured what was known as "improvement" – economic innovation, managerial efficiency and capital accumulation', and 'the people' who 'were committed to the preservation of a traditional, custom-centred culture' and who thus 'rejected [the market's] demoralized conception of their place in the social order'.[58] Some historians have, more recently, presented a similarly bipolar model while employing a slightly different vocabulary. Hence, there was – according to Adrian Randall, Andrew Charlesworth, and others – a 'marked contrast' between 'the plebeian culture of the market' based on 'the regulatory economy of the past' and 'the free market culture of the Classical Econ-

---

[55] For 'the middling sort' see Steve Poole, 'Scarcity and the Civic Tradition: Market Management in Bristol, 1709–1815' and Simon Renton, 'The Moral Economy of the English Middling Sort in the Eighteenth Century: The Case of Norwich in 1766 and 1767', both in Randall and Charlesworth (eds), *Markets*, pp. 91–114, 115–36.

[56] Walter and Wrightson, 'Dearth', pp. 24, 31, 41. Much more recently, Walter described a 'politics of subsistence' based on 'the moral economy' which opposed the economic culture of 'commodification': Walter, *Crowds and Popular Politics in Early Modern England* (Manchester, 2006), pp. 18–20, 25.

[57] David Underdown, *Revel, Riot and Rebellion: Popular Politics and Culture in England, 1603–1660* (Oxford, 1985), pp. 116–19, quote at p. 118. Likewise, proletarianisation and the resulting labour indiscipline supposedly brought to the surface 'the contradiction between the moral economy of patriarchalism and the political economy of capitalism': David Levine, *Reproducing Families: The Political Economy of English Population History* (Cambridge, 1987), p. 51.

[58] Robert Malcolmson, *Life and Labour in England, 1700–1780* (London, 1981), pp. 123, 134.

omists'.[59] For these scholars, early modern economic beliefs can ultimately be sorted into just two categories, each of which became a contender in a long-running duel.

Attempts to characterise the chronological progress of this struggle demonstrate the third substantial problem with 'moral economy' scholarship: teleology. Indeed, time is the most common axis upon which the moral/amoral dichotomy has been projected. The genealogy of this notion is too long to trace systematically here, but its modern proponents clearly owe much to the nostalgic commonplaces of their predecessors – indeed, for thousands of years, Western culture has propagated the myth of a harmonious 'Golden Age' degenerating into a strife-filled 'Iron Age' and, similarly, the idea of humankind's 'Fall' from a prelapsarian 'Eden'. In early modern England this theme found popular expression in stories about vanished 'Anglo-Saxon liberties' and in ballads describing 'Old England' that complained of the growth of greed and vanity, the decline of charity, and the weakening of social ties.[60] Such pastoral lamentation continued during the period of parliamentary enclosure and the early years of industrialisation, when men such as Oliver Goldsmith, John Clare, and William Cobbett wrote social eulogies that continue to be read today.[61] However, this teleology soon became much more 'scientific'. It was in the nineteenth century that both positive and negative conceptions of economic 'modernisation' were proclaimed most explicitly.[62] For Sir Henry Maine the transition was from communal to individual property and from 'status' to 'contract' relations; for Ferdinand Tönnies it was from cooperative 'community' to competitive 'society'; and, for Karl Marx, it was from 'feudalism' to 'capitalism'.[63] What-

---

[59] Randall et al., 'Introduction', in Randall and Charlesworth (eds), *Markets*, pp. 12, 16. Elsewhere they refer the former as 'an ideology' based on 'common "rights" and customary practice' as well as 'the sanction of law' offered by the 'paternal model of political economy': Adrian Randall and Andrew Charlesworth, 'The Moral Economy: Riots, Markets and Social Conflict', in idem (eds), *Moral Economy*, pp. 5, 20.

[60] For pre-Norman equity see Christopher Hill, 'The Norman Yoke', in his *Puritanism and Revolution: Studies in Interpretation of the English Revolution of the Seventeenth Century* (London, 1958), pp. 50–122. For 'the politics of cockanye' see John Walter, 'A "rising of the people"? The Oxfordshire Rising of 1596', *Past & Present*, 107 (1985), pp. 90–143; Steve Hindle, 'Imagining Insurrection in Seventeenth-Century England: Representations of the Midland Rising of 1607', *History Workshop Journal*, 66 (2008), pp. 36, 57 n. 96. For the decline of hospitality and of other 'paternalism' see below pp. 109–12.

[61] Oliver Goldsmith, 'The Deserted Village' (1770), and, John Clare, 'The Mores' (c.1821–24), discussed in Thompson, *Customs in Common*, pp. 179–84; William Cobbett, *Rural Rides* (2 vols, 1830), I, pp. 38, 123–4, 134, 265–8.

[62] For a summary see Richard Smith, '"Modernization" and the Corporate Village Community in England: Some Sceptical Reflections', in Alan R. H. Baker and Derek Gregory (eds), *Explorations in Historical Geography: Interpretative Essays* (Cambridge, 1984), pp. 150–55. See also Phil Withington, *Society in Early Modern England: The Vernacular Origins of Some Powerful Ideas* (Cambridge, 2010), ch. 1–2.

[63] See below Chapter 1.6, Chapter 2.5, Chapter 3.6.

ever their differences, they agreed that 'modern' economic relations were more 'rational' than what had come before.

Inspired by this tradition of teleological thinking, numerous historians have seen the process of economic 'modernisation' – essentially the shift from a 'moral economy' to an 'amoral economy' – unfolding in early modern England. The most powerful formulation surely came from Richard Tawney, whose faith in Christian Socialism clearly inspired much of his historical writing. He argued that, by the late seventeenth century, moral restrictions on individual acquisitiveness were 'relics of medieval doctrine which linger[ed] embalmed' in only a handful of archaic texts.[64] This narrative became a historiographical orthodoxy, one which clearly shaped the most prominent work on the subject in the 1960s and 1970s. It seems, for example, to have served as the structure for Peter Laslett's evocative depiction of the 'pre-industrial' world of hierarchy and community as 'the world we have lost'.[65] The influence of Marx and Tawney is also obvious in Christopher Hill's voluminous work on the 'the making of modern English society' in the early modern period.[66] For Hill, the mid-seventeenth century was 'a turning point in the establishment of a competitive business society'; thus the 'Bourgeois Revolution' was symptomatic of growth of modern 'ways of thought' culminating in Smith's *Wealth of Nations*.[67] Historians who have focused on the economic opinions of early modern intellectuals have drawn this contrast between 'pre-modern morality' and 'modern amorality' especially starkly. According to C. B. Macpherson, for example, the belief 'that human society is essentially a series of market relations' became the 'dominant' opinion in England after Locke 'erased the moral disability' afflicting 'unlimited capitalist appropriation'.[68] Likewise, Joyce Appleby has claimed that 'a change of consciousness' allowed 'the dramatic reorganisation of social priorities around production for private profit', ensuring that many economic issues 'escaped the purview of moralists' as modernity overcame 'mindless traditionalism'.[69]

Scholars have, in more recent decades, continued to use this convenient conceptual binary to describe the historical trajectory of various aspects of early modern economic culture. Whether implicit or explicit, it has

---

[64] Tawney, *Religion*, p. 243. This belief in a transition from a political economy based on Christianity and paternalism to one based on *laissez-faire* can also be seen in the writings of William Cunningham and E. M. Leonard over a century ago: Anthony Fletcher, *Reform in the Provinces: The Government of Stuart England* (New Haven, 1986), p. 354.

[65] Peter Laslett, *The World We Have Lost: Further Explored* (3rd edition, London, 1983).

[66] Christopher Hill, *Reformation to Industrial Revolution: A Social and Economic History of Britain, 1530–1780* (London, 1967), p. 168.

[67] Ibid., pp. 6–10.

[68] Macpherson, *Political Theory*, pp. 221, 270–73.

[69] Appleby, *Economic Thought*, pp. 24, 115, 245–6.

remained a popular model of change.[70] For example, as will be seen, discussions of the relationship between religious belief and worldly affairs have usually conformed to this convention. Accordingly, Norman Jones and C. J. Sommerville have described a transition from an economic world shaped by religious ethics to one ruled by secular rationality. Others, such as Andrew McRae, have followed Weber in arguing that the sixteenth and seventeenth centuries witnessed the birth of a more individualist, profit-orientated religious outlook, supposedly a precursor for the mindset of modern capitalism. On the question of 'paternalism' and 'patriarchalism', historians have employed a similar dichotomy. In this interpretation, the quasi-familial ties between 'superiors' and 'inferiors' – including masters and servants, landlords and tenants, governors and governed – were breaking down during the early modern period, creating an increasingly 'contractual' and 'bureaucratic' social system over the course of the seventeenth and eighteenth centuries. Indeed, perhaps the most influential recent characterisation of the early modern social order – namely, Keith Wrightson's notion of a transition from functional 'estates' to hierarchical 'degrees' and ultimately to antagonistic 'sorts' – rests on the assumption that 'ideals' such as 'duty' and 'harmony' came to be replaced by the 'bald facts of relative wealth, status, and power'.[71] Finally, teleology has also inflected much writing on later Stuart economic communities. Although several historians have criticised this form of the 'modernisation' paradigm in the last decade, the supposed disintegration of collective solidarities has long been central to the historiography of craft associations, urban corporations, rural villages, and 'neighbourliness'. Even some professed sceptics of such dichotomies have argued that the boundaries of mutuality became more narrow and selective. When all of these various depictions of early modern economic culture are considered together, one cannot help but notice the ubiquitous tendency to rely on a chronology that begins with a 'moral economy' and ends with an 'amoral economy'.

The problems inherent in so much of this scholarship seem to have reinforced one another. The focus on dramatic episodes of conflict made it easy to reduce manifold economic beliefs to two opposing ideologies, both of which were then readily incorporated into a narrative of 'development' that implies 'a moral economy in retreat' which, as the following chapters are intended to demonstrate, simply does not seem to have existed in later Stuart England.[72] Yet such obvious simplifications have also more recently been challenged. Riots and other forms of 'resistance', for example, are no longer as central to analyses of economic culture as they once were. The scholars who have orientated their investigations towards less inherently

---

[70] For fuller analysis (and references) of the historiography described in this paragraph see the conclusions of Chapters 1–3.

[71] See below pp. 144–5.

[72] Appleby, *Economic Thought*, ch. 3.

combative social ideas – such as 'hospitality', 'credit', 'commonwealth', 'neighbourliness', and 'giving' – have not always explicitly rejected Thompson's approach, but their research has provided an implicit counter-argument to the assumption that collective protest reveals the essence of popular mentalities.[73] Some historians have also attempted to undermine the teleological structure inherent to conventional histories of economic culture. For the most part, this critical response has involved drawing attention to early modernists' uncritical use of crude 'modernisation' narratives inherited from nineteenth-century social theorists.[74] In a few cases, scholars have gone further and shown how certain types of 'moral economy' were not merely surviving but thriving in later Stuart England – as seen, for example, in the recent work of Naomi Tadmor and Ilana Krausman Ben-Amos.[75] As a result of the accumulated pressure of these various critiques, it is no longer possible to hide the cracks in the foundation of the historiography of early modern economic culture.

The binaries that can be found embedded in so much of the work on these themes have impeded our ability to understand the diversity and complexity of past beliefs. By attempting to compress a whole panoply of different social and cultural norms into two antagonistic 'economies', Thompson and many of his successors have produced a deeply problematic representation of both early modern thinking and economic relations in this period. We must disaggregate these supposedly dichotomous ideologies and, in so doing, demonstrate the inadequacy of unilinear trajectories of change. The vigour and variety of later Stuart 'moral economies' are simply too profuse to be contained within the limited confines of the conventional model.

A New Approach

So, while the work of previous scholars has been both vast and valuable, much of it has also remained encumbered with chronological weaknesses and problematic assumptions. Its flaws necessitate a new approach, one which has begun to emerge through the work of a new generation of historians over the last decade or so. One of the first and most persistent among them has been Craig Muldrew, who has forcefully argued that 'thinking of the

[73] Heal, *Hospitality*; Muldrew, *Economy of Obligation*; Withington, *Politics of Commonwealth*, esp. ch. 6; Tadmor, *Social Universe*, ch. 1; Ben-Amos, *Culture of Giving*.
[74] Smith, 'Modernization', pp. 141–6; Muldrew, 'Interpreting the Market', pp. 166–7; Keith Wrightson, 'Mutualities and Obligations: Changing Social Relationships in Early Modern England', *Proceedings of the British Academy*, 139 (2006), esp. pp. 158–61; idem, '"Decline of Neighbourliness"', pp. 19–21, 33; Garthine Walker, 'Modernization', in eadem (ed.), *Writing Early Modern History* (London, 2005), pp. 25–48; Withington, *Society*, ch. 1–2.
[75] Tadmor, *Social Universe*, pp. 47–9; Ben-Amos, *Culture of Giving*.

market as an "invisible hand" is a self-imposed ethical myopia preventing us from finding our way', when in reality moral language and ethical ideals 'dominated the way market relations were conceived' throughout the early modern period.[76] He has shown that socially constructed personal 'credit', networks of 'mutual interdependence' and carefully bounded 'moral communities' were not undermined by the expansion of commercial relations but rather were vital to England's long-term economic development.[77] This emphasis on the strength and vigour of a moralised economic culture has been reiterated by several other historians. For example, Naomi Tadmor and Ilana Ben-Amos have shown that the biblical idioms of 'neighbourly love' and 'good service' as well as the reciprocal bonds of 'gift relations' and 'mutual aid' permeated social relations long after their supposed post-Reformation 'decline'.[78] Likewise, Phil Withington, Joseph Ward, Steve Hindle, and Keith Snell have all recently stressed how the local economic 'communities' of parish, guild, town, and city were adapted, expanded or intensified during the late seventeenth and early eighteenth centuries.[79] As the medievalist James Davis has argued, the complex and flexible 'market morality' of the thirteenth century shows 'striking similarities' with that of Stuart and Hanovarian England, suggesting the resilience rather than the disintegration of moralised economic culture.[80] These and other historians have created a wave of innovative scholarship that, although not always engaging with our inherited narratives as directly or explicitly as I do here, has made possible alterative ways of thinking about early modern economic life.

This book is an attempt to build on this new work by drawing on a broad array of sources and focusing on the specific circumstances of this era. The primary sources used in this study are thus diverse. The countless pages of printed media published during these decades provide one key form of evidence for understanding the most common norms and sentiments. Specifically, this study makes extensive use of several types of printed material: almost 100 short printed texts, including chapbooks, tracts, pamphlets, and almanacs; about 150 broadside ballads gathered from five major collec-

[76] Muldrew, *Economy of Obligation*, pp. 11, 152. For his initial attempt to push against these 'whiggish' historiographical tendencies see Muldrew, 'Interpreting the Market', esp. p. 168.

[77] Ibid., esp. pp. 124–5, 149, 209, 298; idem, 'From a "Light Cloak" to an "Iron Cage": Historical Changes in the Relations between Community and Individualism', in Alexandra Shepard and Phil Withington (eds), *Communities in Early Modern England* (Manchester, 2000), pp. 156–77.

[78] Tadmor, *Social Universe*; Ben-Amos, *Culture of Giving*.

[79] Withington, *Politics of Commonwealth*, esp. ch. 6; idem, 'Citizens, Community and Political Culture in Restoration England', in Shepard and Withington (eds), *Communities*, pp. 134–55; idem, *Society*, ch. 5; Ward, *Metropolitan Communities*; Hindle, *On the Parish*; Snell, *Parish and Belonging*.

[80] James Davis, *Medieval Market Morality: Life, Law and Ethics in the English Marketplace, 1200–1500* (Cambridge, 2011), ch. 4, quotation at p. 447.

tions; and over 50 works of religious instruction, consisting of sermons and catechisms.[81] Nearly all of these texts were intended to reach a very broad audience through their cheap price, their oral transmission, or both. As many other scholars have already shown, these sorts of texts pervaded the cultures of all levels of English society by the late seventeenth century if not before, offering invaluable examples of the ideas most frequently encountered by ordinary people.[82] However, this material cannot be examined in isolation. It is thus placed in context by drawing on a variety of local and national records, especially those of London, Coventry, Essex, Hertfordshire, Yorkshire, and the central government.[83] The documents produced or collected by state officials, county magistrates, urban corporations, craft guilds, and village officers show how economic attitudes manifested themselves in daily life. In addition, four substantial troves of petitions to magistrates, amounting to several hundred items in total, demonstrate some of the ways in which ordinary people reacted to moments of material hard-

[81] Specifically, the ballads are drawn from the Pepys, Roxburghe, Wood, Euing, and Rosebery collections.

[82] To rehearse the various historiographical debates about extent of literacy, the nature of 'popular culture' and the effectiveness of religious ministry in early modern England would make for a very long diversion. It must suffice to say that there are now few scholars who would suggest that these types of sources can tell us little or nothing about widespread ideas and beliefs. Key studies that emphasise the reach and influence of these sources include Bernard Capp, *Astrology and the Popular Press: English Almanacs, 1500–1800* (London, 1979); David Cressy, *Literacy and the Social Order: Reading and Writing in Tudor and Stuart England* (Cambridge, 1980); Margaret Spufford, *Small Books and Pleasant Histories: Popular Fiction and Its Readership in Seventeenth-Century England* (London, 1981); Barry Reay (ed.), *Popular Culture in Seventeenth-Century England* (London, 1985); Tessa Watt, *Cheap Print and Popular Piety, 1550–1640* (Cambridge, 1991); Tim Harris (ed.), *Popular Culture in England, c. 1500–1850* (Houndmills, 1995); Ian Green, *The Christian's ABC: Catechism and Catechizing in England, c. 1530–1740* (Oxford, 1996); Barry Reay, *Popular Cultures in England, 1550–1750* (London, 1998); Adam Fox, *Oral and Literate Culture in England, 1500–1700* (Oxford, 2000); Ian Green, *Print and Protestantism in Early Modern England* (Oxford, 2000); Lori Anne Ferrell and Peter McCullough (eds), *The English Sermon Revised: Religion, Literature and History, 1600–1750* (Manchester, 2001); Adam Fox and Daniel Woolf (eds), *The Spoken Word: Oral Culture in Britain, 1500–1850* (Manchester, 2002); Julia Crick and Alexandra Walsham (eds), *The Uses of Script and Print, 1300–1700* (Cambridge, 2004); Patricia Fumerton, Anita Guerrini and Kris McAbee (eds), *Ballads and Broadsides in Britain, 1500–1800* (Farnham, 2010); Christopher Marsh, *Music and Society in Early Modern England* (Cambridge, 2010), ch. 5–6, esp. pp. 251–70; Angela McShane, *Political Broadside Ballads of Seventeenth-Century England: A Critical Bibliography* (London, 2011). For a summary of the difficulties associated with this pursuit see Robert Scribner, 'Is a History of Popular Culture Possible?', *History of European Ideas*, 10:2 (1989), pp. 174–91.

[83] A full list of the eighteen record offices and libraries holding manuscripts used in this study can be found in the bibliography.

ship and the rhetoric they used to describe their plight.[84] Together, this broad range of texts illuminates both prescription and practice in English economic culture.

The core of this book consists of three main chapters focusing on a trinity of motifs. In Chapter 1, I examine the economic implications of the constantly reiterated concept of divine omnipotence, expressed in both frequent heavenly intervention in earthly affairs and God's ultimate authority over all worldly property. I demonstrate, for instance, that the heartfelt belief in religious concepts such as 'providence' and 'steward-ship' continued to shape economic conduct even in an era of supposedly increasing secularism. In Chapter 2, I investigate the later Stuart obsession with interdependence, duty, and discipline, as indicated in the popularity of 'the household' as a metaphor for social and economic relations. Specifically, I show how the assumptions associated with patriarchy and paternalism shaped attitudes towards, among other things, employment, commercial regulation, and hospitality. In Chapter 3, I survey how the powerful bonds of common identity and exclusivity created economically powerful 'imag-ined communities' both large (e.g. the nation) and small (e.g. the parish). I consider, for example, the ways in which traditional social ideals such as 'the neighbourhood' and 'the trade' intertwined with the novel values asso-ciated with the parish state and the 'national interest'. Together, these three chapters show the links between the actions of ordinary people and the cultural landscapes in which those actions took place. Thus, my analysis of these moralised discourses is paired with brief studies of particular instances of individual or collective action, such as begging, cursing, petitioning, and rioting. I show that the habits of mind which arose from these pervasive moralities influenced the economic lives both of poor families and of their social superiors over many generations.

This conclusion leads me to close by exploring the implications of this approach for the study of early modern economic culture. In contrast to existing historiographical approaches, this book shows the diversity and vitality of early modern 'moral economies'. Ultimately, I hope, it provides a rough prototype for achieving a better understanding of the links between cultural and economic systems, a task which may be more pressing now than it has been in many years past.

[84] The main collections of petitions are those of the quarter sessions of Hertfordshire (HA, QSR), the North Riding of Yorkshire (NYCRO, QSB) and the West Riding of Yorkshire (WYAS–W, QS 1), and those of the London Court of Aldermen (LMA, COL/CA/05). For further discussion see Chapter 2.4 below.

1

God's Will: Judgement, Providence, and the Prayers of the Poor

For faithful Christians, there could be no doubt that God was a sovereign whose dominion encompassed both this world and the next. The dire fate that awaited dying sinners was well known, but it was also clear that he might intervene directly or indirectly in human affairs. God overthrew popish tyrants, foiled assassins, smote murderers, and burned great cities to the ground.[1] And this vengeful, interventionist deity also had a role to play in dealings that modern commentators might regard as purely economic. God ordained society's vast inequalities in wealth, rewarded the industrious poor and the charitable rich, punished ruthless money-lenders and food-hoarders, and responded quickly to pious individuals afflicted by sudden material hardships. Though some widely held assumptions about divine influence and otherworldly intervention were theologically dubious, they supported a whole web of early modern beliefs about property, accumulation, charity, finance, and trade.

Previous work on the later Stuart period has almost entirely neglected these manifold connections between religious ideas and economic culture, in some cases simply denying such links even existed. Richard Tawney argued that late seventeenth-century Protestantism 'left little room for religious teaching as to economic morality'.[2] Unfortunately, many scholars have followed his lead and, even in recent decades, the 'secularisation' of later Stuart social relations has often been regarded as a self-evident fact.[3]

---

[1] For just a few of the countless examples that could be cited see John Evelyn, *The Diary of John Evelyn*, E. S. de Beer ed. (6 vols, Oxford, 1955), V, pp. 100–101, 233–4, 475; Richard Gough, *The History of Myddle*, David Hey ed. (Harmondsworth, 1981), pp. 59–60, 122; John Thomlinson, 'Diary [1717–1722]' in *Six North Country Diaries*, John Crawford Hodgson ed. (Surtees Society, vol. 118, Durham, 1911), p. 76 (27 Aug 1717). For many more examples see Chapter 1.4 below and the works cited therein.

[2] Tawney, *Religion*, p. 195. For fuller discussion of the problematic historiography noted in this introduction see Chapter 1.6 below.

[3] C. J. Sommerville, *The Secularization of Early Modern England: From Religious Culture to Religious Faith* (Oxford and New York, 1992), pp. 143, 147–9; idem, *Popular Religion in Restoration England* (Gainesville, 1977), p. 140; Appleby, *Economic Thought*, pp. 50,

However, evidence to support this view is actually much more difficult to find than that which contradicts it. Indeed, preachers and tract-writers continued to attempt to shape people's conduct through numerous, often elaborate discussions of topics such as poverty and commerce. By analysing the economic implications of popular religiosity, this chapter challenges the many attempts which have been made to apply the 'secularisation' model to the early modern marketplace.

Some historians have also used a simplified form of Max Weber's 'Protestant ethic' thesis to describe the religious discourse of this period. They have argued that the teachings of seventeenth-century clergymen increasingly promoted proto-capitalist ideals such as acquisitive individualism and profit maximisation.[4] As with the 'secularisation' model, this characterisation of early modern Protestantism is seriously flawed. Weber was correct to point to the clerical emphasis on hard work and self-discipline, but he and his followers misrepresented later Stuart religious teaching when they argued that it somehow endorsed limitless accumulation and self-aggrandisement.[5] According to most commentators, Christian virtues such as industrious labour were part of a much wider set of duties that included, for example, redistributing superfluities, forgiving debts, disciplining profiteers, and selling goods at discounted rates to needy neighbours. Merciless merchants and farmers, on the other hand, often found themselves vilified; some were reportedly consigned to hell for their greed while others were struck down by God in dramatic acts of heavenly fury. What follows is thus an attempt to review the influence of later Stuart theological assumptions on everyday economic conduct, which will incidentally demonstrate the misleading narrowness of Weberian accounts of the era.

Although it addresses both 'secularisation' and 'capitalist spirit' theses,

---

70, 188, 276; Norman Jones, *God and the Moneylenders: Usury and Law in Early Modern England* (Oxford, 1989), p. 199; Andrew McRae, *God Speed the Plough: The Representation of Agrarian England, 1500–1660* (Cambridge, 1996), p. 7.

4   Weber, *Protestant Ethic*, pp. 109–10, 115–17, 312; Tawney, *Religion*, pp. 233, 246–7, 251; Richard Schlatter, *The Social Ideas of Religious Leaders, 1660–1688* (New York, 1971), pp. 197–8; McRae, *God Speed*, pp. 77–9; Jones, *God*, p. 203; Gordon Marshall, *Presbyteries and Profits: Calvinism and the Development of Capitalism in Scotland, 1560–1707* (Edinburgh, 1992), p. 343 n. 119. Confusingly, some of these historians (e.g. Tawney, McRae, and Jones) seem to have argued that clergymen were *sacralising* capitalist individualism at the very moment when they began *desacralising* economic conduct in general. These contradictory positions are discussed more fully in the concluding section of this chapter.

5   For a critique of Weber's problematic conflation of the 'work ethic' with the 'profit ethic' see Michael H. Lessnoff, *The Spirit of Capitalism and the Protestant Ethic: An Enquiry into the Weber Thesis* (Aldershot, 1994), esp. pp. 9, 21, 57–8. For evidence of a clear distinction between the virtue of diligence and that of profit in the mind of a mid-seventeenth-century Puritan artisan see Paul Seaver, *Wallington's World: A Puritan Artisan in Seventeenth-Century London* (London, 1985), ch. 5, esp. pp. 132–3.

this chapter is intended to be more than just an act of academic iconoclasm. It begins, therefore, with a section tracing the limits imposed on property rights by the ubiquitous notion of 'stewardship'. The second section examines the many ways in which contemporaries routinely connected the single-minded pursuit of wealth to the idolatrous worship of false gods. In the following two sections, the analysis focuses on the consequences which were thought to arise from specific economic sins or virtues, addressing in particular the practice of adapting and augmenting biblical motifs to suit later Stuart society. These sections demonstrate the continuing importance of supernatural judgements – heaven, hell, and divine providence – as sanctions on everyday economic interaction. The fifth section is a discussion of the opportunities for action left open to the poor themselves in a world governed by God's will. Specifically, it explores the sometimes ambiguous early modern attitudes toward repentance, prayer, blessing, cursing, and even theft. Finally, the conclusion returns to the historiographical issues mentioned above by interrogating the assumptions inherited from Weber, Tawney, and other early scholars of this subject. The chapter as a whole, by examining how economic behaviour might have been seen through the lens of popular Christianity, shows that the forces of poverty and piety, wealth and worship intersected in remarkable ways in early modern England, many of which remain largely misunderstood or unexplored.

1 Stewardship

Ideas about ownership and rightful possession are fundamental to every social system, so the religious context in which they arise provides an ideal starting point for an exploration of economic relations. In a world where a heavenly being exercises absolute authority over every twig, rock, and insect, the question of who owns the 'fruits of the earth' is not reserved only for lawyers. Philosophers had grappled with this issue since the earliest years of Christianity and the doctrine which eventually became orthodox was well established by the time early modern commentators set about elucidating it. The essential premise was tidily summed up in the official *Book of Homilies* and preached to generations of English church-goers. 'God is the giver of riches,' it declared, so 'be more diligent well to spend them to Gods glory, and to the profit of our neighbour, that we may make a good account at the last, and be praised for good stewards.'[6] Incorporating elements of biblical parable and patristic theology, this notion of temporary stewardship was a

---

6 'Homily for Rogation Week, [pt. II]', in *Certain Sermons or Homilies, Appointed to be Read in Churches* (2 vols, 1673), II, p. 295.

commonplace for moralists demanding the correct use of earthly wealth.[7] Whether they conveyed their message in a learned sermon or humble ballad, all commentators agreed that mere men had no real claim to ownership beyond that delegated to them on the whim of their Creator. 'Our Interest is a Deputation, a Stewardship', preached William Thomas, bishop of Worcester in 1688. We are no more than 'Trustees' or 'Treasurers for the Poor, nay, for Himself, who sues for Succours in his distressed Members'.[8] Archbishop Tillotson, whose sermons were read (and plagiarised) by many lesser clergy, relied on a similar formulation. For him, worldly estates are only granted 'to us in trust, and the greater they are, the more we are to account for', because 'we are but *Trustees, and Stewards*'.[9]

---

[7] Preachers and catechists often cited Luke 16 (Christ's parable of the unjust steward), Luke 12:48, 1 Cor. 4:1–2, Psa. 50:10–12, along with the writings of St Basil of Caesarea (c.330–379). For a brief, useful, and amusingly titled survey of patristic theories of property and stewardship see John Ryan, 'Were the Church Fathers Communists?' *International Journal of Ethics*, 14:1 (1903), pp. 26–39. The few existing discussions of early modern notions of stewardship are usually extremely brief and most do not even mention its implications for property rights: Tawney, *Religion*, pp. 44–5, 153–4; Schlatter, *Social Ideas*, pp. 125–9; Hindle, *On the Parish?* p. 101; Lessnoff, *Spirit*, pp. 55–8, 83, 88; E. D. Bebb, *Nonconformity and Social and Economic Life: Some Problems of the Present as They Appeared in the Past* (Philadelphia, 1980), ch. 6; Patrick Collinson, 'Puritanism and the Poor', in Rosemary Horrox and Sarah Rees Jones (eds), *Pragmatic Utopias: Ideals and Communities, 1200–1630* (Cambridge, 2001), p. 245; idem, 'Christian Socialism in Elizabethan Suffolk: Thomas Carew and his Caveat for Clothiers', in Carole Rawcliffe, Roger Virgoe, and Richard G. Wilson (eds), *Counties and Communities: Essays on East Anglian History: Presented to Hassell Smith* (Norwich, 1996), pp. 170–71.
[8] William Thomas, *The Mammon of Unrighteousness Detected and Purified in a Sermon Preached at the Cathedral Church of Worcester* (1688), p. 23 and passim.
[9] John Tillotson, *Sixteen Sermons, Preached on Several Subjects ... Being the Third Volume* (1696), pp. 199–200. See also Thomas Cartwright, *The Danger of Riches, Discovered in a Sermon Preach'd at St. Pauls ... before the Right Honorable the Lord Mayor* (1662), pp. 14–15; John Hart, *The Charitable Christian: or, A Word of Comfort ... to such as are Truly Poor And a Word of Christian Counsel and Advice to such as are Worldly Rich* (8th edn, 1662), sig. B1r; Richard Younge, *The Poors Advocate Epitomized: Or, Christ's call To Rich Men, in Behalf of his Poor Members* (1665), p. 19; *Avaritia Coram Tribunali: Or, The Miser Arraign'd at the Bar of Scripture and Reason; for his Sinful Neglect of Charity* (1666), pp. 7–9; Richard Steele, *The Husbandmans Calling: Shewing the Excellencies, Temptations, Graces, Duties, &c. of the Christian Husbandman Being the Substance of XII Sermons* (1668), pp. 95–6; Isaac Barrow, *The Duty and Reward of Bounty to the Poor: In a Sermon Preached at the Spittal upon Wednesday in Easter Week* (1671), pp. 70–81, 123–4; William Durham, *Encouragement to Charity: A Sermon Preached at the Charter-House Chapel ... at an Anniversary Meeting in Commemoration of the Founder* (1679), p. 9; Andrew Jones, *The Black Book of Conscience, or, Gods High Court of Justice in the Soul* (36th edn, 1679), fol. A5r–v; George Hickes, *A Sermon Preached at the Church of St. Bridget on Easter-Tuesday ... Upon the Subject of Alms-Giving* (1684), pp. 8–9; Thomas Pittis, *A Spittle Sermon Preach'd in St Brides Parish-Church, on Wednesday in Easter Week* (1684), p. 21; David Jones, *A Sermon Preached at Christ-Church, London, November the 2nd* (1690), p. 23; David Clarkson, 'Sermon 10', in *Sermons and Discourses on Several Divine Subjects* (1696),

For the poor, who might be 'Trustees' of little more than the food on their table and the clothes on their backs, the obligations that came with their material possessions were depressingly few. Hence, preachers such as Robert Moss stressed the 'Duty of the poor, quietly and patiently to acquiesce in the Sovereign Disposals of His good Providence' and 'to rest contented with that State or Condition in which it hath pleas'd God to rank him'.[10] That Moss should so firmly emphasise the need to raise no complaint against pre-ordained poverty is partly explained by the fact that he was speaking before 3,000 children from London's charity schools, but the sentiment was not exceptional.[11] The pervasiveness of this belief helped it find its way into less explicitly prescriptive texts such as ballads and almanacs. A broadsheet on *The Poor-Man's Comfort*, for instance, insisted that those with little must simply trust in the Lord, be 'contented' with 'Every morsel of bread' that

---

esp. pp. 311, 324–45; Matthew Hale, *Some Necessary and Important Considerations …taken out of (that late Worthy and Renowed Judge) Sir Matthew Hale's Writings* (9th edn, 1697), p. 9; Richard Croft, *The Wise Steward: Being a Sermon Preached the Thursday in Whitson-week, 1696: In the Parish Church of Feckenham, in the County of Worcester* (1697), p. 53; John Bellers, *Essays About the Poor, Manufactures, Trade, Plantations, & Immorality* (1699), pp. 14–15; Henry Cornwallis, *Set on the Great Pot: A Sermon Upon Hospitality, Preach'd at a Late Visitation at Tunbridge in Kent* (1703), p. 19; Charles Brent, *Persuasions to a Publick Spirit: A Sermon Preach'd Before the Court of Guardians of the Poor in the City of Bristol, at St. Peter's Church* (1704), pp. 5–6; George Stanhope, *The Danger of Hard-heartedness to the Poor: A Sermon Preach'd in the Parish-Church of St. Sepulchers, May 31, 1705, Being Thursday in Whitson Week* (1705), p. 3. The notion of 'stuard for the poor' even appeared in a few broadsheets: *Time's Darling* (c.1684–6), in *PB*, II, p. 11; Lawrence White, *God's Great and Wonderful Work in Somerset-shire* (1676) in *WB*, Wood 276b (101); *A Threefold Alphabet of Rules, Concerning Christian-Practice* (1681), s.v. 'N'. Unsurprisingly, the 'steward' motif also features in Richard Baxter's directions to the rich in his influential discussion of 'Christian Oeconomicks' in *A Christian Directory: or, A Summ of Practical Theologie, and Cases of Conscience* (1673), pp. 495, 631–3.
[10] Robert Moss, *The Providential Division of Men into Rich and Poor, and the Respective Duties thence Arising, Briefly Consider'd in a Sermon* (1708), pp. 7–8.
[11] Similar, though usually less condescending, sentiments can be found in Steele, *The Husbandmans Calling*, pp. 63–9, 76–83; Thomas Gouge, *The Principles of Christian Religion Explained to the Capacity of the Meanest* (1675), p. 35; Humphrey Bralesford, *The Poor Man's Help: Being, I. An Abridgement of Bishop Pearson on the Creed … II. A Short Exposition of the Lord's Prayer … III. The Ten Commandments Explain'd* (1689), p. 29; Stanhope, *The Danger of Hard-heartedness*, pp. 11–15, 19; Clarkson, *Sermons and Discourses*, pp. 333–5; John Stevens, *The Whole Parable of Dives and Lazarus, Explain'd and Apply'd: being Several Sermons Preached in Cripplegate and Lothbury Churches* (1697), p. 25; Henry Hammond, *A Practical Catechism: Whereunto is Added The Reasonableness of Christian Religion* (7th edn, 1662), pp. 282–3; Adam Littleton, *Solomons Gate, or, An Entrance into the Church being a Familiar Explanation of the Grounds of Religion Conteined in the Fowr Heads of Catechism* (1662), pp. 83, 90–91; John Williams, *A Brief Exposition of the Church-Catechism, with Proofs from Scripture* (3rd edn, 1691), pp. 50–51; William Wake, *The Principles of the Christian Religion Explained: In a Brief Commentary upon the Church Catechism* (1699), p. 139.

he provides, and look forward to death, that 'stingless friend' of the poor.[12] If God, whose infinite wisdom was impossible to deny, assigned one family great riches and other practically nothing, the chief duty of the poor family was to bear such hardship patiently.

Admonitions like these, when looked at in isolation, might seem merely to reinforce Marx's pithy remark about religion as 'the opium of the people', a tool used by authorities to pacify the masses.[13] Yet, while the passivity demanded in these texts is an aspect that cannot be ignored, such an interpretation would rely on a rather myopic reading of the sources. In fact, most writers who employed the notion of stewardship thought that it was the rich who had the most to learn from this doctrine. For instance, a short religious tract noted that '*principally*, and especially, this duty [of stewardship] belongeth unto *rich men*'.[14] The same emphasis can be seen in a ballad published in the 1680s. The song began by insisting that one should avoid the temptations of covetousness irrespective of one's present 'Estate', for there is 'No Wealth like a contented mind', but later verses included a more socially specific admonition. The 'Rich', claimed the ballad-writer, ought to remember that 'If God hath lent thee treasure store, / Thou art but the Steward for the Poor' and must 'give account' in 'Heavens Court of Justice high', especially if you 'by oppression wrong the Poor' or 'turn the poor man's Cause away'.[15] Drawing on the proverbial wisdom of the day, this song turned a brief plea for the joys of contentment into a wide-ranging elaboration of the duties of earthly 'Trustees'.[16] Patience in the face of poverty may

---

[12] *England's Mercies in the Midst of Miserys* (1685), in *PB*, II, p. 226. See also John Houghton, *England's Great Happiness: Or, A Dialogue Between Content and Complaint* (1677); Thomas Jordan, *An Honest Mans Delight* (c.1660–74) in *WB*, Wood E 25(50); *Time's Darling* (c.1684–6), in *PB*, II, p. 11; *The Poor Mans Councillor* (c.1684–6), in *PB*, II, 86; *The Poor Man put to a Pinch* (n.d.), in *PB*, IV, p. 299; *A Threefold Alphabet of Rules*, s.v. 'S'; Capp, *Astrology*, pp. 102–3. For a similar portrayal of death as 'the best friend' of the godly poor see John Hart, *Heavens Glory And Hells Horror: or, the Parable of Dives and Lazarus Opened and Applied* (1662), sig. B2v.

[13] Karl Marx, 'Contribution to a Critique of Hegel's Philosophy of the Right' (1844), in *Selected Writings in Sociology and Social Philosophy*, T. B. Bottomore and Maximilien Rubel eds (2nd edn, Harmondsworth and Ringwood, 1970), p. 41. Several Marxist historians, whose analysis of religion is elsewhere quite nuanced, have sometimes reinforced this view: Thompson, *Making of the English Working Class*, ch. 11 (but cf. ch. 2); Hill, *World Turned Upside Down*, pp. 324–31, 350–53 (but cf. ch. 7, 9, etc.). Richard Schlatter went so far as to describe Restoration religious teaching on poverty as 'a drug' that dampened revolutionary impulses: *Social Ideas*, p. 155.

[14] Younge, *The Poors Advocate*, p. 19. Nearly all the passages cited in n. 9 above are explicitly directed at the wealthy.

[15] *Time's Darling* (c.1684–6), in *PB*, II, p. 11. One can also find a wonderfully literal inversion of this notion condemned in another ballad from the same period, for which see pp. 58–9 below.

[16] It integrates several popular axioms on contentment along with the commonplace about 'rich men' as 'stewards to the poor': Morris Tilley, *A Dictionary of Proverbs in*

have been a virtue, but this was usually just one element in a multifaceted evocation of economic morality.

Even more specific was John Bellers, the respected Quaker merchant and philanthropist. In a short essay published in 1699, he reminded rich men to make 'a consideration of the great Stewardship they are in and must give an account of, whilst they possess manifold more than there is in Proportion for the Body of the Nation'.[17] Like most commentators, he insisted that the greater men's riches, 'the greater Stewards' they must be. Thus, 'every Master of such an Estate' must 'consider how far he shall be answerable for the Stewardship of it, and for the present Comfort and future Happiness of all such Dependents, he in a degree Ruleth over'. However, Bellers went much further than other writers in attempting to formulate an equation that would determine the extent of one's obligations, claiming that 'whatever any enjoys more than 40l. for every Head in his Family' must be used to 'imploy' and 'direct the Poor in their Labour' at the rate at one dependant for every £40 in excess. It seems that quantitative methods – so often regarded as signs of economic modernity when used in 'political arithmetick' – might just as easily be employed in promoting ideals of Christian charity.

While it was rarely acknowledged directly, texts that represented property as a 'Deputation' from God were endorsing a concept that was inherently antithetical to conventional proprietary theories of ownership. Faith in the all-encompassing power of the Almighty was the bedrock upon which stewardship was based and this absolutist notion of authority gave little scope to those who claimed exclusive dominion over material possessions. For one catechist, writing just after the Restoration, the ideal way to teach this doctrine to those of 'Vulgar Understanding' was through the Lord's Prayer. According to him, if our heavenly Father is kind enough to give us more than just our daily bread, we are obliged to 'communicate God's goodness, and to distribute it amongst the poor', for our superfluities are 'a trust to be laid out for the good of the community'. This ought to be a warning to 'worldly men, [who] consider none but themselves' and 'ingross the whole stock of His blessings' – only the most 'sacrilegious and profane' dared to try to 'cheat God himself of his due'.[18] It was broadly accepted that individuals were entitled to maintain themselves at a level appropriate to their rank or station in life, but such self-indulgence had indisputable limits. None but

England in the Sixteenth and Seventeenth Centuries (Ann Arbor, 1950), pp. 117–18, 438, 713.

[17] Bellers, *Essays About the Poor*, pp. 14–15.

[18] Littleton, *Solomons Gate*, pp. 81–92. For another catechistic explanation of the Lord's Prayer with much the same message see Gouge, *The Principles of Christian Religion*, p. 35. Regarding the idea of poor stewardship as sacrilege, Clarkson preached that it was '*virtual Atheism*; and no less in effect than Treason against the Most High', while Moss agreed that it was 'Disobedience to his Lord': Clarkson, *Sermons and Discourses*, pp. 329–30; Moss, *The Providential Division*, pp. 8–12.

atheists could believe that temporal possessions lay completely at the whim of their mortal possessor.

Legalist notions of exclusive property rights may have won some converts among philosophers and jurists, but more popular sources remind us that they clearly had tough competition.[19] In fact, even for learned political thinkers, wholly 'possessive' conceptions of wealth and goods were never more than one idea among many. For example, one of the most famous judges of this era, Sir Matthew Hale, was popularly represented as a traditionalist in his attitude toward economic stewardship. In a brief tract pieced together from parts of his devotional essays, Hale declared that 'a Faithful Steward' is like 'the Lords Baily, or the Merchants Cash-keeper', who knows that his 'Dispensation' is only granted on 'Trust'.[20] Given their pervasiveness, such sentiments cannot be regarded as mere remnants of an obsolete religious morality. Even the thoroughly proprietary writings of John Locke included – and were tempered by – a belief in stewardship.[21] However, the most interesting evocations of divine ownership are to be found in texts intended for people of a more 'Vulgar Understanding'.

One of the fullest expressions of this doctrine can be found in a tract by the writer Richard Younge of Essex. Originally published during the interregnum as a longish work called *The Poores Advocate*, it was republished in 1665 as a short pamphlet whose title page announced Younge's intention to focus much of his attention on 'Rich Men' who fail in 'the faithfull discharge of their stewardships'. Relying on the authority of both scripture and the Church Fathers, he declared:

> we are not *owners* but *almoners*; *Stewards*, not independent *Lords* of what we possess.... The *wealth of the rich*, is but deposited in their hands, to supply the *necessities of the poor* ... [who are] the owners of our superfluities.... It is the *bread* of the hungry which mouldeth in thy *cupboard*, it is the *coat* of the naked which hangeth useless in thy chamber or wardrobe, they are the *shooes* of him that goeth *barefoot*, which ly rotting by thee; it is the *silver* of the needy which *rusteth* in thy chest.[22]

---

[19] For arguments that legal and political theorists of this period saw property in increasingly exclusivist terms see Macpherson, *Political Theory*; Appleby, *Economic Thought*; G. E. Aylmer, 'The Meaning and Definition of "Property" in Seventeenth-Century England', *Past & Present*, 86 (1980), pp. 87–97.

[20] Hale, *Some Necessary and Important Considerations*, pp. 5–6, 9, 15. According to the title-page, this was the ninth edition of the tract and was apparently 'freely given away' by the publisher.

[21] Ian Shapiro, 'Resources, Capacities, and Ownership: The Workmanship Ideal and Distributive Justice', in John Brewer and Susan Staves (eds), *Early Modern Conceptions of Property* (London, 1995), pp. 21–42. For Locke's balance between 'inclusive' and 'exclusive' property rights more generally see Thomas Horne, *Property Rights and Poverty: Political Argument in Britain, 1605–1834* (Chapel Hill, 1990), ch. 2.

[22] Younge, *The Poors Advocate*, pp. 4–5 (paraphrasing Prov. 2:27 and St Basil). His

In this formulation, goods belonged to their possessor only so long as he or she required them. If they were no more than 'superfluities', their owner-ship immediately transferred to 'the needy' and their possessor was forced to assume the responsibility of faithfully distributing them. For most moralists, it seems that God's gifts came with clear and unavoidable obligations.

These denunciations of ungodly behaviour sometimes pushed the notion of property as 'a trust' still further by presenting uncharitableness as a crim-inal act of misappropriation.[23] After all, the selfish accumulation of wealth had long been associated with criminality. Later Stuart preachers echoed their predecessors when they declared that 'the Man that lays up, not to use [charitably], but to keep and possess his Wealth', would rather 'rob' God than be a good 'Steward' to him.[24] David Clarkson, preaching to his nonconformist congregation at Mortlake (Surrey) in the 1670s or 1680s, warned his flock against this scandalous practice: 'Every one who imploys not what he hath for God, is a Thief to God' and such malefactors are 'Thieves to Men also, *viz.* To those, for whose Relief and Refreshment that [misemployed wealth] was due'.[25] Because sharing one's God-given resources with the poor was said to be sanctioned by divine law, its inversion came to be seen as an illicit breach of the same. To treat charity as a mere 'Arbitrary' option, claimed clerics and catechists, is to 'Rob' from the distressed under 'a black Criminal Hue', for anything 'which thou storest up, without regard to the necessities of others, is unlawfully detained by thee'.[26] In the minds of the faithful, the mere act of private possession might be transformed into a spiritual felony by the mercilessness or ingratitude of a false steward. Still worse, there were some rich men who claimed that what God had trusted them with was not enough. Such were the 'oppressor', 'extortioner', 'griping usurer' or 'couzning trades man', each of whom 'breaks open the exchequer, and plunders divine bounty' by seeking gain at the expense of his neigh-bours.[27]

---

contemporaries noted that Younge was in 'the habit of selling works at below cost price, or lending copies (on deposit of 2d.), or even giving them away': *ODNB*.

[23] This paragraph examines the metaphor of criminality only within the theological framework of 'stewardship'. For uses of illegality as a trope see below pp. 132, 171–2.

[24] William Talbot, *The Foolish Abuse and Wise Use of Riches: A Sermon Preach'd in the Parish-Church of Bromsgrove in Worcester-shire* (1695), p. 8.

[25] Clarkson, *Sermons and Discourses*, pp. 329, 341.

[26] Thomas, *The Mammon of Unrighteousness*, p. 25; Tillotson, *Sixteen Sermons*, p. 219. See also Younge, *The Poors Advocate*, p. 24; Barrow, *The Duty and Reward of Bounty*, pp. 77–80; Durham, *Encouragement to Charity*, p. 9; Jones, *A Sermon Preached at Christ-Church*, p. 25. One wonders if this doctrine was what inspired Pierre-Joseph Proudhon to declare that 'property is theft' almost 200 years later. Perhaps both formulations owe something to the proverb, common since St Jerome, that 'every rich man is either unjust or the heir of an unjust man': Tilley, *Proverbs*, p. 426.

[27] Littleton, *Solomons Gate*, pp. 89–90.

God, it seems, intended his gifts to be used charitably. This was the central claim that emerged from the notion of stewardship and, throughout the early modern era, it remained a universal point of agreement. The implications of this injunction, however, were not always spelled out. When they were, as in the moralised descriptions of corn-dealing published in ballads and cheap octavo pamphlets, it becomes clear that 'charity' meant much more than mere occasional philanthropy by the 'better sort'.[28] In an oft-repeated account of greedy Somersetshire farmers, for instance, it was reported that this group of 'Churlish Nabals' raised their prices to profit from the dearth which struck the western counties in the mid-1670s. Clearly they had forgotten that corn – like all temporal goods – 'is but lent to us by the Lord, who expects it to be improved to his Service and the Good of our fellow-Creatures'.[29] During the lean years of the 1690s, commentators were even less forgiving. One grain hoarder – because of his 'cruel and covetous mind' – was said to have cursed a plentiful harvest and vowed to hold his corn until the price rose again. According to the ballad-writer, this 'oppressor' did 'not deserve … the name of a christian', because he desired only 'to see [his] poor brethren starve' and confined the 'sweet blessings of God' sent from heaven to 'nourish the race of mankind' to his 'barns for profit' rather than graciously distributing them.[30] Even catechists taught that God, 'in his providence, designed the rich man to be his Steward, [and] the wealthy mans barn to be the poor mans store-house'.[31] The duty of charity that came with each earthly 'Deputation' was one which reached into every sphere of economic life and was as likely to affect the dynamics of weekly market days as to influence death-bed testaments or informal poor relief.

The material consequences that might have emerged from this doctrine should not be overestimated, but neither should they be ignored. In the hands of preachers such as Robert Moss, stewardship was never more than a rhetorical device with which to prod stingy rich men and reassure the poor of God's grand plan. However, even these rather mild sentiments contained a much more troublesome philosophical kernel. Since all property ultimately

---

[28] 'Charity', in the words of one preacher, was 'A word so big and comprehensive … that it points out the whole duty of man', while other clergymen included neighbourly love under this heading and defined it as '*essential* to true Christianity', the crowning virtue, the highest law, and the plainest mark of godliness: Pittis, *A Spittle Sermon*, p. 1; Durham, *Encouragement to Charity*, p. 8; Edward Stillingfleet, *Protestant Charity: A Sermon Preached at S. Sepulchres Church, on Tuesday in Easter Week* (1681), p. 10; Isaac Barrow, *Of the Love of God and Our Neighbour, in Several Sermons* (1680), esp. pp. 75–7, 135–7.

[29] *God's Great and Wonderful Work in Somerset-shire: Or the Charitable Farmer Miraculously Rewarded* (1674), p. 5. For the story of Nabal, who is killed by God after refusing to provision David's men, see 1 Sam. 25.

[30] *The West-Country Miser* (c.1692–1703), in *PB*, IV, p. 236. For a few of the many variants of this story see the ballads and pamphlets cited below p. 58 n. 115.

[31] Hammond, *A Practical Catechism*, p. 282.

belonged to an absolute authority beyond the mortal realm, no individual had an exclusive claim to his or her possessions. The possibilities opened up by this were immense and John Edwards, preaching at the 'Opening of a Great Fair', made one of them explicit. By misusing our 'worldly Blessings', he declared, we 'dishonour our Great Benefactor' and 'if thus we pervert the Intentions of the Donor, it is but just that we should be deprived of them'.[32] Edwards obviously intended that God should do the depriving, but one wonders if hungry members of his audience would have interpreted it this way.

Like most sources from this era that allude to temporal trusteeship, this sermon was certainly not radical in any conventional sense. The religious truism upon which it relied, however, could never be entirely purged of its distinctly anti-proprietary implications. It was simply impossible for rational, self-interested *homo economicus* to function unimpinged while most people still believed that God attached conditions to every worldly gift. An almanac writer of 1685 was not alone when he affirmed that 'we now cry, Every man for himself and God for us all; but ... where every man is for himself, *Non Deus sed Diabolus*, the Devil is for all'.[33]

2 Mammonism

Obedience to the jealous deity of seventeenth-century Protestantism required a total and unambiguous commitment. Equivocation was no better than heresy. Militant monotheism of this sort was, theologically at least, impossible to reconcile with any deep interest in worldly affairs and those who seemed too devoted to the pursuit of earthly gain risked accusations of idolatry.[34] Christ himself made this clear in his gloss of the first commandment: 'No man can serve two masters: for either he will hate the one, and

---

[32] John Edwards, *Sermons On Special Occasions and Subjects* (1698), p. 145. One tract-writer claimed that 'the relief of [the poor's] common necessities is none of the least Conditions whereby [the rich man] holds all his *Good things*; which when that Tenure is forfeited by his default, he may justly expect some Judgement to ensue; or else that those riches wherby he prizes himself so extravagantly, may shortly be taken from him': *The Mowing-Devil: Or, Strange News out of Hartford-shire* (1678), pp. 3–4. Likewise, God decreed that 'the Poor have always *a Right* to some part of the Possessions of the Rich': Stanhope, *The Danger of Hard-heartedness*, p. 10 (emphasis added). For the implications of these views for strategies for redress see pp. 75–7 below.

[33] John Wing, *Olympia Domata, or, An Almanack* (Cambridge, 1685), sig. C5r. See also Vincent Wing, *Olympia Domata, or, An Almanack* (1668), sig. C6r–v; Tilley, *Proverbs*, p. 410.

[34] There were presumably connections between theologically inspired iconoclastic idioms and the politicised role of anti-popery. The economic aspects of the latter are discussed on pp. 173–5 below.

love the other; or else he will hold to the one, and despise the other. Ye cannot serve God and Mammon.'[35]

The equation was quite simple, but it seems that the people of later Stuart England needed constant reminders. Many detailed explanations of the dangers of 'Mammonism' were, accordingly, preached or published during this period. An extreme example of this persistent reiteration can be found on almost every page of a short tract by the Quaker leader George Fox, published in 1679. Citing numerous passages from both the Old and New Testaments, Fox unremittingly equated covetousness and the 'love of money' with 'Idolatrous Practice' that 'must be purged out'.[36] But this was not just an issue for zealots emerging out of the radicalism of the Interregnum; even the most conventional religious ministry made the connection. One of the official homilies, for example, condemned 'covetous persons ... worshipping indeed, not onely the images, but also the matter of them, gold and silver, as that vice is of all others in the Scriptures peculiarly called idolatry'.[37] No genre of religious instruction or popular literature seems to have lacked an allusion to this particular metaphor – its truth was proverbial.[38]

In its plainest form, the denunciation of Mammonism focused on material riches as a temptation likely to incite the unwarranted devotion of weak mortals. 'This [worldly wealth] is array'd in gorgeous apparel', noted renowned preacher William Dawes in 1698; we are thus prone to 'bow down to it, and worship it, and call whatsoever it dictates the voice of God'.[39] Many other clergy, including Archbishop Tillotson, felt similarly obliged to remind their audiences that 'the *Covetous* Man sets up his *Riches* in the place of *God*', and a Restoration catechist instructed every Christian to attempt an intellectual 'amputation of all those superfluous burthensome cares of the Worldling or Mammonist'.[40] Given its prevalence in religious discourse, it is

---

[35] Mat. 6:24 and Luke 16:13.

[36] George Fox, *This is a Warning to All that Profess Christianity and Others: To Beware of Covetousness, which is Idolatry* (1679). Variants of this metaphor are found on eleven of the tract's sixteen pages.

[37] 'Homily Against Peril of Idolatry, [pt. I]', in *Certain Sermons or Homilies*, II, p. 103 (citing Eph. 5:5 and Col. 3:5). For further discussion of this and other examples of 'idolatry' as a rhetoric device in earlier preaching on economic issues see Brodie Waddell, 'Economic Immorality and Social Reformation in English Popular Preaching, 1585–1625', *Cultural and Social History*, 5:2 (2008), pp. 167–8.

[38] Tilley, *Proverbs*, p. 264.

[39] William Dawes, *Wor[l]dly Men Wiser, in Their Way than Christians, in Theirs. A Sermon Preach'd at Saint James's in Lent, 1698* (1707), p. 13.

[40] Tillotson, *Sixteen Sermons*, pp. 134–5, 156, 177–82; Hammond, *A Practical Catechism*, p. 289. Hammond's advice was part of a detailed exposition of Mat. 6:19–24 centered on the dangers of 'Mammonism' in ibid., pp. 265–89. For analogous warnings about 'Mammon, the Idol Paramount', see Thomas, *The Mammon of Unrighteousness*, p. 10; Barrow, *The Duty and Reward of Bounty*, pp. 98–9, 103–4, 198; Jones, *A Sermon Preached at Christ-Church*, p. 26; Moss, *The Providential Division*, p. 9. For a slightly different

perhaps unsurprising that this trope also appeared in the ubiquitous ballads and pamphlets published to lament the avaricious nature of contemporary social life. Several cheap printed verses produced during the last decades of the seventeenth century claimed, for instance, that 'Madam Money' had become an 'adored Idol' for the whole country and 'the Worldling's *Primum Mobile*'.[41] One ballad took this personification still further (Fig. 1.1). Probably published in the early 1690s, this rhyming tale described how the Devil appeared and tempted a 'Vertuous Young Man' from the London parish of St Giles. Satan claimed 'he would furnish him with Baggs of Gold and Silver', but the youth resisted his offer and declared: 'Deceitful Wretch begon, I cannot brook / Thy Golden Baits, nor yet thy Silver Hook'.[42] Such stories of enrichment through diabolical pacts, despite their reliance on well-worn tropes, reaffirmed the link between wealth and sin. Indeed, often these under-developed analogies were neither particularly original in their form nor especially potent in their appeal, but they show that the Mammonist's presence in the mental landscapes of the time is undeniable. More importantly, further investigation reveals that these brief and sometimes superficial allusions rested on a much more substantial conceptual foundation.

The biblical passages quoted at the beginning of this section ought to remind us that such concerns were a perpetually recurring feature in the Mosaic tradition. In the sixteenth and seventeenth centuries, however, the iconoclastic impulse reached new levels of intensity and its analogical strength gave it an enhanced role in the kingdom's socio-political affairs.[43] The theorist Jean-Joseph Goux has demonstrated how easy it is for a philosophical critique of religious imagery to evolve into an attempt to abolish economic idolatry. For Judaeo-Christian ideologues, the context of this

analogy, wherein the rich glutton will 'worship no God but *his Belly* ... His Morning-Devotion seems to have lain among his Hounds, and the drowning of his Senses was his *Evening-Sacrifice*', see Richard Theed, *Admonition from the Other World: Or, The Story of Dives and Lazarus Practically Improv'd, in Two Sermons, Preach'd at Sutton-Cofield, in Warwickshire, on Sunday, October the 22d MDCCX* (1711), p. 2.
41 *Pecunia's Departure* (c.1696–9), in *PB*, IV, p. 325; *The Nature, Nobility, Character and Complement of Money* (1684). For pamphlets see Richard Younge, *A Precious Mithridate for the Soule made up of those Two Poysons, Covetousness and Prodigality* (1661), pp. 2–3; Hart, *The Charitable Christian*, sig. A4v, A7r; Younge, *The Poors Advocate*, pp. 29–31; Edward Stephens, *An Admonition Concerning a Publick Fast, the Just Causes we have for It, from the Full Growth of Sin, and the Near Approaches of God's Judgments* (1691), p. 18. See also the famous depiction of 'Lucre Hill' as 'a dangerous Hill' holding a 'treasure [which] is a snare to those who seek it' leading many weak mortals to be 'slain': Bunyan, *Pilgrim's Progress*, pp. 141–2.
42 *The Young-mans Victory Over the Power of the Devil: Or, Strange and Wonderful News from the City of London* (c.1693).
43 Literature on this subject is increasingly voluminous. For two insightful examples see Margaret Aston's research, including *England's Iconoclasts* (Oxford, 1988), and John Walter's '"Abolishing Superstition with Sedition"? The Politics of Popular Iconoclasm in England, 1640–1642', *Past & Present*, 183 (2004), pp. 79–123.

Figure 1.1. An image from *The Young-mans Victory Over the Power of the Devil* (c.1693) made literal the commonplace notion that those eager for riches were likely to abandon Christian principles in favour of diabolical impulses.

particular sin was insignificant – because, whether religious or economic, 'fetishism is always … the overvalorization of the *thing*, as opposed to a relationship'.[44] Hence, just as spiritual idolaters were said to have turned their divine master into an object that could be possessed, economic idolaters reified their wealth, granting it an intrinsic rather than a 'social' value. In either case, this was a dangerous species of hubris. The essential problem, according to contemporaries, was not merely that the world was a distraction from more spiritual concerns, but that worldly riches gave their mortal possessors a false sense of their own power.

This conflation of spiritual idolatry and economic egoism could lead to some tremendously detailed rhetorical attacks from would-be iconoclasts. On 2 November 1690, for example, the wealthy parishioners of London's Lombard Street experienced just such an assault from the pulpit of their young minister, David Jones. The ferocious preacher declared that, like Judas, 'rich men' are often

---

[44] Jean-Joseph Goux, *Symbolic Economies: After Marx and Freud* (Ithaca, 1990), ch. 7, (quotation at p. 158). Following Goux's lead, the literary critic David Hawkes has looked at this issue through the work of authors like Shakespeare, Milton, Donne, and Bunyan in his *Idols of the Marketplace: Idolatry and Commodity Fetishism in English Literature, 1580–1680* (New York, 2001).

so Proud, that they despise and undervalue the best of Men at so great a rate, as to value the Lord of Life, and King of Glory at no more than Thirty pieces of Silver… [H]e will not only forget the Lord that made him, but he will also treat Him with the greatest Scorn and Contempt imaginable; … he will use Him in the vilest manner, he will lift up his heels against Him, he will kick at Him, and trample with his Feet upon the Lord that brought him.[45]

This vitriol was part of a larger onslaught that Jones launched against the banking district's complaisant attitude toward extortion and covetousness. His habit of excommunicating usurers made him enough powerful enemies to ensure that he was soon dismissed from this post, but his assumptions about the link between pride, riches, and idolatry were hardly controversial.[46] Other preachers followed a similar line of reasoning, incorporating the doctrine of stewardship as well. Rather than regarding wealth as a gift granted conditionally by God, worldly affluence led weak mortals to regard it as an exclusive possession and to neglect their social duties. The insatiable rich man 'doth not *possess* his estate, but is *possest by it*, which if it not be the *same* is *as bad* as being *possest by the Devil*'.[47] Paradoxically, by believing that riches are entirely our own, we make them 'our Lord and Master' and give them hold 'a Sovereignty and Empire over us' that ought to belong only to the Almighty.[48] In early modern homiletics, those who insisted on their personal authority over material possessions became slaves to an idol, whereas those who accepted the obligations of Christian stewardship actually liberated themselves from this sinful servitude.

In the vast majority of sermons published during the period, this theological elaboration remained fairly abstract. With the revealing exception of the ill-fated David Jones, most clergy who discussed the bond connecting religious and economic idolatry used the inoffensive, time-worn terminology of 'covetousness' and 'charity' to describe the relevant sins and

---

[45] Jones, A *Sermon Preached at Christ-Church*, pp. 17–18.

[46] David Jones, A *Farewel-Sermon Preached to the United Parishes of St. Mary Woolnoth, & St. Mary Woolchurch-Haw in Lombard-Street* (1692), esp. pp. 31–9. Throughout his career he was regularly a 'frustration to his congregations', although he drew large audiences and his farewell-sermon's popularity provoked four additional editions: ODNB.

[47] Cartwright, *The Danger of Riches*, p. 22. Like Jones's, this sermon also seems to have courted controversy, although Cartwright went on to become a royal favourite rather than being ousted from his post. For similar passages about rich men as idolaters and Satan-worshippers see ibid., pp. 2, 12, 15, 18–19, 23. For the controversy that arose from the sermon see p. 82 below.

[48] Tillotson, *Sixteen Sermons*, p. 144; Dawes, *Wor[l]dly Men Wiser*, p. 13; Younge, *The Poors Advocate*, p. 29. Hawkes has pointed out that in Bunyan's allegories both Mr Badman and Mr By-Ends have 'illusions of chimerical independence' and 'fantasies of autonomy', but are actually just reprobation personified and thus completely subjugated by their sinful self-interest: David Hawkes, 'Commodification and Subjectivity in John Bunyan's Fiction', *Eighteenth Century: Theory and Interpretation*, 41:1 (2000), pp. 40, 50.

virtues. Instead of citing particular practices or occupations, they tended to rely on biblical parables or classical allusions to convince their audiences of the dangers of Mammonism.[49] However, in the more anonymous world of pamphlets and broadsides such abuses often became at least slightly more specific. One of the more common variants of the stereotypical idolater was the greedy miser who was decried not only for his lack of charity but also because he prevented the country's scarce currency from circulating. In 1689, for example, a pamphleteer writing under the pseudonym 'Poor Robin' complained that 'Rich Misers and wealthy Chuffs, who go by the name of Christians, make a God of their Gold, and commit Idolatry'.[50] The ballads in Samuel Pepys's collection employed much the same language to fault 'Misers' because they 'horded' and 'worshipt' their money, killing trade by 'raking' in coin rather than relieving the poor.[51] In the early modern imagination, this image of niggardly accumulation might be associated with almost anyone who had wealth, but its most common practitioner was thought to be the professional money-lender. Even when the terms were not simply used as synonyms, both the 'miser' and the 'usurer' were regarded as idolatrously inclined. The rhetorically astute 'tradesman' who authored a purportedly desperate complaint in 1663 reported that these usurious creditors turn their 'lovely Bags' into a 'God' and became the 'Devils Brokers' for each 'loves his Money … more then soul and body'.[52] Charging poor debtors heavy interest or ruthlessly pursuing defaulters may have had little more than a metaphorical connection to the supposed fetishism of popery or paganism, but the link was still a strong one. Although such occupationally specific allegations of idolatry were not particularly common in later Stuart preaching, they certainly appeared in other genres and built on the imagery found in the religious discourse of previous generations.[53]

Miserly creditors were not the only social group to find themselves targeted by writers drawing on the iconoclastic fervour of the Reformation. Along with those whose whole profession centred on the commodification and reproduction of money, practically anyone who enjoyed some measure

---

[49] The parable in Luke 12:13–21, for example, was paraphrased and glossed in Talbot, *The Foolish Abuse*, p. 5.

[50] 'Poor Robin', *A Hue and Cry after Money* (1689), p. 3. 'Chuff', in this instance, simply meant 'a close avaricious man': *OED*.

[51] *Conscience by Scruples and Money by Ounces* (1697), in *PB*, IV, p. 307; *The Naked Truth* (c.1688–96), in *PB*, IV, p. 314; *England's Mercies in the Midst of Miserys* (1685), in *PB*, II, p. 226. For the social aspects of the perennial scarcity of hard currency in early modern England, especially in the decades leading up to the recoinage of 1696, see Craig Muldrew, '"Hard Food for Midas': Cash and Its Social Value in Early Modern England', *Past & Present*, 170 (2001), pp. 78–120; idem, *Economy of Obligation*, esp. pp. 98–103; Malcolm Gaskill, *Crime and Mentalities in Early Modern England* (Cambridge, 2000), ch. 4–5, esp. pp. 162–4.

[52] *The Citizens Complaint for Want of Trade* (1663), p. 6.

[53] For earlier examples see Waddell, 'Economic Immorality', pp. 167–8.

of economic power over others might be accused of Mammonism. When employers attempted to increase their profits at the expense of their workers, they provided authors such as Lawrence White with an opportunity appeal to their readers' religiosity. At the end of his providential tract against grain hoarders, for instance, White went on to condemn those so 'greedy of gain' that they

> deceive the poor laborers out of their wages: gripe them that which is their due, & think they never work cheap enough to inrich their covetous desires, for they lie hoarding up their money, & *make it their god*, for where their riches lyes there their heart is also, but know, oh man, that the Lord will bring you to a reckoning at last.[54]

A more wide-ranging critique appeared in 1700 in the form of a detailed biographical parody penned by Edward Ward. He recounted the tale of 'John Sharp', a fast-rising merchant who severely mistreated his apprentices, lied to customers, cheated local paupers, and hoarded every penny that passed his way – all because 'Gold [was] his Heav'n'. One wonders if it was merely a coincidence that one of Sharp's most profitable frauds was said to have been embezzling funds from his numerous projects to 'gilt' and beautify his parish church.[55] For the hack writers and satirists of the later Stuart publishing trade, it was clearly uncontroversial to conflate specific economic sins with more heinous offences against the first and second commandments. This homology must have come naturally to authors and audiences whose religious education had taught them that 'the denunciation of idols' could include a 'critique of economic fetishism'.[56] In this world, the unequal social relations created through bonds of credit, employment or retail exchange were all open to abuse by those whose only deity was material wealth.

---

[54] Lawrence White, *The Charitable Farmer of Somersetshire: or, God's Great and Wonderful Work* (1674?), p. 7 (emphasis added). A century later, accusations of idolatry were still being levelled in times of dearth. The gentlemen of Newbury, for example, received an anonymous warning in 1772 saying 'Donte make a god of your mony' by starving 'the pore', and later still, in 1795, Cornish tinners threatened an 'Averishes Woman' who apparently hoarded corn, saying 'We are … determined to assemble and immediately to march till we come to your Idol, or your God or your Mows [of hoarded grain], whome you esteem as such and pull it down and likewise your House': Thompson, *Customs in Common*, p. 255.

[55] Edward Ward, *The Wealthy Shop-keeper, or, The Charitable Citizen: A Poem* (1700).

[56] Goux, *Symbolic Economies*, p. 160. Indeed, this trope remained a part of mainstream economic discourse even in the mid-nineteenth century: G. R. Searle, *Morality and the Market in Victorian Britain* (Oxford, 1998), p. 81. Compare this to the claim that, by the eighteenth century, 'there was no consciousness of an acute tension between the claims of religion and the glittering allurements of commercial civilization': Tawney, *Religion*, p. 274.

'The carking infidelity of the worldling' drew him into 'the service of Mammon' which 'prescribeth violence to every man, oppressing the poor righteous man, any that stands in our way to our espoused gain'.[57] This was the near-universal anxiety framing these sacralised condemnations of particular offences. The atheistic disavowal of divine power implied in even relatively minor acts of worldly self-aggrandisement evidently led directly to much graver sins, whether religious or economic. In cases like that of the satirical 'John Sharp', the specifics of this socio-spiritual descent were described in meticulous detail, but more often they were just insinuated or assumed. Preachers and authors could rely on their audiences making the connections for themselves. Accustomed to thinking in dichotomies, contemporaries imagined Christ's stark division between 'God and Mammon' as two mutually illuminating ideas – an allusion to either might invoke a whole constellation of powerful imagery. Hence, just as the true worship of God was always thought to include graciously fulfilling the neighbourly duties outlined in the 'second table' of the Decalogue, a corrupt faith in the world necessarily implied a more general social malevolence. This is why Bishop William Thomas paired his call to relieve 'our indigent Brethren', 'the living Temples of the everliving God', with an attack on 'Mammon, the Idol Paramount'.[58] Likewise, the 'Homily of Alms-Deeds' represented the binary as that between the greedy, who 'choose with pinching covetousness, rather to lean unto the Devil', and the pious, who 'by charitable merciful-ness, either to come unto Christ, or to suffer Christ to come unto them'.[59] Economic virtues demonstrated obedience to God, while economic vices implied a darker master.

3 Heaven and Hell

Worldly 'mammonists' – and 'good stewards' – faced a variety of conse-quences at the hands of divine justice, but the most intense effects were always associated with the world to come. Although theologians might debate the logistics of the operation, every Christian knew that death led

---

[57] Hammond, A Practical Catechism, p. 267. By 'carking' was meant 'fretting', 'anxious', 'miserly' or 'niggardly': OED.

[58] Thomas, The Mammon of Unrighteousness, pp. 10, 37 (citing Mat. 25:34–36). For a similar conflation of 'Covetousness', 'Idolatry', 'Unmercifulness', and 'Unbelief' in the context of a demand for charity see Hart, The Charitable Christian, sig. A4v–A5r.

[59] 'Homily of Alms-Deeds, [pt. III]', in Certain Sermons or Homilies, II, p. 238. For a more detailed homiletic attack on the Satanism of 'the Merchant and the worldly occupier' who 'increase themselves by usury, by extortion, [etc.]' see 'Homily for Rogation Week, [pt. II]' in Certain Sermons or Homilies, II, p. 295. For less theologically inspired allusions to diabolism see pp. 159–60 below.

either to endless torments or eternal bliss, and, owing to the absence of purgatory in Protestant theology, the division between them was strict.[60] The impact of this belief on later Stuart economic behaviour is unquantifiable, but for many individuals anxiety about the afterlife was something that significantly shaped their conduct in earthly affairs.[61] The connection between this life and the world hereafter had been firmly established by Christ himself and it was hardly fading away in the late seventeenth century. Instead, the renewed emphasis on moral conduct in Restoration religious teaching –a reaction against the single-minded predestinarianism of the 'puritans' – made this an essential part of the search for salvation.[62]

Like the doctrine of stewardship, a conviction that divine justice would be meted out in the afterlife was sometimes invoked in unambiguous demands for plebeian passivity and obedience. Scriptural passages such as Luke 6:20, where Jesus told his disciples that 'Blessed be ye poor: for yours is the kingdom of God', may have provided the impoverished with vital spiritual and psychological solace in times of hardship, but they were hardly likely to spur social action. A published sermon by Robert Johnson, for instance, espoused exactly this sort of pacifistic interpretation and proved popular enough to reach its twenty-second edition by 1684. In it, Johnson described Christ's parable of Lazarus and Dives as one in which 'He doth comfort all poor men, that although they are afflicted in this life with great miseries and calamities, yet they shall be comforted in the life to come, and rest in Abrahams bosom.'[63] This tendency to see earthly poverty as a precursor to heavenly riches was also regularly inverted. After all, it was 'easier for a camel to go through the eye of a needle, than for a rich man to enter into the kingdom of God'.[64] The publishers who presented Johnson's sermon to its Restoration audience clearly understood the appeal of this simple dichotomy as they used an old cracked wood-cut to express the point in a language understood by even the most illiterate of readers (Fig. 1.2).

[60] Philip Almond, *Heaven and Hell in Enlightenment England* (Cambridge, 1994), pp. 67–72.

[61] As Richard Schlatter pointed out many years ago, 'an active belief in the rewards of heaven and the punishments of hell … had important social consequences': Schlatter, *Social Ideas*, p. 147.

[62] John Spurr, *The Restoration Church of England, 1646–1689* (New Haven, 1991), ch. 6, esp. pp. 296–322; Green, *Print and Protestantism*, pp. 351–60, 369–71, 443, 589–90.

[63] Robert Johnson, *Dives and Lazarus, Or Rather Devilish Dives: Delivered in a Sermon at Paul's Cross* (22nd edn, 1684), sig. A4v.

[64] Matthew 19:23–24 (cf. Mark 10:24–25 and Luke 18:24–25). For reiterations of this point see Tilley, *Proverbs*, p. 570; Hart, *The Charitable Christian*, sig. B2r; Younge, *The Poors Advocate*, p. 30; Steele, *The Husbandmans Calling*, p. 82; Barrow, *The Duty and Reward of Bounty*, p. 178; Jones, *A Sermon Preached at Christ-Church*, p. 24; Clarkson, *Sermons and Discourses*, pp. 343–4; Stevens, *The Whole Parable*, p. 10; Theed, *Admonition from the Other World*, p. 35; Deuel Pead, *The Wicked Man's Misery, and the Poor Man's Hope and Comfort: Being a Sermon upon the Parable of Dives and Lazarus* (1699), p. 5.

Figure 1.2. The frontispiece to Robert Johnson's *Dives and Lazarus, Or Rather Devilish Dives* (1677) depicted the rich, uncharitable Dives feasting while 'clothed in purple and fine linen' – oblivious to the judgement about to strike him down from above. In contrast, the beggar Lazarus, despite being starved and 'full of sores', was shown to be crowned by God's blessing.

Here, the beggar's future bliss hangs over him as a glowing crown while the rich man's damnation sweeps down towards him in the form of a divine sword.

For most later Stuart moralists, however, the parable of Lazarus and Dives was more than just a consolation for the poor – it was also a call for reform. Christ condemned the rich man not because he was rich, but because he refused to share even the crumbs from his table with the starving beggar at his gate. This unambiguous act of mercilessness gave commentators an opportunity to launch into an often wide-ranging discussion of the importance of 'charity', which, it must be remembered, was a word that meant much more than just alms. Richard Younge conveyed the underlying sentiment clearly and directly when, in his 1665 tract, he declared that 'charity' was vital because 'the *sentence of absolution* or *condemnation*, shall be pronounced, either for or against us, according as we have *performed* or *neglected* this duty'.[65] Preaching almost thirty years later, William Sherlock, a royal chaplain and dean of St Paul's, put it even more bluntly. According to him, it had been 'plainly and expressly taught' by Christ and all his disciples that 'Heaven is the Reward of Charity; [and] that Hell is the Punishment for Uncharitableness.'[66] Such direct equations of 'good works' with salvation were far removed from the Calvinist predestinarianism of the early seventeenth century, but it was the logical interpretation of a great many later Stuart religious discussions of social and economic ethics.

Strict 'solifidians' doubtlessly would have objected even more strongly to the willingness of many preachers and tract-writers to use the language of accountancy when offering everlasting rewards to the charitable. The terminology of spiritual 'loans' and 'debts', inherited from medieval teaching and reinforced by the early modern era's pervasive 'culture of credit', imbued even the smallest of transactions with spiritual import.[67] William Talbot's 1695 sermon on *The Foolish Abuse and Wise Use of Riches* was typical in this respect. 'He that hath pity on the Poor, lendeth unto the Lord', claimed Talbot, and God will 'repay us with usury ... both here and hereafter'.[68] This

---

[65] Younge, *The Poors Advocate*, p. 3 (citing Mat. 25:33–46). Isaac Barrow is similarly emphatic in his sermon on *The Duty and Reward of Bounty*, pp. 58–63.

[66] Richard Sherlock, *The Charity of Lending without Usury ... In a Sermon Preach'd before the Right Honourable the Lord Mayor, at St. Bridget's Church* (2nd edn, 1692), p. 4.

[67] For medieval spiritual 'accounting' see John Bossy, 'Moral Arithmetic: Seven Sins into Ten Commandments', in Edmund Leites, *Conscience and Casuistry in Early Modern Europe* (Cambridge, 1988), p. 219. For the culture of credit see Muldrew, *Economy of Obligation*.

[68] Talbot, *The Foolish Abuse*, pp. 16, 23 (quoting Prov. 19:17). For more allusions to charity as 'the most growing Interest, with a most infallible Security to the Principle' see Stanhope, *The Danger of Hard-heartedness*, p. 27; Steele, *The Husbandmans Calling*, p. 97; Barrow, *The Duty and Reward of Bounty*, pp. 68, 189–190; Cornwallis, *Set on the Great Pot*, p. 10; Dawes, *Wor[l]dly Men Wiser*, p. 10; Edward Welchman, *The Duty and Reward of Charity, Especially as it Regardeth the Education of Poor Children: A Sermon*

drift into financial parlance must have been distasteful to those who valued only selfless altruism, but it may well have helped keep alive the many forms of informal support after the institutionalisation of parish relief in the Elizabethan statutes. Perhaps this is why Richard Croft, vicar of Stratford-upon-Avon, employed this idiom in his laudatory sermon on the endowment of 'a free-school and public charity' in 1696 wherein he declared that 'the necessitous and afflicted, the needy and the out-casts … will prove the best *Factors* to Negotiate our Affairs above, by laying up for us everlasting *Funds*, and fixing us Banks that shall be more durable'.[69] Such language was not, however, restricted to sycophantic preachers. Even the certificates granted by magistrates to those deemed 'fit objects of charity' sometimes included such sentiments, suggesting that 'what itt shall please the Almighty to move your heart [to give to the bearer] … you may be assured is but lent unto God and he will in his due time recompense you again'.[70] Similarly, in a twopenny tract which went through at least eleven editions in the late seventeenth century, John Hart used much the same imagery: 'O give, give unto the poor, and make God as much as you can indebted to you; [for] He is a good sure pay-master.' But optimistic promises like these often transformed into a threat. 'If you will not make God your Debter by giving', continued Hart, 'He will be your Judge for not giving.'[71]

The sheer popularity of the Lazarus and Dives parable attests to the menacing shadow which hung over early modern conceptions of uncharitableness. Its pervasiveness is remarkable. On 31 May 1705, for instance, George Stanhope used the parable as the basis for an entire sermon, directed at the patrons and pupils of London's charity schools, in which he focused mostly on how 'the Love and the Abuse of Money' consigned Dives 'to the Flames of Hell'.[72] His emphasis was hardly unique.[73] The reach of this story

Preach'd at Banbury in Oxfordshire (1707), p. 14; *A Voice from Heaven To the Youth of Great Britain: Containing, A Dialogue Between Christ, Youth, and the Devil* (c.1714), B1v; Tilley, *Proverbs*, p. 549. For charity as 'the best sort of *purchase*, even a *purchase* of eternal life' see Durham, *Encouragement to Charity*, p. 19. For medieval tales of charity repaid 'a hundredfold' after death see Frederic Tubach, *Index Exemplorum: A Handbook of Medieval Religious Tales* (Helsinki, 1969), p. 20 (no. 176).

[69] Croft, *The Wise Steward*, p. 21. Similarly, a later preacher described charity as the best 'Way to provide a good Security, and lay up *Treasures* for our selves in the Bank of *Heaven*, … [because] in our *grand* Account; it shall be allow'd us with ample Interest': Brent, *Persuasions to a Publick Spirit*, p. 13.

[70] *Minutes of Proceedings in Quarter Sessions Held for the Parts of Kesteven in the County of Lincoln, 1674–1695*, S. A. Peyton, ed. (Lincoln Record Society, nos. 25–26, 2 vols, Lincoln, 1931), II, p. 400.

[71] Hart, *The Charitable Christian*, sig. B3r–B3v.

[72] Stanhope, *The Danger of Hard-heartedness*, p. 20.

[73] For other extended treatments of the socio-economic implications of the parable see Hart, *Heavens Glory And Hells Horror*, esp. sig. A4r–B3v; Johnson, *Dives and Lazarus*; Stevens, *The Whole Parable*, esp. 'Sermon V'; Pead, *The Wicked Man's Misery*. For briefer

even stretched beyond print and preaching. It was one of the most common topics for post-Reformation wall paintings and decorative cloth hangings, while in the early eighteenth century one can find a broadside advertising 'a PLAY call'd Dives and Lazarus, Shewing how poor Lazarus went to Dives's Gate to seek Relief; and how instead of relieving him, he set the Dogs to bite him'.[74] This narrative of hellish punishment was also sung by English and Scottish balladeers, who warned their listeners to beware of the 'heavy Rod' that struck that 'wealthy Glutton' Dives.[75] The image of the rich man, stripped of his robes of 'purple and fine linen', endlessly tortured by the teeth and claws of Satan's demons (Fig. 1.3), must have been seared into the minds of educated and illiterate alike.[76]

Nonetheless, these biblical tropes are less interesting for their omnipresence than for the ways in which they were reformulated to apply to the social world of early modern England. Although some later Stuart authors refused

allusions see Cartwright, *The Danger of Riches*, pp. 25, 29; Younge, *A Precious Mithridate*, p. 10; Hart, *The Charitable Christian*, sig. A7r–A7v; Younge, *The Poors Advocate*, pp. 7–8; *Avaritia Coram Tribunali*, pp. 12–13; Steele, *The Husbandmans Calling*, p. 79; Croft, *The Wise Steward*, pp. 6, 15, 23; Theed, *Admonition from the Other World*, pp. 22–3; *A Voice from Heaven*, B1r–B2v; White, *The Charitable Farmer*, p. 6; Jones, *The Black Book*, B3v; George Fox, *Christs Parable of Dives and Lazarus* (1677); John Rawlet, *The Christian Monitor, Containing an Earnest Exhortation to an Holy Life, with some Directions in order Thereto: Written in a Plain and Easie Style* (2nd edn, 1686), p. 25; *Youths Divine Pastime: Containing Forty Remarkable Scripture Histories* (1691), pp. 70–71; Timothy Cruso, *Discourses upon the Rich Man and Lazarus* (1697); *The Workhouse Cruelty, Being a Full and True Account of one Mrs. Mary Whistle, a Poor Woman* (c.1731). It is telling that one of the first books to be printed in English was Richard Pynson's edition of *Dyalogue of Diues [and] Paup[er]* (1493). For further medieval antecedents see Tubach, *Index*, pp. 20 (no. 169), 138 (no. 1690).

74 Watt, *Cheap Print*, pp. 194, 202, 205, 208–9; Robert Sheppard, *By His Majesty's Permission ... a Play call'd, Dives and Lazarus* (1720?). The play's broad audience is indicated by the fact that the advertisement also promised jigs, puppets, and a wondrous 'Piece of Machinery', as well as 'several other ingenious curiousities'. This parable was even used to decorate a piece of eighteenth-century earthenware: Michael Ashby, 'Religion and the Governance of Consumption, 1675–1725' (M.A. thesis, University of Cambridge, 2011), p. 10.

75 *A Letter for a Christian Family* (c.1684–6), in PB, II, pp. 33v and 3.102v; *The Meal Mongers Garland* (1700?) in RyB, Ry.III.a.10(079). Though it does not mention Dives, for another ballad that warns 'thy ill-got Goods [will] make thee to lament' see *The Worldlings Farewell* (c.1666–78), in PB, II, p. 15. Apparently the story was still regularly being sung by young carol-singers at Christmas in early nineteenth-century Worcestershire: 'Dives and Lazarus' in *The English and Scottish Popular Ballads*, Francis James Child ed. (5 vols, New York, 1965), II, pp. 10–12 (no. 56).

76 Another powerful (though less commonly cited) image was the weeping and howling 'rich men' in Jam. 5:1–5, who were variously described as 'oppressors' or 'misers': Cartwright, *The Danger of Riches*, p. 9; Younge, *The Poors Advocate*, p. 8; Barrow, *The Duty and Reward of Bounty*, p. 162; Sherlock, *The Charity of Lending*, p. 20; Talbot, *The Foolish Abuse*, p. 14; Tillotson, *Sixteen Sermons*, pp. 198–9.

Figure 1.3. In 'A Dialogue between Dives and Lazarus' in *A Voice from Heaven to the Youth* (c.1714), 'the Youth of Great Britain' were told that in the afterlife 'Poor Men rejoice, whilst rich Men cry: As pleases best the Deity'. Here even illiterate children could see the merciless rich man about to be savaged by fiends in Hell.

to do more than warn of the consequences in store for those who failed to act charitably, others provided their audiences with a much clearer picture of the sinner and his sins. William Thomas merely reminded his Worcester audience that 'the Treasures of the Earth are the Borders of Hell, the Mines of Gold and Silver are at a great Distance from Heaven', but many moralists linked hellfire to particular people or offences.[77] In 1711, for instance, the London clergyman Richard Theed identified the heightened risk of damnation attached to titles and privileges. His sermon vividly portrayed Dives as the sort of 'Lewd Nobleman' or 'Right Worshipful Criminal' that might be

---

[77] Thomas, *The Mammon of Unrighteousness*, p. 7. Likewise, everyone knew that 'riches and sin are oft married together': Tilley, *Proverbs*, p. 570.

found in a great many country houses and metropolitan mansions.[78] He was just one of many who vernacularised the social ethics found in scripture by reclothing biblical sinners in contemporary garb.[79]

Practices that had vexed moral commentators for generations, or even millennia, were attacked in an idiom that resonated with the issues of the day. The most obvious example is found in threats issued against uncharitableness – a perennial concern, but one that was especially acute in an age of increasingly institutionalised poor relief.[80] A ballad from the 1670s, for example, reported that 'some Rich Cormudgeons … gripe and grind the poor, / and care not if they starve', because they think only of 'earthly riches' instead of their final 'account' before God. The rich had to be reminded that hardheartedness was liable to lead them to 'hells hot burning flame'.[81] A tract published in 1666 expressed this belief even more vividly by describing a divine tribunal in which 'those who die for default of seasonable Administrations [of charity are] Witnesses, Conscience the Accuser, God the Judge, the Devil the Executioner'.[82] Similarly singled out were wealthy hypocrites who claimed to be religious but offered no concrete help to their distressed brethren. Preaching in 1709, Luke Milbourne told his London flock that 'the Rich and Worldly' who gave only 'a few good Words' to 'the Poor in a naked, destitute, starving Condition' would be cast 'into Everlasting Fire'.[83]

However, Milbourne reserved the brunt of his attack for another apparently damnable crew: namely, merciless lenders. Whether one was a professional usurer or just a shopkeeper offering credit, 'Judgment without Mercy' awaited 'Unchristian Creditors' who threw 'unfortunate Debtors … into Prison till they have paid the utmost Farthing'. Even if these unforgiving men were to 'escape the Lash of Humane Laws in this World, … yet they'll find

---

[78] Theed, *Admonition from the Other World*, pp. 22–3. John Bunyan's allegorical reprobates were 'almost obsessively labelled as lords and ladies, gentlemen and gentlewomen'; meanwhile, for Richard Baxter, 'hell was a world of social reversal – a Puritan's revenge for what he saw as the sins of the social elite': Christopher Hill, *A Turbulent, Seditious, and Factious People: John Bunyan and His Church, 1628–1688* (Oxford, 1988), p. 215; Almond, *Heaven and Hell*, p. 82. For ballads in which sins are personified as rich and virtues as poor see *Poor Robin's Dream, Commonly called Poor Charity* (c.1686–93 and c.1728–31), in *RB*, III, pp. 472–3, 895; *The Good Christians Complaint; or, Poor Charity's Languishing Lamentation* (1692), in *RB*, III, p. 851.

[79] Tadmor, *Social Universe*.

[80] Slack, *Poverty and Policy*, ch. 8–9; Hindle, *On the Parish?* esp. pp. 107, 122–3, 144.

[81] *The Wicked-mans Warning-peice* (c.1674–9), in *PB*, II, p. 23. See also Lawrence White ['L. W.'], *All Things be Dear but Poor Mens Labour* (c.1674) in *WB*, Wood E 25(199); *The Good Christians Complaint; or, Poor Charity's Languishing Lamentation* (1692), in *RB*, III, p. 851.

[82] *Avaritia Coram Tribunali*, p. 21.

[83] Luke Milbourne, *Debtor and Creditor Made Easy: or, The Judgment of the Unmerciful Demonstrated, in a Sermon* (1709), p. 3. A similar message was preached by Barrow, *The Duty and Reward of Bounty*, pp. 111–12.

it hard to escape the Damnation of Hell'.[84] The fact that nearly everyone, at all levels of society, was involved in some sort of debtor–lender relationship gave such sentiments added poignancy.[85] This universal applicability helps to explain why similar threats appear in ballads and cheap religious tracts. It would have been impossible for the vast majority of the population who lacked hard currency to survive, or for the economy to maintain flexibility, if creditors used their power to 'gripe and grind the faces of the Poor'. Thus, such 'cruel' lenders were repeatedly told that they had started down 'the road to hell' and if they continued they would soon learn that 'the hottest place in hell will be too cool' for their tortured souls.[86] Men and women who pushed their debtors to the point of bankruptcy endangered the social fabric of early modern England, so it is hardly surprising that the menace of divine retribution should be invoked to stimulate their cooperation.

Landlords, on the other hand, seem to have been rather less threatened by everlasting damnation. Although there was no shortage of precedents in earlier moralist preaching, the clergy of later Stuart England do not appear to have spent much time proclaiming the sinfulness of enclosure and rent-racking. Whether in parochial sermons or in learned treatises, 'divines had less to say about depopulation … than in Latimer's day' and at least a few of them voiced their approval for dividing up common land.[87] When such behaviour was critiqued it was generally in less respectable media, such as the almanacs published by John and Vincent Wing in the reign of Charles II:

> I see men so hard and miserable, caring not to grinde their poor Tenants to Powder, to maintain their pride and wickedness; but be it known to them that they must one day make a severe account for the same, when they shall wish again and again, they had in time been more charitable to their poor distressed Brethren…. Wo to you depopulators, that joyns house to house, and land to land, till there be no place left for the poor.

According to the Wings, miserable thraldom was still the most likely fate for these 'oppressing Landlords'.[88] As Bernard Capp has pointed out, the

---

[84] Milbourne, *Debtor and Creditor*, pp. 3, 19 (citing Jas. 2:13).

[85] Muldrew, *Economy of Obligation*.

[86] Jones, *The Black Book*, A4v–A5r; *The Poor Peoples Complaint of Unconscionable Brokers and Talley-men* (c.1680–1703), in *PB*, IV, p. 353. For medieval tales of hell-bound creditors see Davis, *Market Morality*, p. 127; Tubach, *Index*, pp. 380–83.

[87] Schlatter, *Social Ideas*, pp. 77–81, quote at p. 78. For examples of the importance of enclosure in pre-1640 economic morality see McRae, *God Speed*, ch. 1–2; Tawney, *Religion*, pp. 142–54.

[88] Wing, *Almanack* (1685), sigs. C4v–C5r (quoting Isa. 5:8). Similar statements can be found in the Wing almanacs of 1668 and 1669. Although he did not mention depopulation, Richard Steele briefly noted that if landlords 'make their Tenants grown by the racking of their Rents, … they will have a full cup of wrath made ready for them in due time': *The Husbandmans Calling*, p. 79. Likewise, Robert South preached a sermon

fact that these astrologers continued to complain about 'depopulation' may have been due primarily to their residence in Rutland, which was part of one of the few English regions that had problems associated with enclosure during this period. This could explain why complaints of this sort reappear in the late eighteenth century when depopulating enclosure re-emerged as a central issue.[89] In general, however, 'depopulators' and their ilk seem to have featured only very occasionally in published descriptions of doomed sinners published during the decades following the Restoration.

When adapting the Word of God to the economic circumstances of early modern England, one of these authors' most common targets was the seller of foodstuffs. Sometimes, the biblical reference was overt and unambiguous, as in the Scottish ballad – probably published following the famine of the late 1690s – that compared those who 'took unlawful gains' and 'grew rich with selling Meal' to 'The wealthy Glutton [who] would not *Lazarus* feed, / But let him starve and die for want of Bread'. By their dedication to 'giving so little a Peck / And taking so mickle gain', meal hoarders forfeited their souls and were, like Dives, 'convey'd to endless misery'.[90] In a similar rhetorical process, the many Old Testament admonitions against fraudulent retailing were employed as cautions against dealers 'who run head-long to the pit of destruction' by 'overselling'.[91] These texts explicitly linked the dangerous temptations involved in marketing necessities to specific scriptural threats of hellfire, thus proving their points with evidence that only the most impious could have denied. Such interpretations of biblical tenets built on the long tradition, stretching back to the Middle Ages, of frightening fraudulent victuallers and avaricious grain-dealers with images of looming damnation.[92]

While these reformulations of time-tested injunctions were certainly forceful, the most direct warning to be published during this period was a ballad written by Lawrence White in response to hardship caused by the scarcity and high prices of 1673–5. This remarkable song – said to be describing the situation in the west midlands – condemned greedy employers for paying poor labourers little or nothing and decried 'covetous' farmers who 'hoard for better profit'. It even singled out one 'Rich man' in Staffordshire who had 'hop'd to sell his Corn so dear … as Grocers do their Pepper'. It is entirely possible that at the very moment crowds were gathering to seize grain in several of this region's markets, balladeers were singing White's bitter words:

to the elite audience at Westminster Abbey in 1676 that showed mixed feelings toward enclosers: Schlatter, *Social Ideas*, p. 78.
[89] Capp, *Astrology*, pp. 105–6, 257, 265, 409 (n. 20).
[90] *The Meal Mongers Garland* (1700?) in *RyB*, Ry.III.a.10(079). In addition to the allusion to Luke 16, it elsewhere paraphrases Prov. 11:26 and Amos 8:4–7.
[91] Jones, *The Black Book*, A6v.
[92] Davis, *Market Morality*, pp. 105–11.

> It makes my very heart to ake,
>   to hear poor people thus complaining,
> For all their care and pains they take,
>   rich men the poor are still disdaining
> But let Rich Misers consider well
>   the poor, and show to them some favour
> Or else their soules will hang in Hell,
>   all things are dear but poor mens labour.[93]

Perhaps employers and grain dealers sometimes needed more immediate threats to rouse their Christian charity.

Historians should not, however, make too strict a division between the effects of a belief that one's soul might 'hang in Hell' and those engendered by the possibility that one's grain might be taken by an angry crowd. Both were seen as the unpleasant consequences of economic immorality, and both were widely assumed to be very real possibilities. Yet, while historians have readily acknowledged the social impact of popular protest, they have rarely tried to account for the ways in which warnings about fire and brimstone may have influenced behaviour in the marketplace. Even when particular individuals were willing to risk their soul for the sake of a quick profit, they might have found themselves punished by earthly authorities worried about their own spiritual fate. Preachers reminded reluctant magistrates that 'the Great and Powerful' would be counted amongst the reprobate if they failed 'to deliver their poor Brethren out of the cruel Hands of the Oppressor'.[94] Over time, these constant warnings about the agonies awaiting sinners in the afterlife shaped the beliefs and, in turn, the actions of all those wealthy laypeople who thought of themselves as good Christians. John Evelyn, for instance, reacted to sermons on hell with heartfelt self-reflection and contrition.[95] He may not be typical, but he was hardly unique.

---

[93] Lawrence White, *All Things be Dear but Poor Mens Labour* (c.1674) in *WB*, Wood E 25(199). According to its introduction, 'This Song was begun at Worcester, the middle at Shrewsbury, the end at Coventry'. For similar but less geographically specific complaints about the combination of low wages and high prices see *The Troubles of this World* (1688–1702), in *PB*, II, p. 87. For a slightly more detailed account of the wicked 'Rich man' in Wolverhampton (Staffs.) and for even more threats of fiery damnation directed at exploitative employers, as well as more discussion of the high prices and food riots of these years, see White, *The Charitable Farmer of Somersetshire*, pp. 3, 7. See also the sermons that described how 'unjust and cruel Masters' will be punished with hellfire by their '*Master that is in Heaven*' and that claimed that those who defraud or oppress their neighbours will 'suffer the Vengeance of *Eternal Fire*, and ... the vindicative *Justice* of an angry and incensed God': William Fleetwood, *The Relative Duties ... in Sixteen Sermons* (1705), p. 414 (quoting Col. 4:1); Thomas Pargiter, *A Sermon Preached before ... the Lord Mayor* (1682), pp. 22–4, 29–35, quote at p. 24.

[94] Milbourne, *Debtor and Creditor*, p. 3.

[95] Evelyn, *Diary*, V, pp. 153, 534. Earlier in the century, a London artisan fearfully

For the poor, a faith in other-worldly justice was far more likely to offer mental consolation than to inspire a programme of direct action. In times of distress, it might be satisfying to hear that 'it seldom happens that the Riches of this World and those of the next go together', but such a doctrine could offer only patience and prayer as remedies for the afflicted.[96] Nonetheless, it still had a potentially positive influence on many people's material lives, if only indirectly. For instance, the prospect of 'unspeakable torments' in a 'lake of fire' was a strong disincentive for those tempted to take 'unlawful gains' at the expense of their co-religionists.[97] Heaven was also an important factor in such calculations, and the hunt for everlasting rewards must have underlain a great many of the innumerable acts of charity – both formal and informal – which helped to mitigate the effects of economic deprivation. In this sense, these beliefs meant that acts of worldliness or avarice, which otherwise might have just fleetingly pricked the conscience, could come with a sharp psychological sting.

4 Providence

In the minds of early modern Protestants, divine judgement stretched across the boundary separating the living from the dead with unnerving frequency. The final account before God was just the culmination of a life filled with opportunities to witness, sometimes first-hand, exemplary instruction in the form of divine signs and providences. This tenet, according to Alexandra Walsham, arose as a logical corollary of the Protestant reiteration of heavenly omnipotence and omnipresence. The Reformation produced a nation of men and women who saw their God as 'a vigilant and interventionist deity' partaking in 'direct and dynamic government of the terrestrial realm'.[98]

recorded having been visited in a dream by 'a man in black ready to destroy me' after committing a minor act of dishonesty in order to keep a customer: Seaver, *Wallington's World*, p. 140.

[96] Jones, *A Sermon Preached at Christ-Church*, p. 24.

[97] For two attempts to simply overwhelm their audiences with terrifying images of hell from scripture see Hart, *Heavens Glory And Hells Horror*, sig. B4r–B4v; Theed, *Admonition from the Other World*, pp. 7–9. For the continuing importance of images of infernal punishment in popular religious literature and mainstream theology see Sommerville, *Popular Religion*, pp. 84–5; Almond, *Heaven and Hell*, esp. pp. 81–95. Even D. P. Walker's seminal work on the subject notes that any 'decline' in this belief was restricted to a tiny minority: *The Decline of Hell: Seventeenth-Century Discussions of Eternal Torment* (London, 1964).

[98] Alexandra Walsham, *Providence in Early Modern England* (Oxford, 1999), pp. 10, 225. Following the example of previous scholars, I have treated providence as 'a loosely bound category' which included prodigies, miracles, omens, and judgements, because these phenomena were readily conflated by practically everyone other than learned theo-

Even at the end of the seventeenth century, 'the idea of a *deus absconditus* who had abandoned his creation to its own devices was reprehensible' to a people who 'universally assumed' and 'routinely asserted' providential explanations of events.[99] Whether a fall from a horse or a fantastic battle in the sky, everything that occurred was somehow part of God's plan and ultimately reflected his sovereignty over earthly affairs. This gave even the most banal experience a deeper meaning and imbued truly unusual phenomena with a powerful moral charge.

The importance of this belief for social and economic relations is plain enough: by linking sin and virtue to material punishments and rewards, it added a second layer of consequences to those of the afterlife. Moreover, most texts from this period made no attempt to disaggregate these two fields of divine justice. '[C]harity and bounty to the Poor', for example, were said to bring 'reward, to us and ours, both here and hereafter'.[100] The official homily on 'Alms-deeds' reiterated this point, while also stressing that uncharitableness would be punished with both poverty and hellfire.[101] It is thus hardly surprising that, among the less educated, 'temporal punishment and eternal torment were readily confused'.[102] The relationship between providentialism and the expectation of final judgement was ambiguous, but often mutually reinforcing, and moralists were not hesitant to use this to strengthen their arguments. In his attempt to promote the cause of Christ's 'Poor Members', for instance, Richard Younge provided many pages of examples to prove that 'God hath promised to bless the merciful man, in his *temporal, civil, spiritual and eternal estate*', for the charitable dealings of the godly bring '*blessings upon their Souls, Bodies, Estates, Names, [and] Posterity*'.[103] Here, the perpetuity of the Almighty's power was matched only by its immediacy.

One cannot examine providential expressions of economic morality without first recognising that they made up only one facet of God's role in the lives of the poor. For many people, his providence was a more literal process of providing them with the resources needed to 'make shift'. Instead of asking for supernatural reprisals against their exploiters, those distressed Christians who turned to the Lord's Prayer asked only for their daily bread

logians: William Burns, *An Age of Wonders: Prodigies, Politics and Providence in England, 1657–1727* (Manchester, 2002), pp. 2–3; Walsham, *Providence*, p. 230; eadem, 'Miracles in Post-Reformation England', *Studies in Church History*, 41 (2005), pp. 286–8.

[99] Keith Thomas, *Religion and the Decline of Magic* (Harmondsworth, 1973), ch. 4, quotation at p. 93; Sommerville, *Popular Religion*, p. 81; Walsham, 'Miracles', pp. 288, 301–6.

[100] Younge, *The Poors Advocate*, p. 1. See also Hammond, *A Practical Catechism*, p. 213; Barrow, *The Duty and Reward of Bounty*, p. 54; Stillingfleet, *Protestant Charity*, pp. 38–41; Brent, *Persuasions to a Publick Spirit*, pp. 11, 13; Welchman, *The Duty and Reward of Charity*, pp. 14–16.

[101] *Certain Sermons or Homilies*, II, pp. 230–40.

[102] Walsham, *Providence*, p. 95.

[103] Younge, *The Poors Advocate*, pp. 8, 18.

and, of course, forgiveness. In 1699, for example, one poor woman reported having only 'maintained and brought upp' her fourteen children 'by the blessing of God' upon her 'honest Labour, Care & Industry'.[104] Likewise, early modern diaries show that people often put so much faith in God granting their needs that they spent time in worship or prayer which might have been spent working to advance their economic position.[105] In some cases this bordered on fatalism, as evidenced by a gentleman's account of life in the Scottish lowlands. Sir James Steuart reported that if one had asked the agricultural labourers of early eighteenth-century Lanarkshire how they survived, 'they would have told you, "By the providence of God". The answer was good and proper. Their industry was then so miscellaneous; the employment they found was so precarious and uncertain that they could not give it a name.'[106] Still, providential favour was usually seen as an adjunct to more practical measures, as indicated by the petition from the inhabitants of Birstwith (Yorks.) in 1710 claiming that an orphan there had 'no depend-ence butt God alone and the charity of the Town'.[107]

In cheap printed texts, divine support tended to be rather more dramatic. An optimistic ballad printed at the turn of century, for instance, gave a 'true Account' of a 'Miraculous wonder' in Essex, where a pious thresher had fallen six months behind in his rent, but when he prayed for relief his orchard produced 'a vast encrease' by 'the wonderful hand of Providence'. This merciful act of direct heavenly intervention allowed him to pay his 'harsh' landlord and even buy a pair of cows with the money that was left.[108] The thresher's successful petition to God was mirrored in the oft-reprinted tale of 'a poor distressed Widdow' from Kent who laboured hard at her spin-ning wheel and pawned everything she owned, but was still unable to feed 'her hungry Children small'. Unlike her Essex counterpart, however, after praying for heavenly mercy she also addressed herself to earthly sources of potential relief. Finding her brother-in-law selling corn in the town, she pleaded with him to lend her some grain 'till the next Market-day'. In the end, God proved more merciful than man, for her 'churlish' relative refused her request whereas God sent her a burnt loaf which miraculously sustained her family for seven full weeks. To drive the point home, these ballads reported that her heartless refuser found 'his corn was washt away ... by a

---

[104] WYAS–W, QS 1/38/4/6 (petition of Francis Firth, 1699). See also Mary Hudson's claim to have 'maintaind [her two children] by Gods blessing upon her endeavours & with a very small Allowance from the Town of Steeton': WYAS–W, QS 1/49/5/6 (1710).

[105] Seaver, *Wallington's World*, ch. 5, esp. pp. 126–7. For more examples see Muldrew, *Economy of Obligation*, pp. 144–5.

[106] Wrightson, *Earthly Necessities*, pp. 313–14.

[107] WYAS–W, QS 1/49/5/6.

[108] *The Essex Miracle* (1692–1703), in PB, II, p. 79.

mighty Flood' on the very next day.[109] Here, as in so many other later Stuart texts, the prospect of divine intervention mixed a promise with a threat. To the humble poor, it offered the hope of supernatural succour. For the niggardly rich, it predicted only punishment 'both here and hereafter'.

This conception of a heavenly judge holding bounty in one hand and wrath in the other was the foundation upon which all providentialist narratives of economic morality and immorality were built. However, in contrast to the stories of the Essex thresher and the Kentish widow, many seemed to draw their lessons from the behaviour of people with power over the poor, rather than focusing on the poor themselves. In these tales, the actions of 'the better sort' provide examples of virtue as well as vice. One ballad from the 1680s or 1690s, for instance, compared a wealthy Somerset knight to his prodigal son. The former found that 'blessings from Heaven replenish'd his store' because he clothed, fed, and educated the poor, while the latter 'Rid to *London* in Court for to live, / And unto the Poor not a Tester wou'd give', instead spending it all on 'Wine, Harlots and Dice'. Predictably, he died in debtors' prison.[110] Whether this report actually led to the reform of any 'young gallants' is doubtful, but if nothing else it added yet another angle from which to critique the gentry for their supposedly declining hospitality. This sort of concrete illustration also helped to sustain the more general belief that social ethics were likely to be enforced by the firm hand of God's providence.

Preachers were well-supplied with scriptural proofs to back up their claims on the subject and these phrases were an obvious source of inspiration for many moralists in search of a story idea. It is remarkable how often figurative axioms on this subject might manifest themselves quite literally in the streets or fields of early modern England. Biblical depictions of rewards as 'harvests', for example, prompted Richard Steele to tell his rural congregation in north Wales that 'charity is good Husbandry, for it

---

[109] Earlier, she had been robbed by a 'Cut-purse Man' who 'broke his neck ... E're he of this poor widdows mony / one single penny had spent': *The Kentish Miracle* (c.1684), in *PB*, II, p. 54. For other versions of this story, including medieval and Elizabethan precursors, see *The Worlds Wonder ... shewed to a Poor Distressed Widdow* (c.1624–63), in *EB*, fol. 401; *The Tryal of Patience; Being a Relation of a Widdow in York-shire* (c.1672–96), in *RB*, II, pp. 476–7; Walsham, *Providence*, p. 93 n. 101; Tubach, *Index*, p. 63 (no. 763). The story was probably inspired by the charitable widow of 1 Kings 17, who was incidentally alluded to in Younge, *The Poors Advocate*, p. 24. For another story of 'how good Providence still does take care, / Of the Poor and the Needy' despite uncharitable earthly superiors see *The Cruel Land-Lord: Or, The Fortunate Husband-man* (1685?), in *RB*, II, p. 186.

[110] *The Bountiful Knight of Sommersetshire* (c.1688–96), in *PB*, II, p. 57. For other providence-themed comparisons between gentlemanly and ungentlemanly attitudes to the poor see *A True Sence of Sorrow* (1685–8), in *PB*, II, p. 53; Jonathan Dove, *Speculum Anni à Partu Virginis MDCLXXII, or, an Almanack* (1672), sig. B4r. On the importance of munificence to the ideal of gentility see pp. 109–12 below, and Heal, *Hospitality*.

brings a certain and plentiful Harvest'.[111] In the hands of poetasters and pamphleteers, this simple agrarian metaphor became an elaborate tale of rural social relations. Although the locale varied between Maidstone (Kent) and Welling (Somerset), all the accounts focused on a farmer who earned a 'very good Repute among his Neighbours, especially the poorer sort, for his Charitable Inclination'. His fellow farmers 'derided' him 'for under-selling his Corn' during a scarcity, but he replied that 'God had given him all he had' and made him 'no more then stuard for the poor', so they 'should have the benefit of it'. The heavens seem to have been listening; his good stewardship was rewarded with a miraculous 'crop of wheat / the like no mortal man before did reap'.[112] If, in Steele's words, 'The way to have *full Barns*, is to have *free hands*', then the charitable farmer's prodigious harvest was the physical embodiment of this truth.[113]

But in the 'vulgar' literature of ballads and chapbooks – and even in many elegant printed sermons – uplifting stories of morality rewarded were far outweighed by the great mass of narratives describing the horrible fates of sinners. Despite regularly setting out material incentives for charitable practices such as forgiving debts or 'under-selling' foodstuffs, the overwhelming majority of providential discourse stressed punishments rather than rewards.[114] God smote individuals for their economic immorality with dreadful regularity. Merciless creditors died at the hands of demonic assailants; covetous grain-hoarders saw their crops and lives ruined; wasteful gentlewomen bore monstrous children; uncharitable misers and ruthless enclosers sank into abject poverty; oppressive tax-collectors suffered humiliating robberies; and other exploiters of all sorts provoked various acts of

---

[111] Steele, *The Husbandmans Calling*, pp. 93–8, quotation at p. 98 (citing Prov. 11:25). These sermons, which were popular enough to reach a fourth edition, were preached while Steele was minister at Hanmer (Flints.) between 1654 and 1662.

[112] This story was recorded in at least two ballads and three chapbooks: *The Maidstone Miracle* (c.1683–96), in *PB*, II, p. 78; Lawrence White, *God's Great and Wonderful Work in Somerset-shire* (1676) in *WB*, Wood 276b (101); *God's Great and Wonderful Work in Somerset-shire: Or the Charitable Farmer Miraculously Rewarded* (1674); White, *The Charitable Farmer of Somersetshire*, pp. 5–7.

[113] Steele, *The Husbandmans Calling*, p. 96. The prodigy was also concrete proof that 'if we but *sow the seeds* of our benificence, we shall ... *reap an earthly crop of spiritual and temporal blessings*', whereas 'parsemony is no good husbandry': Younge, *The Poors Advocate*, pp. 8–14, quotations at pp. 12, 14. See also the parable of a man who made clothes for the poor, 'yet his bundle or roll of cloth was never the less' and the riddle of 'A man there was, though some did count him mad, / the more he cast away, the more he had', thus 'He that bestows goods upon the poor, / Shall have as much again, and ten times more': Bunyan, *Pilgrim's Progress*, pp. 318, 344. For a medieval tale of full barns as a reward for charity see Tubach, *Index*, p. 159 (no. 1975).

[114] This mirrors the emphasis on hell (rather than heaven) evident in the texts discussed in the preceding section.

dreadful vengeance.[115] Indeed, the notion that 'ill-gotten goods' would not last was proverbial.[116] Given the sheer number and complexity of these sorts of providential stories, it would be easy to devote an entire chapter to the issue. However, in the interests of brevity, the following outline is restricted to a single fascinating case.

The tale, recounted in at least two ballads printed in 1684, was that of Dorothy Winterbottom, known to her neighbours in Southwark as 'Dirty Doll' and 'notorious' for her anti-social behaviour.[117] Not only did she drink,

[115] For creditors see below. For corn hoarders see *The Countrey-Miser or the Unhappy Farmers Dear Market* (1693); *A Sad, Amazing and Dreadful Relation of a Farmer's Wife, near Wallingford in Barkshire* (1697); *The Wretched Miser* (c.1682–96), in *PB*, IV, p. 331; *The West-Country Miser* (c.1692–1703), in *PB*, IV, p. 236; *The Kentish Wonder* (c.1692–1702), in *PB*, II, p. 189; *A Looking-glass for a Covetous Miser* (c.1666–78), in *PB*, II, p. 19; *The Rich Farmer's Ruine* (c.1685–88), in *RB*, II, p. 396; *The Meal Mongers Garland* (1700?) in *RyB*, Ry.III.a.10(079); Walsham, *Providence*, p. 77. For proud women who waste money on 'curious and costly attire' see Andrew Jones, *Morbus Satanicus, The Devils Disease: Or The Sin of Pride Arraigned and Condemned* (27th edn, 1677), sig. B1v–B2r; *The Downfal of Pride* (c.1688–96), in *PB*, II, p. 59; *Prides Fall* (c.1684–6), in *PB*, II, pp. 66–7; *A Fair Warning for Pride* (1691), in *PB*, IV, p. 310; Burns, *Age of Wonders*, pp. 140–41; Walsham, *Providence*, p. 195. For uncharitable 'worldlings' see *The Death and Burial of Mistress Money* (1678); *A Most Excellent Ballad of an Old Man and his Wife* (1678–80), in *RB*, I, pp. 332–3; Jones, *A Sermon Preached at Christ-Church*, pp. 25–6; Barrow, *The Duty and Reward of Bounty*, pp. 56, 184–5; Johnson, *Dives and Lazarus*, sig. B3r; *Bloudy News from Germany* (c.1670–96), in *RB*, II, pp. 38–9; *The Kentish Miracle* (c.1684), in *PB*, II, p. 54; *The Bountiful Knight of Sommersetshire* (c.1688–96), in *PB*, II, p. 57; *A True Sence of Sorrow* (1685–8), in *PB*, II, p. 53; *Strange, Dreadful, and Amazing News from York: Giving a Sad and Terrible Account of God's Fearful Judgment on one Winam Tendin, near Rippon* (1697); Younge, *The Poors Advocate*, pp. 24–5. For enclosers see Thomas, *Religion*, p. 113. For exploitative masters see *The Mowing-Devil*; Stephens, *An Admonition Concerning a Publick Fast*, p. 15. For greedy tax-collectors see *The Chimney-man's Lamentation* (c.1688–9), in *PB*, II, p. 172v. For other providential warnings against economic injustice see Steele, *The Husbandmans Calling*, pp. 120–32; John Powel, *The Assize of Bread* (1671), sig. B2r; Pargiter, *A Sermon Preached before ... the Lord Mayor*, pp. 17–20, 31–3; John Jeffery, *The Duty and Encouragement of Religious Artificers Described in a Sermon* (1693), p. 20; Edwards, *Sermons On Special Occasions*, pp. 152–5. For medieval precedents see Davis, *Market Morality*, pp. 128–9; Tubach, *Index*, pp. 19–20 (no. 160–161, 174), 40 (no. 455), 261 (no. 3357).

[116] Specifically, it was claimed that 'ill-gotten riches' would not last for three crops or, more often, for three generations: Tilley, *Proverbs*, p. 267; Younge, *A Precious Mithridate*, p. 9; Henry Peacham, *The Worth of a Peny* (1664), p. 9; Steele, *The Husbandmans Calling*, pp. 125–6; *The Death and Burial of Mistress Money*, sig. B2v; Gough, *History of Myddle*, pp. 126, 138, 226.

[117] All quotes in this paragraph are taken from *Sad and Dreadful News from Horsly Down* (1684), in *PB*, II, p. 152, and *Dirty Dolls Farewel* (1684), in *PB*, III, p. 223v. The two accounts differ in only minor respects. There was at least an element of truth to these stories, as 'Dorothy Winterbottum' was in fact buried in St Olave's, Southwark, on 29 August 1684, just as claimed in the ballads. Sadly, the entry in the parish register lacks any annotation about the reputed cause of death: LMA, X015/198, p. 302.

curse, and beg without need, but she also mercilessly 'pinch[ed] the poor' at every opportunity by lending out money 'upon the Tally'. Winterbottom even inverted the doctrine of stewardship by claiming that she exploited her neighbours because 'The Devil had lent her and she must repay', instead of regarding her wealth as a trust granted by God to be repaid through charity. In short, to the late seventeenth-century mind she was the very personification of moral disorder. The final stroke came on 17 or 18 August 1684, when she grew so frustrated with her penniless debtors that she threatened to have them arrested and invoked the devil as a witness. This proved to be a step too far. In response, God sent three demons 'in humane shapes' to visit Winterbottom that night, and they beat her with such violence she 'was much bruised, so that one of her Arms was a black as a Cole, and her Thumb almost pinched off'. Although she survived this assault, gangrene soon set in and about a week later, muttering of money, she died. At her funeral, overjoyed by this wondrous act of divine justice, her neighbours added their own voices to that of the Lord:

> Oh there goes Dirty Doll,
>   aloud the people cry'd,
> Now she will grind the poor no more
>   'tis well for them she dy'd.

Her 'extortion' had thus been repaid with brutal supernatural violence and a vitriolic public hostility that followed her all the way to the grave: such was the punishment meted out for grievous breaches of economic morality.[118]

Later Stuart print and preaching was saturated with tales like these, yet belief in supernatural punishment for economic misbehaviour was not just found in ballads, tracts, and sermons. It was also expressed in less prescriptive sources. In the late 1660s, for example, the gentleman Edward Moore privately warned his son to treat his tenants charitably, because 'if you grind the face of the poor, the Lord God of Abraham, Isaac and Jacob, will revenge their cause, because they have no other to relieve them; and will save them, not for their sakes, but for his own honour'.[119] John Aubrey showed a similar sentiment when writing about enclosers. According to him, landowners in Northamptonshire and Buckinghamshire who depopulated the countryside were fated to have their estates wither away within three generations.[120] Others saw the economic impact of divine will much more immediately. For example, Samuel Jeake frequently used his diary to record direct evidence

---

[118] Stories of extortionate creditors meeting violent ends, including one of usurers carried off by demons, had been circulating since at least the Middle Ages: Tubach, *Index*, pp. 380–83, esp. p. 383 (no. 5057).
[119] Edward Moore, *The Moore Rental*, Thomas Heywood, ed. (Chetham Society, Manchester, 1847), pp. 60–61.
[120] Thomas, *Religion*, p. 113.

of the 'gracious Providence of God' in the vicissitudes of his trading affairs, and Oliver Heywood interpreted his father's bankruptcy as a result of having 'sinned in changing his calling, in too eager pursuit of the world, in unfaithful dealing, in not keeping his word, in pleasuring himself with hopes of riches or imagining a kind of contentment in worldly injoyments'.[121]

Of course, simple ethical binaries promising rewards for virtue and punishments for vice had much wider implications. Observers such as John Aubrey or Oliver Heywood, who saw a divine hand directing every earthly affair, naturally concluded that poverty and hardship might be the products of sin. Prosperity, on the other hand, could be seen as a potential upshot of godliness. This interpretation of early modern social morality has been endorsed by many eminent historians since its initial formulation in the work of Max Weber, and there is certainly evidence to support it.[122] The Shropshire yeoman Richard Gough, for example, readily identified sins such as adultery and lewdness with impoverishment in his illuminating parish history.[123] However, no one from this period was so blind as to believe that English society was a meritocracy. It was obvious to even the most opti-mistic commentators that the best did not always flourish and most popular religious authors (even the Weberian exemplar Richard Baxter) saw little 'providential connection' between poverty and sin: 'In fact, the prosperity of the wicked was sometimes contrasted with the sufferings of God's people.'[124] Hence, Robert Moss, a resolute apologist for the established order, argued that often one person can 'suffer undeservedly even for being Good, and the other flourish and triumph in his Wickedness'.[125] In this analysis, material hardships could never be categorically blamed on sin and, according to one tract, only fiendish men like Dives would dare to try to use this as an excuse for uncharitableness.[126]

The reason for this apparently contradictory outlook is actually to be found within the doctrine of providentialism itself. Divine intervention could not be universal or there would be no need for Christian ethics at

---

[121] Samuel Jeake, *An Astrological Diary of the Seventeenth Century: Samuel Jeake of Rye, 1652–1699*, Michael Hunter and Annabel Gregory eds (Oxford, 1988), pp. 133, 137, 209, 219, 246, 249; Hunt, *Middling Sort*, p. 36.

[122] Among many examples of this position see Weber, *Protestant Ethic*, pp. 111, 200; Tawney, *Religion*, esp. pp. 251–70; Schlatter, *Social Ideas*, pp. 203–4; Christopher Hill, 'Puritans and the Poor', *Past & Present*, 2 (1952), pp. 32–50; Wrightson and Levine, *Poverty and Piety*, pp. 179–82, 203, 211; Slack, *Poverty and Policy*, pp. 25–6, 103. For an early discussion of providentialist understandings of inequality and a critique of the Weberian position see Jacob Viner, *The Role of Providence in the Social Order: An Essay in Intellectual History* (Philadelphia, 1972), ch. 4, esp. pp. 106–7.

[123] Gough, *History of Myddle*, pp. 101, 218–19.

[124] Sommerville, *Popular Religion*, pp. 81, 101, 104–6; Thomas, *Religion*, ch. 4, esp. p. 95; Viner, *Providence*, pp. 106–7.

[125] Moss, *The Providential Division*, p. 6.

[126] Johnson, *Dives and Lazarus*, sig. B1v.

all. It must, therefore, be *exemplary*. The judgements witnessed in this world were merely precursors to those of the world to come, providing guidance for weak mortals in need of correction. The fate of Dorothy Winterbottom, for instance, was said to be 'A Warning' and 'sad Example' to those tempted to oppress the poor for gain.[127] Moreover, such judgements might be directed not just at an individual but at an entire community. Plagues like those that struck Egypt continued to punish erring nations for their sins long after the Pharaoh freed the Israelites. Pestilence, earthquakes, storms, fires, and military defeats were all regarded as cautions against ungodliness which would be perilous to ignore.

These vivid manifestations of God's power, like the fates of particularly wicked individuals, could simply reinforce conventional social norms, but in some cases the relationship was slightly more complex. The awful effects of dearth and depression are obvious examples of this ambiguity.[128] Some commentators thought that such events were judgements like any other and thus presumed that their sufferers must somehow be at fault. Several ballads and tracts included this assumption, claiming that the impoverished ought to be content even if a trade slump or the 'heavier Curse' of 'Famine' brings hunger and privation, because 'It is our Sins that causeth all the same', so only God can 'mend' these calamities.[129] Likewise, John Edwards preached a sermon at the opening of a fair arguing 'That Decay of Trade and Commerce, and Consequently of Wealth, is the Natural Product and Just Penalty of Vice in a Nation'.[130] These were probably common sentiments and one must not dismiss their importance, but a counter-discourse existed as well. In 1699, for example, *The Poor Man's Plea Against the Extravagant Price of Corn* emphatically denied that dearth resulted from sin, or that it could be redressed with fasts or official 'Days of Humiliation'. '[T]he present Dearness is not occasioned by a Scarcity, or real want of Corn', but rather the result of covetous men who 'make a Pretence of God's Judgements' in order 'to set an Extravagant Price'.[131] According to the pamphlet's author,

---

[127] *Sad and Dreadful News from Horsly Down* (1684), in PB, II, p. 152.

[128] The following discussion builds on points made in Walter and Wrightson, 'Dearth', esp. pp. 27–34; and in Steve Hindle, 'Dearth, Fasting and Alms: The Campaign for General Hospitality in Late Elizabethan England', *Past & Present*, 172 (2001), pp. 44–86.

[129] *The Poor Man put to a Pinch* (n.d.), in PB, IV, p. 299; *London Mourning in Ashes* (1666), in PB, IV, p. 228; *The Troubles of these Times* (c.1672–96), in RB, II, p. 456; John Dunton, *Englands Alarum, or Warning-Piece: Declaring by Ten Infallible Evidences, that Her Ruine and Destruction is at Hand* (1693), p. 4; *Causes of a Solemn National Fast and Humiliation, Agreed upon by the Commissioners of the late General Assembly* (Edinburgh, 1696); Thomas Johnson, *A General Proposal for the Building of Granaries* (1696), p. 1.

[130] Edwards, *Sermons On Special Occasions*, pp. 133ff.

[131] *The Poor Man's Plea against the Extravagant Price of Corn* (1699), pp. 3–4, 10, 13. Similarly, a ballad writer had a 'poor man' complain of 'the many Abuses' of 'Ingrossers of Corn' and 'Brandy Stillers' who create 'a Scarcity in a time of Plenty': *The Present State of England: Containing The Poor Man's Complaint* (c.1690–1703), in PB, II, p. 77.

the remedy for the poor's suffering was energetic government management of the distribution and pricing of foodstuffs. Prayer and fasting could not remedy a man-made dearth.

In many cases, elements of these two positions were melded together by moralists seeking objects of blame. For these commentators, the great judgements which befell later Stuart England arose as punishment for the nation's avaricious conduct and merciless attitude to the needy. The cause of communal hardship still lay in immorality, but here the provocation was identified as the economic injustice of the rich rather than the moral failings of the poor. This view was expressed in a variety of texts, including a ballad from 1690 which purportedly recounted the observations of a travelling shoemaker. Looking around him, he saw 'greedie Usurers' and 'Merchant men' growing rich by committing 'grievous sinnes', while widows and orphans were 'wel-nigh starved'. Realising the danger of this situation, the shoemaker lamented that 'great plagues will us befall' unless people quickly found a way to overcome their gluttony and greed.[132] The official homily for Rogation week was darker still: 'God in his ire doth root up whole kingdoms for Wrongs and Oppressions, ... for unrighteous dealing, for Wrongs and Riches gotten by deceit.'[133] These ominous warnings fitted neatly into the providentialist assumptions of the age and drew strength from the recurrent campaigns to reform the country's morals, but they also left a great deal of space for positive action.[134]

It might not seem especially remarkable to find these sorts of claims for persistent, dramatic divine intervention emphasised in homilies written by Elizabethan divines. Yet their recurrent appearance in the mainstream religious discourse of later Stuart England ought to give pause for thought. Historians have long claimed that belief in supernatural explanations grew increasingly marginalised from the mid-seventeenth century onwards.[135]

---

[132] An Excellent Song, called, The Shooe-makers Travell (1690) in WB, Wood 401(69). See also Edward Stillingfleet, A Sermon Preached before the Honourable House of Commons ... Being the Fast-day Appointed for the Late Dreadfull Fire in the City of London (4th edn, 1666), pp. 25–7; Vincent Wing, Olympia Domata, or, An Almanack (1669), sig. C5v; Pargiter, A Sermon Preached before ... the Lord Mayor, pp. 20–22 (citing Zach. 7); Edward Stephens, Relief of Apprentices Wronged by their Masters (1687), p. 12; Stephens, An Admonition Concerning a Publick Fast, pp. 14–15; Dunton, Englands Alarum, pp. 8–9, 11–12, 21. In one lengthy 'complaint', the author variously blamed the trade slumps and dearths of the 1690s on taxes, coin-clippers, bankers, 'close-Fisted Gentlemen', and regrating grain merchants, along with the 'Vice and Wickedness' of the whole nation: Richard Newnam, The Complaint of English Subjects, Delivered in Two Parts (1700).

[133] 'An Exhortation ... in Rogation Week', in Certain Sermons or Homilies, II, p. 305.

[134] For the providential context of politico-religious drives for moral reformation see Burns, Age of Wonders, ch. 4; Walsham, Providence, p. 139.

[135] For suggestions that the credibility of providentialism was undermined and that belief in divine intervention significantly declined see Blair Worden, 'The Question of Secularization', in Alan Houston and Steve Pincus (eds), A Nation Transformed: England

In light of the evidence considered here, this argument seems somewhat dubious. It is entirely possible, as William Burns has argued, that learned attitudes towards providence and prodigies were 'drastically reorganized' in the second half of the seventeenth century.[136] However, the writings of natural scientists and philosophical advocates of 'rational religion' should not be taken as indicative of widespread attitudes. The scepticism shown by a handful of later Stuart intellectuals may have been a precursor of things to come, but it was confined to a tiny minority.[137] Indeed, Alexandra Walsham, whose knowledge of English providentialism is unsurpassed, has recently argued that 'assumptions about miracles, prodigies and providence ... survived and adapted to the intellectual and cultural challenges of a period immortalized as the "Age of Reason"'.[138] For instance, although the fact that Ralph Josselin and other godly enthusiasts held providentialist convictions is perhaps predictable, one also finds these among well-educated, orthodox laypeople such as Richard Gough, John Evelyn, and even Queen Mary herself.[139] Thus, when the heir of Thomas Bouchier, the notorious lawyer, died of smallpox in 1695, some Oxford fellows regarded it 'a great judgement for his covetuousness and grinding the poore'.[140] In many ways, a belief in exemplary divine intervention appears to have suffered little diminution

---

after the Restoration (Cambridge, 2001), pp. 32–6; Sommerville, *Popular Religion*, p. 81; Walsham, *Providence*, pp. 221, 333–4. See also the proponents of a more general 'secularisation thesis' cited below pp. 78–80.

[136] Burns, *Age of Wonders*, p. 9. Hence, Keith Thomas described the providentialism of this period as a 'survival' rather than 'a coherent theory': *Religion*, p. 129. For a counterargument to this division between elite scepticism and popular providentialism see J. C. D. Clark, 'Providence, Predestination and Progress: or, Did the Enlightenment Fail?', *Albion*, 35:4 (2004), pp. 559–89.

[137] For a thorough discussion of the many religious and scientific 'rationalists' of this era who argued for a 'reasoned' belief in providence, and their sceptical opponents, see John Spurr, '"Rational religion" in Restoration England', *Journal of the History of Ideas*, 49:4 (1988), pp. 563–85; Jane Shaw, *Miracles in Englightenment England* (New Haven, 2006), esp. ch. 4–6.

[138] Alexandra Walsham, 'The Reformation and "the Disenchantment of the World" Reassessed', *Historical Journal*, 51:2 (2008), p. 501. See also Walsham, 'Miracles', pp. 288, 301–6; Shaw, *Miracles*; Jerome Friedman, *Miracles and the Pulp Press during the English Revolution: The Battle of the Frogs and Fairford's Flies* (London, 1993), esp. pp. 259–62.

[139] Gough, *History of Myddle*, pp. 59–60, 101, 122, 248–9; Evelyn, *Diary*, V, pp. 100–102, 133, 152–3, 268, 293, 366, 422–3, 550; Craig Rose, *England in the 1690s: Revolution, Religion and War* (Oxford and Malden, 1999) p. 204. See also the almost obsessive recording of providences in Jeake, *Diary*; Ralph Josselin, *The Diary of Ralph Josselin, 1616–1683*, Alan Macfarlane ed. (London, 1976); and the diary of the Suffolk gentleman-farmer William Coe (1662–1729) in *Two East Anglian Diaries: 1641–1729: Isaac Archer and William Coe*, Matthew Storey ed. (Suffolk Records Society, 38, Woodbridge, 1994).

[140] Anthony Wood, *The Life and Times of Anthony Wood, Antiquary, of Oxford, 1632–95*, A. Clark ed. (Oxford Historical Society, 5 vols, Oxford, 1881–1900), III, p. 488.

since the first wave of Protestant providentialism in the late sixteenth and early seventeenth centuries.

As a result, the meddlesome God who had presided over England before the Civil Wars remained quite lively at the end of the century and beyond. For most Christians, providentialist interpretations of the world still received constant reinforcement through the evidence so regularly recounted in tracts and at the pulpit, evidence which remained largely uncontested until the popular scientism of the nineteenth century.[141] Economic life was not excluded from such assumptions. In 1753, for example, a devious Wiltshire woman was 'struck Dead' by God while trying to cheat a farmer when buying some wheat in the Devizes marketplace, an event commemorated with an engraving on the market cross and one which continued to be invoked as a lesson in morality long after.[142] Even in the Victorian era, people were still being taught many of the same lessons that their predecessors had heard two centuries earlier. So, when dearth struck in 1847, the Church did not shy from promoting official prayers that set out a providentialist interpretation of the calamity.[143] The message offered to young readers at this time was equally clear. John Ruskin's story of *The King of the Golden River*, for example, described how two rich landowners – who cheated their servants of wages, hoarded corn, refused to give charity, and allowed beggars to starve at their door – eventually received supernatural punishment for their insatiable greed, whereas their abused brother – who was merciful, charitable, and hospitable – was rewarded with a fruitful estate.[144]

In this context, heavenly intrusions in the mortal world gave ethical precepts a much harder edge. 'The general assumption that virtue and vice would gain their true deserts acted as a powerful sanction for the morality of the day', and economic morality was no exception.[145] The prospect of material consequences augmented the already formidable incentive provided by the promise of either everlasting bliss or fiery damnation. Together, these twin systems of reward and punishment formed a coercive psychological apparatus that worked to sustain the sacralised social order, though never

---

[141] For examples of both elite and popular providentialism in Georgian Britain see Burns, *Age of Wonders*, p. 174; Thomlinson, 'Diary', p. 76 (27 Aug. 1717); Viner, *Providence*, pp. 46, 60; Clark, 'Providence'; idem, *English Society, 1660–1832: Religion, Ideology and Politics during the Ancien Regime* (2nd edition, Cambridge, 2000), pp. 87–9, 107–14, 282–4; Margaret Jacob and Matthew Kadane, 'Missing, Now Found in the Eighteenth Century: Weber's Protestant Ethic', *American Historical Review*, 108:1 (2003), pp. 25, 28–9, 36, 47 n. 124; Charles Varlo, *The Modern Farmers Guide* (2 vols, Edinburgh, 1768), I, pp. 47–8, 56, 96–100.

[142] Randall et al., 'Introduction', p. 13.

[143] R. B. Outhwaite, *Dearth, Public Policy and Social Disturbance in England, 1550–1800* (Houndmills, 1991), p. 7.

[144] John Ruskin, *The King of the Golden River, or the Black Brothers* (1851). It sold out three editions.

[145] Thomas, *Religion*, p. 107.

with more than mixed success. Religiously inspired archetypes such as 'the steward of the poor' or 'the idolatrous worldling' left an indelible impression on the economic lives of ordinary people, but only because the fates of rich Dives, greedy Dorothy Winterbottom, and the charitable farmer of Somerset were such common knowledge.

5 Redress: Prayers and Curses

God's authority to enforce economic justice was an unambiguous article of faith for many people in later Stuart England. Less clear, however, was the role of 'the lower orders' themselves. Everyone could agree that their primary duty was to bear patiently the cross of earthly afflictions, but many preachers and writers also hinted at opportunities for redress in which the oppressed played a more active part. Taking their models of social relations from scripture, commentators granted a degree of autonomy to the godly poor in their dealings with rich sinners, while simultaneously insisting that God alone was the final arbiter. Several paths for redress lay open, though the route with the highest recommendations from moralists was not always the route chosen by needy members of their audience.

Economic hardship, whether individual or communal, could be mitigated – and even averted altogether – through sincere, heartfelt repentance. This was universally acknowledged as the most fitting response for a good Christian, and religious commentators affirmed its centrality at every turn. Under Elizabeth, the government had responded to dearth in 1596–7 with an extensive campaign to promote public fasting and charity, and proclamations issued a generation later, in 1630, had much the same intent, though rather less impact.[146] Collective rituals of penitence and contrition were also deemed an appropriate response to dearth under Charles II. In 1662, when the heavens sent incessant rains which threatened to cause 'Scarcity and Famine', the authorities ordered a day of public fasting and issued a prayer to be read out in every parish church. Congregations collectively pleaded with God to forgive 'our grievous and heinous sins, and grant us true and hearty sorrow and repentance for them all', in the hope that the Lord might then 'send us such wholesome Seasons, that we may continue in health, and strength, and safety, and use all them all to thy honor and glory'.[147] The fast-day prayer even included a reading of Joel 2:12–32 to remind parishioners of the utopian plenty that could come from true repentance.[148] The process

146 Hindle, 'Dearth, Fasting and Alms'.
147 'Morning and Evening Prayers: First Collect', in *A Form of Prayer, To be Used Upon … the Several Days Appointed for a General Fast* (1662), sig. C2v–C3v, G2r–G3r.
148 'Morning Prayer: Epistle', in ibid., sig. E2r–E2v. The assigned passages declared that if you 'rend your heart, and not your garments, and turn unto the Lord', then 'the floors

was repeated in 1674 and this time the official proclamation was reinforced by a newspaper-style pamphlet reminding readers that 'undoubtedly the Ocean of our sins has brought upon us these Deluges of Water, which will be best dried up and stopt for the future by Floods of Repentant Tears'.[149]

When the harvest was threatened in 1693, the bookseller John Dunton authored a tract calling for 'a general Repentance and Reformation' in the form of fasting and prayer.[150] This time, however, the official response was more minimal. Although there were numerous national 'Days of Humiliation' declared during this period in an effort to support the war effort, the prayers issued for these fast-days focused exclusively on military affairs. At least one preacher in Essex used one of these occasions to suggest that penitence would be the best way to counteract the current 'Scarcity of Bread', but it is impossible to know whether he was typical.[151] Perhaps clerics simply employed the forms designated for use 'In Time of Dearth and Famine' which had been included in the new *Book of Common Prayer*.[152] Given that the language of these texts echoed the special fast-day prayer of 1662, the Church may have simply assumed that initiatives for 'Repentance and Reformation' could be safely left to the parochial clergy. The primary exceptions to this were in Scotland, where religious leaders ordered days of public penitence at least twice in response to the 'pinching Dearth' of William's reign, and in London, where the crown commanded that every minister preach on the virtue of charity in response to the 'Hardships and Distresses' of 1693 and 1696.[153] Although the Scottish Kirk seems to have been more active than its southern counterpart during this decade, this contrast may merely be a product of the very different magnitudes of crisis that struck England

shall be full of wheat, and the vats shall overflow with wine and oil'. During this winter Ralph Josselin reported from Essex 'such a dearth of corne that flesh is to bee allowed this Lent' and complained that, despite the 'publick fast to seeke god', 'oh how few lay any of gods judgments to heart': *Diary*, pp. 484–6 (esp. 17 Nov. 1661; 19 and 22 Jan. 1662; 2 and 9 Feb. 1662).

149 *Sad News from the Countrey, or A True and Full Relation of the Late Wonderful Floods in Divers Parts of England* (1674), p. 8. It was published just before the fast-day in February 'as a Preparative' to provoke humbled reflection and included extracts 'from Letters from several Parts' describing the 'National Calamity'. The fast proclamation itself called on 'all Preachers to Exhort their Congregations on the said respective Days, to Mercy and Liberality to the Poor, in this time of Dearth and Scarcity': Charles II, *A Proclamation for a General Fast* (1674).

150 Dunton, *Englands Alarum*, pp. 4, 21.

151 ERO, D/DBm Z10, not paginated (26 Nov 1693).

152 'Prayers and Thanksgivings' in *The Book of Common Prayer and the Administration of the Sacraments* (1662). These included requests 'For Rain' and 'For Fair Weather', in addition to the two used 'In Time of Dearth and Famine'.

153 *Causes of a Solemn National Fast* (Edinburgh, 1696); *Act of the General Assembly, anent a Solemn National Fast and Humiliation* (Edinburgh, 1700); TNA, SP 44/163, pp. 51–2, 82–3.

and Scotland.[154] Ultimately, the faithful of both countries continued to regard repentance as part of the solution to any earthly problem.

These appeals for divine forgiveness reflect the foundational place occupied by petitionary prayer in late seventeenth-century thinking, a habit of mind that remains one of the most persistent aspects of early modern culture.[155] Individuals, families, parishes, and nations all sought relief from their material sufferings by speaking directly to the Almighty. One of the era's most popular tracts, *The Christian Monitor*, reminded the impoverished of 'the good effects' that could come from 'devoutly applying themselves to God by Prayer': 'Would the poor Man seek as earnestly to God for relief, as he does to his rich Neighbour, he would find it the surest course to have his wants supplied.'[156] This remedial strategy was also a basic component in many later Stuart ballads. In the oft-reprinted story of the Kentish widow, for example, the devout woman responded to the threat of starvation with a long, abject, and eventually successful plea for miraculous divine intervention.[157] Likewise, when the economy slumped, an anonymous balladeer instructed listeners to 'Pray God that Trading may be good again, / And every one that hears now, say Amen'.[158] These songs dutifully recorded the happy results that came from each suitably humble request and, in so doing, clearly established the direct line of communication between the poor and their Heavenly Father.[159]

If the prayers of distressed Christians could provoke providential relief, they might also bring about other forms of supernatural interces-

---

[154] Karen Cullen, *Famine in Scotland: The 'Ill Years' of the 1690s* (Edinburgh, 2010); Robert Houston, *Social Change in the Age of the Enlightenment: Edinburgh, 1660–1760* (Oxford, 1994), pp. 253, 273, 286–7.

[155] For a brief review of the analogical (and sometimes symbiotic) relationship between prayer and petition in Christianity see David Nicholls, 'Addressing God as Ruler: Prayer and Petition', *British Journal of Sociology*, 44:1 (1993), pp. 125–41. Ralph Josselin alluded to the closeness of petitioning God and petitioning the king when he declared that 'I fear Holland and France think England is broken, and our glory and trade will fall into their hands while we groan under misery … now the K. will admit no addresses to him, we will go [to] god who will hear': *Diary*, p. 626 (26 Jan 1680).

[156] Rawlet, *The Christian Monitor*, pp. 21, 36 (citing Psalm 34:15). This tract had gone through twenty-seven editions by 1701 and, five years earlier, the title-page claimed that more than 95,000 copies had been sold.

[157] *The Kentish Miracle* (1684), in *PB*, II, p. 54. Her prayer filled six stanzas and referenced four different biblical stories of God providing for the faithful.

[158] *The Poor Man put to a Pinch* (n.d.), in *PB*, IV, p. 299. According to another ballad, if a poor man is burdened with hungry children, 'Let his Prayers be still unto the Lord, / Then relief for them He will afford': *An Antidote of Rare Physick* (1685), in *PB*, II, p. 46. Similar advice was provided by 'a poor Husband-man' and by 'Queen Mary' herself: *A Looking-glass for a Covetous Miser* (c.1666–78), in *PB*, II, p. 19; *The Bedford-shire Widow* (c.1689–96), in *PB*, II, p. 75.

[159] For the importance of petitionary models to social relations in a less theocentric context see Chapter 2.4 below.

sion. According to popular tradition, the effects of their appeals for God's sympathy were as likely to be felt by their superiors as by the petitioners themselves. For example, in return for dealing justly and charitably with their neighbours, benevolent gentlemen could expect to receive the most efficacious of all blessings, the praise of the poor. Richard Croft, preaching in Worcestershire in 1696, was very specific on this count. He recommended using charity to 'Purchase or Bribe' the affections of 'the necessitous and afflicted, the needy and the out-casts, whose Prayer and Intercessions for us ... will be infinitely better Advocates for us at the Throne of Grace, then all the rich and haughty Men in the World'.[160] Although God was still the ultimate judge in this formulation, the indigent were indispensable as attorneys. They performed a similar role in some providential ballads and in these stories the rewards for good works were much more immediate. In one song from the 1680s, for instance, a penniless Yorkshireman, while seeking food for his starving family, met a kindly squire who took pity and relieved him. 'I hope the Lord will bless this honest Gentleman', said the poor man, 'For every penny that he gave me, the Lord may send him ten.' Of course, God 'heard his prayer' and sent his liberal benefactor 'a plenty'.[161] Evidence of a belief in the efficacy of such prayers was not confined to sermons and broadsides. After Sir John Nicholas had his steward distribute meat to the poor on his Wiltshire estate in 1700, the steward wrote back to say that when 'the prayers of the poor are prevalent you are to expect health and long life'.[162]

These ideas can also been seen in the appeals made by the poor them-selves (or at least their scriveners). Petitions to magistrates and other authorities nearly always ended with the petitioner offering a prayer on the patron's behalf, a rhetorical claim which had in fact become so conventional by the late seventeenth century that most of these letters simply ended with 'And your petitioners shall ever pray &c.'. When made explicit, such prayers often focused on the material rewards of charity to the distressed – hence, justices received many petitions from widows, invalids, and other supplicants claiming that they would 'pray for all your worships health and happinesse' or 'pray that God may always preserve you & yours in Safety

---

[160] Croft, *The Wise Steward*, p. 21. He later qualifies this starkly Pelagian outlook by noting 'I dare not say, that good Works can purchase or merit Heaven; for when we have done the best we can, we must humbly bow our Heads and say, we are *unprofitable Servants*' in ibid, p. 47. For a topical ballad which praises the 'brave noble Men [who] gain'd the Prayers of the Poor' by relieving them during the distress caused by the recoinage see *The New and True Touch of the Times* (1696), in *PB*, IV, p. 332.

[161] *A True Sence of Sorrow* (1685–8), in *PB*, II, p. 53.

[162] D. R. Hainsworth, *Stewards, Lords and People: The Estate Steward and his World in Later Stuart England* (Cambridge, 1992), p. 163. See also the assumption that 'a Gentleman of great Hospitality' would be rewarded when the prayers of his benificiaries 'pierce through the Clouds': Samuel Izacke, *Remarkable Antiquities of the City of Exeter* (1722), p. 200.

to your lives end'.[163] Others, however, offered even greater rewards. For example, when Richard Piercy, a cooper from the village of Harome in the Vale of Pickering, sought aid at the quarter sessions after losing his home to 'a sad & dreadfull fire' in 1696, he concluded his plea by attesting his 'great hopes through your Christian charity of Relief, your poore petitioner will be deeply obledged to bless God for you, ever be mindfull of his benefactors & for your felicity here & hereafter send up his weak and incessant prayers'. The justices, in response, granted £5 towards relieving his 'necessitous condition'.[164] Even petitioners who did not conclude their requests with a 'prayer' might nonetheless remind potential benefactors that God's eyes were upon them. In 1708, an English merchant at Bergen in Norway received one such petition from twelve Newcastle seamen shipwrecked there:

> As you would desire the life of so many *Christians* here att the point of Starving for want of food & clothing, We earnestly desire & request, over and over again *for God Almightys sake*, to help and assist us in this our most doelfull & lamentable starving condition upon whom the hard hearted people in this place will take no pity. Our Requests is unto you, Most Noble Seir and as you would desire *the blessednesse of Heaven*, help *for God sake*.[165]

The godly duty of charity to distressed Christians, and the divine favour that would result, could not be clearer.

It would be misleading, however, to focus solely on the blessings available through the intercessions of grateful poor people. As in contemporaneous discussions of providence or the afterlife, threats were often more prominent than promises. Everyone knew that petitionary prayer was a useful tool, but

---

163 HA, QSR 12/1664/938, QSR 19/1684/588, QSR 22/1691/181; NYRCO, QSB 1686/128, QSB 1699/197; WYAS–W, QS 1/57/6/6 (petition of imprisoned debtors in Rothwell gaol, 1720); DRO, QS/4, box 132 (petition of Edward Wichhalce, Sep 1692); LMA, COL/CA/05/01/0010 (petition of the poor tankard-bearers, 1709; petition of Thomas Veasey, 1709); TNA, ADM 106/487/123, ADM 106/494/390; *Leic. Boro. Recs*, VII, p. 20.

164 NYCRO, QSB 1696/152. For other petitioners – including the minister at London's Newgate prison – who pledged to 'pray unto the Allmightie God for all your Honours and Worships healthes prospertie and happinesse in this world and eternall joye and happiness in the worlde to come' see HA, QSR 16/1674/311, QSR 22/1691/180; NYRCO, QSB 1699/197; LMA, COL/CA/05/01/0010 (petition of Paul Lorrain, 1709); *Leic. Boro. Recs*, V, pp. 39–40. For the tendency of London beggars to promise 'future returns' see Tim Hitchcock, 'The Publicity of Poverty in Early Eighteenth-Century London', in Julia F. Merritt (ed.), *Imagining Early Modern London: Perceptions and Portrayals of the City from Stow to Strype, 1598–1720* (Cambridge, 2001), pp. 172–3.

165 TNA, SP 42/8/1. Emphasis added. The merchant, David Cristy, forwarded the request to Lord Pembroke, who ordered that a letter be sent to the magistrates of Bergen 'to support these poor Men (to prevent their perishing), & to send them to Great Britain by the first shipping': TNA, SP 42/8/7.

they were also aware of how easily it could be transformed into a devastating weapon for, as Keith Thomas has pointed out, 'the line dividing a curse from a prayer was extremely thin'.[166] So thin, in fact, that at least one preacher thought it reasonable to use the abundant biblical evidence on the effectiveness of cursing in order to draw attention to its more positive counterpart. The well-known cleric Isaac Barrow, in one of his sermons on neighbourly love, declared:

> if the complaints and curses of those who are oppressed or neglected by uncharitable dealing do certainly reach God's ears, and pull down vengence from above; how much more will the intercessions and blessings of the [well-treated] poor pierce the heavens, and thence draw recompence?[167]

The power to bless benefactors was inexorably intertwined with the power to injure superiors who failed to live up to their social and economic commitments. Moreover, as Barrow's statement indicates, later Stuart audiences seem to have been more familiar with the dangers of the latter than with the rewards of the former. Ballad-writers, knowing the ubiquity of this belief, even used as a stock comic character the beggar who met every refusal of alms with 'a volley of Curses' such as 'The Divel confound your good worship'.[168] Then again, they also saw humour in the 'meal monger' who claimed to 'care not a fig' for 'all the Curses' occasioned by his hoarding – only a fool would ignore such legitimate complaints.[169]

Although this outlook probably had primeval roots, good Protestants seeking justification for their belief did not need to look any further than God's Word. 'If thou afflict [any widow or orphan] in any wise, and they cry at all unto me, I will surely hear their cry', declared Jehovah to the Israelites, 'And my wrath shall wax hot, and I will kill you with the sword; and your wives shall be widows, and your children fatherless.'[170] Elsewhere in the Bible, this was expanded to include the 'curses' and 'cries' of strangers, beggars, neighbours, rural labourers, hired servants, and poor consumers.[171] Taken together, this would have meant practically every economically

---

[166] Thomas, *Religion*, p. 605.

[167] Barrow, *Of the Love of God and Our Neighbour*, p. 213.

[168] *The Joviall Crew, or, Beggars-Bush* (c.1660–63) in *EB*, fol. 150. Likewise, another ballad has beggars saying 'Take pitty on the Fatherless, / That God Almighty may you bless', but 'If some will not pull out their Purse, / In heart we oft lend them a Curse': *The Jovial Beggars Merry Crew* (1684), in *RB*, IV, p. 51.

[169] *The Meal Mongers Garland* (1700?) in *RyB*, Ry.III.a.10(079).

[170] Exod. 22:22–24.

[171] For strangers, widows, and orphans see Deut. 27:19. For those in need of charity see Deut. 15:8–9; Prov. 28:27. For neighbours with land rights see Deut. 27:17. For wage-earning farm workers, hired servants, and slaves see Jam. 5:4; Deut. 24:14–15; Exod. 3:7. For buyers of corn see Deut. 27:17. Even after the Reformation put an end to some types of ecclesiastically sanctioned curses, other forms continued to be used by the Church in

vulnerable person in later Stuart England. Even so, it was not enough for Luke Milbourne, preaching in early eighteenth-century London. He lengthened the list still further by adding innocent debtors and emphatically warned 'unmerciful Creditor[s]' not to provoke 'the weighty and terrible Curses' of their victims.[172] Predictably, these biblical axioms were glossed and paraphrased in widely read texts, in some cases even being put into the mouths of particular characters.[173] But the most fascinating evidence for the strength of these religious ideals comes from the way they converged with social practice.

The tangible effects of cursing only very rarely appear on the historical record. Most of the time, people either believed in the power of the curse, and hence modified their behaviour to avoid it, or they were sceptical enough to simply ignore it altogether. Only in the few cases where the 'victims' of curses responded with legal prosecution, rather than an attempt at conciliation, do early modern sources record concrete examples of lowly individuals attempting to seek redress through evocations of divine (or at least supernatural) power. By accusing a poor person of witchcraft, for instance, these guilt-ridden individuals plainly showed that they feared the cries of their supplicants and, more importantly, often left a record in the form of legal testimony or cheap printed accounts. These provide a rare opportunity for historians to see the poor responding to 'a breach of charity or neighbourliness' by calling down other-worldly retribution.[174] In both life and literature, numerous examples can found of beggars cursing the uncharitable, tenants cursing evicting landlords, gleaners cursing unjust employers,

---

its liturgy. This included, for example, regularly reading through the curses and blessings in Deut. 28 as part of the service: Thomas, *Religion*, p. 601.

[172] Milbourne, *Debtor and Creditor*, pp. 20–21 (citing Psalm 12:5 and 146:9). See also Newnam, *The Complaint of English Subjects*, p. 28; Edmund Archer, *A Sermon Preach'd at the Parish Church of St Martin … for the Charity Schools of the City of Oxford* (Oxford, 1713), p. 17.

[173] For the owner of 'great Estates' regretfully repeating Jam. 5:4 see Jones, *The Black Book*, sig. A5r–A5v.

[174] Thomas, *Religion*, pp. 660–67. In the historiography this subject is often discussed under the rubric of 'the beggar's curse'. I have avoided this term as it tends to conflate beggars or paupers with 'the poor' as a whole and, moreover, it does not seem to have been used in early modern sources. For further discussion of the phenomenon, in addition to the key works cited in the following footnote, see Hindle, *On the Parish?* pp. 73–4; Walter, 'Public Transcripts', pp. 131–3; William Hunt, *The Puritan Moment: The Coming of Revolution in an English County* (Cambridge, MA, 1983), pp. 54–8; Lizanne Henderson, 'The Survival of Witchcraft Prosecutions and Witch Belief in South-West Scotland', *Scottish Historical Review*, 85:1 (2006), pp. 52–74. Of course, socio-economic factors were only one element among many in the witchcraft phenomenon and the following discussion is not intended as an explanation of English witchcraft as a whole. The historiography has developed rapidly since Thomas and Macfarlane's insistence on the primacy of the 'charity evaded' model: Malcolm Gaskill, 'Witchcraft and Evidence in Early Modern England', *Past & Present*, 198 (2008), p. 34, and the works cited there.

debtors cursing creditors who demanded repayment, and even one case of a woman bewitching a malt-dealer who asked too high a price.[175] In England, criminal prosecutions for this sort of behaviour occurred most frequently in the century or so following the passage of the Witchcraft Act of 1563, but even after the Restoration cases continued to surface of economic disputes turning into allegations of malicious cursing.

Landowners who, in the eyes of their tenants or neighbours, abused their property rights were an obvious target. This idea was partly based on Deuteronomy 27:17 – 'Cursed be he that removeth his neighbour's landmark' – yet it was not limited to boundary disputes. In the 1680s, for example, a Suffolk widow named Philippa Munnings met an attempt to evict her with a threat, saying 'Go thy way, thy nose shall lie upward in the church yard before Sunday next.' Vindication came when the landlord died soon after.[176] Many years earlier, on a medieval manor, a similar act of perceived injustice had led a widow and her children to fall 'on their knees imprecating the vengeance of God' upon their evictor and his heirs. One of the merciless gentleman's seventeenth-century descendants, a nonconforming Cornish minister, reported that 'a curse hath remained on the estate ever since'.[177] No one seemed willing to dispute the effectiveness of calling for divine reprisals against men who, in Christ's phrase, devoured widows' houses. A few people, however, felt threatened enough by this power to respond with sometimes deadly legal persecution. Philippa Munnings escaped with an acquittal after being charged with witchcraft in 1684, but the Scottish woman who cursed a man for driving her cattle off his pasture-land was not so lucky: she was executed in Dumfries in 1671.[178]

Of course, land and housing disputes were not the only source of social friction in later Stuart communities and, as with the discussion of providence, it would be easy to fill up many pages with parallel examples. Limited space permits only a very brief review of several other sites of conflict. Refusing to provide charitable relief, for instance, was regarded as a likely cause of petitions for divine intercession. One cheap tract had Christ warn the rich directly: 'You let my poor members cry and call to you for Bread, Bread, for the Lords sake, and you gave it them not; you stopped your ears at the cry of the poor, and now though you cry never so loud, you shall not be heard.'[179]

---

[175] For pre-1660 examples from the courts see Alan Macfarlane, *Witchcraft in Tudor and Stuart England: A Regional and Comparative Study* (London, 1970), pp. 104–5, 151, 159, 164, 170–75, 196–7, 204–6. For pre-1660 examples from literature see Walsham, *Providence*, pp. 81–5; Thomas, *Religion*, pp. 660–67; Tubach, *Index*, p. 112 (no. 1404).

[176] C. L'Estrange Ewen, *Witchcraft and Demonianism: A Concise Account Derived from Sworn Depositions and Confessions Obtained in the Courts of England and Wales* (London, 1933), p. 373.

[177] Theophilus Gale, *The Life and Death of Thomas Tregosse* (1671), pp. 3–4.

[178] Henderson, 'Survival', pp. 56–7.

[179] Hart, *Heavens Glory And Hells Horror*, sig. A7v. For similar statements see Hart,

This helps to explain why beggars in Northumberland were given alms 'for fear of their curses' in the 1660s, why tight-fisted people in Bedford (1680), Devon (1693), and Hertfordshire (1712) accused their unsuccessful supplicants of witchcraft, and why a dread of supernatural retaliation continued to inspire charity in Cornwall even into the nineteenth century.[180] The biblical curse laid on food hoarders was equally well known.[181] Hence, in the 1670s, when a rich grazier from the village of Eastcote near Northampton found that thirty of his sheep had died after he had refused to sell Anne Foster some mutton, the man immediately blamed their mysterious deaths on Foster's 'murmuring'.[182] Indeed, almost any conflict might give rise to accusations of witchcraft, but they were especially common in situations where someone dealt 'unchristianly' with an individual – usually a poor woman – who lacked any prospect of legal remedy. This appears to have been the root cause of the allegations levelled against Joan Kent of London in 1682. According to her accuser, his refusal to deliver Kent two pigs without being paid in advance led her to wreak supernatural vengeance on his whole family, though the old woman's honest piety convinced the jury otherwise.[183] Similarly, a Somerset woman named Margaret Agar responded to a parish overseer's attempt to force her children into service by striking him down with a fatal curse in 1664.[184] Disadvantaged by their poverty – as well as their age and gender – these women were left with only one route for redress.

The Charitable Christian, sig. A7v; Younge, *The Poors Advocate*, p. 6 (paraphrasing Prov. 21:13); Johnson, *Dives and Lazarus*, sig. B2r. See also Deut. 15:8–9 and Prov. 28:27.

[180] Northumberland comments quoted in John Walter, 'The Social Economy of Dearth in Early Modern England', in John Walter and Roger Schofield (eds), *Famine, Disease and the Social Order in Early Modern Society* (Cambridge, 1989), p. 111; Luppitt (Devon) court case in DRO, QS/4, box 134 (26 Aug 1693); Bedford court case and comments of William Lovett (Cornwall), cited in Thomas, *Religion*, p. 666–7, 675; Walkerne (Herts.) court case recorded in eight pamphlets and a broadside, all cited in Ewen, *Witchcraft*, pp. 384–9. At harvest time in Norfolk, the reapers asked each passer-by for 'pence, as well as Pray'rs', and 'If nothing drops into the gaping Purse, / Ye carry with ye, to be sure a Curse': Matthew Stevenson, 'Upon the Norfolk Largess' in his *Norfolk Drollery: Or, a Compleat Collection of the Newest Songs, Jovial Poems, and Catches, &c.* (1673), p. 33. For similar late seventeenth-century examples of people offering blessings or prayers in exchange for informal charity, and curses in response to refusals, see Ronald Hutton, *Stations of the Sun: A History of the Ritual Year in Britain* (Oxford, 2001), pp. 198–9, 374.
[181] The curse in Prov. 11:26 was not cited just by preachers. It was used as an epigram in White, *The Charitable Farmer of Somersetshire*; mentioned by 'a poor Husband-man' to a rich hoarder in *A Looking-glass for a Covetous Miser* (c.1666–78), in PB, II, p. 19; and repeatedly paraphrased in *The Meal Mongers Garland* (1700?) in RyB, Ry.III.a.10(079).
[182] Ewen, *Witchcraft*, pp. 362–3.
[183] Ibid., pp. 364–5.
[184] Steve Hindle, 'Civility, Honesty and the Identification of the Deserving Poor in Seventeenth-Century England', in Henry French and Jonathan Barry (eds), *Identity and Agency in England, 1500–1800* (Basingstoke, 2004), p. 47.

Although the records relating to these incidents only rarely specify whether the authority invoked was God or the Devil, the very fact that they might end up in court attests to the undeniable other-worldly power invested in the voices of the poor. Luke Milbourne, in his sermon of 1709, must have spoken for many when he said that 'I would choose to meet a Lyon in his Rage, or a Bear in his Fury, rather than to do anything that might bring the Curses of such unfortunate Innocents upon my Head'.[185] Such curses were something to be fearfully avoided. Consequently, in Alan Macfarlane's words, the dread of supernatural retribution 'acted as a sanction in enforcing neighbourly conduct', though clearly the sad fate of some 'witches' indicates that even successful evocations might backfire.[186] This belief sharpened the inflection of otherwise unremarkable censures by giving the vocabulary of condemnation dangerous connotations. To sing, for instance, that 'the poor cry fye upon' rich employers who 'keep their Wages from them', was to raise the spectre of divine intercession without even mentioning God.[187] Inarticulate laments, bitter curses, and desperate cries all had the potential to transform into potent weapons through the idea of petitionary prayer.

This aspect of the doctrine of divine power often incorporated other common elements of early modern religiosity, such as the providentialist assumptions evident in John Hart's warning to the 'unmerciful':

> The poor will curse him, and not onely man, but even God himself curseth them. … [S]ometimes they are wasted at Law, sometimes by Fire or Robbery, sometimes by such secret wayes that none can give a rational account of, but know that the curse of God is there.[188]

Hart, like other providentialists, simply merged divine curses with their mortal counterparts in order to explain the dire effects of unjust behaviour on the lives and estates of the rich. However, official records of this particular manifestation of providentialism became rarer over the course of the later Stuart period. Scepticism about the possibility of proving malicious

---

[185] Milbourne, *Debtor and Creditor*, p. 21.

[186] Macfarlane, *Witchcraft*, p. 105; Thomas, *Religion*, p. 599–611. Paradoxically, both scholars also connect the decline of 'the old tradition of mutual charity' to witchcraft accusations, though whether the former caused the latter or vice versa is probably an unanswerable question: Macfarlane, *Witchcraft*, p. 204; Thomas, *Religion*, pp. 670–77.

[187] Lawrence White, *All Things be Dear but Poor Mens Labour* (c.1674) in WB, Wood E 25(199). This ballad also recounts the poor men's 'many sad Complaints' against miserliness which the 'Rich … will not hear / because Charity's out of fashion'.

[188] Hart, *The Charitable Christian*, sig. A5v–A6r (citing Matt. 25:41, Prov. 28:27, Prov. 3:33, Psalm 41:1). The curses of God and the poor were also treated indiscriminately in *The Meal Mongers Garland* (1700?) in RyB, Ry.III.a.10(079). Interestingly, at least one contemporary attempted to divide these two doctrines by explicitly declaring that the disasters which struck the uncharitable were not witchcraft, but rather providential punishment for miserliness: Thomas, *Religion*, p. 674.

magic spread among the educated men who ran the English legal system and this caused a marked decline in formal charges of 'cursing', eventually leading to the Witchcraft Act of 1736 which 'disenchanted' the offence entirely.[189] But popular faith in magic in general and the mystical powers of the oppressed in particular remained strong. Informal accusations of witchcraft, for example, continued for centuries and generally fitted 'the same old special pattern of charity evaded, followed by misfortune incurred'.[190]

The enduring vitality of the concept of petitionary prayer meant even the most disenfranchised of men and women were never without some degree of agency. They had a unique relationship with the Almighty, a privileged position in the heavenly order that could be invoked as a counter to the earthly strength of their antagonists. In some formulations, they were Christ's holy representatives, who might remind the uncharitable that in 'starving the poor you starve Christ'.[191] '[W]hen the poor man asketh us in Gods Name, or for Gods sake, he doth not usurp or forge, he hath good authority, and a true ground for doing so', claimed Isaac Barrow in 1671. In fact, the godly supplicant 'bears His Name, and wears His Livery, (for the poor mans rags are badges of his relation unto God)'.[192] However, in the vast majority of early modern texts, their 'good authority' was limited to pleading or praying for the intervention of others, whether their immediate superiors on earth or their supreme ruler in heaven. The curses hurled at worldly oppressors might not be particularly deferential, but they became effective only if God choose to fulfil the request. This interpretation of the Bible sanctioned active attempts to seek redress, as long as they were ultimately merely petitions.

In contrast, at least a few authors hinted at possible justifications for a more direct remedy to material hardship: theft. Although explicit state-

---

[189] For the importance of legal and judicial changes (rather than a decline in the belief in witchcraft itself) see Gaskill, 'Witchcraft and Evidence', pp. 62–70.

[190] Thomas, *Religion*, p. 696. For examples see ibid., pp. 539, 547, 550, 675; Henderson, 'Survival'.

[191] Hart, *Heavens Glory And Hells Horror*, sig. A7v (probably based on Matt. 25:34–46). Of course this notion of divine proxy could be inverted. For instance, servants and apprentices were told that their masters were God's representatives and thus serving them was 'obeying *Him*, who requires, and will recompence your diligent and faithful Service to *them* as done to *Himself*': John Waugh, *The Duty of Apprentices* (1713), p. 20, citing Col. 3:22–23.

[192] Barrow, *The Duty and Reward of Bounty*, pp. 67–8, 70. This illustrates perfectly Walsham's contention that those seeking charity – such as women, children, and the elderly – spoke through 'divine ventriloquism': Walsham, *Providence*, p. 207. Regarding the idea of badges as licenses for lawful supplication, the ambiguity inherent in literal attempts to badge the poor has been noted in Steve Hindle, 'Dependency, Shame and Belonging: Badging the Deserving Poor, c. 1550–1750', *Cultural and Social History*, 1:1 (2004), esp. pp. 11–13, 16–18, 29. For beggars' badges in Scotland see Houston, *Social Change*, pp. 261–75.

ments on the subject were undeniably rare, they may be indicative of an attitude shared more widely among the poorer sort than religious writers would have liked to admit. Moreover, the possibility of godly theft was theologically defensible. Using the doctrine of stewardship, wherein wealth was no more than a loan from the True Proprietor, some of the greatest thinkers in Christendom argued for what Scott Swanson has called 'the principle of extreme necessity' via 'the right of subsistence'.[193] Since God had created the fruits of the earth for the provision of humankind, to deny the needy their due was to 'pervert the Intentions of the Donor'.[194] Thomas Aquinas, for instance, was fairly typical in teaching that 'private property is only a means to an end, [so] if it obstructs that end, its legitimacy falls away at that instant'.[195] According to this logic, the 'owners' with the weakest claims over their wealth were those ungodly rich men who not only failed to fulfil their roles as generous stewards but actually grew rich through the suffering of their less-fortunate neighbours. The exhortation in the *Book of Homilies* scheduled for rogation week made this point bluntly: 'God is not bound to defend such possessions as are gotten by the Devil and his counsel.'[196]

As an abstract principle, this theory of property must have seemed self-evident and irrefutable to early modern Christians. Applying it to the world in which they lived proved rather more troublesome. George Stanhope, for example, hinted in passing at the legitimacy of redistribution in 1705 when he declared that 'the Poor have always a Right to some part of the Possessions of the Rich', yet he also employed the example of Lazarus to demand the passive acceptance of the most savage depravations, even starvation.[197] This divided loyalty is perhaps predictable given that Stanhope's sermon was preached to an audience of poor children and their gentry patrons. Moralists generally left the legal implications of their theory of property unspoken or even denied these implications altogether by insisting that obedience to secular law overrode any divinely ordained right of subsistence. The ever-popular *Christian Monitor* was merely following convention when it warned those 'in want' of 'Necessities' to seek 'no unlawful Course for their Relief', especially 'stealing any thing, though of a small value'.[198] Indeed, only

---

[193] Scott Swanson, 'The Medieval Foundations of John Locke's Theory of Natural Rights: Rights of Subsistence and the Principle of Extreme Necessity', *History of Political Thought*, 18:3 (1997), pp. 399–459. For the 'principle of necessity' see Istvan Hont and Michael Ignatieff, 'Needs and Justice in the *Wealth of Nations*: An Introductory Essay', in idem (eds), *Wealth and Virtue: The Shaping of Political Economy in the Scottish Enlightenment* (Cambridge, 1983), pp. 26–8; Schlatter, *Social Ideas*, pp. 96–7; Hindle, *On the Parish?* pp. 81–92; Andrea McKenzie, *Tyburn's Martyrs: Execution in England, 1675–1775* (London, 2007), pp. 75–83.

[194] Edwards, *Sermons On Special Occasions*, p. 145.

[195] Swanson, 'Medieval Foundations', pp. 419–22, quotation at p. 421.

[196] 'An Exhortation … in Rogation Week', *Certain Sermons or Homilies*, II, p. 305.

[197] Stanhope, *The Danger of Hard-heartedness*, p. 10.

[198] Rawlet, *The Christian Monitor*, p. 44; Green, *Christian's ABC*, p. 463; Hindle, *On the*

Richard Younge, that self-declared 'advocate' for the poor, was willing to spell out the principle for a broad audience. '[T]he Rich', he claimed, 'offend more, in not giving their superfluities; then the poor do, in stealing necessaries'.[199] This may have been an obvious corollary to the doctrine of godly stewardship, but Younge alone applied the precept so pointedly.

Later Stuart commentators who based their ethical judgements on a belief in divine sovereignty can hardly be faulted for giving primacy to petitionary rather than direct modes of redress. Mere mortals might repent, pray, and even curse – only God decided if they would be answered. On the whole, however, the qualified support offered to these sorts of actions gave the poor a degree of influence over the behaviour of their rich neighbours which they otherwise would have sorely lacked. Since the cries of needy Christians had unparalleled resonance in heaven, those who were able to present themselves as bearing 'His Name' and wearing 'His Livery' could apply real pressure to antagonists. Their power was no less formidable for being immaterial.

6 Conclusions

Over the last century, discussions of the link between religion and economic culture in early modern society have largely revolved around 'the rise of capitalist modernity'.[200] Some scholars have declared that religious innovation gave birth to modern commerce; others have argued that later Stuart theology merely justified underlying shifts in the economic system; many more have assumed that the secular values of capitalism just pushed Christianity out of the marketplace. None of these positions is entirely without foundation. Nonetheless, this chapter has revealed the profound paucity of this debate when compared to the rich complexities of actual early modern attitudes. Though anchored on the simplest of theological truths – that of God's omnipotence – the concepts of stewardship, idolatry, judgement,

---

Parish? pp. 90–91; Schlatter, *Social Ideas*, pp. 96–7. Moreover, the concept of theft justified by necessity does not appear to have ever been applied 'as a principle of law' in the courts, though there was a distinct tendency for judges and juries to treat such crimes more leniently in the seventeenth century: Swanson, 'Medieval Foundations', p. 410; Hindle, *On the Parish?* pp. 83–4. For related justifications of theft see pp. 137–8 below.

[199] Younge, *The Poors Advocate*, p. 6 (paraphrasing St Lawrence). The idea that stealing in cases of extreme necessity was 'no theft' still found some support in religious texts intended for a more socially select audience: Hindle, *On the Parish?* p. 90; Schlatter, *Social Ideas*, pp. 96–7.

[200] For the beginnings of this debate in the first years of the twentieth century see the chapters by Paul Münch, Harmut Lehmann and Thomas Nipperdey in Hartmut Lehmann and Guenther Roth (eds), *Weber's Protestant Ethic: Origins, Evidence, Context* (Cambridge, 1993).

and redress cannot be reduced to mere epiphenomena. They were not just causes, products or victims of 'capitalism'. Hence, the preceding sections are an attempt to move beyond these century-old debates by focusing on the continuities and ambiguities in the religious beliefs of the era.

After reading through many of the texts of this period, it becomes increasingly difficult to accept the radical post-Reformation discontinuity in economic ethics described in the established narrative. Although Max Weber – with the help of Richard Tawney – spawned a seemingly endless debate among sociologists about 'the Protestant Ethic', historians who have touched on it rarely disagree with the overall chronology established by these pioneers. Both Weber and Tawney regarded the seventeenth century as the pivotal point of transition from 'traditional' Christian social teaching to something quite novel. Weber emphasised the 'capitalist spirit' that supposedly infused post-Reformation religious thinking and argued that this 'ascetic Protestantism' presented 'striving for gain ... as directly willed by God', thus 'liberating the *acquisition of wealth* from the inhibitions of traditionalist ethics'.[201] Tawney argued much the same, but added another layer of complexity by suggesting that this process was compounded by the secularisation of the market. According to him, Christian commentators transformed 'social vices' – including 'limitless increase', 'methodical accumulation' and shameless 'acquisitiveness' – into 'moral virtues'. Yet, paradoxically, he also argued that 'the claim that religion should keep its hands off business' became orthodoxy during this same 'critical period'.[202]

The most obviously incorrect of these assertions is also, curiously, the most unexamined. It has been more than eighty years since Tawney declared that cultural support for 'a Christian standard of economic conduct' had collapsed by 1660, but the absurdity of this statement remains unremarked.[203] Fifty years later, Joyce Appleby echoed it by declaring that after the Civil Wars 'a moral order where economic activities were a means to social ends – God's and man's – fell from public view', a process which allowed for the 'secularization of economic life'.[204] In recent decades, this teleology has found more supporters and suffered amazingly little criticism. Norman Jones, for example, defended a similar model of change in his work on Elizabethan and Jacobean credit relations: 'The theocentric, communal, and theologically defined approach to money-lending had been replaced by one that was secular, individualistic, and defined by economic thought.'[205] Similarly, C. J. Sommerville argued that 'social thought' lost its religious aspects in the late seventeenth century and, as a consequence,

---

[201] Weber, *Protestant Ethic*, p. 115 (emphasis in original).
[202] Tawney, *Religion*, pp. viii–ix, 246–7.
[203] Ibid., p. 23.
[204] Appleby, *Economic Thought*, pp. 70, 50.
[205] Jones, *God and the Moneylenders*, p. 199. In dating the change, he argued that 'the Middle Ages had ended' by 1625.

'social relations were secularized'.[206] Even Margaret Hunt, in her fascinating examination of the culture of the later Stuart middling sort, claimed that 'literate public opinion' increasingly discounted the possibility of supernatural intervention in the market and 'tended more and more to conceive of economic issues within a secular rather than a religious frame'.[207] According to these scholars, religious beliefs were thoroughly excluded from the realm of economic conduct over the course of the seventeenth century.[208]

In fact, the texts discussed in this chapter indicate that preachers and catechists continued to deal with these issues on a regular basis. Daniel Baugh, a rare critic of this aspect of the secularisation thesis, has remarked that 'Tawney's portrait of a society suddenly smothered in secularism, and of a church readily abandoning the task of criticizing the conduct of economic relations "to the rationalist and the humanitarian," does not accord with

[206] Sommerville, *Secularization*, pp. 143, 147–9. After surveying the era's best-selling religious works, he concluded that 'interest in social themes came to be incompatible with a concentration on devotional ones', despite noting that 'nearly half' of these authors 'tried to give some guidance on business ethics' and many more discussed issues such as charity: Sommerville, *Popular Religion*, pp. 126–7, 140. Even more recently, Andrew McRae implied a similar process whereby 'the meaning of agrarian England shifted' from a religious 'moral economy' to 'a modern landscape of capitalist enterprise': McRae, *God Speed*, p. 7. According to yet another historian, the views of Barrow, Bunyan, and Baxter on property and stewardship were 'minority voices' that 'may fairly be described as throwbacks to an earlier Puritan ideology': Whitney R. D. Jones, *The Tree of Commonwealth, 1450–1793* (Cranbury, 2000), p. 244.

[207] Hunt, *Middling Sort*, pp. 35–8. She also has remarked that, despite the influence of the Reformation of Manners campaigns of the 1690s and 1700s, 'there existed a good deal of disagreement within the trading community itself about the role of Providence in everyday business dealings and perhaps even a gathering conviction that, in the end, God favored free enterprise, even on a Sunday': ibid., p. 117.

[208] I have discussed only those works that touch directly on the desacralisation of social and economic ethics. For seventeenth-century 'secularisation' in general see Sommerville, *Secularization*, and the more balanced, but I think still overstated, endorsements of the thesis in the chapters by Worden, Knights, and Pincus in Alan Houston and Steve Pincus (eds), *A Nation Transformed: England after the Restoration* (Cambridge, 2001). For critiques of the thesis see Walsham, '"Disenchantment" Reassessed'; eadem, 'Miracles', pp. 303–6; Clark, *English Society*, esp. pp. 10, 26–33, 124–5; idem, 'Providence'; Brian William Young, 'Religious History and the Eighteenth-Century Historian', *Historical Journal*, 43:3 (2000), pp. 849–68; Tim Harris, Paul Seaward, and Mark Goldie (eds), *The Politics of Religion in Restoration England* (Oxford, 1990), esp. Tim Harris, 'Introduction: Revising the Restoration', pp. 1–28; Jeremy Gregory, '"For all sorts and conditions of men": The Social Life of the Book of Common Prayer during the Long Eighteenth Century: or, Bringing the History of Religion and Social history Together', *Social History*, 34:1 (2009), pp. 29–54. For a wide-ranging critique of the thesis over the long-term see David Nash, 'Reconnecting Religion with Social and Cultural History: Secularization's Failure as a Master Narrative', *Cultural and Social History*, 1:3 (2004), pp. 302–22.

the facts'.[209] Although discussing an earlier period, Ilana Ben-Amos has also voiced disagreement with the Tawneyite position, noting that 'the Reformation led neither to the abandonment of the ideal of charitable giving nor indeed to the secularization of giving'.[210] Most recently, Naomi Tadmor has shown conclusively how the 'social universe' of early modern England was steeped in idioms and ideas drawn from scripture.[211] Although it is impossible to quantify religious instruction with any exactitude, it is telling that Luke 16, a chapter packed full of social implications, continued to be a popular starting point for preachers throughout the early eighteenth century.[212] Peter King has noted that even at the end of the century scriptural defences of gleaning still influenced legal disputes between farmers and the poor.[213] Likewise, depictions of property frequently continued to be based as much on theology as on political economy. David Clarkson was just one of many who argued that God 'never gives away His Interest and Propriety in what He bestows on any', only granting 'an Use limited as He thinks fit, and an answerable Possession of them'.[214] In so doing, Clarkson and his fellow clergymen directly refuted any attempt to see humankind as holding a true dominion over the earth and its fruits. The frequency of such forthright statements ought to make them impossible to ignore, yet many historians have continued to rehearse – or, in the case of Sommerville, expand – the secularisation thesis with little comment.

By contrast, Max Weber's so-called 'spirit of capitalism' thesis has received a great deal of critical attention.[215] Although he was infamously imprecise

---

[209] Daniel Baugh, 'Poverty, Protestantism and Political Economy: English Attitudes towards the Poor 1660–1800', in S. B. Baxter (ed.), *England's Rise to Greatness, 1660–1763* (Berkeley, 1983), p. 75.

[210] Ben-Amos, *Culture of Giving*, p. 245.

[211] Tadmor, *Social Universe*.

[212] For references to dozens of examples see Sampson Letsome, *The Preacher's Assistant* (1753), pp. 145–7.

[213] Peter King, 'Gleaners, Farmers, and the Failure of Legal Sanctions in England, 1750–1850', *Past & Present*, 125 (1989), pp. 140–43. Thompson also mentions in passing that 'old [i.e. religious] precepts resounded throughout the eighteenth century' in disputes about provisioning and quotes examples from 1756, 1757, 1772, and 1795, though he later argues that the 'magical components of the Tudor theory [of economic morality] became much weaker' in the first half of the century: Thompson, *Customs in Common*, pp. 254–5, 269. For the continuing importance of 'Christian Economics' in mainstream nineteenth-century culture see Searle, *Morality*, ch. 2, esp. pp. 22–4.

[214] Clarkson, *Sermons and Discourses*, p. 308.

[215] For the traditional criticisms of the thesis see Peter Baehr and Gordon C. Wells, 'Introduction', in Weber, *Protestant Ethic*, pp. xxi–xxxi; Lehmann and Roth, *Weber's Protestant Ethic*. The vast majority of scholars who have disagreed with Weber have taken issue only with his apparent willingness to blame capitalist individualism on Protestantism. To caricature the positions (including my own), one might say that Weberians have argued that Protestantism made the world capitalist, whereas anti-Weberians have argued that the world made Protestantism capitalist. No one has seemed interested in

about both chronology and causality, Weber clearly believed that there had been a dramatic shift in the relationship between religion and economics during the early modern period. He argues that the elaboration of 'Puritan philosophy' in the seventeenth century allowed wholehearted 'striving for riches' to become 'not only morally permissible, but actually commanded'.[216] The puritans apparently spawned 'a creed which transformed the acquisition of wealth from a drudgery or a temptation into a moral duty', and the Calvinist ideal of 'the calling' served mainly 'as an instrument for increasing profits'.[217] More recent scholars have reiterated this contention. For example, despite his otherwise nuanced analysis of early modern agrarian ideals, Andrew McRae relies on the same basic teleology. There was, he argued, a 'long-term movement away from the moral absolutism of [mid-Tudor] complaint' towards a religious outlook which was, by the 1640s, 'just as likely to celebrate the godly improver of the land within a dynamic market economy'.[218] Likewise, according to Norman Jones and Gordon Marshall, English Protestantism's alleged emphasis on private conscience 'created a rationale that sanctioned economic self-aggrandizement', while Scottish Presbyterian teaching on temporal stewardship supposedly helped to 'reinforce the entrepreneurial tendency' of early modern businessmen by promoting the 'accumulation and reinvestment of capital'.[219] Weber and his followers provide accounts in which those merchants and landowners who sought to justify 'striving for riches' at the expense of their poor neighbours heard excuses preached at the pulpit every Sunday.

No doubt certain individuals in later Stuart England did manage to hear such excuses thanks to a bit of wilful misinterpretation, but clerics usually made their views on this matter extremely clear. Indeed, preachers decried

the possibility that neither the world (in 'spirit' at least) nor Protestantism were particularly 'capitalist' well into the eighteenth century.

[216] Weber, *Protestant Ethic*, pp. 109–10. For two recent critical engagements with this specific aspect of the thesis, both of which fruitfully revisit early modern sources, see Lessnoff, *Spirit of Capitalism*; William Lamont, *Puritanism and Historical Controversy* (London, 1996), ch. 7.

[217] Tawney, *Religion*, p. 251; Schlatter, *Social Ideas*, p. 198. Schlatter's account was much more nuanced than Tawney's, but retains the same underlying assumptions. Both authors had much firmer grip on the English situation than Weber, yet *The Protestant Ethic* benefits from Weber's refusal to get bogged down in specifics.

[218] McRae, *God Speed*, pp. 77–9.

[219] Jones, *God and the Moneylenders*, p. 203; Marshall, *Presbyteries and Profits*, p. 343 n. 119. See also idem, *In Search of the Spirit of Capitalism: An Essay on Max Weber's Protestant Ethic Thesis* (London, 1982), pp. 88–94. This idea is taken quite directly from Weber, *Protestant Ethic*, pp. 110, 116–17, 312. In contrast, Hunt has made the much more reasonable claim that early modern print culture helped to 'justify the ways of commercial folk to the rest of society' and 'improved the spiritual and temporal status of commercial people and commercial modes of reasoning': Hunt, *Middling Sort*, pp. 172–3, 191. In other words, popular literature encouraged positive conceptions of trade without endorsing boundless profit-seeking.

those who attempted to justify hard-dealing or miserliness by euphemisti-
cally calling it 'thrift' or 'good husbandry'.[220] The purveyors of God's word,
like their medieval predecessors, unanimously agreed that Christians had
to redistribute their wealth to the poor and needy rather than saving it
up. To single-mindedly seek one's own material advantage, especially when
such behaviour came at the expense of one's neighbours, was no better than
'Mammonism'.

Religious ethics were not, of course, static. Perceptions had changed
markedly since the days of 'voluntary poverty' and mendicant friars. As has
been noted many times, 'Lady Poverty no longer sat in the seat of honour'
after the Reformation and some parish elites showed a marked 'tendency to
associate ungodliness with the poor'.[221] But attitudes towards wealth changed
much more slowly. The process of loosening some of the assumed ties
between affluence and sinfulness stretched across the whole early modern
period and met with frequent reverses. Indeed, the most vocal critics of the
rich actually appeared in the form of the Diggers and Ranters, long after
Calvin had supposedly swept away such 'archaic' attitudes.[222] Even among
the orthodox Protestants of the Restoration era, fierce denunciations of
wealth could still be heard at certain pulpits. Thomas Cartwright, both an
arch-royalist and grandson of the famous puritan, preached one such impol-
itic sermon at St Paul's on 28 September 1662 to the Lord Mayor and a
large City congregation. For his text, he chose Matt. 19:24 – 'It is easier for
a Camel to go through the eye of a Needle, than for a rich man to enter into
the Kingdom of God' – and firmly asserted that Christ's words on the subject
were no mere hyperbole.[223] In general, however, the radicalism of the 1640s
and 1650s produced an increased awareness of the potentially dangerous
social implications of religious discourse and, as a result, late seventeenth-
century churchmen were often more cautious than their Elizabethan or
early Stuart counterparts. In fact, Cartwright revealed his exceptionality
with the admission that he had only decided to publish the sermon after
being accused of '*libelling* Citizens'.[224] Most of his fellow preachers lacked
this sort of unflinching audacity.

Few religious commentators thus went so far as to dismiss all rich men as
inherently hell-bound. Even fewer, however, regarded the acquisition and
use of wealth with indifference, as somehow falling outside the purview of
moral censure. Enforcing divine ordinances did not just concern, as some

---

[220] Thomas, *The Mammon of Unrighteousness*, p. 21; Stevens, *The Whole Parable*, p. 10.
For more attacks on those who use religion as an 'Excuse' for greed and inhospitality see
pp. 111–12 below.
[221] Schlatter, *Social Ideas*, p. 143; Wrightson and Levine, *Poverty and Piety*, pp. 179–82,
quotation at p. 179; Hill, 'Puritans and the Poor'; Tawney, *Religion*, pp. 251–70.
[222] Hill, *World Turned Upside Down*, ch. 7, 9.
[223] Cartwright, *The Danger of Riches*, p. 5.
[224] Ibid., preface.

historians have implied, 'the vices of the poor'.[225] According to conventional theology, the social responsibilities of 'the better sort' were actually much more acute than those of 'the necessitous and afflicted'. The money, land and goods possessed by the rich belonged ultimately to God and punishment would quickly ensue if they were not treated as such. Wicked people who put their faith in themselves or their riches became worshippers of Mammon, little better than popish idolaters or even satanists. Unless such worldlings immediately repented their ungodly behaviour and recompensed everyone who they had treated uncharitably in their pursuit of ill-gotten goods, these sinners faced the wrath of a notoriously jealous deity.

How and when this wrath would arrive was an open question. Damnation, of course, loomed large. Preachers, catechists, and tract-writers warned their audiences that the fate which befell Dives was incomparably worse than any earthly suffering. The palpable effects this must have had on day-to-day economic conduct should not be underestimated, though obviously it cannot be measured and it is admittedly difficult for secular academics to understand fully the fear of hellfire among early modern Christians. Still, it would also be misleading to argue, following Christopher Hill, that the Restoration banished any possibility of earthly social justice, allowing it only in the world hereafter.[226] The Northampton vicar John Conant, for instance, would certainly have disagreed. 'The weaker he is, and the more unable to defend or right himself, the more unsafe it is to meddle with him', preached Conant, 'For God himself hath undertaken to stand by, and help those who have no power to help themselves.'[227] Penny chapbooks and popular balladry were filled with remarkable examples of God intervening in the mortal realm to punish oppressors and reward benefactors. Indeed, many of these tales would have reminded those with 'no power to help themselves' that they were not quite as defenceless as their superiors might hope. The poor's spiritual status as representatives of Christ rendered their curses, blessings, prayers, and petitions exceptionally effective. When distressed Christians cried to heaven for redress, God listened.

---

[225] Wrightson and Levine, *Poverty and Piety*, p. 211.
[226] Hill, *World Turned Upside Down*, pp. 350–52.
[227] John Conant, *Sermons Preach'd on Several Occasions* (3 vols; 1693–98), I, pp. 248–9 (citing Psalm 12:5, Psalm 35:10, Prov. 22:22–23).

2

Oeconomical Duties: Patriarchy, Paternalism, and Petitioning

No institution had as many functions in early modern society as the household. It was, of course, the birthplace and nursery for each new generation. It competed with the school, the church, and the alehouse as a site of learning, worshipping, and socialising. And it served as a metaphor for a variety of other social relationships, political hierarchies, religious beliefs, and ecclesiastical systems. Hence, given its central place in the social and cultural landscape, it would be impossible to overlook the influence of the household on English economic life. In both practice and theory, the later Stuart economy depended on this crucial institution.

At a practical level, a huge proportion of the nation's production happened in the home – a versatile space which regularly doubled as a farmhouse, workshop or retail store.[1] Until the rise of the factory, the 'household-family' was the primary economic unit, with members of the nuclear family working alongside 'fictive kin' such as journeymen, apprentices, domestic servants, and servants-in-husbandry.[2] In fact, domestic employment probably reached its peak sometime in the late seventeenth or early eighteenth century, a time when a large proportion – probably a majority – of the hired labour force consisted of resident servants and apprentices.[3] Moreover, the

---

[1] For examples of the importance of household-based economic activity, ranging from subsistence farming to 'proto-industry' see Overton et al., *Production and Consumption*, ch. 3–4; Muldrew, *Food*, pp. 241–57; Maxine Berg, *The Age of Manufactures, 1700–1820: Industry, Innovation and Work in Britain* (2nd edition, London, 1996), pp. 66–70; David Hey, *The Fiery Blades of Hallamshire: Sheffield and its Neighbourhood, 1660–1740* (Leicester, 1991), pp. 101–2.

[2] For the clearest elucidation of the concepts of the 'household-family' and 'fictive kin' see Naomi Tadmor, *Family and Friends in Eighteenth-Century England: Household, Kinship, and Patronage* (Cambridge, 2001), ch. 1–2, esp. pp. 21–5. I have followed the early modern practice of using 'household' and 'family' interchangeably.

[3] Both Kussmaul and Snell argue that the proportion of young people who became servants and apprentices probably peaked in the late seventeenth or early eighteenth century, especially in southern and eastern England, though Woodward and Gritt are less convinced: Ann Kussmaul, *Servants in Husbandry in Early Modern England* (Cambridge, 1981), pp. 3–4, 11–19, 173 n. 11 (for proportions), ch. 6 (for trends); Keith Snell, *Annals*

household provided an ideal environment for the growth of 'proto-industry' – both as a primary source of income and as a by-employment. Finally, it must be remembered that these domestic units not only produced most of England's goods and wealth in this period but also provided the chief site for decisions and negotiations concerning the allocation of scarce resources among husbands and wives, parents and children, employers and workers, and various other cohabitants.

More importantly for this study, the direct material contribution of the household to the economy was compounded by its conceptual significance. Early modern thinking about economic matters relied heavily on the ancient model of the *oikos* ('household'), a microcosm thought to exemplify the essence of the macroeconomic order. Indeed, even contemporary lexicons affirm this connection. While 'economy' is a term which now usually refers to the production, distribution, and consumption of resources in a particular locale, it actually evolved directly from *oikonomikē*, a term denoting 'the art of household management', and these two meanings were commonly conflated prior to the rise of 'political economy' in the late eighteenth century.[4] As a result of its antiquity, this 'art' came equipped with a voluminous collection of commentary. After being first propounded by Aristotle and other classical philosophers, the study of *oikonomikē* was revived in the early modern era by humanists and godly reformers, and its values were then constantly reiterated by later Stuart moralists.[5] This venerable

of the Labouring Poor: Social Change and Agrarian England, 1660–1900 (Cambridge, 1985), ch. 2, 5, 7; Bridget Hill, Servants: English Domestics in the Eighteenth Century (Oxford, 1996), pp. 6–7; Donald Woodward, 'Early Modern Servants in Husbandry Revisited', Agricultural History Review, 48:2, (2000), pp. 145–8; Overton et al., Production and Consumption, pp. 80–81; A. J. Gritt, 'The "Survival" of Service in the English Agricultural Labour Force: Lessons from Lancashire, c.1650–1851', Agricultural History Review, 50:1 (2002), pp. 34–6; Peter Linebaugh, The London Hanged: Crime and Civil Society in the Eighteenth Century (London, 1991), pp. 97, 101–2.

[4] OED, s.v. 'economy' and 'economic'. The idea of this etymology as symbolic of early modern economic attitudes I owe to an aside in Walter, 'Social Economy', p. 122. Other terms had similar meanings and were often used as synonyms in this period, including 'husbandry', 'housewifery', 'housekeeping', and 'householding'. Although some thinkers, such as William Petty, had begun to disaggregate these concepts, this was extremely uncommon in both popular and learned discourse.

[5] For classical and humanist discussions of *oikonomikē* translated into English in the early modern period see Aristotles Politiques, or Discourses of Government (1598), I, esp. ch. 3, 5, 7–8; Xenophons Treatise of House-hold (1573); Jean Bodin, Six Bookes of a Commonweale (1606), I, ch. 2. For further examples of this genre, including Plato's The Statesman, pseudo-Aristotle's Oeconomica, and a variety of renaissance thinkers see William James Booth, 'Household and Market: On the Origins of Moral Economic Philosophy', Review of Politics, 56:2 (1994), pp. 207–35; idem, Households: On the Moral Architecture of the Economy (Ithaca, 1993); Gordon Schochet, Patriarchalism in Political Thought: The Authoritarian Family and Political Speculation and Attitudes especially in Seventeenth-century England (Oxford, 1975), ch. 2; Andrea Finkelstein, The Grammar of Profit: The Price

expositive tradition ensured that the model of 'household management' brought with it a host of assumptions about the nature of economic relations. For instance, the household analogy predisposed people to think of their society as one divided according to the function (or 'calling') of each social group, rather than as one organised by differing degrees of wealth. It also legitimated patriarchal regulation, while devaluing individual initiative and competitive self-advancement. In addition, it instilled a longing for equity and balance, but denied the possibility of equality in either property or opportunity. In short, 'the moral economy of the *oikos*' emphasised the ideals of duty, reciprocity, order, and inequality, values which were central to the economic culture of later Stuart England.[6]

Historians have obviously noted the significance of the 'householding' model before, but the scholarship on this issue is often remarkably narrow or teleological. The vast majority of this work has focused on relations within the household itself, especially on the economic implications of gender norms.[7] Although this has resulted in several excellent studies on this topic, no one has yet provided a sustained analysis of the ways in which the familial understanding of economics shaped behaviour *outside* the ties of blood or marriage. Most discussions of 'patriarchalism' in the later Stuart period, for example, have focused on the political debates among the elites rather than on the economic attitudes of the multitude.[8] Even those – such as E. P. Thompson and many of his followers – who have remarked on the occasional 'paternalism' of employers, landowners, and magistrates have tended to strip the term of its analogical meaning and simply use it as a synonym for 'customary' perquisites or 'traditionalist' market regulation.[9]

Revolution in Intellectual Context (Leiden, 2006), pp. 67–71, 89–93, 98–103, 226–7. For the two most influential early works in English see John Dod and Robert Cleaver, *A Godlie Forme of Household Gouernment for the Ordering of Priuate Families, according to the Direction of Gods Word* (1621; first published in 1598); William Gouge, *Of Domesticall Duties* (1622).

6   Booth, 'Household and Market', p. 212.
7   Susan Amussen, *An Ordered Society: Gender and Class in Early Modern England* (New York, 1993), ch. 3; Anthony Fletcher, *Gender, Sex and Subordination in England, 1500–1800* (New Haven, 1995), ch. 12; Sara Heller Mendelson and Patricia Crawford, *Women in Early Modern England, 1550–1720* (Oxford, 1998), ch. 5–6; Alexandra Shepard, 'Manhood, Credit and Patriarchy in Early Modern England c. 1580–1640', *Past & Present*, 167 (2000), pp. 75–106; eadem, *Meanings of Manhood in Early Modern England* (Oxford, 2003), ch. 7; Hunt, *Middling Sort*.
8   See, for example, most of the sources cited in p. 114 n. 105 below.
9   See, for example, Thompson, *Customs in Common*, pp. 38–9, 193–200. Indeed, Thompson's declared dislike for the 'imprecise' nature of the term 'paternalism' (pp. 18–24) did not stop him from constantly using it in this extremely 'imprecise' way. In contrast, the vocabulary used in this chapter has been chosen with care, though offering precise definitions for many conceptually loaded words is impossible. I hope most of my terms are self-explanatory (e.g. 'fatherly', 'childlike', etc.), but some might need clarification. In this chapter, the term 'familial' denotes characteristics associated literally

Hence, this chapter is partly an attempt to remedy the shallowness of the existing historiography. Specifically, it charts the impact of early modern assumptions about the well-ordered household on the dynamics of production and exchange found within larger social constructs, such as the neighbourhood and the nation. It shows that the *oikos* was not just a frequently used analogy; it was the basis for a powerful worldview.

Those historians who have addressed the influence of familial ideals have nearly always depicted them as 'traditional' or 'pre-modern', destined for extinction with the coming of 'the market'. Christopher Hill offered a clear example of this interpretation when he argued that 'there was a new hardening of social divisions' after the Restoration, bringing an end to 'feudal–patriarchal relations' and producing 'a two-class society with a two-class mentality'.[10] While most scholars have been more cautious about the pace of change, recent assessments have continued to imply a unilinear shift away from an economy shaped by 'paternalism' over the course of the sixteenth, seventeenth, and eighteenth centuries. For example, Keith Wrightson, in his nuanced reading of the changing language of social description, has continued to claim that the vertical bonds of 'duty' gave way to the horizontal ties of 'interests'.[11] The later Stuart era, if it features at all in these sorts of narratives, is normally regarded as yet another period witnessing the decline of the old ways and the growth of the new. In fact, as this chapter shows, the flexibility of the householding model made it remarkably resilient, and its influence on economic relations in some types of agriculture and industry actually became stronger.

These historiographical critiques are developed further in the pages that follow, but this chapter is intended to be more inquisitive than disputatious. It is an attempt to describe the nature and influence of a particular economic idea, namely the logic of *oikonomikē*.[12] The analysis is divided into

or metaphorically with the 'household-family'. 'Patriarchal' refers only to the *authority* of the father (or his surrogate), whereas 'paternal' refers to the fatherly role more generally, in which authority is just one of many privileges and responsibilities.

[10] Christopher Hill, *Some Intellectual Consequences of the English Revolution* (London, 1980), pp. 38–9. More examples of this interpretation are mentioned throughout this chapter, especially in 'Conclusions' below.

[11] See pp. 144–5 below.

[12] Although this chapter focuses on 'the moral economy of the *oikos*', other idioms and analogies were used to express the same logic. The notion of society as a human body, for instance, was also popular, and commentators regularly explained economic inequality, interdependence, duty, and authority through anatomical imagery: Finkelstein, *Grammar of Profit*, ch. 5, esp. pp. 142–9; idem, *Harmony*, esp. pp. 21–5; Jones, *Tree of Commonwealth*, pp. 22–8, 35–8, 250, 286; Hindle, 'Imagining Insurrection', pp. 34–5, 37, 39–40, 44–8; Ludovic Desmedt, 'Money in the "Body Politick": The Analysis of Trade and Circulation in the Writings of Seventeenth-Century Political Arithmeticians', *History of Political Economy*, 37:1 (2005), pp. 79–101; Natasha Glaisyer, '"A due circulation in the veins of the publick": Imagining Credit in Late Seventeenth and Early Eighteenth-Century

four main parts. The first section documents the belief that 'every man must labour in his own calling' to support the material welfare of society as a whole.[13] Instead of regarding this attitude as merely a product of Weber's 'Protestant work ethic', this section shows that the valorisation of work emerged from a deep faith in the familial values of mutuality and interdependence. The second section examines ideas about the virtues of provision and hospitality, usually described in the idiom of 'good husbandry'. This includes a discussion of the way commentators reinforced the obligation to provide for one's 'dependants' by contrasting it with the evils of neglect and self-advancement. The third section highlights the duty of governance and its impact on early modern political economy. The main focus of this part of the chapter is on manifestations of patriarchal authority, from the father as manager of the household economy to the explicitly analogous role of the prince as governor of the kingdom's wealth. Lastly, the fourth section describes the role of the poor themselves in the household model, in particular through an analysis of the remarkably flexible petitionary model of redress. It shows that some appellants to authority, despite their claims of deference and dependence, used familial logic to exert a remarkable degree of social and psychological pressure on their supposed 'superiors'.

1 Labour

The long-term viability of the 'household economy' depended on the material contributions of every one of its 'able' members. Accordingly, the need for mutuality and reciprocity was a feature of English family life with which everyone – especially the poor – would have been intimately acquainted. Long before being exposed to catechism or sermons, the children of the poorer sort learned about these ideas first-hand through their dependence on the intense labours of their parents and older siblings. These bonds were then both described and reinforced in cheap printed texts. Several ballads, for example, reminded husbands of 'lowly degree', especially those granted the 'blessing' of children, that they must work constantly to support their households: 'Remember your Children, / and think upon [your wife]; ... At no time be idle, / but follow thy labour'.[14] The seemingly ceaseless toil neces-

---

England', *Eighteenth Century: Theory and Interpretation*, 46:3 (2005), pp. 286–91. The metaphor of the tree or plant was also occasionally used with much the same purpose.
[13] This was a stock phrase used in many of the sources cited below: Tilley, *Proverbs*, p. 77 (paraphrasing 1 Cor. 7:20).
[14] *The Poor Mans Councillor* (c.1684–6), in *PB*, II, p. 86; *A Dainty New Dialogue between Henry and Elizabeth* (c.1679–81), in *PB*, IV, p. 76. One claimed that it was 'no great wrong' to spend 'a Tester' drinking 'with a Friend' as long as you go 'then to your Labour

sitated by family ties was also evident in the response of 'a poor Thresher' when he was asked how he maintained 'his charge' of seven children:

> I Reap and I Mow, and I Harrow and Sow,
> Sometimes I to Hedging and Ditching do go:
> No Work comes amiss, for I Thresh and I Plow,
> Thus I eat my Bread by the sweat of my Brow.[15]

Given the tenuous economic position of many later Stuart families, a householder who pursued 'idleness' instead of 'industry' caused not only personal damnation but also collective suffering.

As a result, when poor men sought aid from county magistrates, they often emphasised their laborious efforts to support their families. Many a pauper noted that he had 'formerly' endeavoured 'to worke & take pains for a living for himself & his wife' or that he had maintained his 'great Charge of Children ... by his hand labour' in previous years.[16] According to these men, their present incapacity – whether due to age, injury or imprisonment – was a sudden and exceptional deviation from an otherwise solid record of diligence and toil. Perhaps the clearest rhetoric of this kind came from a small tenant farmer from Scugdale, on the edge of the North York Moors. Petitioning for charitable relief in 1691, he claimed to have 'Laboured & taken paines for a maintenance for him & his family & by his Labour & Industry had acquired A Compatent Small estate Sufficient to support himselfe & his Wife & family for their Lives', only to be cast into poverty by a 'Dreadfull fyer' which burnt down his house and barn.[17] Such men were, at least in their own eyes, exemplars of the industriousness essential to every good householder.[18]

Yet, while the labours of the *paterfamilias* were usually vital, so too were those of women and youth. Married women supported their families through conventional 'housewifery' and often worked alongside their husbands in crafts, retailing or agriculture, while others had separate occupations of their own.[19] The labour of domestic manufacturing ('the distaff') was just

again' for 'This care will your Houshold maintain': *The Father's Wholesome Admonition* (c.1688–96), in *PB*, II, p. 83.

[15] *The NobleMan's Generous Kindness* (1685–8), in *PB*, II, p. 56.

[16] WYAS–W, QS 1/10/5/6/2; QS 1/13/6/6/7. For similar formulations see NYCRO, QSB 1691/322, QSB 1692/220; WYAS–W, QS 1/38/4/6 (petition of Joseph Rishforth, 1699); HA, QSR 16/1674/31, QSR 16/1675/564, QSR 25/1703/127.

[17] NYCRO, QSB 1691/314.

[18] For the growing emphasis on industriousness and laboriousness more generally see Muldrew, *Food*, ch. 7.

[19] This paragraph is based on the now sizable literature on women's economic roles. For examples see Mendelson and Crawford, *Women*, ch. 5–6, esp. pp. 303–7, 327–36; Amy Louise Erickson, 'Married Women's Occupations in Eighteenth-century London', *Continuity & Change*, 23:2 (2008), pp. 267–307; Amanda Flather, *Gender and Space in*

as important as the labour of child-rearing ('the cradle') according to a contemporary playing card (Fig. 2.1). So, although the patriarchal assumptions of the era limited the types of work available to them, poor women were still expected to provide much of the labour and resources needed to sustain their households – a demanding task which seems to have earned many wives a degree of respect from their menfolk.[20] This positive interpretation of female involvement in economic life appeared even in ballads, typically one of the most misogynistic of early modern sources. One song, printed several times in the seventeenth century, ridiculed a husbandman for disparaging his wife's daily toil and used a detailed description of role reversals to show that 'housewifery' (childrearing, spinning, baking, brewing, milking, cheese-making, butter-churning, poultry-raising) was just as difficult and important as male 'work without doors' (ploughing, carting, hedging, ditching, heaping, mowing, lading, pitching).[21] Likewise, the 'poor Thresher' readily admitted that his family survived, in part, because

> My Wife she is willing to pull in the Yoak,
> We live like two Lambs, and we never provoke
> Each other, but like to the labouring Ant,
> We do our endeavour to keep up from want.[22]

Early Modern England (Woodbridge, 2006), pp. 32–3, 82–93. For a specific discussion of the connection between the honour of a housewife and her diligence or idleness see Garthine Walker, 'Expanding the Boundaries of Female Honour in Early Modern England', *Transactions of the Royal Historical Society*, 6th ser., 6 (1996), pp. 238–40.

[20] Even women who lacked a husband might occasionally receive praise for their contributions, as evidenced by the comments of William Stout, the Lancashire shopkeeper. He lauded his widowed mother and unmarried sister, who were 'not only fully imployed in housewifery', but also worked in farming and retailing, often managing the family's land or William's shop themselves: *The Autobiography of William Stout of Lancaster, 1665–1752*, J. D. Marshall ed. (Manchester, 1967), pp. 68, 75, 90, 151. For other attitudes toward (and experiences of) 'spinsterhood' see Amy M. Froide, *Never Married: Singlewomen in Early Modern England* (Oxford, 2005). For a discussion of women's roles in less-conventional household economies see Laura Gowing, *Domestic Dangers: Women, Words and Sex in Early Modern London* (Oxford, 1996), pp. 14–15, 22–3.

[21] *The Woman to the Plow and The Man to the Hen-Roost* (c.1682–4), in *PB*, IV, p. 100.

[22] *The NobleMan's Generous Kindness* (1685–8), in *PB*, II, p. 56. The notion of a married couple as 'yokefellows' was a commonplace based on Phil. 4:3 and alluded to in 'An Homily of the State of Matrimony' in *Certain Sermons or Homilies*, II, 316. For similar uses of the trope see *The Poor Mans Comfort* (c.1684–6), in *PB*, IV, p. 92; Susana Jesserson, *A Bargain for Bachelors* (1675), p. 7. For a modern anthropological equivalent to this early modern analogy see the discussion of Ralph and Jane Josselin's marriage as a 'joint-role relationship' in Alan Macfarlane, *The Family Life of Ralph Josselin: A Seventeenth-Century Clergyman. An Essay in Historical Anthropology* (London, 1970), pp. 106–10. For more examples which acknowledge (or demand) the economic contributions of wives see Tilley, *Proverbs*, p. 332; Thomas Vincent, *An Explicatory Catechism* (1673), pp. 216–17; *Reflexions upon the Moral State of the Nation: With an Offer at some Amendments Therein*

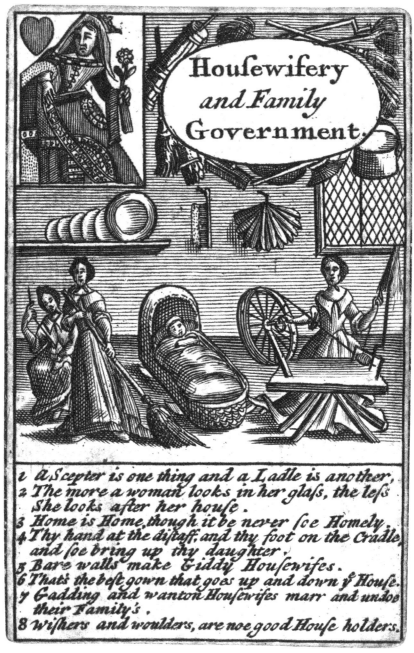

Figure 2.1. A playing card entitled *Housewifery and Family Government* (c.1700) called on women to live with 'Thy hand at the distaff, and thy foot on the Cradle', contributing industriously to the household economy through both spinning wool and raising children.

Even if patriarchal theory left little room for female economic autonomy, early modern gender norms certainly allowed women to participate in the arduous struggle to 'make shift'. In fact, female labour was not so much a privilege as a responsibility, a fact hinted in the petition of 1686 from 'a very poore & impotent Woman … who whilst she was able has beene very Labourous to maintaine herself & poore family'. The magistrates apparently acknowledged the value of her previous hard work, as they granted her a parish pension of six pence per week.[23]

Children born into poor families were also burdened with this duty, often from a very early age. Boys and girls fulfilled their role in the household economy by minding livestock, collecting fuel, weeding fields, preparing wool, or partaking in any number of other menial tasks, which were usually assigned to them sometime between the ages of seven and ten.[24] The contributions of children, like those of women, received particular emphasis in years of crisis. For instance, one ballad recounted the story of a poor man who despaired because 'trading be dead' and 'money be scant', only to have his wife reply that they could overcome this hardship by working as a couple, 'like two Oxen in one yoak together', and by putting their children to work: 'I'le teach my Son Thomas … To work at our Trade … [and] I'le teach pretty Nanny to Card and to Spin'.[25] Everyone recognised that prepubescent children could not match the productive capacity of their parents, and their responsibilities were proportionally lighter, but manual labour was still thought to be a useful and necessary part of a poor child's upbringing. This attitude towards the economic functions of young people reinforced the early modern conception of the family as a composite entity bound together by inequalities in aptitude and obligation.

Shared livelihoods created a need for reciprocity between household members that strengthened the usual ties of blood or marriage – yet this reciprocity also enveloped those outside the nuclear family, particularly 'fictive kin' such as servants and apprentices. By joining their employer's household, these young men and women took on a variety of familial responsibilities. Indeed, according to Humphrey Bralesford, author of a short religious guide entitled *The Poor Man's Help*, the duties they owed to their new 'Civil

(1701), p. 21; Thomas Cooke, *Workhouses the Best Charity: A Sermon Preacht at the Cathedral Church of Worcester* (1702), p. 10.

[23] WYAS–W, QS 1/25/5/6 (petition of Ann Laycock, 1686). For another widow with children who claimed to have 'provided for them to the utmost of my power' before ultimately seeking relief see HA, QSR 25/1701/166. For the case of Mary Poynter, who served a full apprenticeship and sought the freedom of the city in order 'to follow some Imploy where to mainetene her selfe and Children' see LMA, COL/CA/05/01/0005/1699.

[24] For the economic contributions of children see Muldrew, *Food*, pp. 233–6; Hindle, *On the Parish?* pp. 24–6; I. K. Ben-Amos, *Adolescence and Youth in Early Modern England* (London, 1994), pp. 40–7; Jane Humphries, *Childhood and Child Labour in the British Industrial Revolution* (Cambridge, 2010), pp. 237–44.

[25] *The Poor Mans Comfort* (c.1684–6), in *PB*, IV, p. 92.

Parent' – i.e. their master or mistress – were almost exactly the same as those owed to 'the natural Parent that begat and bore' them.[26] Though some moralists insisted on these duties using only the vague language of 'Reverence and Obedience', others specified the exact nature of these obligations and paid particular attention to economic issues.[27] Irrespective of whether one was a promising apprentice or a common drudge, instructions on the nature of true 'service' stayed remarkably consistent.[28] Servants must 'perform all labour willingly', 'without grudging', and they ought to work diligently to 'encrease and improve' the material welfare of their surrogate family. Such conduct exemplified the prized quality of 'Industry', sharply contrasting with the wicked pursuit of 'fulness, ease, and idleness'. They were also expected to be honest, loyal, and provident: obligations which will be examined more closely later in this chapter. These simple moral strictures were preached in sermons, repeated in catechisms, and published in instructional manuals, including at least one handy broadsheet edition, with Dissenter and Anglican alike using almost the same words to describe the duties associated with service. Although later Stuart descriptions were usually derivative of earlier manuals, they remained highly relevant in a society where the labours of servants continued to sustain many of the nation's household economies.[29] The interdependence required to provision an actual family seemed to be a commendable model for the relations between employers and their resident employees.

The family also formed the basis for much early modern political thinking. In many texts, conventional symbolism turned the kingdom into a household and the prince into a parent. Humphrey Bralesford, for example, used

---

[26] Bralesford, *The Poor Man's Help*, p. 40.

[27] These duties (and the following quotations) are found in *Mr Baxters Rules & Directions for Family Duties* (1681); Thomas Watson, *A Body of Practical Divinity Consisting of … Sermons* (1692), pp. 351–2; Richard Mayo, *A Present for Servants* (1693), pp. 27–37; *The Servants Calling; With Some Advice to the Apprentice* (1725), esp. pp. 46–7; Wake, *The Principles of the Christian Religion*, p. 111; Fleetwood, *The Relative Duties*, 'Discourse XIV' and 'XV'; Waugh, *The Duty of Apprentices*, pp. 14–22. The familial nature of the relationship between master and servant was reinforced by the tendency to discuss it in the context of the fifth commandment: Green, *Christian's ABC*, pp. 451–60; Tadmor, *Social Universe*, pp. 108–9. See also the duties outlined in apprenticeship indentures, discussed below p. 103.

[28] Both contemporaries and historians have had great difficulties defining 'service' and often failed to distinguish between 'servants', 'apprentices', and even 'labourers', particularly in the case of 'parish apprentices': Kussmaul, *Servants in Husbandry*, pp. 5–7, 135–42; Mendelson and Crawford, *Women*, pp. 99–102, 263–6; Hill, *Servants*, pp. 11–15; Muldrew, *Food*, p. 219. I have taken an extremely broad definition and thus used the term 'servant' to refer to all resident employees, including apprentices who had paid a premium.

[29] Many seem to have derived their categories and phraseology from the section on 'The Seruants dutie towards their Maisters' in Dod and Cleaver, *A Godlie Forme of Household Gouernment*, sig. Aa4v–Aa7v.

the term 'Civil Parent' to refer to 'the King and his Magistrates, a Master, a Mistriss, or an Husband', and he conflated the duties of English subjects with those of children, wives, and servants.[30] Obviously, the usual duties of obedience, reverence, love, and honour were always considered politically relevant, but most commentators also noted several others directly connected to more material concerns. Bralesford, for instance, specifically mentioned 'Service and Maintenance', implying that one must be willing to devote one's labour and property to the prince and, by extension, to the kingdom.[31] John Sharp, archbishop of York, provided a more detailed description in his sermon at the coronation of Queen Anne in 1702. He noted that her subjects owed her a *'Filial Obedience'* which they ought to express 'by contributing every Man in his Sphere, what Assistance they could to their Prince, for the promoting the common Good'.[32] According to Sharp and other similarly minded preachers, the duty of the loyal subject to work diligently in an honest calling was partly a product of the monarch's patriarchal authority. At the same time, however, this obligation indicated more than just the prince's power over his people – it also hinted at his inescapable dependence on them. The familial connotations which had become embedded in this sort of political relationship implied mutuality as well as inequality. 'The king himself is served by the field', preached John Conant, quoting Solomon's admonitory maxim. It took many hours of bodily toil in planting, growing, harvesting, milling, and baking, 'in which many poor mens hands is necessary, before the King himself can eat a bit of Bread'.[33] Just as fathers, husbands, and masters relied on the contributions of their subordinates to sustain the household economy, monarchs relied on their subjects for the resources needed to govern their dominions.

Moreover, the kingdom as a whole, not just the king himself, was supported by the dutiful labours of the poor. The invaluable contributions of lowly manual workers received, in fact, a remarkable amount of emphasis in the writings and sermons of men such as George Hickes. Preaching to an audience that included the Lord Mayor and other London notables in 1684, Hickes reminded them that

> no Common-weal, little or great, can subsist without Poor.... The Poor are the Hands and Feet of the Body Politick, the *Gibeonites* and *Nethinims* in all Countries, who hew the Wood, and draw the Water of the Rich. They Plow our Lands,

[30] Bralesford, *The Poor Man's Help*, p. 40. The same was true of most other short explanations of the fifth commandment cited below p. 114 n. 106.
[31] Ibid.
[32] John Sharp, *A Sermon Preach'd at the Coronation of Queen Anne* (1702), pp. 22–3. For more examples see pp. 118–19 below.
[33] Conant, *Sermons Preach'd on Several Occasions*, I, p. 222 (quoting Eccl. 5:9).

and dig our Quarries, and cleanse our Streets, ... [and] fight our battels ... for seven pence a day.[34]

His emphasis on the value of the labouring poor was shared by others with very different religious and political loyalties. For instance, although Hickes was a militant royalist and later became a nonjuring bishop, his words were echoed fifteen years later by John Bellers, the innovative Quaker merchant. In one of several short pamphlets which Bellers wrote on the subject, he argued that if the nation were full of 'rich men', but lacked 'Hewers of Wood, and Drawers of Water, Plowmen, and Threshers', then 'we should be under *Midas's Golden Curse*, Starve for want of Bread, tho' had our Hands fill'd with Gold', for 'where there is no Servants, there can be no Masters'.[35]

In some cases, those affirming the worth of labouring folk focused their attention on specific subgroups or 'callings'. This approach was particularly common in ballads, with some songs singling out the contributions of various crafts, while others honoured the daily efforts of those who toiled in the country's fields. In a ballad from the late 1680s, for example, a ploughman from the West Country pointedly reminded 'fine Folk' of the city that 'For all your Rich Jewels you starving may dye, / If we do not bring in a daily supply'.[36] Whether using broad labels like 'the poor' or more specific occupational categories, contemporaries tended to acknowledge the vital contributions of manual workers rather than simply dismissing 'the multitude' as a threat to the order of the commonwealth.[37] Learned observers often insisted that the rich should be grateful, rather than hostile or condescending, to the poor. Even a boy learning a menial trade should be honoured for his service, because every 'Art and Mystery' rendered its practitioners 'useful

[34] Hickes, *A Sermon Preached at the Church of St. Bridget*, pp. 6–7. For more on this metaphor see p. 88 n. 12 above.

[35] Bellers, *Essays About the Poor*, p. 8. For other clergymen and tract-writers who insist that 'Employments which are of least Esteem, are often most necessary: and the great men cannot live without the meanest' see Jeffery, *The Duty and Encouragement*, pp. 13–14; Younge, *The Poors Advocate*, pp. 9, 16; Pittis, *A Spittle Sermon*, pp. 8–9; Conant, *Sermons Preach'd on Several Occasions*, I, pp. 222, 237–8; *Reflexions upon the Moral State* (1675), pp. 18–19; Moss, *The Providential Division*, p. 5 and passim. For other contemporary comments of a similar sort, including several from the mid-eighteenth century, see Malcolmson, *Life and Labour*, pp. 12–13; Keith Thomas, *The Ends of Life: Roads to Fulfilment in Early Modern England* (Oxford and New York, 2009), pp. 87–90.

[36] *Down-Right Dick of the West* (1685–88), in PB, IV, p. 273. In an earlier ballad, both the 'tradesman' and the 'gentleman' admit they 'could not live' without the labour of the 'Country men': *The Honest Tradesmans Honour Vindicated* (c.1666–78), in PB, IV, p. 350. See also Steele, *The Husbandmans Calling*, pp. 17, 37–9. An equally fierce claim to indispensability, this time by weavers, can be found in *Proper New Ballad in Praise of the Gallant Weavers* (Edinburgh, c.1700) in RyB, Ry.III.10(023).

[37] For the larger debate over early modern attitudes towards the labouring poor see the lengthy discussion in Appleby, *Economic Thought*, ch. 6.

to Mankind' by requiring 'Labours that are not only privately beneficial, but conduce to the publick Interest, and Prosperity of his Country', 'to the Good of his Nation and Neighbour'.[38] The 'fine Folk' might hold much more property than the typical ploughman or apprentice, but this did not free the few from their reliance on the labours of the many.

These appreciative depictions of manual workers must have seemed rather obvious to those who actually spent their days in fields or workshops – they already knew that the sweat of their brows sustained the economy. Nonetheless, the stress on the social utility of the poor was just one aspect of a powerful set of beliefs about provision and reciprocity that had a much broader impact. For instance, the song in which the West Country ploughman reminded townspeople that he provided their daily bread inspired *The Londoners Answer* in the form of another ballad.[39] The citizens replied that, while farmers supplied the nation's food, 'Money maintains the Farmers Team', so we must 'give to each one his due. / You must have of us and we must have of you' – mutual dependence lay at the heart of the relationship.

More generally, while the poor had to fulfil their duty by labouring diligently in their lowly callings, the rich and powerful were equally obliged to contribute their share for the welfare of the whole. Idleness was abhorrent irrespective of one's social position. Indeed, comparisons between the rich and poor often presented a rather unflattering image of those fortunate enough to possess ample estates. A broadsheet published in 1688 bitterly reflected on the sad condition of the 'poor man' who 'must live by his Labour', 'like the industrous painful Bee', 'with pains and a sweating Brow'; meanwhile, 'Misers' and 'Landed Men may flourish; / sleeping or waking their Baggs they fill' (Fig. 2.2).[40] Instead of accepting their social obligations, the idle rich spurned their king and country by gleefully embracing a life of ease and luxury, a situation that many commentators regarded with abhorrence.

Yet, despite seemingly unanimous agreement on this point, contemporary understandings of the need for labour were far from simplistic. Each 'calling' demanded a different type of 'labour', so everyone must be 'imployed', but 'some must be imployed in meaner, other in higher Services'.[41] Manual labour was not the only way to contribute to one's household, neighbourhood or

---

[38] *The Servants Calling*, p. 65.

[39] *Down-Right Dick of the West* (1685–88), in PB, IV, p. 273; *The Londoners Answer to Down-right Dick of the West* (1685–8), in PB, IV, p. 274.

[40] *The Rich Mens Joyes* (1688), in PB, V, p. 174v. For a similar condemnation of 'the best Gentlemen' who 'despise honest *callings*' see Younge, *A Precious Mithridate*, pp. 6–7.

[41] Conant, *Sermons Preach'd on Several Occasions*, I, p. 238. As Keith Thomas has recently remarked, gentlemen 'objected not to work as such, but to certain kinds of work'; so, although manual labour was 'thought to be incompatible with gentility', 'service to the commonwealth' was regarded as essential: Thomas, *Ends of Life*, p. 83.

Figure 2.2. Two figures adorned a broadside ballad entitled *The Rich Mens Joyes, or, The Poor Mens Cares and Comforts* (1688), in *Pepys Ballads*, V, p. 174v. The first was 'A poor labouring man making Ropes' with his wife, who 'must trust to their Labour' and endure the 'cruelty' of rich 'Landed men'. The second was 'The Rich Miser', who lived a life of 'delight and ease' while 'ever contriving to wrack the poor'.

nation. While some people supported their community by producing the necessities of life, others distributed these resources, and still others oversaw the operation. In fact, one of the most prominent of these 'higher Services' was the task of assigning differing duties to England's various social groups and, more controversially, punishing those who failed to perform their duties. In the early modern imagination, a stable social order, just like a household, required mutuality, but it also required discipline and inequality. The nature of these 'higher Services', and the unequal relationships they implied, are the basis of the sections which follow.

2 Paternal Provision

The young man who laid down a penny or two for a later Stuart broadside entitled *The New Art of Thriving* would have learned that he must 'make use of his *Head* and his *Hands* to preserve or recover him out of the Quagmire of Want'.[42] No amount of hard work could bring prosperity if it was not

---

[42] All quotations in this paragraph are taken from *The New Art of Thriving: Or, The Way to Get and Keep Money* (c.1685). It was 'Principally intended as an Admonition to *Youth*'

twinned with '*Good Husbandry*', a phrase connoting prudent and profitable management.[43] This guide – with its insistence on '*Industry* and *Frugality*' as preconditions for 'a comfortable subsistence' – seemingly provides outstanding evidence of an increasingly individualist, profit-orientated economic culture in later Stuart England.[44] But this interpretation, while not baseless, would be misguided. Even in these lessons on 'thriving', good husbandry was as much a social duty as a path for personal advancement. Frugality was 'a Virtue that is the Root of all Liberality', for it provides a man with 'a Spring, wheance he can send forth Streams of Bounty upon any necessary Occassion, which Prodigality would soon dry up, and leave him miserable himself, and useless to others'. Thus, a gambler provided an example of ill husbandry by allowing his improvidence to cause 'his poor Wife and Half a Dozen small Children ... to starve for Want of Bread'. To manage one's estate with wisdom and care was praiseworthy not because it brought individual prosperity but because it enabled familial, and therefore social, stability.

At the level of individual homes, farms, and workshops, this duty fell mostly to the head of the household. Just as the *paterfamilias* was expected to labour diligently to produce the necessities of life, he was also expected to manage carefully these resources (and those of his subordinates) for the good of the family.[45] Principally, this meant providing for one's spouse and children by avoiding wasteful vices like extravagance, drunkenness, and whoring. The men who failed to fulfil their duties in this respect were often depicted as unmanly, an attitude that has recently been noted by Alexandra Shepard and others, but which deserves re-emphasis.[46] Status as a 'good husband' – and, by extension, manhood itself – hinged on a willingness

and was mostly a distillation of Henry Peacham's oft-reprinted tract on *The Worth of a Peny*, which went through at least eight editions in the later Stuart period.

[43] For evidence that their economic and familial meanings were intertwined until at least the nineteenth century see *OED*, s.v. 'husband' and 'husbandry' (see also 'housewife' and 'housewifery').

[44] For examples of this interpretation see Glaisyer, *Culture of Commerce*, ch. 3; Hunt, *Middling Sort*, pp. 172–5, 191. According to Laura Stevenson, this was the fundamental difference between Elizabethan and post-Restoration economic cultures – whereas the former had praised 'thrift and diligence' as a tool for fulfilling social duties, the latter supposedly praised these same virtues as part of 'the spirit of capitalism': Laura Caroline Stevenson, *Praise and Paradox: Merchants and Craftsmen in Elizabethan Literature* (Cambridge, 1984), ch. 7, esp. pp. 155–6.

[45] Obviously, a significant portion of households were headed by women (usually widows) who took on this role, but for the sake of simplicity I have here and elsewhere followed the early modern habit of referring to 'the householder' using the masculine pronoun.

[46] Shepard, *Meanings of Manhood*, pp. 84–6, 189–91; Elizabeth Foyster, *Manhood in Early Modern England: Honour, Sex and Marriage* (London, 1999), pp. 65–6, 87; Joanne Bailey, 'Reassessing Parenting in Eighteenth-Century England', in Helen Berry and Elizabeth Foyster (eds), *The Family in Early Modern England* (Cambridge, 2007), p. 220.

to support one's dependants. Ballad-singers, for example, could take on the persona of the reformed drunkard recounting his days as an 'ill Husband', when he would often return from the alehouse to find his 'Wife and Children … waiting and wailing' for him

> To bring them provision, or Cloaths to their back,
> For I knew very well that such they did lack;
> But though I did know it, I never took care,
> Tho their bellies did pinch & their backs did goe bare.[47]

Another former spendthrift regretted that he, like other 'bad husbands', left his vulnerable family crying 'for Bread', but claimed that henceforth he would 'be a Husband to my wife'.[48]

Nor was this attitude confined to published texts. At the beginning of the eighteenth century, the yeoman Richard Gough bitterly recalled many cases wherein 'an idle, drunken, careless husband … consumed his estate notwithstanding his wife's paines, care, and industry' and left her 'distitute'.[49] Wives themselves made similar complaints. In 1663, for example, Alice Lowen of Hoddesdon (Herts.) tried to have the local alehouse shut down, so 'I & my Children may not want Sustenance while he lyeth spending his mony debaysily there'.[50] Other condemnations of paternal neglect can be found in the requests for maintenance orders received by county justices. At the end of the century, John Shaw, a Yorkshireman, found himself denounced because he had 'left his wife and Children' and 'sould their land' – for 'where ought the Charge of the maintenance to lye but upon the said John'?[51]

---

[47] *The Bad Husband's Information of ill Husbandry* (c.1684–96), in *PB*, II, p. 89.

[48] *Folly Plainly Made Manifest by An Extravagant Husband* (c.1671–99), in *PB*, IV, p. 120. For further examples of wastrels and drunkards denounced as 'ill Husbands' see *A Groatsworth of Good Counsel for a Penny* (c.1684–96), in *PB*, IV, p. 78; *The Farmers Reformation* (1687–8), in *PB*, II, p. 91; Rawlet, *The Christian Monitor*, pp. 18, 44, 46. Less specific laments against spendthrifts who impoverish their families (especially through drunkenness and lust) are too numerous to list in detail, but, for a selection, see *PB*, II, pp. 22, 83, 89, 91, 93; IV, pp. 75–7, 79–80, 83, 248, 254–5, 260. This should not, however, be taken to imply that drinking or other forms of 'good fellowship' were seen as inherently unmanly; it was alcoholism (and the resulting negligence), not alcohol, that created 'bad husbands'. For the ambiguity in early modern attitudes toward drinking and masculinity see Mark Hailwood, 'Sociability, Work and Labouring Identity in Seventeenth-Century England', *Cultural and Social History*, 8:1 (2011), pp. 9–29. For clerical condemnations of 'immoderate' consumption see Ashby, 'Religion'.

[49] Gough, *History of Myddle*, p. 276. For similar complaints see ibid., pp. 133, 191–2, 210, 286; Stout, *Autobiography*, p. 125. Similarly, accusations of material neglect were regularly included in complaints about male cruelty and violence by women seeking separations: Gowing, *Domestic Dangers*, pp. 210–15, 224; Flather, *Gender and Space*, pp. 60, 67.

[50] HA, QSR 12/1663/797.

[51] WYAS–W, QS 1/38/4/6 (petition of John Lees, 1699).

Similarly, the parish officers, rector, and inhabitants of Hemyock in Devon demanded redress against Richard Player, 'a Fellow of a Notorious ill life & Conversation, [who] by his wicked Idle Practices bring his family to want & Ruine & now Positively refusing to maintain any of them or so much as to take them into house along with him'.[52] Indeed, sometimes masculinity became an even more explicit issue in contemporary comparisons between dutiful and negligent householders. If you followed the example of 'honest good husbands' who 'take pains' and 'bring home the gains' to their family, then you could 'carry yourself like a man'. If, on the other hand, 'You piss'd all o'th Wall, and come penniless home', then you would 'be counted no man'.[53] Given the prominence of this theme in the rhetoric of the era, Shepard has convincingly argued that 'links between manhood and provision have … received far less scrutiny by historians than the association of femininity with chastity, even though they were as central to the normative gender roles prescribed by early modern moralists'.[54]

Yet, while the importance of 'provision' to manhood should not be ignored, it was also relevant to other social roles – the duty of 'good husbandry' did not apply solely to husbands. The best example comes from a 1675 tract in which Susanna Jesserson described the 'industry and frugality' of an ideal wife: 'her good man dares trust her with his cash without an exact account', because 'she provides liberally for her family, but has an eye that nothing be wasted'.[55] In practice, wives were often the ones who managed household finances, though this fact tended to be minimised by patriarchal commentators who preferred to acknowledge women's roles only indirectly. Rather than praising wives who proved to be able providers, most commentators

---

[52] DRO, QS/4, box 132 (24 Dec 1692). See also the case of Thomas Collup of Ware (Herts.), condemned by his neighbours because he 'being a willfull and obstinante person chuses rather to begg his own bread from door to door, and to suffer his said wife and daughter to become a charge … then to join us in the disposal of [his farm] … or to putt himself in some way to maintain his family as he ought to doe': HA, QSR 19/1683/261. For many cases of fathers of illegitimate children forced to pay maintenance see Patricia Crawford, *Parents of Poor Children in England, 1580–1800* (Oxford, 2010), pp. 96–105.

[53] *A Looking Glass for All Good-fellows* (1685–88), in PB, IV, p. 79; *Tis Money that Makes a Man* (c.1679–81), in PB, IV, p. 254.

[54] Shepard, *Meanings of Manhood*, pp. 186–7.

[55] Jesserson, *A Bargain for Bachelors*, p. 6. Similarly, a broadsheet used a verse by Thomas Tusser to declare that 'The Care of the Husbandman enricheth the Hutch, / The Eye of the Housewife availeth as much. / What he doth provide with Money his Drudge, / She still must look which Way it doth trudge': *The New Art of Thriving* (c.1685). The notion of maternal provision was also sometimes praised in funeral sermons that 'explicitly connected the female sex and charitable giving by evoking images of babies sucking and child rearing, and identifying these actions with acts of charity': Ben-Amos, *Culture of Giving*, pp. 269–70. For a fuller discussion of the honour and virtue associated with 'good housewifery' (and the dishonour of the 'idle huswife') see Walker, 'Expanding the Boundaries', pp. 238–40. For a detailed discussion of the economic responsibilities of poor mothers see Crawford, *Parents*, pp. 117–29.

focused their energy on denouncing those who wasted the familial estate on extravagant fashions and other vanities.[56] Equally villainous were children who, upon reaching maturity, failed to support their aged and impotent parents. A particularly flagrant violation of the intergenerational bond of reciprocity was reported in a news sheet from 1697. It gravely described the dire fate that befell a Yorkshireman named Winam Tendin after he cast his widowed mother out of his house, forcing her to live in a 'Hovel', 'while her ungracious Son kept Revelling and Feasting, not in the least regarding her or sending her any relief'. His mother called on God to revenge her and, in response, his feast turned into plates full of 'ugly venomous Serpents'.[57] Although fathers and mothers were expected to provide for the needs of their young children, these same children were later expected to honour their elderly parents by helping them to maintain an adequate standard of living.

For the most part, however, these duties of wives and children were seen as secondary to those of the male householder. This may help to explain why so many religious commentators made sure their audiences understood the implications of St Paul's stern injunction to Timothy: 'He that provides not for his own, is worse than an Infidel'.[58] William Fleetwood used this passage as the basis for two lengthy sermons on negligent parents, and Richard Younge declared that a dissolute drunkard, who 'taketh no care to provide for thy own family, but drinkest the very blood of [his] Wife, Children and Servants', was 'worse than an Infidel.'[59] In fact, as this quotation indicates, the glosses on this passage offered by Younge and other clergymen expanded this duty still further by conflating, on one hand, 'Children and

---

[56] As with condemnations of wasteful husbands, attacks on extravagant wives are too numerous to name. For one particularly striking example see *The Invincible Pride of Women* (c.1688–96), in *PB*, IV, p. 153.

[57] *Strange, Dreadful, and Amazing News from York* (1697), p. 4. For another story of providential punishment inflicted on uncharitable children see *A Most Excellent Ballad of an Old Man and his Wife* (1678–80), in *RB*, I, pp. 332–3. For a ballad that notes 'shame shall come to such as do / their Parents not Relieve' see *An Hundred Godly Lessons* (c.1686–8), in *PB*, II, pp. 16–17. For general admonitions to children to 'relieve their Parents if they need' see *Mr Baxters Rules & Directions*; Thomas Firmin, *Some Proposals For the Imployment of the Poor, and for the Prevention of Idleness and the Consequence thereof, Begging* (1681), p. 32; Rawlet, *The Christian Monitor*, p. 41; Watson, *A Body of Practical Divinity*, p. 355; Fleetwood, *The Relative Duties*, pp. 60–67. This obligation was also explicitly written into the Elizabethan poor law. For evidence of children supporting elderly parents see Hindle, *On the Parish?* pp. 49–51, 54–5; Ben-Amos, *Culture of Giving*, pp. 30–40; WYAS–W, QS 1/5/1/6/5.

[58] Edward Boughen, *A Short Exposition of the Catechism of the Church of England* (1662), p. 53 (paraphrasing 1 Tim. 5:8). Yet one must not succumb to 'worldly phansies' and believe that this passage endorses hoarding 'estates and riches' for family members: Hammond, *A Practical Catechism*, pp. 274–7.

[59] Fleetwood, *The Relative Duties*, pp. 113–64; Younge, *A Precious Mithridate*, p. 12.

Servants' and, on the other, 'Parents and Masters'.[60] I have already noted, in the previous section, the tendency to represent household employees as family members, but this habit was particularly common in discussions relating to provision. Thomas Watson, preaching to his dissenting congregation sometime before 1686, began with the assumption that 'Masters' are 'the Fathers of Families', leading him to declare:

> Masters must have a care to *provide* for their Servants: As they cut them out Work, so they must give them their *Meat in due season*, [Luke 17:7]. And the Food should be wholsom and sufficing. It is an *unworthy* thing in some Governors of Families, to lay out so much upon their own Backs, as to pinch their Servants Bellies.[61]

Moreover, this duty was directly acknowledged in the indentures signed by masters taking in a new apprentice. For example, the printed forms used by tradesmen in London and elsewhere in the late seventeenth and early eighteenth centuries obliged masters to provide 'Meat, Drink, Lodging, and all other necessaries' and also, of course, to 'Teach and Instruct ... his said Apprentice in the same Art which he useth'.[62] The same fundamental responsibility applied to those who accepted the more menial services of 'pauper apprentices'. Thus, according to an indenture of 1677, a mistress in Doncaster agreed 'to find and provide for her said Apprentice sufficient and wholesome meate drink lodging & washing', and 'a new Suit of Apparrell' at the end of her term.[63] As integral parts of the family, resident employees had to receive a decent maintenance from their familial 'Governors'.

The master's duty to provide for any servants or apprentices who entered his care had a variety of practical implications, many of which can be glimpsed unfolding in households across later Stuart England. Court records reveal that this obligation applied even in times when it would have been in masters' interests to cut expenses by dismissing their workers. Just as Thomas Watson insisted that masters must not follow 'the *Amalekite*, who forsook his Servant when he was sick, ... but be as the good Centurion, who kept his sick Servant, and sought to Christ for a Cure', county magistrates frequently required masters to care for servants who had been disabled by illness or injury.[64] In 1662, for example, Anthony Gray of Standon (Herts.) was

---

60 For 'Parents and Masters' see Boughen, *A Short Exposition*, p. 53.

61 Watson, *A Body of Practical Divinity*, p. 353. For similar expositions of the duty of providing for servants under the rubric of familial duties see Vincent, *An Explicatory Catechism*, p. 220; *Mr Baxters Rules & Directions*; Stephens, *Relief of Apprentices*, p. 5; Wake, *The Principles of the Christian Religion*, p. 112; Fleetwood, *The Relative Duties*, pp. 407–10.

62 LMA, COL/CA/05/01/0005/1699; DA, AB/5/2/92/57; HA, QSR 24/1698/170.

63 DA, AB/5/2/87/10.

64 Watson, *A Body of Practical Divinity*, p. 353 (citing 1 Sam. 30:13 and Mat. 8:6).

required to 'receive, keepe and maintaine' a servant named Jeffrey Salmon after having 'unjustly discharged him' because Salmon had 'fallen sicke and thereby become possessed of strainge fits of Lunacy and Madnesse'.[65] Even when the courts were not involved, some dutiful householders devoted themselves to helping sickly servants. In 1666, for example, Samuel Pepys offered a nurse 20s per week, along with 'clothes and bedding and physic', to care for his family's undermaid after learning 'the ill News that our little Su is sick'.[66] These crucial forms of support could at least temporarily protect those in service from the threat of destitution, but they were also augmented by a wide range of less dramatic manifestations of pseudo-parental provision. Employers regularly offered wedding gifts, or even whole dowries, to trusted servants upon marriage, and dying masters often left bequests in their wills to these 'fictive kin'. Similarly, maids and other domestics could expect to receive perquisites in the form of monetary tips, old clothes, and, in a few cases, subsidised schooling.[67]

Even after these servants had grown too old for service or had left their adoptive households, their relationship with their employers sometimes continued in this familial mode. Some masters kept on servants who were well past their prime while others assisted elderly former servants by granting them pensions or other forms of patronage.[68] Edward Moore, a gentleman who owned extensive properties in and around Liverpool, seems to have shared this attitude. In the late 1660s, for example, he informed his son that a 'good honest poor man' named Henry Mason had once 'had a poor house under me in the Castle street, which was ready to fall down, and I out of charity built [a new] house from the cold ground for him, in regard he had a been an old servant for some fifty years to our family'.[69] The responsibilities of 'the Fathers of Families' were asserted and sometimes fulfilled even when youth, health, and prosperity turned into old age, illness, and hardship.

---

[65] HA, QSR 12/1662/462. For further evidence from the courts on both slumps and sickness see ERO, Q/SO 2, fol. 36; Ben-Amos, *Adolescence and Youth*, pp. 113, 171–2; idem, *Culture of Giving*, p. 350; Kussmaul, *Servants in Husbandry*, p. 32.
[66] Samuel Pepys, *The Diary of Samuel Pepys: A New and Complete Transcription*, Robert Latham and William Matthews eds (11 vols, London, 1970–83), VII, pp. 115–16 (1–3 May 1666). See also Bernard Capp, *When Gossips Meet: Women, Family and Neighbourhood in Early Modern England* (Oxford, 2003), p. 142. For a master who, in 1672, cared for a maid 'as if she had not been a servant but a child' see R. C. Richardson, *Household Servants in Early Modern England* (Manchester, 2010), p. 109.
[67] Ben-Amos, *Adolescence and Youth*, pp. 110–13, 171–3; eadem, *Culture of Giving*, p. 61; Hill, *Servants*, ch. 4; Capp, *When Gossips Meet*, pp. 139, 141–2; Mendelson and Crawford, *Women*, pp. 104–6, 267; Amussen, *Ordered Society*, p. 157; Levine and Wrightson, *Industrial Society*, p. 358.
[68] Capp, *When Gossips Meet*, pp. 140–42; Hill, *Servants*, pp. 96–7; Hainsworth, *Stewards*, p. 160; Ben-Amos, *Culture of Giving*, p. 62.
[69] Moore, *The Moore Rental*, pp. 28–9. For another example of charity to 'a faithful servant of the family' see ibid., pp. 118–19.

Taken together, these assumptions about the duty of provision must have had an impact on the lives of a huge proportion of the labouring population, especially given the fact that perhaps four out of five poor youths went through some form of service.[70] A dutiful master or mistress could blunt many of the sharp edges of the early modern economy.

Of course, the paternalist ethos affected relations well beyond the microcosm of an individual family or household. The obligations instinctually assigned to parents and employers could stretch to apply to almost anyone with a significant amount of wealth, authority or standing. In the process, this attitude incorporated and strengthened the concept of godly stewardship. The faithful saw God as a 'great *pater-familias*' who had created the world 'for the necessary sustenance … of his creatures', and most believed that the Heavenly Father had then delegated his paternal duties to the rich, endowing them with the world's bounty 'in Trust, to *Provide for His Great Household* or Family'.[71] This divine policy, according to George Hickes, was designed to link people at either end of the social spectrum together in a relationship akin to familial dependence. Preaching in 1684, Hickes argued that 'the Rich are Gods Stewards for the Poor, [and] He laies up their Maintenance in their Treasuries, because He would have them depend upon them, and serve them'. Just as fathers had to provision their children, God 'hath Ordained, That the Great and Rich in all places should provide, and allow what is sufficient for the use and maintenance of the Inferior, and Poorer sort'.[72] The inequalities in later Stuart life – whether in families or on a much grander scale – were explained as part of the divine plan to endow superiors with the benevolent authority needed to distribute the fruits of the earth according to needs of dependants. The doctrine of stewardship and the logic of household management were thus mutually reinforcing.

Still, determining the exact responsibilities of each individual or group was never straightforward, and the duty of provision was certainly not shared equally by every propertied Englishman. Indeed, the extent of one's duty was not even thought to be directly proportionate to one's wealth. Rather than calculating obligations based on crude economic metrics, people tended to link them to particular callings or positions. Most of these associations seem self-evident: workers looked to their employers, parishioners to their parsons, tenants to their landlords, commoners to their lords, and subjects to their monarchs. Some positions could overlap each other – as in cases of clerical landowners or gentry employers – and clearly some came with more expectations than others, but they all implied some degree of fatherly benevolence.

---

[70] See above p. 85 n. 3.

[71] Barrow, *Of the Love of God and Our Neighbour*, pp. 50–51; Younge, *The Poors Advocate*, title page.

[72] Hickes, *A Sermon Preached at the Church of St. Bridget*, p. 9. For a fuller discussion of the doctrine of stewardship see Chapter 1.1 above.

Just as this idea influenced relations between masters and servants within the household, it also affected non-resident employees. In Daniel Defoe's retrospective narrative of the 1665 Great Plague, for example, he reported that the pestilence had caused a 'Stagnation of our Manufacturing Trade in the Country, [which] would have put the People there to much greater Difficulties, but that the Master-Workmen, Clothiers and others, to the uttermost of their Stocks and Strength, kept on making their Goods to keep the Poor at Work'.[73] Instead of responding to the trade slump with mass dismissals, these manufacturers duly continued to pay their employees long after it had ceased to be profitable. Likewise, in less difficult times, employers might prove their paternal credentials by conspicuous acts of largesse. According to David Levine and Keith Wrightson, this sort of 'industrial paternalism' actually *expanded* in the Tyneside coalfields in the late seventeenth and early eighteenth centuries. The mine-owners expressed their newfound interest in projecting a fatherly image by partaking in 'myriad minor acts of patronage and assistance to pitmen and their families', including pensions, medical care, and foodstuffs. It also included providing a 'Punch Waggon' with 'fiddlers and pipers' at an event in 1712, and buying the prize plate for a race in 1717.[74] Nor was the impact of this attitude limited to manufacturing and 'industrial' workers. After the harvest of 1674, for instance, Ralph Josselin, in his role as a substantial Essex farmer, described 'feasting' his hired hands, so 'that my labourers might partake of gods bounty and goodness to me'.[75]

On the other hand, Josselin was also a vicar, and he seems to have attended to the charitable duties associated with that role with rather less diligence. His piety is indisputable and his diary indicates that he devoted much of his energy to the spiritual needs of his parishioners, but he clearly did not see their material concerns as part of his clerical responsibilities. In this respect, Josselin was probably typical of his fellow clergymen. While

---

[73] Daniel Defoe, A *Journal of the Plague Year:* ... *During the last Great Visitation In 1665* (1722), p. 257. He admitted that 'none but those Masters that were rich could do thus'. An example of an attempt to enforce such paternalism can be seen in the case of Richard Constable, 'a gentleman of good and plentiful estate' in Mildenhall, who fled his town during the plague in 1666 leaving behind his family and the needy of the parish. In response, the churchwardens fined him five pounds: *Records of the County of Wilts., Being Extracts from the Quarter Sessions Great Rolls of the Seventeenth Century*, B. H. Cunnington ed. (Devizes, 1932), p. 245.

[74] Levine and Wrightson, *Industrial Society*, pp. 365–6; John Hatcher, *The History of the British Coal Industry, Vol. I: Before 1700* (Oxford, 1993), pp. 317, 320–21.

[75] Josselin, *Diary*, p. 579 (16 Oct 1674). See also Macfarlane, *Family Life*, pp. 51–2. For other farmers feasting their workers see Ronald Hutton, *The Rise and Fall of Merry England: The Ritual Year, 1400–1700* (Oxford, 1994), p. 24; idem, *Stations of the Sun*, pp. 332–4. One providential tract implied that farmers had a duty to provide for the 'common necessities' of the poor by hiring labourers at 'a good round Price': *The Mowing-Devil* (1678), pp. 2–3. For further discussion of the perquisites offered to labourers see Muldrew, *Food*, pp. 226–33.

they taught extensively on the duty of provision and many performed regular acts of charity, their role as benefactors had declined markedly since the Reformation. This could explain why the early seventeenth-century rector of Myddle 'kept good hospitality and was very charitable', whereas his successor was 'much blamed for his too much parsimony, or covetouseness, and want of charity'.[76] It would be easy to read too much into a single example, but Felicity Heal has shown that this was part of a larger trend away from clerical munificence.[77] Although theological and ecclesiastical changes contributed to this transition, the main cause was presumably the formalisation of parochial poor relief, a process which shifted the burden of responsibility from the minister to the institution of the parish itself and its lay officers. Hence, when John Russel, a Staffordshire pauper, starved to death in 1674, it was the parish overseer – not the parson – who was singled out for condemnation.[78]

Still, this transition should not be overstated. In the 1690s James Lees, the minster of Saddleworth (Yorks.), supported an abandoned wife and her children for several years, and in the next decade John Crakanthorp, vicar of Fowlmere (Cambs.), frequently gave alms to his poorest parishioners.[79] Likewise, according to Richard Willis, a rector in Nottinghamshire, charity had begun 'to wax cold' among laymen, 'but on ye Parsons shoulders it still rested'. He recorded feasting his parishioners at Christmas and Rogationtide over the course of many years, even complaining in 1701 that his charity 'was expected as a Right'.[80] Similarly, two years later, Henry Cornwallis, speaking to a 'mix'd congregation, made up of Clergy-men and Laymen' in Kent, told his fellow preachers to 'give, according as we are able, to the Necessity of the Poor' and 'be given to Hospitality'.[81] Assumptions about clerical paternalism, while less prevalent than they had been in the sixteenth century, had not disappeared entirely.

---

[76] Gough, *History of Myddle*, p. 41.

[77] Heal, *Hospitality*, ch. 7.

[78] Hindle, *On the Parish?* p. 395. For a fuller examination of the influence of long-term trends in poor relief see ibid., pp. 269–71.

[79] WYAS–W, QS 1/38/4/6 (1699); John Crakanthorp, *Accounts of the Reverend John Crakanthorp of Fowlmere, 1682–1710*, Lambert Brassley and Philip Saunders eds (Cambridgeshire Record Society, vol. 8, Cambridge, 1988), pp. 121–273. See also the 'great Hospitality' to poor neighbours attributed to Edward Trelawney, Dean of Exeter, 1717–1726, and the charity of the nonconformist minister James Forbes (d. 1712): Izacke, *Remarkable Antiquities*, p. 200; Ben-Amos, *Culture of Giving*, pp. 70, 209–13, 263. The gifts offered by Giles Moore provide another example, for which see below p. 159.

[80] Heal, *Hospitality*, p. 297. For more on the minister's role in provisioning Rogationtide festivities see Steve Hindle, 'Beating the Bounds of the Parish: Order, Memory, and Identity in the English Local Community, c.1500–1700', in Michael Halvorson and Karen Spierling (eds), *Defining Community in Early Modern Europe* (Aldershot, 2008), pp. 205–28.

[81] Cornwallis, *Set on the Great Pot*, pp. 18–19.

Perceptions of the duties of the landed classes also underwent slow but undeniable changes in the early modern period. In the chaotic land market and hostile political climate under the Tudors and early Stuarts, an infusion of aggressive newcomers coincided with a decline in the influence of the great noble magnates, creating a situation in which the pseudo-feudal conventions inherited from the Middle Ages suffered severe attrition. But, from the mid-seventeenth century, changing economic conditions necessitated 'a reassertion of paternalist values' among gentry landowners.[82] In fact, many landed gentlemen had little choice in the matter. Faced with stagnating land values, increasingly contested elections, and a shrinking pool of labour, these men found themselves forced to conciliate tenants and other villagers with frequent acts of liberality. The beneficiaries were often middling tenant farmers, but landowners also attempted to prove their gentility and build loyalty by providing for the needs of the poor. Lord Leigh drew upon these sentiments when he memorialised his porter in 1688 at his estate in Warwickshire:

> Here lyes a faithfull Friend of the Poore,
> Who dealt large Alms out of his Lordships Store ...
> If Markets rise, Raile not Against their Rates,
> The Price is still the same at Stone Leigh Gates.[83]

Two ballads published in the late 1680s presented a similar image of the 'honest Gentleman' or 'Nobleman' by recounting tales of impoverished cottagers who ever so gratefully received support from their superiors.[84] Even more vividly, Sir Henry Tichborne of Hampshire provided a telling self-portrait of gentry paternalism when he hired Gillis van Tilborch to paint the *Tichborne Dole* in 1670. By ritually distributing bread to all-comers in an act of highly personalised charity, the Tichborne family publicly proclaimed

---

[82] The process described in this paragraph is elaborated more fully in Felicity Heal and Clive Holmes, *The Gentry in England and Wales, 1500–1700* (Basingstoke, 1994), pp. 102–4, 113–19 (quotation at p. 113); Heal, *Hospitality*, esp. ch. 4; Hainsworth, *Stewards*, esp. ch. 4, 7–8; Bowden, 'Agricultural Prices', pp. 75–85; James M. Rosenheim, 'Landownership, the Aristocracy and the Country Gentry', in Lionel Glassey (ed.), *The Reigns of Charles II and James VII & II* (Houndmills, 1997), pp. 152–70.

[83] Heal, *Hospitality*, p. 394. Thomas Mansell of Margam (Glamorgan) showed a similar inclination when he donated 'lavish' amounts of grain to the poor of his neighbourhood during the dearth years of the Restoration era: Fletcher, *Reform*, p. 200. Likewise, Timothy Burrell, a Sussex gentleman, noted in 1709 giving beef, wheat and barley to the poor 'who apply for it at the door on Sundays ... as long as the dearth of provisions continues': Ben-Amos, *Culture of Giving*, p. 129.

[84] *A True Sence of Sorrow* (1685–8), in *PB*, II, p. 53; *The NobleMan's Generous Kindness* (1685–8), in *PB*, II, p. 56. Of course, the latter ballad also lamented that there were 'few ... such Noble Men ... to be found'.

their allegiance to a resurgent ideal.[85] Many other landowners embraced the duty of provision in similar ways, though few were as indiscriminate in their giving. Edward Moore's gentlemanly benevolence – such as renting to particularly needy tenants, especially widows, at highly discounted rates – was probably more typical.[86] Even landlords who did not offer substantial charity might contribute though minor acts of patronage. In 1686, for example, George Witham, who held land at Cliffe in the North Riding, forbore collecting the great debts owed by one of his cottagers and gave the 'yonge fellow' a recommendation with which to seek alms for his '2 little sisters not yet capable to gett themselves breade'.[87] This version of gentility, as both an image and a practice, had been dulled by years of social strain and political dislocation, but it temporarily regained much of its gleam in the decades following the Restoration.

Tracing the complex shifts in attitudes toward the responsibilities of the landed elite is no easy task. Assumptions about 'hospitality' offer an illuminating example of some of the problems. Felicity Heal, in her exhaustive study of the topic, has shown that the ideal of hospitality was decidedly weaker at the end of the early modern period than at the beginning, and plenty of evidence from the later Stuart period appears to support this conclusion.[88] At the most practical level, the tendency of landowning families to spend more and more time in London certainly impeded hospitality, as indicated by the Earl of Bridgewater's insistence, in 1673, that there should be 'no house kept' when he left his Hertfordshire estate, 'for *I keepe house at London*; and strangers must not expect to be entertain'd while I am away'.[89] Writers of tracts and ballads certainly perceived a decline, one which they usually blamed on the moral degeneration of the rich. For instance, an author using the popular pseudonym of 'Poor Robin' published a bitter pamphlet on the subject in 1687. He claimed that 'Piety, Charity, and Hospitality' along with 'Bounty, Liberality, Good-Housekeeping, and other Vertues befitting a Gentleman' had once helped to relieve 'all the poor People in England', but had since been replaced by wasteful pursuit of

---

[85] Steve Hindle, 'The Growth of Social Stability in Restoration England', *European Legacy*, 5:4 (2000), pp. 563–4.

[86] Moore, *The Moore Rental*, pp. 28–9, 54–5, 60–63, 95–7, 116, 118–19. For more examples of landowners supporting the poor of their localities either directly (though contributions of money and goods) or indirectly (through abatements in rent) see Hainsworth, *Stewards*, ch. 8; Bowden, 'Agricultural Prices', p. 76; Levine and Wrightson, *Industrial Society*, p. 358; John Broad, *Transforming English Rural Society: The Verneys and the Claydons, 1600–1820* (Cambridge, 2004), pp. 184–7.

[87] NYCRO, QSB 1686/123.

[88] My argument about the larger process relies heavily on her extremely nuanced narrative, which is conveniently summarised in Heal, *Hospitality*, p. 400.

[89] Heal, *Hospitality*, pp. 149–50. For more evidence of the 'drift to London' see ibid., pp. 141–53.

'Pride' and 'Leachery'.⁹⁰ Indeed, the notion that landlords were misspending the wealth that had been entrusted to them – and thus neglecting their duty to the poor – arose frequently in discussions of hospitality. Again and again, moralists accused 'rich Cormorants' of greasing the proverbial 'fat Sow' by providing lavish feasts for their rich peers instead of opening their houses to their poorer neighbours.⁹¹ Although they use a slightly different vocabulary, both contemporaries and historians seem to agree that early modern gentlemen turned from charitable conviviality to conspicuous consumption and from hosting the poor to banqueting with equals.

It is, however, risky to presume that something was happening just because contemporaries thought it was happening, especially given that the 'decline of hospitality' was a centuries-old trope, as Felicity Heal has already noted.⁹² In this particular case, the persistent laments about gentlemen neglecting their duties may in fact indicate that these duties were so thoroughly ingrained in the minds of most contemporaries that any deviation from them was met with universal scorn. The vigour of these endless complaints actually suggests that the ideal of hospitality to the needy was not just a Tudor relic; it was still very much alive, and perhaps even resurgent, in the later seventeenth century. Moreover, positive portrayals of charitable hospitality were ubiquitous. To take just one particularly evocative example, Thomas Pittis preached that 'being hospitable' by opening one's gates to the poor helps 'to set a lustre on the different Orders of the World, by shewing a decent mixture of Authority and Wealth' and also 'invites Inferiors ... to an awful and affectionate regard to the hospitable persons'.⁹³ This suggestion appealed directly to the insecurities of England's landed classes, who genu-

---

⁹⁰ *Poor Robins Hue and Cry After Good House-Keeping: Or, A Dialogue betwixt Good House-Keeping, Christmas, and Pride* (1687). For a similar complaint see John Blanch, *The Naked Truth in an Essay upon Trade* (1696), p. 6. For ballads see *Englands Present State* (c.1682–4), in *PB*, II, p. 10; *Make Use of Time* (c.1665–74), in *PB*, IV, p. 248. See also the almanac and ballads cited in Hutton, *Stations of the Sun*, p. 20.
⁹¹ Hart, *Heavens Glory And Hells Horror*, sig. A6r–A6v, A8r–A8v; *The Rich Mens Joyes* (1688), in *PB*, V, p. 174v (paraphrasing the adage 'to grease the fat sow in the arse': Tilley, *Proverbs*, p. 621; *Make Use of Time* (c.1665–74), in *PB*, IV, p. 248; James Bowker, *An Almanack* (1679), sig. B8r; John Bucknall, *Ro'eh, or, The Shepherds Almanack* (1676), sig. C1r; Younge, *The Poors Advocate*, p. 21; Barrow, *The Duty and Reward of Bounty*, pp. 16–17. Many of these accusations cited or paraphrased Luke 14:12–14, which declared: 'When thou makest a dinner or a supper, call not thy friends, nor thy brethren, neither thy kinsmen, nor thy rich neighbours ... But when thou makest a feast, call the poor, the maimed, the lame, the blind'. This passage had long been used as a proof-text in these sorts of complaints, including in the campaign for general hospitality in the 1590s: Hindle, 'Dearth, Fasting and Alms', p. 55.
⁹² Heal, *Hospitality*, p. 93; Daniel Woolf, *The Social Circulation of the Past: English Historical Culture, 1500–1730* (Oxford, 2003), pp. 60–63.
⁹³ Pittis, *A Spittle Sermon*, pp. 11–12. According to one adage, 'Noble housekeepers need no doors': Tilley, *Proverbs*, p. 332. For more examples see *Avaritia Coram Tribunali*, p. 13; William Dade, *A New [Almanack] and [Prognostication]* (1666), sig. C3r; *Old Christmas*

inely feared losing the loyalty and obedience of their meaner neighbours and who sometimes invested heavily in 'good house-keeping'. Gentlemen such as Sir John Reresby and George Evelyn expended considerable sums maintaining their reputations for generosity, and even some absentee land-lords partook in Christmas hospitality, as evidenced by the absent squire who ordered the distribution of sixpenny loaves to poor families who were 'sufferers by my not being there' in 1707.[94]

Of course, some people regarded practices such as these with a degree of wariness, if not hostility. Prodigious or indiscriminate provision for one's inferiors could be dangerous for all sorts of reasons, and several later Stuart commentators warned against overgenerous hospitality. A ballad published in 1670 reminded hearers that 'While you do feast and give good gifts, / keep for your self some store, / For that you do part with all / you then must needs be poor', and William Fleetwood gave similar advice in his sermon on indebtedness in 1718.[95] However, for the most part, these defences of inhospitable behaviour were dismissed as self-serving excuses for niggardli-ness. Interestingly, several commentators singled out religious 'enthusiasm' as a common pretext for covetousness in this regard. Thomas Pittis, for example, preached against the miserliness of puritanical zealots – 'our little, narrow, systematical men' – who complained about the supposed 'abuses of open hospitality, to hide their Avarice under the Mantle of Vertue and a more strict Sobriety'.[96] Other moralists claimed that the 'many great Profes-sors' of piety cloaked their greed with 'good Names, such as Frugality, and good Husbandry', while using the 'Excuse' that 'Good Works are Popishly inclin'd' as a reason to have 'turned good Hous-keeping out of doors'.[97] In

---

Returnd (c.1683–5), in *PB*, I, p. 147–8; 'Poor Robin' *An Almanack* (1690), sig. B7v; *The Choice: A Poem* (1700), p. 4.

[94] Heal, *Hospitality*, pp. 168, 186–7; Evelyn, *Diary*, V, p. 358; Hainsworth, *Stewards*, p. 161. For more examples see Josselin, *Diary*, p. 539 (22–29 Dec. 1667); Gough, *History of Myddle*, pp. 111–13; Hutton, *Rise and Fall*, p. 242; Heal and Holmes, *Gentry*, pp. 284, 287; Thomas, *Ends of Life*, p. 159; Felicity Heal, 'Food Gifts, the Household and the Politics of Exchange in Early Modern England', *Past & Present*, 199 (2008), pp. 69–70. Ben-Amos has noted several more examples from this period, but also suggested that hospitality towards the poor increasingly came to be conducted separately from hospitality toward the host's peers: Ben-Amos, *Culture of Giving*, pp. 215–17.

[95] *Wit Bought at a Dear Rate* (1670), in *PB*, IV, p. 259; William Fleetwood, *The Justice of Paying Debts: A Sermon Preach'd in the City* (1718), p. 19. See also the adage connecting a 'fat kitchen' with 'a lean will' in Tilley, *Proverbs*, pp. 331, 359. Richard Gough recounted the story of a rich man who 'kept good hospitalyty, and was very charitable to the poor', but 'As hee increased in dignity, so hee decreased in riches' and died with great debts: Gough, *History of Myddle*, pp. 160–61.

[96] Pittis, *A Spittle Sermon*, pp. 18–19. See also Thomas, *The Mammon of Unrighteousness*, p. 21; Stevens, *The Whole Parable*, p. 10.

[97] Dunton, *Englands Alarum*, pp. 11–12; 'Poor Robin', *An Almanack* (1697), sigs B8r, C6r. See also Richard Gough's complaints about men and women who were 'sparing, even to a fault': Gough, *History of Myddle*, pp. 113, 138, 162–3.

reality, religious enthusiasts may have been just as likely to be generous as other rich folk and it is impossible to measure whether such attempts to justify a parsimonious attitude towards the poor were any more common in the late seventeenth century than they had been a century earlier. Still, whatever the circumstances, the inhospitable had clearly failed to convince most observers that they were anything but 'bad housekeepers'. The landed men of later Stuart England – whether high-ranking peers, local squires, or even just wealthy yeomen – had responsibilities that could not be lightly brushed off.

The duty of provision also intertwined with more formal manifestations of authority. Civic elites and landed gentlemen, in their roles as local magistrates, often responded to scarcity and economic dislocation by supplying food or money to the poor. For instance, reacting to rising food prices in the winter of 1693, the mayor of Chester, Roger Whitley, worked with city officials to ensure that 'the poore of severall parishes' were fed.[98] Sometimes the king himself took on this obligation. While instances of monarchs distributing aid directly from their own coffers were never more than occasional, they certainly created a powerful image of royal paternalism, especially in times of acute crisis. One particularly explicit example can be seen in a contemporary account of the charity of Charles II after the Great Fire of London. In the words of this broadside ballad:

> Cradles were rock'd in every field,
>   and food was all their cry,
> Till the Kings bowels bread did yield
>   and sent them a supply;
> A father He,
> Of his Countrey,
>   Himself did sweetly shew,
> Both day and night,
> With all His might,
>   He fought to ease our woe.[99]

Usually, however, it was much less exulted political authorities who took up the task of supplying the necessities of the people. The thousands of overseers of the poor created by the Elizabethan Poor Laws were the primary agents for

---

[98] *Roger Whitley's Diary 1684–1697: Bodleian Library*, MS Eng. Hist. c. 711, Michael Stevens transcriber (British History Online, 2004), fol. 167r (15, 18–22 Dec 1693), available at: <www.british-history.ac.uk/source.aspx?pubid=121>.

[99] *London Mourning in Ashes* (1666), in *PB*, IV, p. 228. Similarly, a London clergyman praised William III as 'the truest Father of his Cuntry' for declaring the 'Duty' of 'Provision' for the poor to be 'a National care': Cooke, *Workhouses the Best Charity*, p. 3 (dedication). These sorts of evocations of monarcho-parental care owed much of their resonance to the frequent mentions of Isa. 49:23, for which see below pp. 125, 143.

redistributing the resources of the parish economy to ensure that the need-iest of English subjects were provided for. Moreover, the amount of resources devoted to poor relief increased substantially in the later Stuart period.[100] Yet the expansion of this institutional support system did not necessarily mean the diminution of paternalism. Instead, the appeal process built into the relief system may have actually increased the likelihood of magistrates finding themselves asked to show a fatherly concern for the poor by over-ruling parish officers, especially between 1692 and 1723, when the law made their responsibilities still greater.[101] Even forward-looking proposals for the 'rationalisation' of poor relief used familial idioms. An influential pamphlet authored by Josiah Child, for example, called for the establishment of a class of officials to be known as 'Fathers of the Poor', who would 'have very large and sufficient power in all things relating to the poor', including the powers normally assigned to Justices and many others besides.[102] This proposal for 'Fathers of the Poor', probably first published in 1670, was then borrowed and adapted by several pamphlets in the following decades, including a draft parliamentary bill to reform of the poor laws published at least twice under George I.[103]

The duty of 'good husbandry', providing care and sustenance for needy dependants, thus remained an essential part of the paternal ideal that underlay so many social roles in later Stuart society. Employers, landlords, and wealthy gentlemen – like fathers and husbands – were expected to prove their fatherly status in much the same way as their predecessors, though a few groups (particularly the clergy) may have felt their obligations gradually weaken. For most of those holding some sort of economic authority, familial logic continued to influence their relations with their 'inferiors'.

3 Patriarchal Governance

Differences in social duty were sharpest in the realm of governance where, at least theoretically, one had an obligation simply to rule or to obey. Preachers

---

[100] Hindle, *On the Parish?* pp. 255–6, and the earlier work cited therein.

[101] For the appeal process see below pp. 128–30. For the law of 1692 see Hindle, *On the Parish?* p. 406.

[102] Josiah Child, *Sir Josiah Child's Proposals for the Relief and Employment of the Poor* (c.1670), pp. 4–6. This short proposal was reprinted in 1690 and 1699, and also included in Child's long *Discourse on Trade* in 1690, 1693, 1694, and 1698.

[103] Firmin, *Some Proposals*, p. 29; *A Modest Proposal for the More Certain and yet more Easie Provision for the Poor* (1696), p. 3 and passim; James Puckle, *England's Way to Wealth and Honour* (1699, reprinted in 1700, 1707, 1718, 1737), 39–42; Laurence Braddon, *An Abstract of the Draught of a Bill for relieving, Reforming, and Employing the Poor* (1717?, reprinted in 1723), p. 5. See also Crawford, *Parents*, ch. 5.

such as John Conant and Robert Moss had no doubt about the importance of these two interdependent functions. According to them, God had ordained 'different Stations and Conditions' for rich and poor because of the need for 'different Services and Imployments for procuring and carrying the good and welfare of the Community of Mankind. Some must govern, and others must be governed; or else we shall quickly be ruined'.[104]

The most popular way to conceptualise economic governance was as patriarchy. After all, fathers – both literal and metaphorical – ruled early modern England. Their authority was ordained by God, sanctioned by law, fortified by custom, and sometimes guaranteed by brute force.[105] Moreover, the sheer range of relationships bracketed into the father–child binary was vast. In catechisms and other didactic literature, the injunction in the fifth commandment was extended dramatically, so the poor were taught that 'by *the Father* he ought to honour, is meant all his Superiors', including kings, magistrates, parish officers, military leaders, landlords, benefactors, masters, ministers, teachers, elders, and husbands.[106] These beliefs invested immense power in these individuals and, despite certain pragmatic and ideological limitations, patriarchs were able to exercise a significant degree of control

---

[104] Conant, *Sermons Preach'd on Several Occasions*, I, p. 237. Similarly, the providential 'Disparity of Circumstances betwixt Man and Man' was created to indicate 'who should obey and who should govern': Moss, *The Providential Division*, p. 5.

[105] The historiography of patriarchy is extensive but scattered widely and only a very small proportion of it addresses economic implications in any depth. I cite the most relevant scholarly works in the analysis that follows. For more comprehensive accounts see Schochet, *Patriarchalism*; Amussen, *Ordered Society*, esp. ch. 2; Fletcher, *Gender*; Shepard, 'Manhood, Credit and Patriarchy'; eadem, *Meanings of Manhood*, esp. ch. 3, 5, 7; Capp, *When Gossips Meet*, ch. 1. Weber touched on the topic very briefly, just long enough to assert that '[p]atriarchalism and patrimonialism have an inherent tendency to regulate economic activity in terms of utilitarian, welfare or absolute values … [which] stems from the character of the claim to legitimacy and the interest in the contentment of the subjects': Weber, *Economy and Society*, I, p. 240. Regarding the legitimation of the use of the violence to enforce patriarchal discipline both inside and outside the household see Susan Amussen, 'Punishment, Discipline, and Power: The Social Meanings of Violence in Early Modern England', *Journal of British Studies*, 34:1 (1995), pp. 1–34.

[106] Steele, *The Husbandmans Calling*, p. 104. See also Hammond, *A Practical Catechism*, pp. 183–9; Boughen, *A Short Exposition*, pp. 46–55; Littleton, *Solomons Gate*, p. 336; Richard Sherlock, *The Principles of Holy Christian Religion* (1663), pp. 33–4; Vincent, *An Explicatory Catechism*, p. 213; Gouge, *The Principles of Christian Religion*, p. 28; *Mr Baxters Rules & Directions*; Rawlet, *The Christian Monitor*, p. 41; Bralesford, *The Poor Man's Help*, p. 40; Williams, *A Brief Exposition of the Church-Catechism*, pp. 35–6; Watson, *A Body of Practical Divinity*, p. 350; Wake, *The Principles of the Christian Religion*, p. 107; Thomas Curteis, *Religious Princes the Greatest Blessing and Safety and Safety to the Church and State: A Sermon Preach'd in the Parish Church of Wrotham in Kent* (1716), pp. 6–7; Green, *Christian's ABC*, pp. 451–60. Of course, this commandment actually ordained parental, not just patriarchal, power. Although the commentators firmly placed the emphasis on fathers rather than mothers, the parental aspect was not entirely ignored.

over the political, religious and personal lives of their 'inferiors'. The effects of this philosophy on later Stuart economic relations cannot be ignored.

But one cannot understand the grander implications of patriarchalism until one has addressed the source of this metaphor: the family itself. Here, the theory endowed the *paterfamilias* with the power to employ the collective resources of the family in pursuit of the common good. The most persistent expression of this idea was found in the prejudices of the English legal system. For instance, young people who were trapped in a state of 'nonage' under early modern property law – i.e. children and youth who had not yet reached their twenty-first birthday – had almost no formal economic autonomy. Married women were similarly subordinated, specifically through the doctrine of 'coverture', which designated a wife as a 'feme covert'. In most jurisdictions, despite significant legal loopholes, these women lacked the ability to sign binding contracts or hold property in their own name. The labour, land, and movable wealth of all family members were thus under the control of the patriarch, at least according to the letter of the law.[107]

The legal force of these commonplaces would have been universally known, so it was hardly necessary to reiterate them as moral directives, but they seem to turn up in unofficial injunctions anyway. Tract writers and preachers repeatedly declared that a well-ordered household required more than just industrious labour and good husbandry – it needed a governor. Richard Baxter's monumental *Christian Directory*, for example, touched on several of these points in the section on 'Christian Oeconomicks', some of which was then summarised and reprinted as a broadsheet in 1681. According to *Mr Baxters Rules & Directions for Family Duties*, the wife had a duty 'not to dispose of her Husbands Estate without his consent', for he was the 'chief' authority in the household. Likewise, children must 'be contented with their Parents Allowance and Provisions, and willing and ready to such labour or imployment as they command them', which would be decided ultimately by the father in his role as 'governour of the Family'.[108] Of course, the large numbers of widows who headed their own households meant that not all patriarchs were men, but the gendered idioms used in discussions and the logic that supported them acknowledged only the simple dichotomy between the governor and 'his' familial inferiors.

[107] This extremely broad characterisation of family property law describes only the general thrust of English legal tradition at this time and omits a great many exceptions, both practical and theoretical. Little has been written on the economic implications of 'nonage' (age of minority), but, for the constraints on married women, see Amy Louise Erickson, *Women and Property in Early Modern England* (London, 1993), esp. pp. 24–6, 99–101.
[108] *Mr Baxters Rules & Directions*; Baxter, *A Christian Directory*, pp. 509–11, 533, 550. On the wisdom of obeying one's father 'in the choice of Trade, or Calling', even in cases of parental disagreement, see Fleetwood, *The Relative Duties*, pp. 59–60.

Unsurprisingly, this powerful set of assumptions shaped economic relationships throughout later Stuart society, from the most intimate to the
most abstract. For instance, when considering the administration of the
'household-family', commentators unanimously insisted that servants had a
filial duty to obey their masters and mistresses. In the prescriptive literature of the era, as Gordon Schochet and others have shown, there were
'only slight differences' between subordination to fathers and to masters.[109]
Thomas Watson, in one of his sermons on the Decalogue, made the childlike status of servants even clearer by including 'the *Oeconomical Father*;
that is, the *Master*', under the rubric of the fifth commandment:

> He is *Pater Familias*, the *Father of the Family*. Therefore *Naaman's* Servants called
> their Master *Father* [2 Kings 5:13]. And the *Centurion* calls his Servant *Son*
> [Matt. 8:6]. The Servant is to honour his *Master* as the Father of the Family ...
> by Submission, Diligence, Faithfulness, Love, and humble Silence.[110]

This emphasis on the overwhelming need for obedience must be borne in
mind when considering the practical effects of the familial model. This sort
of infantalisation may have persuaded employers to provide liberally for
their resident workers, but it also gave 'the *Oeconomical Father*' far-reaching
moral authority over his 'inferiors'. John Dunton's grim recollection of his
days as a printer's apprentice bore its imprint plainly: 'I'd reckon my Master
and Mistress as another Father and Mother ... There's no way but this to
make the Chains of a Seven Years Bondage sit easily without galling.'[111]
   These complex attitudes toward employment were not limited to the
confines of the household. Indeed, their convoluted nature was perhaps
illustrated most strikingly in the person of the merchant captain. Marcus
Rediker's work on labour relations among seamen in the early eighteenth
century has shown that the ship's master held the legal authority to physi-
cally 'correct' his men and he exercised it with sometimes brutal regularity, yet the words used to describe this power were very revealing.[112] One

---

[109] Schochet, *Patriarchalism*, pp. 416–17, 424, 428–33, quotation at p. 416; Schlatter,
Social Ideas, pt. 1, ch. 3; S. R. Smith, 'The Ideal and Reality: Apprentice–Master Relationships in Seventeenth-Century London', *History of Education Quarterly*, 21 (1981),
pp. 450–51; idem, 'The London Apprentices as 17th Century Adolescents', *Past &
Present*, 61 (1973), pp. 151–2; Green, *Christian's ABC*, pp. 451–60. Hence, as Alexandra
Shepard has pointed out, a servant or apprentice, in most cases, 'was not yet accounted
an autonomous economic agent': Shepard, *Meanings of Manhood*, p. 207.
[110] Watson, *A Body of Practical Divinity*, pp. 351–2. For many similar statements see the
sources cited above in p. 114, n. 106. The other commonly cited scriptural passages were
Eph. 6:5, Col. 3:22, and 1 Pet. 2:18.
[111] John Dunton, *Life and Errors* (1705), p. 55.
[112] Marcus Rediker, *Between the Devil and the Deep Blue Sea: Merchant Seamen, Pirates,
and the Anglo-American Maritime World, 1700–1750* (Cambridge, 1987), esp. pp. 84,
212–27.

captain called himself the 'Head' of his crew and noted that 'they were the body', while a later observer declared that 'a Captain is like a King at Sea' in his 'Authority' over those aboard. On the other hand, another merchant captain said he 'generally used his Marriners in so kind & tender a Manner that when he speaks to or of his ships Company he calls them Children'.[113] The metaphors used to explain this relationship – anatomy, monarchy, paternity – accounted for both violent punishments and kindly benevolence. As such, these captains and seamen found themselves engaged in an enterprise that involved much more than just the exchange of labour for wages.

Ideals of stern discipline and moral hierarchy also influenced employment relations on land, even in large-scale businesses such as mining and metalwork. For example, the workers at the Gallantry Bank copper mine in Cheshire were told that their 'lord' expected them to pray daily and exhibit 'Christian like behaviour' at the worksite, with the threat of punishment for immorality. According to an instruction issued in 1693, they were also required to contribute to a sickness fund run by the mine owner.[114] Ambrose Crowley, at around the same time, established a similarly hierarchal management regime in his huge County Durham ironworks. Not only did he promise punishment for 'any disorderly or ungovernernable person' accused of offences such as gambling and cursing under his rules for 'Good Government', he also provided relief for sick or aged workers, schooling for their children, and support for their widows. Of course these welfare provisions were funded in part by deductions from the wages of employees themselves, but he retained firm control over disbursements.[115] These sorts of workplace dynamics suggest that early modern conceptions of governance strengthened the employer's claim to be protecting the virtue and welfare of his workers by strictly controlling their energy, resources, and behaviour. Governing one's 'inferiors' was, at least in the minds of some, both a privilege and a duty.

Most people spent at least part of their lives subject to the daily demands of authority as personified in a father, husband or master. However, they – along with even the most well-established independent householders –

---

113   Ibid., pp. 207–8.
114   Andy Wood, 'Custom, Identity and Resistance: English Free Miners and their Law, c.1550–1800', in Paul Griffiths, Adam Fox, and Steve Hindle (eds), *The Experience of Authority in Early Modern England* (Basingstoke, 1996), pp. 273–4. John Wilkins appears to have employed a similar regime to rule his colliers at Silver Hill (Leics.) in the 1690s: Hatcher, *British Coal Industry*, I, pp. 316–17. Likewise, from the late seventeenth century, the owners of the Tyneside coalmines adopted 'a highly paternalistic style', mixing firmer discipline with patronage and charitable support: Levine and Wrightson, *Industrial Society*, pp. 355–69.
115   *The Law Book of the Crowley Ironworks*, M. W. Flinn ed. (Surtees Society, vol. 167, Durham, 1957), pp. 4–8, 154, 164, 167.

also found economic activity constrained by the power of much grander entities, ranging from the hundreds of England's local officers to national political figures in Westminster. Monarchs and, more immediately, magistrates attempted to govern those beneath them through a diverse array of policies and prerogatives. Although their successes were never more than partial and often fleeting, no one seems to have doubted that these men had a special role as social and economic managers – a role dependent in part upon their prominent place in the patriarchal vision of society promoted by so many early modern commentators.[116] Patriarchy, as envisaged in contemporary social analysis, reached from the home to the state and beyond, so every official was thus part of a continuum that harmonised political rule with its domestic and spiritual counterparts.

Of course, at the pinnacle of the whole orderly universe stood God, the greatest of all fathers and the ultimate model of just governance.[117] Likewise, the rule of Old Testament patriarchs provided a seemingly obvious historical reference point for those who sought to understand and explain the nature of godly political authority in an age of biblical literalism. These interlocking conceptions of patriarchal power normally reached the poor through the simple political commonplaces of popular culture. They stressed filial loyalty and obedience above all, but remained remarkably untouched by the debates raging among political theorists in the late seventeenth century. To take just one example, according to an almanac of 1697, all English subjects must 'Honour the King as Sons their Parents do, / For he's thy Father, and thy Countrie's too'.[118] Though published well after the systematic attacks by Locke and Tyrell on Filmer's *Patriarcha*, this concise explanation of patriarchal kingship was probably much more typical of most people's sentiments than the contractual theories elaborated by radical Whig intellectuals. Moreover, the potent symbolism extended to lesser political figures as well. Magistrates and other office-holders – the unpaid local notables who worked to guide the workforce and the market – commonly found themselves represented as 'fathers of the country'.[119]

---

[116] For an excellent survey of the 'patriarchal state' in the seventeenth century see Michael Braddick, *State Formation in Early Modern England, c. 1550–1700* (Cambridge, 2000), pt. 2.

[117] See p. 105 above.

[118] 'Poor Robin', *An Almanack* (1697), sig. A2r. Examples of the patriarchal conception of kingship (many originally from the Roman honorific 'Pater Patriae') are too numerous to mention, but one common variant can be found in the commentaries on the fifth commandment cited above in p. 114, n. 106. In addition to the sources cited here and elsewhere in this section, a very cursory search turned up five more sermons from this period that specifically describe the king as a 'father of his country', so the sentiment must have been exceedingly common.

[119] Fletcher, *Reform*, p. 79; Watson, *A Body of Practical Divinity*, p. 350; Edwards, *Sermons on Special Occasions*, p. 43; John Howe, *A Sermon Preach'd … at the Request of the Societies for Reformation of Manners* (1698), p. 8.

Most scholarly attention has been devoted to the political implications of this ideal, but it also had economic repercussions and these were given voice by preachers and other moralists. Sometimes, as shown in the first section of this chapter, these evocations of patriarchy focused on the need for subjects to offer their wealth to the prince through taxation. Clergymen such as Thomas Curteis informed their parishioners that 'the King, or *Supreme Magistrate*, is very aptly styl'd a *Political Father*, or the Common Parent of his People', so we subjects are 'bound to Honour' our political father 'with our Substance, as well as in our Thoughts and Words; by shewing a chearful Readiness ... [to] answer all publick Necessities of the State' by providing the treasure needed to promote 'the Common Interest'.[120] In other words, everyone must readily pay their taxes, not merely because they had voted for the measure through their representatives but because the monarcho-parental role of their prince required it. At a time when levels of taxation had begun to increase exponentially, the influence of this reasoning could affect the economic lives of practically every person in the kingdom.

Of course, the implications of this model went far beyond just providing a moral justification for extracting resources, and to frame these sorts of assertions as mere propaganda for royal authority would produce a very skewed picture of the logic of 'household management'. Taxation, though important, reflected only one aspect of the complex amalgam of values built on the model of familial governance. After all, authority was seen as an outgrowth of responsibility, rather than the other way around; hence, financial support was only one part of the process of providing this 'Political Father' with the resources he needed to perform his managerial functions. John Sharp made this clear in 1702 when he preached that princes ought to 'look upon the whole *Kingdom* as their own *Family*, and concern themselves as much for the welfare of their *Subjects* as *Parents* do for their own *Children*', using their monarcho-parental '*Powers* or *Prerogatives*' to promote 'the *publick Good*'.[121] The prince and his magistrates had a wide range of paternal responsibilities, so it was only natural that they should also be endowed with the patriarchal power to execute these obligations.

To get a sense of the multitude of duties assigned to these individuals, one need only glance at the jumbled list presented in Richard Saunder's almanac of 1698. After noting that monarchs 'ought to be common Parents' to their people, never favouring one group over another, Saunder lauded those who ensured

the opening and well ballancing of Trade, the cherishing of Manufactures, the banishing of Idleness, the pressing of Waste and Excess by sumptuary Laws, the improvement and husbanding of the Soil, the regulating the prizes of things

---

120 Curteis, *Religious Princes*, pp. 6, 17, 19–22. See also Wake, *The Principles of the Christian Religion*, p. 109.
121 Sharp, *A Sermon Preach'd at the Coronation*, pp. 5–6.

vendible, the moderating of Taxes ... [and] suppressing, or, at the very least keeping a streight hand upon the devouring Trades of Usury, Ingrossing, &c.[122]

This breathless survey certainly confirms that managing the economy was not a minor concern, but even this does not cover every economic duty expected of a good governor. To understand the real impact of these expectations one must examine more closely some of the specific functions assigned to later Stuart political authorities. These can be adduced from the ideals proclaimed in many prescriptive texts, and from the policies implemented by the many 'fathers of the country' who embodied England's government.

Diligent rulers had a number of tasks to fulfil, some of which have already been mentioned. For instance, the duty of provision, discussed in the previous section, lay on kings and parish officers alike. Yet patriarchs had to do more than just relieve needy dependants through royal charity or parish rates; they also had a duty to protect the weak, guide the wayward, and punish the wicked. Because these responsibilities – and the policies employed to discharge them – often overlapped, it is not practical to analyse each of them in turn. Moreover, the sheer number of economic issues that early modern governments tried to address makes a comprehensive overview impractical. Instead, the following discussion focuses exclusively on the two greatest sources of concern in the later Stuart political economy: food and labour.

An efficient, reliable market in grain and other foodstuffs was an essential element in the social order, for nothing did more damage to people's faith in the familial ideal than the spectre of hunger. Knowing this, political patriarchs sought to guarantee that marketplaces were well-stocked with affordable victuals. For instance, magistrates of both cities and counties regularly set prices through the assizes of bread, and there is certainly evidence of justices attempting to enforce this by, for example, punishing delinquent bakers for selling 'underweight' bread.[123] Sometimes, these existing admin-

---

[122] Richard Saunder, *Apollo Anglicanus, The English Apollo* (1698), sigs A7r, B3r–B5r. This was part of a longer discussion about 'sedition' (A5r–B8r), borrowed from Francis Bacon's essay 'Of Seditions and Troubles'.

[123] CUA, T/VII/2; CUA, V.C.Ct/I/14, fol. 87; ERO, Q/SR 397/13, 424/18, 424/27, 434/34–35, 437/30, 438/50, 440/73, 441/18, 441/20, 442/9, 443/3, 446/54, etc.; ERO, T/A 156/1, vol. I (1677), n.p. (18 May 1693); HA, HBR 9/336; LMA, COL/CA/01/01, passim; Northants. RO, Misc. Q.S. Recs, I, n.p. (Oct. 1695, Oct. 1696), NRO, NCR Case 12b/box 1, parcel 2 (8 Oct. 1697); SRO–I, EE 1/H2/1, fol. 7; *The Liverpool Town Books, 1649–71*, Michael Power ed. (Record Society of Lancashire and Cheshire, no. 136, Chester, 1999), pp. 138, 150, 264; *St Albans Corp. Recs*, pp. 95, 99; *VCH: Warwickshire*, VIII, pp. 507; *Middlesex County Records: Calendar of the Sessions Books, 1689 to 1709*, W. J. Hardy ed. (London, 1905), pp. 8, 103; *County of Buckingham: Calendar of the Sessions Records*, William Le Hardy et al. eds (7 vols, Aylesbury, 1933–80), I, pp. 79–80, 181; *Hertford County Records*, William Le Hardy and G. L. Reckitt eds (10 vols, Hertford, 1905–57), I, p. 254; II, p. 55; Beloff, *Public Order*, p. 64; Norma Landau, *The Justices of*

istrative routines provided a sufficient defence against rising grain prices. However, on other occasions when dearth loomed on the horizon the regulative authority of the magistracy was augmented or expanded, and this was often accompanied by conspicuous affirmation of the paternalist position. Hence, when the parliament of 1709 revised and simplified the medieval 'Assiza Panis', the government declared that, because of erratic enforcement of the previous statute, 'Covetous, and Evil-disposed Persons … have for their own Gain and Lucre, Deceived and Oppressed her Majesties Subjects, and more especially the Poorer Sort of People'.[124] The new statute may not have dashed the schemes of every 'Covetous' baker, but it still forcefully proclaimed the logic of paternalism. Indeed, two ballads from the reign of Charles II show that this part of the magistrate's duty had become fixed in the popular consciousness much earlier. One described how bakers selling loaves 'too light' were left 'sore' by city officials who took their bread and gave it 'to the London poor', while the other portrayed an assize-breaking baker forced to dodge the mayor's officers 'For fear they should put my head / into the Pillory'.[125] Although this system for restraining profiteering was neither universally deployed nor consistently enforced, it fitted neatly into later Stuart beliefs about the obligations of political patriarchs. The assize was, according to a repeatedly published handbook on the topic, an invaluable tool 'for holding them in that most loving and member-like duty, which one part oweth unto others, and every of them to the conservation of the whole body in best estate'.[126] Bakers performed a vital function, but only the vigilance of the magistrate could ensure that they sought no more than their due.

In addition to overseeing the retail bread market, governors tried to ensure that every town and village in the country had access to an affordable supply of grain, a task which was often very publicly performed in times of dearth. Indeed, according to an anonymous pamphlet published during the lean years of the 1690s, 'the Poor have a right to the Protection of the Government' against 'Corn-Merchants and Farmers [who] put what Rates and what Prices they please on Corn'.[127] Much like feudal lords defending their vassals from marauding brigands, early modern rulers were theoretically responsible for defending their subjects from the bandits of the marketplace. They thus prosecuted hoarders, sought out unlicensed dealers,

---

the Peace, 1679–1760 (Berkeley, 1984), p. 183; Wendy Thwaites, 'The Assize of Bread in Eighteenth-Century Oxford', Oxoniensia, 51 (1986), pp. 171, 175–6, 180.

124 Statutes of the Realm, pp. 248–51 (8 Anne c. 19).

125 Londons Praise (c.1666–85), in PB, IV, p. 339; Merry Tom of all Trades (c.1682–4), in PB, IV, p. 261.

126 John Powel, The Assize of Bread (1671), sig. B1r.

127 The Poor Man's Plea (1699), p. 26. In more general terms, John Sharp preached that princes must protect their subjects by ensuring that no one can get away with 'oppressing the meanest of the People': Sharp, A Sermon Preach'd at the Coronation, p. 9.

pilloried cheating millers, and occasionally even stopped exporters.[128] The number of traders actually punished under these various policies may have been small, but the case of even one notorious profiteer being brought before the magistrates left a lasting mark on the public consciousness. Not only did these acts of exemplary punishment starkly affirm the limits of acceptable commercial behaviour, they also created a powerful image of fatherly authorities protecting the poor. By publicly disciplining one of the most-hated bogeymen of the popular imagination, these governors loudly proclaimed their allegiance to the familial ideal.

It is tempting to regard magistrates' efforts to guarantee an orderly and equitable food market with some admiration, even affection. Yet, the dutiful gentlemen who threatened greedy grain dealers with the pillory were often the same men who decreed whippings for young servants who fled their masters' service. After all, patriarchal assumptions about disorder and discipline applied just as easily to labour relations as they did to the food trade. For the hundreds of officeholders who liked to style themselves 'fathers of the country', this translated into a series of duties ranging from repressing able-bodied idlers to chastising disorderly servants to restraining excessive wage demands – though zealous implementation of these policies was far from universal.[129] While these tasks were usually handled by individual householders, magistrates sometimes assumed the role of master to the

---

[128] ERO, Q/SR 388/65, 393/11, 399/15, 411/58, 437/25, 441/18, 442/9, 448/41, 488/63, 497/60, etc.; HA, HBR 20&21, p. 221; LMA, COL/CA/01/01/107, pp. 43–6; Northants. RO, Misc. Q.S. Recs, I, n.p. (Jan. 1697, Oct. 1698, Jun. 1699, Oct. 1699, Jun. 1700); NRO, NCR Case 12b/box 1, parcel 2 (10 Sep. 1698, 2 Mar. 1699); NYCRO, QSB 1686/124, QSB 1699/87–89; SRO–I, B/105/2/12, n.p. (22 Jul. 1695); SRO–I, EE 1/H2/1, fols 1, 6, 10; YCA, F.7, p. 510; F.8, p. 278; *Liverpool Town Books*, pp. 159, 197, 203; *Middlesex Sessions Books*, pp. 344, 348–9; *County of Buckingham Sessions Records*, I, pp. 213, 225; II, pp. 130, 138, 252; III, 177, 189, 204, 190, 235; *Minutes of Quarter Sessions of Kesteven*, I, pp. 7, 12–13, 24, 63, 65, 67, 71, 96, 108, 158; HMC, *The Manuscripts of S. H. Le Fleming, esq., of Rydall Hall: Twelfth Report, Appendix VII* (no. 25, London, 1890), p. 107; *Nott. Boro. Recs*, pp. 332–4; *Hertford County Records*, I, pp. 140, 144, 166, 171, 253, 255, 292–3, 311, 315–16, 318, 329; II, pp. 2–3, 28; Narcissus Luttrell, *A Brief Historical Relation of State Affairs, from September 1678 to April 1714* (6 vols, Oxford, 1857), III, p. 209; Landau, *Justices*, p. 242; Wrightson and Levine, *Poverty and Piety*, p. 25; J. A. Sharpe, *Crime in Seventeenth-Century England: A County Study* (Cambridge, 1983), pp. 40–3, 183; Wendy Thwaites, 'The Corn Market and Economic Change: Oxford in the Eighteenth Century', *Midland History*, 16 (1991), p. 114; Outhwaite, *Dearth*, p. 29. Interestingly, even after the victory of free trade ideology lifted most barriers in the grain trade in the nineteenth century, mainstream commentators did not shy from calling for government to intervene directly in the food trade to protect consumers from adulteration: Searle, *Morality*, pp. 91–7.

[129] Thompson, on the other hand, claimed that the harsh punishment of disobedient 'inferiors' was evidence of the *absence* of 'paternalism', ignoring the interconnected nature of patriarchal authority and paternal duty: Thompson, *Customs in Common*, pp. 47–9.

masterless by directly intervening to subdue the perceived insolence of 'inferiors'. For example, 'if Parents or Masters neglect to redress so great an Evil as that of *Idleness* in their Families, the Magistrate himself is obliged to look after it', noted Peter Nourse in his 1708 homily on the subject. Failure to smother this 'Vice' in its infancy would, he argued, inevitably lead not only to ungodliness but also to 'the ruin of Societies'.[130] The whole social order thus depended on the willingness of political authorities to reform forcibly anyone who appeared unwilling to work, and some local office-holders embarked on this quest with fearsome enthusiasm.

Thomas Cooke, preaching at Worcester Cathedral in 1702, gave the civic officials in his audience another reason to fulfil this particular patriarchal duty:

> If Men are naturally prone to sloth, it is more kind to Correct them by a Rod, than by a Gibbet; Idleness is such a path way to Destruction that to indulge Men in it, is to lull them into a Lethargy, and to foment and aggravate the Distemper.

In order to save these poor souls from their self-destructive habits, Cooke suggested that perhaps 'the best Charity' would be the discipline provided by the workhouse, which could both 'compel the Lazy' and 'succour the distressed'.[131] This attitude was typical of the great mass of sermons and pamphlets produced on this subject, especially those ardent polemics by men associated with the Societies for the Reformation of Manners and the Society for the Promotion of Christian Knowledge, but it also found expression in the threats and coercion employed by magistrates trying to 'Correct' disorder in the labour market.[132] Children in charity schools, paupers in

---

130 Peter Nourse, *Practical Discourses on Several Subjects being Some Select Homilies of the Church of England, Put into a New Method and Modern Style* (2 vols, 1708), I, p. 127. This was explicitly based on the Elizabethan 'Homily Against Idleness' which likewise described the duty of 'all Masters of households' and 'all Officers' in the same breath: *Certain Sermons or Homilies*, II, p. 323. For more general denunciations of idleness see pp. 89–90, 94, 97, 100–101 above.

131 Cooke, *Workhouses the Best Charity*, pp. 21, 24–5. Two years later, parliament passed 'An Act for the erecting a Work-House in the City of Worcester, and for setting the Poor on Work there': *Statutes of the Realm*, VIII, pp. 262–8 (2&3 Anne c.8).

132 For more on the logic and polemic of labour discipline see Slack, *From Reformation*, pp. 110–14, 133–41; Slack, *Poverty and Policy*, pp. 195–200; chapters by Fissell and Hitchcock in Lee Davison, Tim Hitchcock, and Robert Shoemaker (eds), *Stilling the Grumbling Hive: The Response to Social and Economic Problems in England, 1689–1750* (Stroud, 1992); Joanna Innes, 'Prisons for the Poor: English Bridewells, 1555–1800', in Francis Snyder and Douglas Hay (eds), *Labour, Law and Crime: An Historical Perspective* (London, 1987), pp. 77–92; Steve Hindle, 'Labour Discipline, Agricultural Service and the Households of the Poor in England, c.1640–1730', in Joanne McEwan and Pamela Sharpe (eds), *Accommodating Poverty: The Housing and Living Arrangements of the English Poor, c.1600–1850* (Houndmills, 2011), pp. 169–90. For examples of implementation see the sources cited below p. 124 n. 135.

workhouses, vagrants in bridewells: all potentially faced the wrath of a dedicated governor insisting on the necessity of 'industry'. Even those poor people who never set foot inside one of these intimidating institutions might be pressured into a lengthy term of service – as a 'parish apprentice' or simply as a servant – by county justices at the petty sessions. This expansive conception of patriarchal authority can be heard most clearly in the words of one pamphleteer writing at the end of the seventeenth century: 'if a Master, or Overseer of one Family, have such an Independant Right [to discipline his inferiors], in the *Paternal* and *Domestick* Government thereof, shall a Master or Overseer of many Families (*for so an Overseer of the Poor is*) have less Power, or not assert it?'[133]

Hostility to wilful idleness was usually accompanied by a harsh attitude towards insubordination among employees, which could include defying convention by seeking high wages. According to the logic of familial interdependence, if bakers and corn-dealers had no right to take excessive profits, then surely craftsmen and other manual workers had no right to take advantage of labour shortages by demanding higher rates for their services. These sentiments regularly received public expression in laws and magisterial orders. Hence the parliament of 1666 announced the passage of an act to prevent London building workers from using 'the common calamity' of the fire as 'a pretence to extort unreasonable or excessive wages'.[134] A similar situation appears to have arisen in Hertfordshire in the late 1680s, provoking the county's justices to issue the following order:

> Whereas the Licentious humours of some servants have prevailed so far upon the Lenity and good Nature of their Masters, that they have advanced the charge of their Wages ... [and] they will not worke but at such times, and in such manner as they please; and when their worke is most necessary, they oftentimes Leave the same, if not their services; ... [the justices believe] that the execution of the Lawes heretofore made against the disorders and misdemeanours of such servants is the best expedient to remedy the same.

So, in an effort to stave off the advance of licentiousness, they proceeded to set the wages rates 'for the several artificers, Labourers and Servants in the County' and demand the strict enforcement of the Statute of Artificers 'for their better government'.[135] Such idioms reveal the underlying logic that

---

[133] Richard Dunning, *Bread for the Poor* (1698), p. 11.
[134] *Statutes of the Realm*, V, pp. 603–12 (19 Car. II, c. 8). This act gave justices additional powers in setting building wage rates and prices of building materials.
[135] *Hertford County Records*, VI, p. 405. For more examples of the implementation of wage rate and compulsory service see CA, Q/SO1, pp. 20, 118, 122, 166; DRO, 1579A/9/35, pp. 47–48; ERO, Q/SBb 47/8; Northants. RO, Misc. Q.S. Recs, I, n.p. (Oct. 1695); SRO–I, B/105/2/5, fol. 37, B/105/2/10, fol. 127; *Minutes of Quarter Sessions of Kesteven*, II, p. 417; HMC, *Reports on Manuscripts in Various Collections* (8 vols, no. 55,

made policies such as these so popular among the gentry. Inspired by a deep commitment to patriarchal authority, the magistracy of later Stuart England loudly condemned any sign of assertiveness as insubordination, especially if it seemed to threaten the master's ability to manage his household economy as he saw fit.

The common thread weaving together all these diverse elements in the fabric of governance was a familial understanding of political authority. This logic gave seemingly incongruous policies an underlying unity which is too easily elided by conventional categories of analysis. If one used more modern terminology, some of these would be defined as social welfare, some as consumer protection, some as labour regulation, and so on. But this approach, by relying on the framework used in twenty-first-century public policy discussions, would obscure the way analogical thinking influenced the later Stuart political economy – instead, it is essential to look at the words contemporaries themselves used. Here, even into the eighteenth century, the master was an 'Oeconomical Father' to his household, the magistrate was a 'father of the country', and the king was a 'Common Parent to his People'. These idioms suggest an authority akin to the sort advocated by sixteenth-century commentators, far removed from the bureaucratised power of today's corporate hierarchies or political directives.[136] The frequency with which contemporaries evoked Isaiah 49:23 – wherein kings are 'nursing fathers' and queens are 'nursing mothers' – attests to the central place of the familial model in later Stuart culture.[137] Indeed, several scholars have noted that the magistrates of Georgian Britain (and their apologists) often seem to have agreed with these sentiments.[138]

Nonetheless, cultural continuities should not be mistaken for stasis. Even the briefest of comparisons between the political economies of the sixteenth, seventeenth, and eighteenth centuries reveals significant shifts in policy and its implementation. Changes in the economic climate meant different governments often confronted very different sets of issues, and long-term trends could shift obligations from one branch of the tree of state to another. This was, in fact, one of the chief strengths of the patriarchal conception

London, 1901–13), I, pp. 322–33; W. E. Minchinton (ed.), *Wage Regulation in Pre-Industrial England* (Newton Abbot, 1972), pp. 124–9, 181–6 and passim; Donald Woodward, 'The Determination of Wage Rates in the Early Modern North of England', *Economic History Review*, New Series, 47:1 (1994), pp. 27–8; Kussmaul, *Servants*, pp. 166–7, 203 n. 3; Landau, *Justices*, pp. 215, 217–18 (table 7); Hindle, 'Labour Discipline'.

[136] For a typical sixteenth-century equation of patriarchal, political and economic authority see Desiderius Erasmus, *The Education of a Christian Prince*, Lester Born ed. and trans. (1516; New York, 1963), pp. 170–71.

[137] Josselin, *Diary*, p. 464 (10 Jan 1660); Capp, *Astrology*, p. 103. At least ten sermons on this passage were published between 1680 and 1716, and it was often mentioned even if it was not used as base-text: Letsome, *The Preacher's Assistant*, p. 85.

[138] Clark, *English Society*, pp. 173–86, 267–71; Jones, *Tree of Commonwealth*, p. 267; Richard Price, *British Society, 1680–1880* (Cambridge, 1999), pp. 300, 324.

of political authority: its flexibility. Rather than demanding uniform administration of pre-established policy, this model assumed that a dutiful 'father of his country' would exercise his own discretion in deciding whether to resolve a particular problem through private pressure, public intervention, exemplary punishment, personal largesse, or some combination thereof. It could thus inspire the sweeping patriarchal initiatives of the Tudors and early Stuarts, such as the Books of Orders and the Depopulation Commissions, but it could also redirect this political energy into the 'routine' paternalism of 'self-activating' local magistrates, a group which became ever-more influential in the late seventeenth century.[139] The familial mode of governance, instead of being inextricably linked to a particular policy or office, depended on a broadly shared faith in certain moral precepts. If authority was still inseparable from the duties of provision and protection, if inequality was still regarded as the foundation of social well-being, if deferential subordination was still lauded as a virtue, then the looming figure of the father would continue to cast his long shadow over English economic culture.

4 Redress: Petitions and Appeals

The 'well-ordered' world described by moralists did not, of course, exist in practice. Neither lowly servants and labourers nor prosperous masters and gentlemen unerringly performed their social duties with the level of devotion expected of them. The moralists themselves recognised the gap between principle and practice, many of them loudly condemning this disparity in jeremiads bewailing England's apparent decent into laxity, vice, and disorder. The issue, then, was how to remedy this dangerous state of affairs.

When 'dependants' failed to perform their assigned social functions there were numerous options open to their aggrieved 'superiors', and the foregoing discussion has described some of these disciplinary possibilities: corporal punishment, public humiliation, fines, imprisonment, or some combination thereof. Exponents of the familial model lauded 'due correction' as a legitimate and necessary response to disobedience, insubordination, and other acts of 'petty treason'.[140] But a complication arose when it was actually these 'inferiors' who were the aggrieved party, because conventional notions of order and governance assumed that injustices could only be redressed by

---

[139] Braddick, *State Formation*, p. 165. It is thus hardly surprising to learn that the 'highly serviceable authority system' of 'paternalism' continued to show itself to be 'infinitely adaptable' in the nineteenth century: Price, *British Society*, pp. 300, 305.

[140] For examples of the tendency to equate disobedience or resistance among employees to 'petty treason' and 'treachery' see Levine and Wrightson, *Industrial Society*, p. 376; *The Servants Calling* (1725), p. 32.

the 'head' of the relevant social unit. This right (and duty) belonged solely to the patriarchal leader of the family or nation. We may experience great 'Sufferings' or 'Oppression', noted a minister preaching at the Gloucester assizes of 1706, yet 'we can have no Redress but from the Magistrate'.[141]

This lack of legitimate authority did not translate into an acceptance of passivity. In its place, one finds near universal support for the principle and practice of petitioning as the ideal means of redress. Reinforced by centuries of Christian teaching on prayer and supplication, the petitionary model had long been an essential part of English political culture and it became even more conspicuous over the course of the seventeenth century.[142] In moments of crisis, especially periods such as 1647–50 and 1679–80, tens of thousands of people signed their names to mass petitions addressed to the king or parliament, while in less turbulent times smaller groups of citizens routinely employed this method in order to capture the attention of government authorities.[143] By the end of the seventeenth century this had become a crucial component in almost every political campaign, and people from all ranks of society were able to voice complaints about affairs of state through the petitioning process. Yet these formalised written appeals, backed by a list of signatures or marks, represented only one manifestation of the petitionary style. The same logic could produce 'petitions' that were public or private, generic or personalised, written or spoken, communal or individual.

Unsurprisingly, this mode of seeking redress was not confined to partisan politics – indeed, most later Stuart petitions probably focused on more material concerns. This was certainly the case for those received by county or borough magistrates. A sample of 243 sent to the justices at quarter sessions in the West and North Ridings of Yorkshire during this period reveal a pattern that was probably mirrored elsewhere.[144] Poor relief was the central issue in fully half (51%), but rates and taxation were also important (13%). The rest concerned a variety of other issues ranging from those with direct material implications – such as reimbursements of various expenses, orders for payment of withheld wages, and the release of poor imprisoned debtors – to those with little economic relevance – such as complaints about legal proceedings and requests for discharge from onerous offices. Those sent to

---

[141] Luke Beaulieu, *The Reciprocal Duty Betwixt Kings and Subjects, Impartially Stated, in a Sermon … in the Cathedral Church of Gloucester at the Assizes* (1706), p. 13.

[142] For a sociological analysis of the way that, in 'both form and content, petitions to God and to political authorities have had much in common' see Nicholls, 'Addressing God', p. 125. See also Ch. 3.5 below

[143] David Zaret, *Origins of Democratic Culture: Printing, Petitions and the Public Sphere in Early-Modern England* (Princeton, 2000), ch. 8; Knights, *Representation and Misrepresentation*, ch. 3; idem, 'Participation and Representation before Democracy: Petitions and Addresses in Pre-Modern Britain', in Ian Shapiro, Susan C. Stokes, Elizabeth Jean Wood, and Alexander S. Kirshner (eds), *Political Representation* (Cambridge, 2009), pp. 35–60.

[144] WYAS–W, QS 1/1–57; NYCRO, QSB 1696–1699.

the London Court of Aldermen were even more likely to relate to economic matters.[145] Here, most petitioners sought 'the freedom of the city', which granted a right to practise a trade, though many others requested release from apprenticeships or appointments to civic posts.

The petitions addressed to national authorities were less overwhelmingly economic in intent. Nonetheless, here too politics and religion were only occasionally the central concern. For example, later Stuart monarchs (and their councillors) received countless pleas from their subjects for pensions, corporate privileges, and other forms of economic patronage.[146] The petitions with greatest impact, however, were normally addressed to parliament, and these often focused directly on matters of trade, manufacturing or taxation. Many such petitions were noted in the *Journal of the House of Commons*, including the one received from 'the Fraternity of Skinners and Glovers' of Ludlow on 1 April 1697, which declared that the industry was 'a great Support to the poor People' of the town,

> but, of late, the great Taxes laid upon Salt, Alum, and Oil, with which the said Leather is dressed, hath so diminished the said Trade, that Half the working Glovers are already like to starve, for want of Work; and, if there should any further Tax be laid upon Leather it would prove almost, if not a total Destruction thereunto.[147]

This plaintive request was an entirely typical example of the numerous pleas received by parliament – indeed, its only distinction came from the fact that it was part of a much larger campaign in which English leatherworkers from all parts of the country presented over 150 petitions against the leather duty passed under William III.[148] The fact that a relatively minor issue could inspire a mobilisation of this size gives some indication of the prevalence of national petitioning during this era.

Each of these petitions incorporated elements from a common store of form and rhetoric. Nearly all of them – even those with undercurrents of criticism or menace – shared the idiom of loyalty, humility, and inferiority. Proclamations of subservience were never clearer than in the pleas of those seeking charity, especially the poor men and women who petitioned for relief from wealthier neighbours, parish officers, charitable trusts, and urban corporations. Scholars such as Steve Hindle and Ilana Ben-Amos have shown how these paupers routinely fell into rhetorical 'postures of humility'

---

[145] LMA, COL/CA/05/01/0001–0023.

[146] Some individual examples are cited below, but hundreds of these can be found in TNA, SP 29–35 and SP 44, especially SP 44/235–236, 249. In addition, other governmental bodies, such the Treasury Board (TNA, T 1) and the Navy Board (TNA, ADM 106) received large substantial numbers of petitions.

[147] *JHC*, XI, p. 764. For more examples see ibid., XII, pp. 57, 181, 556, etc.

[148] Brewer, *Sinews*, p. 233.

Reported reasons for needing relief in petitions to Quarter Sessions.

	Cumberland, 1686–1749	Yorkshire, 1666–1720
Age	186 (40%)	30 (36%)
Lameness	64 (14%)	15 (18%)
Blindness	40 (9%)	6 (7%)
Illness	25 (5%)	5 (6%)
Two or more children	93 (20%)	25 (30%)

Sources: Hindle, *On the Parish?* pp. 408–11 (465 petitions); WYAS–W, QS 1/5–57 (53 petitions); NYCRO, QSB 1686–1699 (30 petitions)

before potential benefactors, just as casual beggars knelt in a literal 'gesture of submission and gratitude'.[149] One imprisoned labourer in Northampton-shire even explicitly declared that he sought 'Charitable Compassion' of the magistrates 'with bleeding heart and bended knee'.[150] Paupers emphasised above all their dependency, often listing a whole series of reasons why they had to rely on the support of their superiors rather than 'making shift' on their own. Typical is the successful petition of Jane Stansfield of Horsforth (Yorks.) in 1705. She described herself as

> a distressed and destitute Widdow ... having formerly lived well By hard Labour and Industry, but now by reason of Age & infirmities, with other miseries inci-dent to the Body Attending this Life, Insomuch that she is Become very Indigent and poor, her Eye sight being very much Impared, & shee Aged above seventy years, Is not able to procure a Livelyhood without the speedy assistance of mone-thly Relief to supply her present want & necessity.[151]

Her plea included many of the claims found in other petitions of this sort. References to old age were especially common, with petitioners frequently complaining that they were 'past labour' and 'alltogether unable by reason of Infirmaties which commonly attends old age to procure unto themselves Mentenace to sustain their bodily healths'.[152] Many paupers mentioned specific disabilities or illnesses: crippled limbs, fading eyes, dismal wounds,

---

149 Hindle, *On the Parish?* p. 164; Ben-Amos, *Culture of Giving*, p. 1.

150 Northants. RO, QSR 1/153 (petition of Thomas Plackett of Helliden, 1694).

151 WYAS–W, QS 1/44/6/6. For more examples see Jeremy Boulton, 'Going on the Parish: The Parish Pension and its Meaning in the London Suburbs, 1640–1724', in Tim Hitchcock, Peter King, and Pamela Sharpe (eds), *Chronicling Poverty: The Voices and Strategies of the English Poor, 1640–1840* (London, 1997), pp. 26–32; Hindle, *On the Parish?* pp. 155–64, 407–28; Ben-Amos, *Culture of Giving*, ch. 6, esp. pp. 202–3.

152 HA, QSR 22/1692/391; WYAS–W, QS 1/20/7/6/4. For similar examples see NYCRO, QSB 1686/119; QSB 1691/335; QSB 1696/150.

and distempered minds (see table above).[153] One woman wrote of being 'sore afflicted with a cancer in her face so that her nose is consumed therewith & lives in great sorrow & paine & not able work', but asked only for enough to pay a doctor.[154] Such graphic testaments to their helplessness made clear their profound reliance on the munificence fatherly benefactors, a point often re-emphasised in a concluding line wherein the petitioners 'Humbly Implore your Worships so to pitty their deplorable Condicion'.[155] By actively embracing their subordinate position, the thousands of desperately poor individuals like Jane Stansfield who made appeals for aid implicitly invoked the familial model with its attendant duties of paternal provision.

Simple pleas for support made up the vast majority of requests received from those seeking parish relief or other forms of charity. Other types of petition, however, often included rhetorical elements that added several layers of complexity to otherwise generic texts. For instance, many displays of public supplication mixed conventional self-effacement with a hard edge of presumption, perhaps even of entitlement. In March 1702, for example, 'the Mercers, Lacemen, Milliners, Weavers and Wyerdrawers … of London' published 'an humble Address' to the new queen:

> All hail, Great Lady; may Your happy reign
> With Glories shine, our sinking Arts maintain;
> Let all th' Angellick Choir, Your Fame resound
> That Sacred Minute, when Your Head is Crown'd;
> Whilst we Your Loyal Subjects, Suffer e'en
> Reduc'd t' extremity; Yet always seen,
> And heard to Pray, good God Protect the Queen.
> And now Dread Madam know; without Your Care,
> We're quite neglected: Mournings cause Despair;
> But questionless, Your Royal Princely Breast,
> Like Providence, will not forget the least:
> For thousands now will pinch with Jaws of Want,
> Unless You do us help; which pray God grant.[156]

While this petition used deferential terminology ('humble', 'Loyal', 'Pray'), it actually left little room for the queen's prerogative. By simultaneously raising and dismissing the possibility of royal neglect, the London tradesmen tried to make their preferred outcome into the 'questionless' result, a strategy

---

[153] HA, QS 24/1698/155 ('Afflicted with the Numbe Palsey'); WYAS–W, QS1/20/6/6/9 ('hir shoulder boone & her arme broken'); HA, QSR 22/1692/391 ('almost blind'); NYCRO, QSB 1686/126 ('grieviously wounded by a fall from a house'); WYAS–W, QS 1/44/6/6('distempered').

[154] WYAS–W, QS 1/44/6/6 (petition of Mary Denton, 1705).

[155] WYAS–W, QS 1/13/6/6/8, and passim.

[156] *An Elegy, From the Mercers, Lacemen, Milliners, Weavers and Wyerdrawers* (1702).

implicitly applying the pressure of public opinion while loudly reiterating their reverence for the power of the crown. The kingdom's shoemakers adopted the same approach when they published a 'humble Petition to the Queen and Parliament' several years later. In rousing verse, they announced that they would drink to the health of 'our gracious Sovereign' and 'Our noble Peers' in the expectation that the government 'could do no less' than grant them 'Redress without Delay' on the issue of leather exports.[157] By accompanying fulsome praise with confident predictions of imminent paternalist support, these tradesmen and craftsmen helped to set public expectations and thus actively shaped the contours of political discussion.

Other petitioners used a more overt, unambiguous vocabulary: the idiom of disorder and disobedience. According to these types of appeals, some crucial pillar in the edifice of social hierarchy rested on the very same ground threatened by the particular grievance they sought to have redressed. In the case of petitioners seeking poor relief, this often meant drawing attention to parish officers who flouted the authority of the county magistrates. For instance, some paupers cited relief orders previously granted by the court which the overseers had then refused to pay. In 1720, for example, an needy old man named Abraham Midgley appealed to the justices of the West Riding of Yorkshire, claiming that a local magistrate had ordered an increase in his allowance but 'the Present Overseer Denies to Perform the Order' and, moreover, 'your Petitioner having often been putt off by Promissess of Amendment but hath received none but instead thereof Part of his former Allowance taken off so that the more Incapable he is of working the Less releef he receives'.[158] Even darker allegations were made by John Preston of Holyfield (Yorks.) in 1686. According to him, not only did the parish officers disobey a previous relief order, they also beat Preston and brazenly 'saye that the Justices of Peace shall not Command their purses'.[159] In response, the magistrates promptly issued a warrant against the officers for this act of gross insubordination. Other petty authorities could also be criticised using these idioms. John Brown, a poor debtor imprisoned in Northampton gaol, had been ordered to be discharged after agreeing to go into military service, but he claimed that the gaoler, 'loving mony more then loyalty', refused to obey the order until paid a large fee.[160] Such perfidious behaviour – ignoring

---

[157] *The Gentle Craft's Complaint: or, the Jolly Shoe-makers Humble Petition to the Queen and Parliament* (1710?), in *RB*, III, pp. 662–3.
[158] WYAS–W, QS 1/57/6/6. For other examples of parochial officers' alleged disobedience see WYAS–W, QS 1/17/1/6/5; QS 1/20/6/6/8; QS 1/49/5/6 (petition of Christopher Coats, 1710); NYCRO, QSB 1686/128; QSB 1691/332. For a governor of a house of correction accused of 'misbehaviour' for not providing a sufficient allowance to poor prisoners whereby 'two of them have been lately starved to death' see *Middlesex Sessions Books*, p. 191.
[159] WYAS–W, QS 1/25/5/6.
[160] Northants. RO, QSR 1/153 (petition of John Brown, 1694).

the dominion of the magistracy and the security of the state for the sake of personal gain – was unlikely to be tolerated.

A similar rhetoric sometimes appeared in print. It was not difficult, for instance, to present hard-dealing middlemen as defiant opponents of the government's right to enforce order in the marketplace, and angry consumers provided a clear example of this reasoning in 1710 when they published a plea for parliament to quash 'the Insolence of the Bakers in and about the City of London' by reaffirming the Assize of Bread. The petition described the bakers as impudent men who 'bid Defiance to the Magistrates' by over-pricing their bread 'as tho' there had been no Laws, or Magistrates in this City'. Allegedly, these audacious criminals had even threatened to 'make a Famine' and 'made their Boasts of late, that there is no Law to Punish them'.[161] The consumers who spoke out against this 'Insolence' obviously believed that redress for their concerns would be more likely if parliamentar-ians saw the 'Defiance' of the bakers as imperilling the authority of London's magistracy, and they were very probably right – though the impact of this petition is unknown, the bill was soon passed. Laceworkers adopted a similar tone during the public debate about ribbons and top-knots in the late 1680s. Their appeal was slightly more complex, but they essentially framed it as a defence of hierarchy 'against the *Rude Rabble*' who condemned these fash-ions because they wanted to 'keep their Betters in awe' by publicly 'flouting' their 'Gentile Mode' of dress. In response, the weavers urged: 'Let Gallants go still like Persons of Fame, / since they are most Nobly descended: / And as for those that will be so rude … By some strict Order let them be subdu'd'.[162] Here, the petitioners claimed to be defending the privilege of gentlefolk to distinguish themselves from the commons, thus protecting the very founda-tion of gentility.

In many other cases, it was the patriarchal family that appeared to be at risk of collapse, imperilled by the inability of poor householders to provide for their dependants. John Vitty of Bedale (Yorks.), an old soldier, was one such father. His petition of 1686 described how he had 'falen into decay and hath fower smale children & little to releive them on' and asked for 'the honorable Bench to bestow some thing on him towards the releife of himselfe wife & children', which they soon did.[163] Vitter was hardly alone in citing the need to support a family as a reason for granting aid – around 20 to 30 per cent of the petitioners in Yorkshire and Cumberland who sought poor relief mentioned having two or more children (see table above). Nor were paupers the only petitioners to use this rhetoric. For instance, a prisoner pleaded for release because he had 'a poore wife at home and

161 *Reasons Humbly offer'd to … Parliament assembled, for … the Assize of Bread* (1710). For more on law and criminality see below pp. 171–2.
162 *The Weavers Request* (1685–8), in *PB*, IV, p. 355. For the examples from debate about top-knots see *PB*, VI, pp. 310, 362–3, 365–7; V, p. 412.
163 NYCRO, QSB 1686/127.

Six children who are in a very poore and distressed condicion for want of your petitioner being at home to work for their maintainance', and an impoverished former grocer requested a chapman's permit because then he 'could much contribute towards the support and maintainance of himself, his wife and foure Children'.[164] Moreover, the trope of starving wives and children regularly appeared in printed complaints and in published tales of petitionary situations.[165] Indeed, some complainants explicitly invoked the possible collapse of the 'well-ordered household' as the primary reason for declaring their grievances, as did an appeal received by the justices of the North Riding in 1696. Here, the petitioner claimed that, because of a fire which burned down his home and workshop, he had 'to apply Himselfe to your Honorable Bench humbly to crave theire charity & Kindness in this necessitous condition, that his wife & family starve not, nor poore Small Children *forced to the loose and idle life of begging*'.[166] By linking the inadequacy of paternal provision to the breakdown of familial order, these petitioners spoke directly to the anxieties of 'superiors' of all sorts.

Yet sometimes the patriarchs themselves were the source of disorder and this too could provoke demands for redress that played upon familial logic. This type of multi-tiered vertical relationship was actually a particularly common feature in later Stuart petitioning. One often finds aggrieved men and women appealing to a higher authority against their more immediate superiors, though some commentators only reluctantly endorsed the legitimacy of such a practice, despite its firm foundation in both law and tradition. Richard Mayo, a dissenting minister based in London, addressed this issue in his *Present for Servants*, first published in 1693 and reprinted twice in the early eighteenth century:

Is there no Remedy for a poor *Servant oppress'd* by a Churlish *Nabal*, no way to avoid his Rigour, and unjust Severity? Why Yes, He may for the present

---

164 WYAS–W, QS 1/38/4/6 (petition of Joseph Rishforth, 1699); QS 1/49/5/6 (petition of Thomas Benson, 1710). Other petitioners who mentioned the demands of needy children included a man seeking a minor court office and a sailor seeking unpaid wages: ERO, Q/SBb 14/7; TNA, ADM 106/483/108.

165 For examples of paternal anxiety about starving families and the complaints or petitions this engendered see *The Citizens Complaint* (1663), p. 3; *Reasons Humbly Offered to ... Parliament by the Drapers, Mercers, Haberdashers, Grocers, Hosiers, and other Trading House-keepers* (1675); *A True Sence of Sorrow* (1685–8), in PB, II, p. 53; *The Sea Martyrs* (1691), in PB, V, p. 375; *The Humble Petition of the Poor Journymen Shooe-makers of the City of London, Westminster and Southwark, and their Brethern of the Countrey* (1691?); 26 Nov., 1711, *Spectator*, issue 232; *The Female Manufacturer's Complaint* (1719), p. 7. For an excellent analysis of the role of gendered and familial ideals in popular protest see Walter, 'Faces', pp. 96–125. See also the discussion of women's role as defenders of 'household' or 'common' property in Garthine Walker, 'Keeping it in the Family: Crime and the Early Modern Household', in Berry and Foyster (ed.), *Family*, esp. pp. 92, 94.

166 NYCRO, QSB 1696/152 (emphasis added).

withdraw himself prudently to avoid his Master's rage; and tho' in case of the utmost extremity the Servant may obtain the help of the Magistrate against an unreasonable Master, yet usually the Apostle's Caution is sufficient, to forbear all muttering returns.[167]

So, while Mayo taught that patient passivity ought to be the usual response to abusive patriarchs, he also raised the possibility of a servant seeking 'help' from further up the social or political hierarchy.

The poor and disenfranchised, unlike educated casuists, embraced this notion boldly and unreservedly. Notions of familial duty were clearest in the case of appeals from wives and mothers who had been cursed with merciless husbands. A Norfolk woman named Elizabeth Cordy provided a sad example of this in 1699 when she sought the intervention of the county magistrates because her husband, Elias, not only 'frequently Beat & Bruise her' but also granted only a few shillings each year for the 'Maintenance' of their two children and refused to pay anything toward their rent. His reckless violence and paternal neglect set Elias in direct opposition to the ideal of 'good husbandry' and meant that he had forfeited the authority that normally came with the role of householder.[168] Magistrates also received great numbers of petitions on behalf of apprentices and servants against undutiful masters. These complaints provide a grim compendium of the numerous ways in which masters might fail to fulfil the obligations that they owed to their young charges: withholding their wages, refusing to instruct them in a trade, denying them food and necessities, sexually mistreating them, or crippling them through brutal beatings.[169] Hence, when the apprentice John Webster was subjected to repeated 'abuses' from his master in 1668, his mother appealed to the magistrates of York for remedy and they responded by releasing Webster from his apprenticeship.[170] The master's failure to be a dutiful patriarch forced the 'natural' parent to appeal to the paternal instincts of the political authorities: a situation showing both the strength and complexity of assumptions about parental duty.

Other types of workers who had complaints against their employers put them into practice by addressing themselves to local notables, influential

---

[167] Mayo, A Present for Servants, p. 36 (citing Titus 2:9).

[168] NRO, NCR Case 12b (1), pt. 2 (information of Elizabeth Cordy, 30 Jun 1699). See also the petition of 1681 from Elizabeth Ward of Wearley (Yorks.), who requests an order for her estranged husband to contribute to the maintenance of their children in 1681: WYAS–W, QS 1/20/6/6/5.

[169] CA, Q/SO2, pp. 40, 57; ERO, Q/SO 3, pp. 345–6, Q/SO 5, pp. 94–5; ERO, Q/SBb 15/29; HA, QSR 29/1716/20; SRO–I, B/105/2/5, fol. 33; YCA, F.7, pp. 480, 510; F.8, pp. 82–3, 146, 171.

[170] YCA, F.8, pp. 151, 156. For more examples of parents petitioning on behalf of their children against abusive or negligent masters see CUA, V.C.Ct/I/14, fols 25–6; Amussen, Ordered Society, p. 160; Capp, When Gossips Meet, pp. 135–6; Paul Griffiths, Youth and Authority: Formative Experiences in England, 1560–1640 (Oxford, 1996), pp. 312, 317.

officeholders, government officials, and sometimes even the king or queen. The shipwrights and caulkers of Chatham naval yard, for example, petitioned the Navy Commissioners in June of 1668 for long overdue wages to 'preserve their families from ruin', complaining bitterly that their manager refused to pay them and, with two years of salaries in arrear, 'their families are denied trust [i.e. credit], and cannot subsist'. Less than a week later the government sent a large sum 'for paying men off in the yards'.[171] Examples of other workmen seeking redress through similar processes are not difficult to find: Tyneside colliers successfully complained about unpaid wages and other 'great oppression' by mine owners in a petition 'to be presented to his Majesty' in 1662; the weavers and shearmen of Tamworth requested aid from Lord Weymouth as an antidote to 'their poor condition and the severity of their masters' in 1711; and commercial seamen regularly petitioned the High Court of Admiralty during this period against captains who failed to provide adequate food or who abused their authority.[172]

Likewise, tenants sometimes successfully appealed to landlords against the 'arbitrary and tyrannical' behaviour of estate stewards, occasionally trekking all the way to London to make their case.[173] Perhaps the most famous appeared in the balladeer's tale of the poor tenant of the Crown in Northumberland who, when threatened with eviction by a local lawyer-bailiff, travelled to the royal court and petitioned the king directly. Despite his 'bold' attitude, the 'plain' man soon received redress thanks to 'the Kings great mercy in Righting wrongs'.[174] In other cases, it was the landlords themselves who were condemned. In 1691, for example, Yorkshire magistrates received petitions from two tenants of William Thompson, esq., of Beverley, complaining that they had been 'thrown out of possession by his Consent' and were 'now destitute of houseing'. They asked to 'be Relieved accordingly as you think Convenient', suggesting that they hoped for aid from their former parish and perhaps direct intervention on their behalf.[175]

The potential impact of these petitions varied enormously, with some complainants showing much more persistence and sophistication than others. One particularly concerted effort was the campaign by the 'market

---

[171] CSPD, Charles II, 1667–8, pp. 443, 455, 463, 473. Five days earlier Col. Thomas Middleton claimed to have been 'almost torn to pieces by the workmen at the yard for their weekly pay'. See also the reports of similar incidents at the Woolwich shipyard around the same time: ibid., pp. 225–6, 456, 463.

[172] Extracts from the Records of the Company of Hostmen of Newcastle-upon-Tyne (Surtees Society, vol. 105, Durham, 1901), p. 127; Hainsworth, Stewards, p. 159; Rediker, Between, pp. 222–3. Unsurprisingly, the steward who passed the poor tradesmen's message to Lord Weymouth noted that 'many of them have great families to maintain'.

[173] Hainsworth, Stewards, pp. 51–2.

[174] The King & Northern-man (c.1684–6), in PB, I, pp. 538–9. This ballad was first licensed to Richard Cotes in 1633, re-entered in 1675, and reprinted at least five times by 1705.

[175] NYCRO, QSB 1961/336–337.

people' of London against the 'many Enormities and Oppressions committed by the Farmers [i.e. lessees] of the City Markets', which apparently included 'extorting' unreasonable rates and other 'Ill Usages' that caused 'the Inhancing the Rates of Provisions, &c.'. They made a successful 'Complaint' to a parliamentary committee in 1676, but by the end of the century they felt forced to 'Humbly' publish a petition to the mayor and council claiming that the new manager 'Repeats and Continues the Abuses your Petitioners formerly complained of, to our very great Burden and Oppression'. They then 'Humbly' threatened to make an 'Application to the next Sessions of Parliament, unless this Honourable Court do in the mean time take our deplorable Condition into their serious Consideration … And otherwise provide for our Redress according to the Merits of our Case'.[176] The superficially humble language of the market traders indicated that they clearly understood their place at the bottom the London hierarchy, but also knew that the authority of the lessees could be trumped by the civic magistrates who could, in turn, be overruled by the power of parliament. Yet, this long-running, highly articulate campaign was very different from the more common attempts to use petitions to turn the power of one patriarch against the abuses of another.

Much more typical were the countless requests for intervention sent to magistrates from paupers who had been denied relief by parish overseers or vestrymen. Hundreds of these appeals have survived from the later Stuart period and, as Steve Hindle has shown, they offer 'narratives distilled from a volatile compound of frustration, desperation, and obsequiousness'.[177] Only a few appellants claimed that parochial authorities tried to 'abuse' or 'threaten' them and even fewer directly condemned overseers as 'uncharitable and inhumane' or 'unmerciful and savage'.[178] But all of these petitions – by their very existence – proclaimed that the poor might have a part in calling their superiors to account.

Of course, the people of later Stuart England knew that sometimes expressing themselves through words on page was not enough. A long list of signatures at the bottom of a cogent petition could certainly have an impact, but seeing those signatures embodied in a large crowd noisily arriving outside one's door could make a much deeper impression. Sir John Brownley of Stamford, Lincolnshire, had one such experience at the height of the

---

[176] *The Petition of the Oppressed Market People, Humbly offer'd to the Consideration of the Lord Mayor, Aldermen, and Common Council of the City of London* (1699), pp. 1–2, 17–19. 'Reprinted for the Public Good' in *The Oppressions of the Market-people: or, The Extortions of the Farmers of the City-Markets* (1720). For more on this case see LMA, COL/CC/01/01/050, fols 84–5, 92–3.
[177] Hindle, *On the Parish?* pp. 361, 405–32, 445–6 (quotation at p. 415).
[178] WYAS–W, QS 1/20/6/6/9; QS 1/25/5/6 (petition of John Preston, 1686); QS 1/49/5/6 (petition of Catherine Robinson, 1710); HA, QSR 12/1662/467; Hindle, *On the Parish?* p. 414.

recoinage crisis in June of 1696, when 'a great company' of local people got together and marched to Brownley's house, where they proclaimed their deep allegiance to the government and the church but also pleaded for aid, claiming to not have any passable coin. In response, Brownley offered them £15 and 'let them go to the cellar, where they drunk God bless King William, the Church of England and all the loyal healths that they could think on'.[179] The crowd remained unimpeachably submissive throughout the whole event – incessantly declaring their loyalty to every possible authority, beseeching mercy rather than demanding redress – and yet they must have inspired fear as well as pity. Of course, this is merely one example among many. Whether assembling in the thousands outside parliament or camping in a family on the porch of a parish church, the poor who used their own presence to publicise their grievances were part of a long tradition of 'petitioning in word and deed'.[180]

The endless variation in the issues, audience, and rhetoric found in early modern petitions cannot obscure the essential similarity of the assumptions shared by every one of them, for they each had at their heart an apparent paradox – they relied on both assertiveness and deference. After all, as the examples above indicate, most people had no qualms about reminding patriarchs of their social duties and even elite commentators grudgingly accepted the legitimacy of this approach. However, these same appeals were also inherently deferential, as they ultimately 'deferred' to their superiors for solutions rather than attempting to solve their grievances through direct action. The power to grant aid, change policy or punish abuses belonged to those who received the petition, not to those who sent it. Thus, petitionary logic strengthened hierarchy and inequality even while it offered a voice to the poor, making the relationship between ruler and ruled flexible enough to withstand otherwise dangerous tensions.

A few desperate men and women took the notion of familial obligations still further, using the threat of famished children to attempt to justify

---

[179] Abraham de la Pryme, *The Diary of Abraham de la Pryme, the Yorkshire Antiquary*, Charles Jackson ed. (Surtees Society, vol. 54, Durham, 1870), pp. 95–6.

[180] Walter and Wrightson, 'Dearth', p. 41. For examples of demonstrations outside Parliament, namely those of the shoemakers in 1714 and of the weavers in 1675, 1689, 1696, 1697, and 1720, see HMC, *Report on the Manuscripts of His Grace the Duke of Portland, Preserved at Welbeck Abbey* (no. 29, 8 vols, London, 1891–1931), V, pp. 452, 454; *Correspondence of the Family of Hatton*, Edward Maunde ed. (2 vols, Camden Society, n.s., 22–23, 1878), II, pp. 138–9; *JHL*, XIV, pp. 311–15; James Vernon, *Letters Illustrative of the Reign of William III from 1696 to 1708 Addressed to the Duke of Shrewsbury by James Vernon*, G. P. R. James ed. (3 vols, London, 1841), I, pp. 76–7; Luttrell, *Brief Historical Relation*, IV, pp. 167, 172, 174–5, 177, 179; William Maitland, *History and Survey of London* (3rd edn, 2 vols, 1760), p. 530. For squatters on church porches see Hindle, *On the Parish?* pp. 319–21.

distinctly undeferential acts of theft and violence.[181] However, as might be expected, educated commentators – including the clergymen who reported these convicts' unsettling excuses – roundly condemned any such excuses for overtly criminal attempts at redress. The petitionary model, on the other hand, could be embraced by both rich and poor alike, appealing to the prejudices of the powerful while conveying the grievances of the weak. By the early modern period, petitioning had become an indispensable element not only in political culture but also in economic and social relations more generally. Although appellate logic had an exceedingly ancient lineage, it thrived in the conditions of the late seventeenth century thanks to the rise of novel institutions such as the poor relief system and the growing eminence of older ones such as parliament. Moreover, this logic stretched along a continuum extending from abject pleas by individual paupers through to noisy demonstrations by menacing crowds and national campaigns by well-organised artisanal groups.[182] Of course, these appeals must have met failure at least as often as they achieved success, but they were nonetheless unparalleled in their ubiquity and diversity. The poor pushed their superiors into action by following a petitionary instinct instilled through many years of struggle.

5 Conclusions

As we now know, the household was the engine of the English economy well into the eighteenth century. Familial logic, the less tangible partner of the household itself, had similarly deep and enduring economic influence. Yet, the impact of this mode of thought does not feature prominently in most of our histories of later Stuart society.[183] Even when scholars have acknowledged the presence of this powerful image in economic discourse, they have often portrayed this type of analogical thinking as an archaic tradition soon marginalised by the rise of more 'modern' conceptual systems. Thus, much of the historiography has continued to rely on a theory of unilinear social development inherited from Marx and other nineteenth-century thinkers.

---

[181] For food rioters claiming that they had to feed their 'poor little Babes' see White, *The Charitable Farmer of Somersetshire*, pp. 2–3. For condemned thieves claiming that their crimes resulted from their 'Duty' to 'keep [their families] from Starving' see McKenzie, *Tyburn's Martyrs*, pp. 80–82.

[182] This continuum parallels the one described in Walter, 'Public Transcripts', pp. 128–46.

[183] For important books that include remarkably little discussion of the analogy of the household see Appleby, *Economic Thought*; Muldrew, *Economy of Obligation*; Glaisyer, *The Culture of Commerce*; Hunt, *Middling Sort*. For the main exception, which is focused almost exclusively on the economic thought of learned gentlemen, see Finkelstein, *Grammar of Profit*; eadem, *Harmony*.

According to this model, 'pre-modern' economic relations based on notions such as 'honour' or 'duty' inevitably collapsed when challenged by the incessant advance of English capitalism over the course of the seventeenth and eighteenth centuries.

This teleology, in which the ties that had once bound together superiors and inferiors became unloosed over the course of the sixteenth, seventeenth, and eighteenth centuries, can be found in most conventional accounts of social relations in early modern England. The terms used to describe this process are many and various – the decay of 'paternalism' and 'patriarchy', the growth of 'class' and 'contract' – but the long-term trajectory seems unmistakable. Hence, many scholars have depicted the later Stuart era as the culmination of these early modern trends, reducing this period to a minor tracking point on the 'great arch' of English social history.[184] Although the scholarship examining this issue is usually more nuanced than the historiography produced by Weber's 'spirit of capitalism' thesis, only a few historians have avoided subsuming this era into a larger narrative of economic 'modernisation'. As a result of these assumptions, the economic implications of the familial ideal have been obscured.

Traditionally, social historians have followed the formula first set out by Marx in his early polemical works, where he describes the brutal transition from 'feudalism' to 'capitalism':

> The bourgeoisie, wherever it has got the upper hand, has put an end to all feudal, patriarchal, idyllic relations. It has pitilessly torn asunder the motley feudal ties that bound man to his 'natural superiors', and has left remaining no other nexus between man and man than naked self-interest, than callous 'cash payment'.[185]

Specifically, he argued that 'the advent of manufacture' after the collapse of 'feudalism' changed the relationship between worker and employer. Although employment apparently retained 'a patriarchal tinge' in older sectors of the economy, Marx claimed that labour relations in 'manufacturing' soon 'lost almost all patriarchal complexion'.[186] This influential narrative was refined by Christopher Hill and E. P. Thompson, who together portrayed a world in which employers and workers ceased to think in terms of familial dependence, deference or duty. This trend, according to them, stretched across the seventeenth and eighteenth centuries, so that Defoe's

---

[184] This notion was coined, but not elaborated, in E. P. Thompson's 1965 essay 'The Peculiarities of the English', in *The Poverty of Theory and Other Essays* (London, 1978), pp. 47, 57, 86.

[185] Marx and Engels, *Communist Manifesto*, p. 82.

[186] Karl Marx, *The German Ideology*, C. J. Arthur ed. (London, 1974), p. 74. Based on context, he seems to date this development in England to the sixteenth and seventeenth centuries, and he is certainly referring to unmechanised 'manufacturing' (p. 72–4) rather than 'big industry' (p. 79).

spleeny complaint about 'the Insolence and Unsufferable Behaviour of Servants' in 1724 became a typical account of how 'economic rationalization nibbled (and had long been nibbling) through the bonds of paternalism'.[187] Other scholars have followed their lead, portraying the later Stuart period as a stepping stone on the path from the close, personal relations of the household to the contractual, self-interested relations of factory. John Rule, Robert Malcolmson, and Marcus Rediker have all described this as an era of 'proletarianization' in which employees experienced 'the movement from paternalistic forms of labour control to the contested forms of waged work'.[188] Historians have even argued that the relationship between masters and resident workers lost its 'patriarchal complexion' despite remaining ensconced in the family home. Bridget Hill and Ilana Ben-Amos, for example, have argued that 'the older paternalistic relationship between masters and servants was giving way to a stricter contractual one' in the late seventeenth century, thus rendering the household economy increasingly 'impersonal'. Apparently this soon led to weaker social bonds and fewer perceived obligations.[189] Andrea Finkelstein, despite her welcome attention to the economics of the familial analogy, has recently provided an apt summary of this interpretation. For her, the people of early modern England increasingly experienced a 'separation of the family from the workplace, in spirit if not in fact', and a growing division 'between the domestic and commercial spheres'.[190]

Measuring the 'spirit' of an economic activity is no simple task, but the evidence presented in this chapter does not easily accord with the picture painted by these scholars of a relationship rapidly losing its 'patriarchal complexion'. Instead, the ubiquitous images of masters as 'Fathers of Families' or 'Oeconomical Fathers' indicate the continuing strength of a deeply familial conception of labour relations, a conception occasionally voiced directly by the participants themselves. This was especially true in

[187] Christopher Hill, 'Pottage for Freeborn Englishmen', in his *Change and Continuity in Seventeenth-Century England* (London, 1974), pp. 219–38; idem, *Reformation to Industrial Revolution*, pp. 135–43, 216–18; Thompson, *Customs in Common*, pp. 36–42 (quotations at pp. 37, 39). In fact, Defoe's intemperate griping indicates that he had a very traditional, non-contractual view of the duties of the poor.

[188] Rediker, *Between*, esp. pp. 114–15, 199–204, 288–94 (quotation at p. 114). According to Rule, 'there was a tendency for employers [and employees] to opt out of the reciprocities implied in the traditional rhetoric of the master–servant relationship': John Rule, 'Employment and Authority: Masters and Men in Eighteenth-Century Manufacturing', in Paul Griffiths, Adam Fox, and Steve Hindle (eds), *The Experience of Authority in Early Modern England* (Basingstoke, 1996), p. 295. Malcolmson concentrated more on the late eighteenth century, but he too thought 'the demise of industrial paternalism' had begun in this earlier period: Malcolmson, *Life and Labour*, pp. 149–53 (quote at p. 152). For another discussion of labour 'being removed from the orbit of patriarchalism' over the long-term see Levine, *Reproducing Families*, ch. 2, quotation at p. 51.

[189] Hill, *Servants*, pp. 5, 17, 88–92; Ben-Amos, *Adolescence and Youth*, pp. 321–8.

[190] Finkelstein, *Grammar of Profit*, p. 314.

the case of resident servants and apprentices. Oliver Heywood, for example, declared that his maid, Martha Bairstow, was 'my child as well as my servant', and in 1705 Lord Fitzwilliam conflated his most trusted servants with 'our children'.[191] Naomi Tadmor has shown that eighteenth-century diarists reflexively thought of servants as family members, just as some legal examinants did with apprentices.[192] Moreover, the innumerable minor acts of pseudo-parental support and benevolence offered by masters indicate that these paternalist sentiments had real effects, though these cannot be separated from the violent 'discipline' sometimes inflicted on young resident employees by masters with patriarchal assumptions about their role. The persistence of familial logic manifested itself in both generosity and brutality.

Indeed, even with regard to non-resident employment, evidence from the late seventeenth and early eighteenth centuries indicates that this process of 'proletarianisation' and 'economic rationalisation' has been over-emphasised. The continuing conflation of 'employer' with 'master' and 'employee' with 'servant' meant that labour relations outside the confines of the household often obeyed the same familial logic as those within.[193] For example, the patriarchal strictures set out in commentaries on the fifth commandment theoretically applied as much to outworkers as to apprentices or servants, thus investing employers with the powers and responsibilities of a *paterfamilias*. Moreover, many of the most seemingly 'modern' workplaces of this period – Tyneside collieries, Cheshire copper mines, Ambrose Crowley's ironworks – operated according to 'a highly visible paternalistic style' which was often 'a relatively recent development'.[194] Even the Atlantic merchant ships, depicted as a prototype of capitalist labour relations by Marcus Rediker, fostered a social dynamic remarkably similar at times to that found in a tightly knit workshop ruled by a domineering master. Although it is not the intention here to dispute the decline of workplace paternalism in the late eighteenth century, attempts to extend this trend back into the later Stuart period are unconvincing. If nothing else, I hope that this chapter has shown the inadequacy of narratives that describe workers and their employers vigorously nibbling through the bonds of paternalism in the decades after the Restoration.

---

191 Capp, *When Gossips Meet*, p. 139; Hainsworth, *Stewards*, p. 251.

192 Tadmor, *Family and Friends*; Snell, *Annals*, p. 258.

193 For the contemporary tendency to not distinguish between 'servants', 'apprentices', and 'labourers' see above p. 94 n. 28. This persistent equation of non-resident employment with 'service' was exemplified in the so-called 'Master and Servant Acts' of the eighteenth century, which ironically did not apply to domestic servants: Douglas Hay, 'England, 1562–1875: The Law and Its Uses', in Douglas Hay and Paul Craven (eds), *Masters, Servants, and Magistrates in Britain and the Empire, 1562–1955* (Chapel Hill, 2004), pp. 59–116.

194 Levine and Wrightson, *Industrial Society*, pp. 356, 359.

GOD, DUTY AND COMMUNITY IN ENGLISH ECONOMIC LIFE

While 'masters and men' have received the most attention, some scholars have also tried to apply this formula to other types of relationship, such as the one between the 'common folk' and their 'natural rulers' – the gentry, the aristocracy, and the monarchy. In their role as landlords, gentlemen apparently became increasingly stingy towards their tenants and neighbours. For example, Susan Whyman used the small private funeral of Sir Ralph Verney in 1696 as a symbol of the 'decline of county hospitality' and Steve Hindle claimed that 'hospitality was ground under the wheels of coaches trundling to the metropolis' because of growing absenteeism after the Restoration.[195] Both historians go on to provide fairly nuanced discussions of the complicated process of change, but their initial statements show the ease with which subtopics can be subsumed within the story of 'modernisation'. A more extensive case of overeager schematisation can be seen in the description offered by James M. Rosenheim: 'the gentry's sense of paternalist obligation to govern and provide hospitality in the country was being undercut' in the decades immediately after the Restoration by 'a slow drift away from traditional roles, such as the patriarchal landlord, towards new identities such as absentee or "man of mode" or party politician'.[196] Nor is Rosenheim the only historian to regard the supposed decline of landed hospitality as paralleled by changing attitudes toward local governance and political authority more generally. According to Robert Malcolmson and others, for example, 'the paternalistic policy of industrial regulation' had begun to be 'decisively jettisoned' even before Adam Smith published his merciless critique of such practices.[197] Scholars discussing the larger political order have often shown much more analytical subtlety, though sometimes they too have lapsed into simplistic schematisation. Gordon Schochet has thoroughly documented the ubiquity of patriarchal attitudes in popular political discourse, yet he also claimed that this outlook 'was bound to become outmoded, irrelevant, and therefore unacceptable', because people had begun to see 'a fundamental distinction between political and social authority'.[198] Likewise, the insightful account of 'the patriarchal state' offered by Mike Braddick is difficult to reconcile with his assertion that 'the analogy between household order and political order was for most people looser' by the late seventeenth century.[199] Although all these historians agree that political paternalism still had at least some effect on social policy long after the Restoration, they also seem to regard the later Stuart period as one in which this long-term decline gained momentum.

Susan Whyman, *Sociability and Power in Late-Stuart England: The Cultural Worlds of the Verneys, 1660–1720* (Oxford, 1999), p. 34; Hindle, *On the Parish?* p. 106.
[196] Rosenheim, 'Landownership', pp. 156, 169.
[197] Malcolmson, *Life and Labour*, p. 151. See also the works of Thompson, Rediker, and Rule cited on p. 140 above.
[198] Schochet, *Patriarchalism*, ch. 10–11 (for ubiquity), quote at p. 57.
[199] Braddick, *State Formation*, p. 175.

The evidence presented in this chapter indicates that this declension narrative is seriously flawed. The reverse actually seems to have been the case in some aspects of social relations. For instance, the pressure on landowners to project an image of generosity and benevolence may have *increased* during this period of scarce labour, anxious tenants, and frequent elections.[200] Sir John Verney, the merchant-turned-landowner, learned this through personal experience. After his parsimony lost him an election to a more hospitable opponent in 1696, Verney invested considerable sums in acts of conspicuous benevolence, including Whitsun ales, feasting, dancing, music, and other inducements to loyalty.[201] By making 'the country his child' and treating it kindly, he won the elections in 1710 and 1713 handily.[202] It is equally difficult to find confirmation of a straightforward decline in the importance of familial logic to political governance. Instead, preachers, pamphleteers, and even almanac-writers continued to describe monarchs and magistrates as 'fathers of the country', an idiom that linked political office to both privileges and responsibilities. In 1705, for example, Richard Stephens centred his sermon on the passage from the Book of Isaiah which made this parental analogy explicit: 'Our Sacred Queen is a *Nursing-Mother* to her people', who 'empties her Private Purse for the ease and advantage of her Subjects'. According to Stephens, Queen Anne's 'Charity and Compassion' mean that fallen soldiers can confidently 'bequeath their miserable Widdows and Orphans under the shade and covering of her Maternal Wings'.[203] This sermon is a reminder of the adaptability of familial idioms – 'paternalism' might have become 'maternalism' with the accession of a female monarch, but the emphasis on dependency and provision remained intact. Likewise, changes in administrative procedure or regulatory focus – such as the shift from privy council to petty sessions or from enclosure commissions to labour regulation – still fit easily within a model of governance founded on the logic of household management.

These assumptions about workplace relations, gentry paternalism, and political authority are, in sum, symptomatic of a more fundamental problem: the tendency to envision a culture in which 'the moral economy of the *oikos*' was slowly, relentlessly demolished.[204] Here, history marches from the 'traditional' to the 'modern'. It begins in an economy suffused with a deeply

---

[200] See pp. 108–12 above.

[201] Whyman, *Sociability and Power*, pp. 163, 167, 171–2.

[202] Ibid., p. 173. Similarly, another contemporary suggested in 1710 that the way to win elections was to 'go into the country, lay aside the merchant, and spend and speak like a gentleman': ibid., p. 163.

[203] Earlier, he noted a good monarch is like 'a Parent' who governs so 'that every Branch in his Family may be Prosperous and Flourishing': Richard Stephens, *The Queen a Nursing Mother: A Sermon Preach'd on … the Anniversary Day of Her Majesty's Happy Accession to the Throne* (1705), pp. 8, 10–12 (quoting Isa. 49:23).

[204] Booth, 'Household and Market', p. 212.

'patriarchal complexion', based as much on 'status' as on 'contract', and inhabited by people aware of their differing but interdependent functions. It finishes in an economy drained of its familial tone, dependent entirely on individual property rights, and split between groups who imagine themselves to be intrinsically opposed.[205] This vision of the past certainly has a long history of its own – aspects of it can be glimpsed in Marx's 'feudalism to capitalism', in William Cobbett's *Rural Rides*, in John Langhorne's *The Country Justice*, and of course in the many earlier laments about the decline of deference and hospitality.[206] The first attempt to apply it directly to the later Stuart era seems to have been Richard Tawney's assertion that, soon after the Restoration, society came to be seen as 'a joint-stock company rather than an organism', turning the state into a mere guarantor of 'contractual freedom'.[207] Susan Amussen, many years later, described a similar process, though rather less dramatically. According to her, 'the organic conception of society' – specifically the identification of the family and the socio-political order – suffered 'gradual erosion' in the late seventeenth century.[208]

Keith Wrightson has provided the fullest account of this supposed transformation in social ideals. The process began, according to Wrightson, in the mid-sixteenth century, when 'the conception of a society of estates defended by the commonwealthsmen truly decomposed in England, crumbling in a tide of economic expansion and commercial intensification'. It was replaced by the 'hierarchy of degrees', 'a perception of the social order which was concerned less with universal ideals than with present realities, less with function than with place, less with vocational and occupational differentials than with the bald facts of relative wealth, status, and power'. By the end of the seventeenth century, however, even the 'hierarchy of degrees' could not contain the emergent commercial order and was becoming 'archaic'. Instead, the people of later Stuart England tended to divide themselves into two or three 'sorts', using 'a language of dissociation'. This was an idiom 'pregnant with conflict', one that assumed a 'clash of interests' between

---

[205] Perhaps the most unambiguous use of this dichotomy can be found in title and text of Laslett, *The World We Have Lost*. It must be noted, however, that he dated the change to the coming of 'industrialization' in the late eighteenth century.

[206] For early modern examples of these sorts of complaints see those cited above on pp. 17, 109–10. For a discussion of 'paternalism' as an ever-receding 'golden age' see Raymond Williams, *The Country and the City* (Oxford, 1975), pp. 9–12, 79–86; Thompson, *Customs in Common*, pp. 23–24; Heal, *Hospitality*, p. 93.

[207] Tawney, *Religion*, p. 192.

[208] Amussen, *Ordered Society*, pp. 63–5, 185–9 (quote at p. 188). She made clear that familial conceptions 'survived on a popular level even after it disappeared from theory', but she was equally clear that it declined steadily after the Restoration. David Underdown, focusing on the early seventeenth century, has described a similar process in his *Revel, Riot and Rebellion*, pp. 18–20, 284.

England's social groups and thus prefigured the antagonistic identities of 'class'.[209]

No doubt people did indeed shift from the terminology of 'estates' to 'degrees' and then to 'sorts'. However, the meaning Wrightson drew from this process is open to dispute. In actuality, the mentality he associated with the language of 'estates' manifested itself in a variety of different idioms long after it had supposedly 'decomposed' in the sixteenth century. His summary of the medieval conception sounds remarkably familiar:

> Each estate had its God-appointed duties, and each also had its all-too-human failings or "defections". Social harmony and divine favour depended upon the proper performance of their duties by the members of each estate.[210]

If one replaces the word 'estate' with 'calling' or 'office', the homology with the familial ideal becomes unmistakable. Paternal figures – from masters to kings – had to provision and govern, while avoiding the failings of laxity or tyranny. Filial figures – from servants to subjects – had to labour and obey, while avoiding the failings of sloth and insubordination. As this chapter has shown, this supposedly 'medieval' way of looking at society, a perspective that emphasised duty and interdependence, remained common throughout the later Stuart period, and probably long after.[211]

At the very least, one would have to agree with the handful of prominent scholars who have argued that 'paternalism' (or 'patriarchalism') dominated economic thinking much longer than is normally assumed by early modernists. Peter Laslett, Jonathan Clark, and E. P. Thompson have disagreed about many things, but they agreed about this. The culprits usually suspected of causing its demise – enclosure, puritanism, social polarisation, the two revolutions, and Lockean liberalism – were less effective than Christopher Hill and company had feared. For example, despite the alleged advance of contractual attitudes, a great many petitions and complaints about wages and other 'modern' issues invoked familial ideals to make their point. Hence, a pamphlet published in 1739 accused the textile bosses in Wiltshire of exploiting their workers by 'more and more falling their wages, increasing their oppressions, and adding fresh miseries to their misfortunes',

---

[209] Wrightson, *Earthly Necessities*, p. 333; idem, *English Society*, pp. 26–31, 230–36; idem, 'Estates, Degrees, and Sorts: Changing Perceptions of Society in Tudor and Stuart England', in Penelope Corfield (ed.), *Language, History and Class* (Oxford, 1991), pp. 42–3, 51–2. For a critique of his analysis of 'middling sort' see Henry French, 'Social Status, Localism and the "Middle Sort of People" in England 1620–1750', *Past & Present*, 166 (2000), pp. 66–99.

[210] Wrightson, 'Estates, Degrees, and Sorts', p. 30.

[211] Even the supposedly antagonistic 'language of sorts' could be used to assign duties to various social groups. Wrightson himself records instances of people insisting on the charitable and governmental responsibilities of 'the better sort', 'the richer sort', and 'the gentlemen of the country and some of the better sort' in the 1590s: ibid., pp. 46–7.

thus becoming 'un-masterlike masters'.[212] Only in an economic culture steeped in paternalist ideals would it make sense to condemn aggressive profit-seeking as 'un-masterlike' behaviour.

However, simply redating the end of 'paternalism' to sometime after the accession of George I is unsatisfying. Certain aspects of later Stuart economic relations raise troubling questions about the whole 'great arch' of English social and economic history. Why was there 'a reassertion of paternalist values' in vital sectors of the economy during an era of rapidly expanding markets and intense commercial development?[213] Why were some of the most 'advanced' industrial enterprises characterised by 'paternalist' forms of authority and munificence? Specific answers to these questions have been offered in the preceding pages, but these 'irregularities' also hint at the problems inherent in the conventional account of 'the rise of capitalist modernity'. It is beyond the scope of this chapter to venture very far into this subject. Still, the many sources discussed above indicate that familial logic may not have been antithetical to the modern marketplace after all.

Max Weber's distinction between 'householding' (Haushalt) and 'profit-making' (Erwerben) may be of use here. For him, 'householding' was any economic activity ultimately orientated to 'consumption', whereas 'profit-making' was orientated to expanding 'profitability'. The key point, however, is that Weber did not try to fit these two concepts into a 'modernisation' paradigm, noting, for example, that the budgeting of modern families and governments can often be categorised as 'householding', and that this same label can be applied to socialist societies. He was right to insist that the 'householding' ideal 'is not something more "primitive" than profit-seeking'.[214] As evidence, one need only note the 'revival of paternalism' in mid-Victorian England or the 'deferential worldview' among many Norfolk agricultural workers in the 1970s.[215] The petitionary model seems to have

---

[212] Miseries of the Miserable: or, An Essay Towards Laying Open the Decay of the Fine Wollen Trade (1739), p. 6. Compare the much earlier denunciation of 'ungentle gentlemen' who oppress the poor in Thomas Becon, The Fortresse of the Faythfull (1550), sig. E4r.

[213] Heal and Holmes, Gentry, p. 113.

[214] Weber, Economy and Society, I, pp. 86–100, 207 n. 14–15. In this edition, Haushalt has been translated as 'budgetary management', but I have followed the more literal translation offered in Richard Swedberg, Max Weber and the Idea of Economic Sociology (Princeton, 1998), pp. 30–31. Weber explicitly drew on Aristotle's distinction between 'the art of household management' (oikonomikē) and 'the art of acquiring' (chrēmastitkē): Aristotle, Politics: Books I and II, Trevor J. Saunders ed. (Oxford, 1995), bk. I, ch. 8–10, esp. 1256b26–1257a5. Likewise, Karl Polanyi drew on Aristotle (and Weber) in his suggestive discussion of the economic concepts of 'householding', 'reciprocity' and 'redistribution': Karl Polanyi, The Great Transformation (Boston, 1957), ch. 4, esp. pp. 53–5.

[215] Patrick Joyce, Work, Society and Politics: Culture of the Factory in Later Victorian England (London, 1980), esp. ch. 4–5; Richard Price, Labour in British Society: An Interpretive History (London, 1990), pp. 62–8; Howard Newby, The Deferential Worker: A Study of Farm Workers in East Anglia (London, 1977), esp. pp. 397–406.

been similarly adaptable. After all, people have continued to use the moral pressure of the petition or demonstration to call attention to their grievances long after they ceased praising monarchs and magistrates as 'fathers of the country'. So perhaps the history of 'the moral economy of the *oikos*' in the later Stuart period can serve as a reminder of the danger of dismissing an attitude as 'archaic' or 'irrational'. The influence of 'paternalism' and 'patriarchy' did not merely limp onwards in the years after the Restoration – some elements actually emerged stronger. Then, as now, many economic relations relied on an ideal modelled on the mutuality, reciprocity, and authority of the family.

3

Communal Bonds:
Solidarity, Alterity, and Collective Action

Belonging to a community – whether local, political, occupational or religious – was a vital part of 'making-shift' in early modern England. To be a 'neighbour' or 'citizen', rather than a 'stranger' or 'foreigner', had a profound effect on one's economic situation. Likewise, gaining settlement in a parish or earning admission to a trade brought with it a range of important rights and privileges, whereas being officially branded as a 'vagrant' or 'intruder' could have dire consequences. All these economic communities were, in a sense, 'imagined', but they nonetheless had a potent influence on the dynamics of production and exchange.[1] Of course, communities took many forms during this period.[2] They varied in size from a single neighbourhood or fellowship to the entire nation or even the whole of humanity. Some had strong institutional structures to regulate the process of inclusion and exclusion while others existed only as a shared sense of common identity or communal solidarity. But whatever their size and complexity, each depended on a basic division between insiders and outsiders, between 'us' and 'them'.

Economic communities in early modern England have received a significant amount of scholarly attention and some recent studies – such as the explorations of urban and rural communities offered by Phil Withington, Joseph Ward, Steve Hindle, Naomi Tadmor, Keith Snell, and others – provide analysis worthy of emulation.[3] Yet, some aspects of the historiography remain problematic. Specifically, for many decades this scholarship built on a simplistic model of decline – crudely summarised as a shift from 'community' to 'society', from *Gemeinschaft* to *Gesellschaft* – inherited from

---

[1] The notion of an 'imagined community' is borrowed from Benedict Anderson, *Imagined Communities: Reflections on the Origin and Spread of Nationalism* (London, 1983).
[2] Note that I have used an extremely expansive definition of 'community'. For a more concrete (but, for my purposes, less useful) definition see Alexandra Shepard and Phil Withington, 'Introduction: Communities in Early Modern England', in Alexandra Shepard and Phil Withington (eds), *Communities in Early Modern England: Networks, Place, Rhetoric* (Manchester and New York, 2000), pp. 1–15.
[3] Cited above, pp. 3–4.

nineteenth-century social theory.[4] Although more recent research has effectively demolished this model's intellectual credibility, only a small number of scholars have focused on the continuing relevance of 'community' after 1660.[5] Hence, the objectives of this chapter are to augment this growing body of knowledge with an examination of the 'communalist' ideal in later Stuart culture and to integrate this often tightly focused previous work into a more holistic analysis of the logic that underlay these various types of economic solidarities and identities. While historians have addressed this subject in a variety of specific contexts, this chapter offers a glimpse of responses to a wide cross section of economic issues rather than a highly contextualised examination of attitudes within one particular trade or locality.

In addition, this chapter also shows the importance of understanding the less amicable side of community.[6] It is impossible to make sense of collective bonds without investigating the power of alterity, exclusivity, xenophobia, and occasional violence. Contemporaries habitually emphasised the importance of securing one's trade, parish, city or nation against economic 'intruders'. Commentators and polemicists used 'outsider' stereotypes – such as vagabonds and itinerant peddlers, French and Dutch interlopers, Catholics and Puritans – as key characters in their narratives of poverty and distress. This chapter shows how perceived cultural divisions could overlap with economic resentments in the minds of contemporaries, turning a dispute over trade or labour into a rejection of 'the Other'. It also examines the practical manifestations of these tendencies. After all, workers and traders energetically defended their occupations from 'strangers' who had arrived from another parish or another country. Well-established locals could gain access to common land and poor relief, whereas needy travellers often met harsh receptions. Neighbours extended informal forms of credit and support to other neighbours, but excluded those deemed to be outside the community. Moreover, this economic xenophobia became even more pronounced during hard times. In places such as London and Norwich local workers targeted their 'foreign' opponents with threats and violence, while petitioning authorities to take more formal measures. Likewise, in market towns, crowds rioted in response to attempts to export scarce foodstuffs to other regions or countries. When the threat of hunger or destitution loomed, hostility to outsiders was often heightened and the defence of one's own economic 'community' became paramount. This chapter thus examines the complex interactions between economic conditions, popular attitudes, and collective action. When all these factors are analysed together, the darker side of community becomes more explicable.

---

[4]   Ferdinand Tönnies, *Community and Society*, Charles P. Loomis ed. and trans. (Mineola, 2002).
[5]   For critiques and recent research see Chapter 3.6 below.
[6]   For the tradition of conceptualising 'community' as a purely positive phenomenon see Shepard and Withington, 'Introduction', pp. 2–4.

The chapter is divided into five sections. The first is an analysis of the broadest of all common identities: the brotherhood of humankind. It examines the universalising ideal of Christian charity, but also its inverse, the concepts of 'inhumanity' and 'monstrosity'. The second discusses the economic implications that emerged from widely held assumptions about the 'national interest' and political allegiance. This part of the chapter also discusses how perceived profiteers could be conflated with civil enemies – rebels, traitors, and criminals – in later Stuart culture. The third section surveys the force of locality in economic culture. It discusses not only local support networks but also the conflicts that often divided 'neighbours' from 'strangers'. The fourth section focuses on occupational communities such as craft guilds and workers' associations, and investigates the methods used by craftsmen and labourers to establish bonds of fraternal solidarity while excluding those who might imperil the interests of the group. The fifth section analyses the diverse range of options open to those who 'belonged' when faced with an economic threat, which could involve direct action by the group itself, with often violent results. This section shows how tumultuous strikes and bloody riots could emerge from the very same set of assumptions that inspired informal charity and parochial processions. Finally, this chapter concludes with a survey of the basic contours of change over the period, emphasising the diversity of stories that can be told about later Stuart economic communities. The strength of some solidarities (e.g. national identity) clearly increased dramatically, whereas the tangible effectiveness of others (e.g. spiritual communion) did not fare quite as well. So, while the effects of this dichotomous logic on early modern economic relations cannot be ignored, neither can they be reduced to a straightforward narrative of rise, decline or continuity. This chapter thus reveals both the immeasurable impact of these communities but also their undeniable complexity.

1 Flesh and Blood

'Blood is thicker than water', claimed the proverb. Blood was indeed thick in early modern England, and it created social bonds that influenced the economic lives of ordinary people in a multitude of ways. In addition to the obvious example of the nuclear family, the impact of kinship ties can be seen in the tendency of siblings, cousins, and other relatives to support each other with loans, jobs, apprenticeships and innumerable acts of charity.[7] Yet, the concept of shared 'blood' could create solidarities that extended far beyond the limits of immediate kinship. After all, the whole of humanity

---

[7]   Ben-Amos, *Culture of Giving*, pp. 47–58; Hindle, *On the Parish?* ch. 1.3.

was descended from a single couple, so even strangers ought to be regarded as 'kin'.

This imagined community, holding all of humankind in its wide embrace, appeared frequently in contemporary discussions of economic morality, especially those focused on the duty of charity. Ministers such as George Hickes argued that a charitable attitude towards one's fellows was not just virtuous, it was inherent to human nature. The fact 'that all men have the same common Nature, and Parentage, and have derived it in all Countrys from the same common Stock, founds the first Obligation to Charity', preached Hickes in 1684, 'and therefore the Rich ought to nourish and cherish the Poor, as their Brethren, as flesh of their flesh, and bone of their bone'.[8] Of course the concept of a universal bond of kinship originated in scripture, a fact which every commentator was sure to mention. In his oft-printed tract on *The Charitable Christian*, for example, John Hart spliced his own idioms with biblical paraphrases and direct quotations:

> The poor are our own flesh, Mal. 2:10, Have not we all one father? ... if a man be naked or hungry, he will seek to cloathe and feed himself, he will not hate his own flesh.... When men therefore refuse to strengthen the hand of the poor and needy, they despise and hate their own flesh, they are unnatural.[9]

Through the vocabulary of 'flesh' and 'blood', wherein humanity became as an all-encompassing 'brotherhood', charity towards strangers was transformed from mere voluntary kindness into fraternal duty.

Moralists often described the community of Christendom using similarly visceral imagery, emphasising the economic obligations owed to fellow Christians 'joined to us by the bands of spiritual Consanguinity'.[10] Following a venerable tradition, they declared that every believer was a 'member' of a larger sacred 'body' with Christ as its 'head', united by shared faith and mutual love. As a result, according to commentators, there was a 'near union between Him, the poor and us, being but one *mysticall body*'; thus, 'when we feed and comfort [our poor neighbour], we do sustain and cherish a member of our own body'.[11] Perhaps the clearest late seventeenth-century expression of this idea can be seen in Edward Stillingfleet's Easter sermon of 1681. 'True Christian Charity', he preached, 'is the Life and Spirit of that Body whereof Christ is the Head; it passeth from one member to another

---

[8] Hickes, *A Sermon Preached at the Church of St. Bridget*, pp. 4–6.

[9] Hart, *The Charitable Christian*, sig. A5r–A5v (also citing Prov. 22:2, Eph. 5:29, Isa. 58:7). See also Barrow, *The Duty and Reward of Bounty*, pp. 131–2; Welchman, *The Duty and Reward of Charity*, pp. 12–13.

[10] Barrow, *The Duty and Reward of Bounty*, p. 135. The most commonly cited scriptural passages were Eph. 4:15–16, Rom. 12:4–5, 1 Cor. 10:17, and 1 Cor. 12:27.

[11] Younge, *The Poors Advocate*, pp. 9, 22–3, 25; Barrow, *The Duty and Reward of Bounty*, pp. 133–4.

… and so by a constant motion and course through the Body it keeps heat and union in all the Parts'.[12] Here, the vitality of the faith depended on the continuous circulation of charity among the faithful.

Moreover, although this bodily conception of the Christian community had plenty of direct scriptural support, it was also strengthened by the contemporary theological emphasis on the power of 'spiritual Consanguinity' as manifested in the ritual of communion. Each communicant, by symbolically partaking in God's blood, became subsumed in the larger whole.[13] Edward Welchman, an undistinguished country clergyman preaching in Banbury in 1707, explained it using the same idioms as his predecessors: 'The *Communion* of particular Christians with one another, and of all with *Christ*, is so strict and close, that it unites us into one *Body*, of which he is the *Head*.' This 'Unity', according to Welchman, created inescapable material obligations, because 'Can anything be dearer to a Man, than the *Members* of his own *Body*, his own *Flesh*, and his own *Bones*?'[14] As these examples show, preachers insisted on the necessity of Christian mutuality using a mixture of theological commonplaces and biblical citations, but the emotional force of their message came primarily from the corporal imagery in which it was expressed.

The concept of 'human nature' created another opportunity for moralists to insist on the intrinsic and unavoidable obligations created by these imagined communities. Hence, William Durham, preaching in 1678, employed a familiar terminology:

> The Law of *Love* and *Charity*, and *Compassion*, … has a direct foundation in *Nature* it self, being interwoven in the very frame and contexture of our Bodies; We are not hewn out of a Rock that is obdurante and insensible, but are made up of the softer and more relenting Principles of Flesh and Blood, which … incline us to be kind, merciful, and compassionate.[15]

Knowing that not everyone would agree with this characterisation, some commentators briefly noted possible objections before dismissing them. Thomas Pargiter, for instance, appealed to 'the Law of Nature' rather than the law of charity to warn his London audience against unjust or deceitful trading practices. 'We are not born Wild and Savage Creatures, and Beasts of Prey', he declared, 'The State of Nature is not a State of Rapine and

---

12 Stillingfleet, *Protestant Charity*, p. 18.
13 For the link between taking communion and being 'in charity' with neighbours see Arnold Hunt, 'The Lord's Supper in Early Modern England', *Past and Present*, 161 (1998), esp. pp. 47–51, 62–3, 71; Wrightson, 'Decline', pp. 29–30.
14 Welchman, *The Duty and Reward of Charity*, p. 13. See also Barrow, *The Duty and Reward of Bounty*, pp. 136–7.
15 Durham, *Encouragement to Charity*, pp. 9–12, quote at p. 12.

Violence, as ... the great *Leviathan* of Atheism ... hath scurrilously asserted.'[16] In this interpretation, equity and generosity were attributes inherent to the human condition, thus invalidating one of the most common excuses for economic injustice.

Policing the limits of expansive communities such as 'humanity' or 'Christendom' was no easy task. Initially, these ideals seem much more likely to promote an inclusive universality than to provide a rhetoric for demeaning and excluding economic deviants. Yet, in practice, the symbolic expulsion of particular people from the bosom of human society was extremely common. The language used to praise individuals for recognising the economic obligations of common parentage and shared blood could be easily inverted to condemn those who neglected or ignored these same bonds.

The inverse of 'humanity' was, of course, 'inhumanity', a term which appeared with notable regularity in the discourse of the period. In a sermon published in 1680, for instance, Isaac Barrow declared that charity 'hath ever been styled humanity, and the disposition from whence it floweth is called good-nature', whereas uncharitableness has been 'termed inhumanity, and its source ill-nature; as thwarting the common notions and inclinations of mankind, devesting us of our manhood, and rendring us a sort of monsters among men'.[17] To deny the uncharitable their 'manhood', to figuratively 'dehumanise' them, was a bold rhetorical move, but entirely typical of even the most staid writing on the topic of economic morality. Preachers, tract-writers, balladeers, and sometimes the poor themselves employed these idioms of exclusion, attempting to push offenders beyond the imagined edge of the human community.

Although the lexicon used to denounce such 'inhumanity' was limited only by the imagination of the accuser, certain words and phrases occurred repeatedly. Unsurprisingly, the Bible served as the most popular source for such imagery, especially the passages describing oppressors as devourers of men.[18] These allusions to scripture, even when it was not cited directly, also invested otherwise strident accusations with a degree of authority and propriety. Similarly, some commentators used classical examples as precedents for their assertions. In 1703, for instance, Henry Cornwallis noted approvingly that 'the Antients ... banished inhospitable Men from the Society of Mankind, and ranked them among the Wolves and Tygers'. Even

[16] Pargiter, A *Sermon Preached before ... the Lord Mayor*, pp. 6–7. Likewise, Durham warned that 'Atheistical Persons ... scandalize *Humane Nature*, representing Men as Wolves and Tygres, and Beasts of Prey', an argument which he regarded as 'an impudent and malicious Slander': Durham, *Encouragement to Charity*, pp. 11–12.
[17] Barrow, *Of the Love of God and Our Neighbour*, p. 124. See also Hickes, A *Sermon Preached at the Church of St. Bridget*, pp. 4–6. For earlier uses of monstrosity as a rhetoric device in preaching on economic issues see Waddell, 'Economic Immorality', pp. 170–73.
[18] Compare the examples quoted in the paragraphs which follow with the language in Mark 12:40, Psalm 14:4, Mic. 3:2–3, Ezek. 22:27, and Prov. 30:14.

'the Heathens' understood that selfish misers 'were not fit for the Company of Men, and therefore they ranked them among the worser sort of Beasts'.[19] Whatever the inspiration, the impulse to expel economic deviants from the body of mankind appears to have been very strong.

Emphasised above all was the predatory nature of such offenders. Isaac Barrow, Richard Younge, and other vocal advocates of charity described how the 'most *fruitfull in their estates*' prefer to '*make prey*' of the poor rather than relieving them, whereby the rich man turned into 'a Fox, or a Wolf; either cunningly lurching, or violently ravening for prey: ... devouring every one that is weaker than himself, or who cannot defend himself from his paws and teeth'.[20] To ignore the pleas of the poor was a tacit admission of inhumanity; worse still, by continuing to rake up riches while one's fellow man lacked the necessities of life, the miser seemed to be actively redirecting resources from the needy to himself. According to these commentators, this bestial behaviour was akin to swallowing up the weakest rather than feeding them. Hence, a providential pamphlet published in response to the Great Plague of London in 1666 roundly condemned 'ye *Nimrods*, ye mighty Hunters, and Unsatiable Birds of prey' who 'Wallow in the complacency of Honour and Riches' even as 'the indigent starve'.[21] Such language transformed the passive offence of miserliness into the active offence of oppression.

The portrayal of economic injustice as cannibalistic was even more common in cases of unambiguous exploitation. The problem of fraudulent commercial dealings, for instance, gave Richard Steele a chance to prove this point using concise but impeccable logic: 'He whom thou defraud is *thy brother*, wilt thou eat up thine owne flesh?'[22] Likewise, a sensational eight-page crime pamphlet published in 1675 used this trope in its denunciation of a cruel landlord in Southwark who reportedly not only evicted a poor family and seized their 'pitiful moveables', but also was 'so unmanly and inhumane as to assault and beat' the poor tenant's wife in a 'barbarous manner'. This landlord was, according to the pamphlet, just one example of the many 'Wolves and Tygers', 'Savages', 'Canibals', and 'Men-eaters, that devour Orphans and Widows, and cannot live without every day a large Mornings-draught of intermingled Blood and Tears'.[23] Here, the idioms of masculinity, humanity, and barbarity share a page with those of bestiality,

---

[19] Cornwallis, *Set on the Great Pot*, p. 3. For another advocate of the policy of banishment, though without the direct invocation of 'the Antients', see Welchman, *The Duty and Reward of Charity*, p. 4.

[20] Younge, *The Poors Advocate*, p. 19; Barrow, *Of the Love of God and Our Neighbour*, p. 194; Welchman, *The Duty and Reward of Charity*, p. 4.

[21] *Avaritia Coram Tribunali*, pp. 21–2.

[22] Steele, *The Husbandmans Calling*, p. 123 (citing 1 Thes. 4:6).

[23] *Lamentable News From Southwark: Or the Cruel Landlord* (1675), esp. pp. 1, 5.

savagery, and cannibalism.[24] It would be difficult to find a more comprehensive attempt to metaphorically eject an offender from human society.

The frequency with which certain words and phrases appear in attacks on economic oppression indicates that they had become commonplaces, particular associations firmly embedded in early modern culture. The image of oppressors as 'beasts of prey', for example, seems to have been universal. It can be found in ballads, such as the broadside which attacked 'A Wealthy man, a Farmer' who 'resolved to hoard up his store / That he might then make a prey of the poor'; and it can also be found in pamphlets, such as Poor Robin's description of pawn-brokers, tally-men, and bailiffs as 'a parcel of *Beasts of prey*, worse than ever *Africk* bred; and more *Unclean* than any that entered into *Noah's* Ark: yet *Cloven-footed*, in imitation of their *Syre*'.[25] Even the most distinguished preachers of the era, men such as Edward Stillingfleet and John Tillotson, used this metaphor. Indeed, Archbishop Tillotson's words were particularly poignant:

> the Covetous Man [who] oppresseth his Neighbour, ... is of that most hateful kind of Beasts of Prey, that kill other Creatures, not to eat them, but that they may see them lie dead by them. Lyons and Wolves kill out of hunger; but the Covetous Man, like a Serpent, or Scorpion, stings and bites others to death, not for his need, but for his pleasure and recreation.[26]

Moreover, many other commentators made the same connection by using images of crocodiles, pikes, sharks, and other stereotypical predators.[27]

Visions of wild animals tearing at the flesh of the poor were not the only examples of zoomorphism used to imagine economic malfeasance. The other popular metaphor was that of the parasite. Anyone perceived to profit from the misfortune of others was liable to become associated with this type of creature, so money-lenders and pawn-brokers made especially apt subjects. Ballads and pamphlets described them as '*Drones, nay, Cankers, in the Common-wealth*', '*Horse-leeches*', and '*Catterpillers* [who] will eat and

---

[24] For an example which uses a similarly wide selection of imagery (i.e. inhumanity, cannibalism, and six different predatory animals) see Milbourne, *Debtor and Creditor*, pp. 4, 18, 22.

[25] *The Rich Farmer's Ruine* (c.1685–88), in *RB*, II, p. 396; 'Poor Robin', *Four for a Penny* (1678), p. 2. For other examples from these media see *The Poets Dream* (1679), in *PB*, IV, p. 302; Younge, *The Poors Advocate*, p. 19. For medieval tales that associated usurers with kites and other predators see Tubach, *Index*, p. 383 (no. 5059).

[26] Tillotson, *Sixteen Sermons*, p. 153. See also Stillingfleet, *A Sermon Preached before the Honourable House of Commons*, pp. 8–9.

[27] For crocodiles, lions, pikes, sharks, ravens, wolves, vultures, eels, bears, hounds, and cats see *The Poets Dream* (1679), in *PB*, IV, p. 302; *The Chimney-Men's Grief* (1689), in *PB*, IV, p. 309; Milbourne, *Debtor and Creditor*, pp. 4, 18, 22; 'Poor Robin', *Four for a Penny*, pp. 7–8; Welchman, *The Duty and Reward of Charity*, p. 4; *The Citizens Complaint*, pp. 4–5; Jones, *Tree of Commonwealth*, p. 231.

destroy / The Substance that honest poor Men should enjoy'.[28] Likewise, Luke Milbourne, preaching in 1709, denounced extortionate lending as 'a Cancerous Humour in the Flesh, which frets, corrupts and consumes the whole Body: It's a Practice which effectually devours Houses and Lands, Living Men and all their Families'.[29] But this parasitical imagery could also be applied to more marginal figures on the economic landscape. For instance, a broadside printed in the 1690s accused Scotch peddlers of being a 'Swarm of Catterpillers, who ... Devour our Shopkeepers ... [and] the poor of our Nation' though 'false Dealing', beggary and, theft.[30] So while certain wealthy creditors might find themselves ostracised for their 'inhumanity', the itinerant poor could also be targeted using images of ravaging vermin or bloodsucking insects.

Alongside this veritable bestiary, expressions borrowed from scripture also entered into the culture of the time. Obviously, some biblical passages were quoted or cited in almost every sermon touching on economic injustice, but these phrases appeared in less explicitly religious contexts as well. For instance, a ballad narrated by a 'poor true and honest' man claimed that some landlords are 'covetous Cormorants' who 'devours / Widdows houses and all'.[31] This paraphrase of Mark 12:40 may have added to the authority of his otherwise generic invocation of carnivorousness. Similarly, Poor Robin's humorous portrait of avaricious creditors incorporated a well-known quote from Psalm 14. According to him, merciless tally-men 'Eateth up the Poor (to use a sacred Phrase) even as Bread' by selling 'sorry Commodities' to vulnerable consumers at usurious rates of interest and then demanding rapid repayment.[32] The opportunity 'to use a sacred Phrase' to dehumanise perceived offenders was seldom ignored even in decidedly lowbrow publications.

Ultimately, however, the logic of human brotherhood (and its inverse) relied more on visceral, emotive rhetoric than on biblical allusions. By habitually presenting economic relations in terms of humanity and alterity

---

[28] Thomas Culpeper, *Plain English, in a Familiar Conference* (1673), p. 3; 'Poor Robin', *Four for a Penny*, pp. 5–6; *The Naked Truth* (c.1688–96), in *PB*, IV, p. 314. Bunyan called them 'the pest and Vermin of the Common-Wealth, not fit for the society of men': Bunyan, *Mr. Badman*, p. 216.

[29] Milbourne, *Debtor and Creditor*, p. 8. For more examples of the usurer (and usury) described as 'a catching Disease', a 'Distemper', 'a Fever', and 'a Dropie' see Culpeper, *Plain English*, pp. 9, 23; 'Poor Robin', *Four for a Penny*, p. 4; Tillotson, *Sixteen Sermons*, p. 159.

[30] *The Crafty Scotch Pedler* (c.1692–9), in *PB*, IV, p. 326. Similarly, Sir Peter Leicester in a charge to a Cheshire grand jury in the 1660s or 1670s denounced vagrants as 'the very scabs and vermin of a state': Fletcher, *Reform*, p. 172.

[31] Thomas Jordan, *An Honest Mans Delight* (c.1660–74) in *WB*, Wood E 25(50). For similar metaphors of cormorancy see Hart, *Heavens Glory And Hells Horror*, sig. A6v; Younge, *The Poors Advocate*, p. 8; Younge, *A Precious Mithridate*, pp. 1–3.

[32] 'Poor Robin', *Four for a Penny*, p. 6 (paraphrasing Psalm 14:4). For a much more extended use of this image see Thomas, *The Mammon of Unrighteousness*, pp. 12–13.

these commentators tried to fortify the boundary between acceptable and unacceptable behaviour, turning the former into the 'natural' result of a common paternity and the latter into the 'unnatural' product of an inherent monstrosity. Ethics thus became instinct, while avarice became aberration.

Just as the concept of a shared humanity led to numerous accusations of inhumanity, the related notion of 'spiritual Consanguinity' necessarily implied the possibility of anti-Christian behaviour as well. For example, although denunciations of 'Mammonism', as shown in an earlier chapter, seem to have drawn most of their strength from contemporary beliefs about divine omnipotence, they also could be interpreted as attempts to exclude certain types of individuals from the Christian community.[33] On one side stood 'true professors' who reinforced the bonds of communion through acts of charity; on the other side stood 'worldlings' whose covetousness and oppression publicised their reprobate status. Hence, while it may be that the *word* 'community' had been 'desanctified' by the early seventeenth century, the *concept* certainly had not.[34] In fact it appears to have remained thoroughly ingrained in later Stuart religious belief.

This emerges even more clearly in sources that make no attempt to allude to abstract theological concerns, instead invoking simple images of diabolical malevolence. In these instances the issue is not the betrayal of God, but rather an open hostility to Christendom. A Scottish ballad, for example, claimed that anyone willing 'to starve thy Christian Brother' by hoarding grain must have 'made a league with Hell' and 'struck hands with *Belzebub*'.[35] Economic immorality was thus linked to the larger struggle between the God's people and the demonic forces who sought to harm them. This association is also evident in the labels applied to merciless creditors in later Stuart chapbooks where they are variously described as 'Old Nick's Warehouse-keeper', 'Wandering Mephistophilus', 'The Devil's Rent-gatherer', and the 'Devils Brokers'.[36] One might be tempted to dismiss such phrases as generic insults, divested of any meaningful connection to contemporary ideas about the borders of the Christian community. Yet the belief that rich profiteers might have entered into a diabolical pact could be very real indeed. For instance, John Grigsby, the notoriously unscrupulous accountant of the South Sea Company, was 'vulgarly reputed' to be a practitioner of black magic.[37] In the minds of some, such men might well be

---

[33] See Chapter 1.2 above.
[34] Shepard and Withington, 'Introduction', p. 10.
[35] *The Meal Mongers Garland* (1700?) in *RyB*, Ry.III.a.10(079). For a ballad describing the coal merchant as a 'covetous Devil' and 'damnable Fiend' who uses the 'Colliers-Caball' to drive up the price so 'the wretched and Poor ... might starve within door' see *A New-Years-Gift for Covetous Colliers* (c.1690–91), in *PB*, IV, p. 323.
[36] 'Poor Robin', *Four for a Penny*, pp. 3–6; *The Citizens Complaint* (1663), p. 6.
[37] P. G. M. Dickson, *The Financial Revolution in England: A Study in the Development of Public Credit, 1688–1756* (London, 1967), p. 116.

seen as possible agents of Satan, conspiring to undermine Christendom by targeting its weakest members.

Ideals of 'Humanity' and 'Christianity' were certainly not the most tangible forms of economic community and they lacked much of the practical institutional support that made other types so effective. Yet, these beliefs about 'human nature' and 'spiritual communion' still influenced individual behaviour. The sphere in which this may have most often occurred was charitable giving. Those seeking aid certainly seem to have drawn on the rhetoric of pious solidarity. One regularly finds poor petitioners asking potential benefactors for 'Such benevolence as they in their Christian Commiseration shall be pleased to bestow', and groups of parishioners lauding a distressed neighbour as 'An object of Great pity To the Charitable Benevolence of all Well disposed Xtians'.[38] Unfortunately, one of the most common avenues of relief – casual interpersonal charity – has left very few marks on the historical record, so it is nearly impossible to reconstruct these sorts of appeals or the motives for granting them.[39] However, it would be difficult to deny that much of this informal giving was predicated on a sense of common humanity or Christian brotherhood. Perhaps this is what motivated the Sussex minister Giles Moore who, in addition to paying the parish rate and giving informally to the local poor, also treated passing strangers charitably. He offered sixpence to a travelling 'Highlander' in 1664 and to 'a begging Welshman' at a wedding at year later.[40] Similarly, the seaman Edward Barlow successfully begged for food and lodging several times while travelling without money in an unfamiliar locale during this same decade.[41] Forty years later, John Crakanthorp, a rector in rural Cambridgeshire, gave regularly to those he described as 'strangers', including fourpence to 'a Scotchman … going to London in want' in 1705.[42] He also helped to relieve those whom he saw as spiritual brethren, giving a shilling to 'a Neapolitan and Capuchin – out of conscience of Popish errours became Protestant – and is yet unsetld', and more than two shillings to a brief 'for the Palatine's Protestants'.[43] These sorts of everyday manifestations of the belief in a broad Christian community, wherein charity was an expression of 'spiritual Consanguinity', even received an explicit pictorial endorsement

---

[38] WYAS–W, QS 1/39/10/6 (petition of John Bingley, 1700); NYCRO, QSB 1696/148 (certificate for John Medd, 1696).

[39] For casual giving as a 'dark figure' and 'an elusive historical quarry' see Ben-Amos, *Culture of Giving*, pp. 3–4; Hindle, *On the Parish?* p. 58. For one attempt to undertake just such a reconstruction see Hitchcock, 'Publicity of Poverty'.

[40] Giles Moore, 'Day Book, 1655–1680', in F. Stenton Eardley, *Horsted Keynes, Sussex: The Church and the Parish of St. Giles* (London, 1939), pp. 93, 95, etc.

[41] Patricia Fumerton, *Unsettled: The Culture of Mobility and the Working Poor in Early Modern England* (Chicago, 2006), p. 97. For more examples of charity offered to travelling strangers see Ben-Amos, *Culture of Giving*, pp. 104, 299, etc.

[42] Crakanthorp, *Accounts*, pp. 125, 131–2.

[43] Ibid., pp. 261, 268.

on the front of one of the most pervasive and authoritative religious documents of the era. The frontispiece to a 1700 edition of *The Book of Common Prayer* featured two beggars requesting aid from church-goers, with one shown receiving alms from a pious woman (Fig. 3.1). Perhaps this explains why so many beggars in early eighteenth-century London – a city notorious for its heartlessness – crowded around church doors on Sundays.[44]

The spiritual bonds that sometimes inspired such acts of indiscriminate charity had much weaker mechanisms for excluding wayward individuals. But they did not lack them entirely. St Paul, in the first epistle to the Corinthians, made this clear when he urged Christians 'not to keep company' with 'a fornicator, or *covetous*, or an idolater, or a railer, or a drunkard, or an *extortioner*; with such an one no not to eat'.[45] Some later Stuart preachers reiterated the importance of excommunication as a collective censure against the 'uncharitable'. Luke Milbourne, for example, argued in 1709 that 'the Pastors and Governors of the Church, [ought] to take Cognizance of such Wickedness and Inhumanity' as was practised by merciless creditors who live 'by cruel Rapine and Oppression'. The man with 'the Blood of so many Innocents hanging about him', he insisted, should not 'approach the Table of the Lord, the Feast of Love'.[46] Milbourne's unambiguous rhetoric indicates that he saw moneylenders as likely candidates for excommunication, though it is unknown whether this ever happened in his parish. For the fiery clergyman David Jones, on the other hand, this issue was impossible to avoid. His parishioners included the rich bankers of London's Lombard Street and, at some point around 1692, he decided to take a stand. Unsurprisingly, he soon found himself preaching a farewell sermon, but even then he continued to defend this policy:

> every Minister and every Churchwarden throughout England, are actually perjured and forsworn by the 109th Canon of our Church, if they suffer any Usurer to come to the Sacrament, till he be reformed. And there is no Reformation without Restitution.[47]

Although his uncompromising stance evidently lacked the parochial support needed for any effective excommunication, it also serves as a reminder of the potential usefulness of this process as an instrument of collective will. Still, the rarity with which such arguments appear in print, when combined with other shifts in institutional religion, indicate that banning economic

[44] Hitchcock, 'Publicity of Poverty', p. 175.
[45] 1 Cor. 5:11 (emphasis added). The same offenders were named in 'An Homily Against Gluttony and Drunkness', in *Certain Sermons or Homilies*, II, p. 192.
[46] Milbourne, *Debtor and Creditor*, p. 21.
[47] Jones, *A Farewel-Sermon*, pp. 31, 34–9, quote at p. 34. The canon does indeed include usury among the list of punishable sins: 'Canon CIX' in *Constitutions and Canons Ecclesiastical* (1660), sig. M3v.

deviants from 'the Feast of Love' probably had a minimal impact at best. The gradual disintegration of the ecclesiastical courts and the end of the Church's official monopoly in 1689 made formal excommunication increas-- ingly irrelevant.[48] By this time, informal pressures such as ostracism probably functioned much more effectively than withholding communion.

The beliefs that underpinned these practical manifestations of commu- nity were strengthened by vividly corporeal representations of collectivity and alterity – positive images of shared blood and well-nurtured bodies; negative images of torn flesh and cancerous infection. Their proponents also had access to a terrifying menagerie crowded with ferocious beasts, noisome parasites, and malevolent fiends. So, despite the undeniably diffuse nature of this particular imagined community, evidence from the print and preaching of later Stuart England indicates that many people habitually divided economic conduct into the human and the inhumane, the Chris- tian and the anti-Christian. This symbolic split provided both an impetus for charity and a battery of rhetorical ammunition with which to harass perceived oppressors.

2 England and Her Enemies

Within the wide domain of Christian society there existed a number of smaller civil dominions, each with its own expressions of communal senti- ment and economic morality. The grandest of these was the nation, a construct which was rarely defined but often invoked in the period after 1660. The institutions and identities associated with the English polity unmistakably inflected the economic culture of the era, creating a vision of community that could promote solidarity among 'citizens' while simul- taneously excluding those regarded as 'enemies' or 'aliens'. The growing importance of 'Englishness' and 'foreignness' – whether expressed in simple slogans or complicated conspiracy theories – provided yet another set of moralised idioms which could be used to discuss issues such as commerce, employment or fiscal policy.[49]

---

[48] Donald Spaeth, *The Church in an Age of Danger: Parson and Parishioners, 1660–1740* (Cambridge, 2000), ch. 3; Spurr, *Restoration Church*, pp. 209, 213–17. For the weakening of the 'spiritual parish' in the seventeenth century and eighteenth centuries see below pp. 223–4.

[49] Most primary sources interchangeably used 'the nation', 'the country', 'the kingdom', and 'England'. I have followed this convention, though obviously the concept of 'Britishness' was growing in importance, especially after 1707: Linda Colley, *Britons: Forging the Nation, 1707–1837* (London, 1992), ch. 1–3. The economics of the Union with Scotland provoked considerable debate, but for reasons of space I have not attempted to discuss this complex issue here. For an able summary see Christopher

Figure 3.1. One edition of *The Book of Common Prayer* (1700) was beautified by an etching that showed a church-goer fulfilling her Christian duty by offering charity to a crippled beggar standing at the church door.

Ever since Adam Smith denounced his predecessors for their idolisation of the 'mercantile system', the centrality of 'national' concerns in early modern economic theory has been well known.[50] More recently, of course, scholars have shown that the picture presented by Smith was something of a caricature. They have emphasised the diversity and complexity of thinkers of the later Stuart era, noting the presence of 'economic liberals' and advocates of 'free trade'.[51] Yet even Joyce Appleby, who has provided the most influential version of this narrative, recognised that this flowering of arguments for commercial 'freedom' was brief and had little effect on government policy. Ultimately, the 'balance-of-trade' theorists 'were able to ignore the theoretical sophistication of their opponents and summon patriotism,

Whatley, 'Scotland, England and "the Golden Ball": Putting Economics in the Union of 1707', *The Historian*, 51 (1996), pp. 9–13.
[50] Smith, *Wealth of Nations*, bk. IV.
[51] Appleby, *Economic Thought*, esp. ch. 7; Finkelstein, *Harmony*, ch. 13; Terrence Hutchison, *Before Adam Smith: The Emergence of Political Economy, 1662–1776* (Oxford, 1988), pp. 50, 59–60, 77–8, 82–6.

common sense, and xenophobia to their cause'.[52] Debates amongst the learned elite may have raised the possibility of global prosperity in a border-less marketplace, but only a handful of writers proved willing to endorse such a vision. Most remained convinced that each country had a separate interest to defend, and that each countryman was bound to defend it.

Outside the complex disputations in the coffeehouses of London's Exchange Alley, appeals to the 'National Interest' were even more common. For most commentators, this meant insisting that all Englishmen should put public benefit before private gain. 'Fellow-Subjects' ought to behave 'as if they dwelt together in one Family', preached Archbishop John Sharp in 1702: 'They would have no *Interests* separate from the *Common-wealth*; nor would they for the advancing themselves, ever seek the ruin of others.'[53] Hence, virtuous citizens and civic leaders should suppress any desire for a personal fortune and instead devote themselves to promoting the economic health of the whole body-politic. This exaltation of selfless patriotism manifested itself in a variety of contexts: royal proclamations and acts of parliament presented new economic policies as advancing 'the good of the country'; amateur projectors sought to build support for their finan-cial schemes with promises of English greatness; and every economic group portrayed its own concerns as essential to the nation's welfare.[54] Foremost among the latter were the workers and traders involved in textile produc-tion. Their numbers and organisational acumen allowed them to regularly publish patriotic public appeals and they had many vocal allies (including paid advocates such as Daniel Defoe), especially during the long-running furore over Indian calicoes.[55] Indeed, this issue resulted in the publication of countless attempts to elide any possible divergence between 'the *Common*

---

[52] Appleby, *Economic Thought*, p. 194. See also Pincus, 'From Holy Cause', esp. pp. 283–92; idem, *1688*, ch. 12. For an article which focuses on thinkers who challenged 'mercantilist' orthodoxy while acknowledging the importance of considerations of 'national interest' see Slack, 'Politics of Consumption'.

[53] Sharp, *A Sermon Preach'd at the Coronation*, p. 23.

[54] For an example of an Act citing 'the Publick Wealth, Honour and Safety of this Kingdom' as reasons for its passage see *Statutes of the Realm*, VII, pp. 513–14 (10 Will. III, c. 13). For an economic example of a typical royal proclamation purportedly to strengthen the 'principal happiness of this Our Realm' and 'to promote the Good and Welfare of Our Kingdoms' against 'divers persons evilly disposed to the Welfare of this Our Kingdom' see James II, *A Proclamation ... for the Preventing the Exportation of Sheep, Wooll, ... and Fulling-Clay* (1688). For a selection of later Stuart pamphlets offering schemes for 'England's Improvement' see those cited in Slack, *From Reformation*, pp. 96–7, 106.

[55] For more context on the anti-calico campaign, which began in the late seventeenth century but became loudest in c.1719–20, see Alfred Plummer, *The London Weavers' Company, 1600–1970* (London, 1972), ch. 14; Beverly Lemire, *Fashion's Favourite: The Cotton Trade and the Consumer in Britain, 1660–1800* (Oxford, 1991), pp. 29–42; Chloe Wigston Smith, '"Callico Madams": Servants, Consumption, and the Calico Crisis', *Eighteenth Century Life*, 31:2 (2007), pp. 29–55.

Good of the *whole Nation*' and the strength of the domestic textile industry.[56] According to pamphlets like these, every Englishman had a stake in promoting domestic manufacturing.

Perhaps the most intriguing attempt to bind the fortunes of these crafts to the fortunes of the national community took the form of an illustrated broadsheet entitled *England's Great Joy and Gratitude*, probably printed around 1700 in response to the prohibition placed on importing printed silks from Asia (Fig. 3.2).[57] The symbolism it employed was not subtle. The engraver had incorporated a variety of patriotic imagery: the royal coat of arms, lambs carrying St George's Cross, a pair of royal lions, and 'God Preserve Our King and Parliament'. But, alongside these, it also featured the company crests of the Cloth Workers, the Weavers, and the Worsted Weavers. This message was rendered still more explicit by the two figures who announced: 'Preserve your fleece / Employ your poore / you'll then have Coyn / and People Store'. The promised prosperity was represented by overflowing horns of plenty and images of all the industries supposedly helped by the statute, including not just wool-workers but also farmers, landlords, sailors, and even alehouses. Finally, at centre, a large and diverse gathering of people danced around a bonfire singing 'Now Let us / all Joyne Hand in Hand / T'advance what most / Promotes our Land'. Taken together, the iconography of this broadsheet told an unambiguous tale in which England heroically defended her domestic craftsmen, thus bringing about an era of communal abundance and shared success.

The weavers also devoted considerable energy to presenting themselves as good Englishmen. For instance, they printed (and presumably sang) broadside ballads which emphasised their patriotism and their devotion to the national interest. One printed in 1689 entitled *The Weavers Loyal Resolution* described their willingness to defend their country, their love for their

---

[56] Claudius Rey, *The Weavers True Case* (1719), pp. 3, 20; Edward Johnson, *The Weavers Case* (1719), p. 12. Similarly, another pamphleteer with obvious sympathy for the weavers began by forswearing 'any particular Interest' and claimed to be solely 'desirous of the good of the Nation'; he then alluded to the 'Profit to the Nation' or 'the great loss to this Nation' on almost every page of this twenty-four page pamphlet against the calico imports: *The Profit and Loss of the East-India-Trade, Stated, and Humbly Offer'd to the Consideration of the Present Parliament* (1700). For similarly nationalist defences of the cloth industry in the Elizabethan and early Stuart period see Roze Hentschell, *The Culture of Cloth in Early Modern England* (Aldershot, 2008), esp. ch. 2.

[57] This refers to *Statutes of the Realm*, VII, pp. 598–99 (11 Will. III, c. 10). There were, however, many other protectionist acts of this sort: Ralph Davis, 'The Rise of Protection in England, 1689–1786', *Economic History Review*, New Series, 19:2 (1966), pp. 307–13; Patrick O'Brien, Trevor Griffiths, and Philip Hunt, 'Political Components of the Industrial Revolution: Parliament and the English Cotton Textile Industry, 1660–1774', *Economic History Review*, 2nd ser., 44 (1991), pp. 395–423; David Ormrod, *The Rise of Commercial Empires: England and the Netherlands in the Age of Mercantilism, 1650–1770* (Cambridge, 2003).

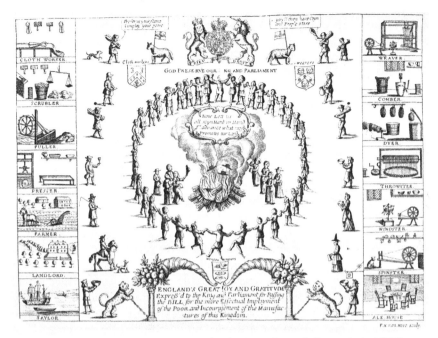

Figure 3.2. A broadsheet expressing *England's Great Joy and Gratitude* (c.1700) at a new bill prohibiting East Indian imports was filled with symbolic images of both the nation-state and the broad array of trades that together supposedly represented the 'national interest'.

new king and queen, and their gratitude to the parliament for supporting their trade.[58] According to this balladeer, 'The Weaver at all times firmly stood, / And would Work or Fight for his Country's Good', especially since 'Good Parliament' had just rejected a bill which would have ruined their livelihoods. The *Loyal Resolution* thus called on weavers to join together to 'for the Nations Wellfare' and reaffirmed their fealty to the English polity, at least as long as their rulers continued to 'let us freely our Trades Enjoy'. By repeatedly alluding to the state's role as the protector of industry, this ballad implicitly reminded lawmakers that the patriotism of artisanal workers was closely linked to parliament's ability to foster 'Justice and Prospertie'.

These laudatory portrayals of commercial policy were part of an expansive discourse about the economics of 'Englishness'. Their subject matter – the fortunes of the textile trades – was entirely typical, but their uniformly optimistic narratives were unusual. Complaints and petitions were much more common than acclamations and panegyrics. Some handicraft workers, for example, argued that the growing numbers of unskilled labourers imper-

---

[58] *A New Coppy of Verses of The Weavers Loyal Resolution* (1689) in PB, V, p. 138.

illed the strength of the kingdom as a whole. Hence, in the 1680s, a group claiming to represent the weavers, clothworkers, combers, and many others in the textile trade 'within this Realme of England' tried to alert parliament to the national danger caused by unrestricted labour markets. They argued that, although these trades were vital 'to the supportation of the Comon Wealth', many of those who now practised these 'Misteryes' had never served full apprenticeships. As a result of their 'want of skill & ability', these illicit workers made 'badd' products which 'hath caused our cloath & stuffes & other manufactures of wooll to bee disesteemed & unliked' both at home and abroad. This, in turn, impoverished lawful workers, discouraged potential apprentices, prompted the emigration of skilled craftsmen, and ultimately disadvantaged the entire English economy.[59]

The central role of textile production in each of the preceding examples is no accident, for the men and women involved in these 'Misteryes' were the most numerous and, at times, the most assertive 'artificers' in the realm. They had potent craft organisations and often enjoyed the support of influential members of the merchant community, features which could make their claims to represent the national interest particularly persuasive. But they were not the only trade to appeal to the spirit of patriotism. For instance, when a number of shipwrights petitioned for the creation of a national corporation in the 1690s, they claimed that this would allow them to 'restrain Vagrants and other Uncapable Persons from practising at the Shipwright's Trade' and 'Breed a more Useful and Deserving Number of Experienced Able Journey-men Shipwrights and Calkers'.[60] They firmly insisted that this corporation would bring 'a great Benefit ... to His Majesty's Service and Merchants' as well as 'the Encouragement and Safety of Navigation in general'. In the rhetoric of these and other occupational groups, the needs of the craft aligned closely with the needs of the national 'Comon Wealth'.

However, despite the prevalence of these patriotic appeals, the real power of Englishness as a unifying ideal came from its opposites: foreignness and treachery. As is well known, identities tend to emerge through constant juxtaposition with supposed alterity, and this was no exception. Indeed, 'the Other' was a prominent fixture on the economic landscape, and one which deserves further attention. As this section shows, this threat could take the form of immigrants, imports, consumers, merchants, financiers, or even rulers. Moreover, the proposed geographic origin of these villains shifted repeatedly over the course of the later Stuart period. Yet, despite this variability, the concept of a foreign danger had real force in English economic

---

[59] CHC, PA 100/16/8. Opposition to calico imports produced similar appeals: *The Just Complaint of the Poor Weavers* (1719), pp. 5–7.

[60] *Reasons for the Regular Re-Establishment of the Corporation of Shipwrights of England* (c.1696), p. 4. On the importance of 'ability', 'experience', and 'skill' in the minds of workers see John Rule, 'The Property of Skill in the Period of Manufacture', in Patrick Joyce (ed.), *The Historical Meaning of Work* (Cambridge, 1987), pp. 99–118.

culture, becoming a focal point for much complaint and protest throughout the era.

In the minds of some labouring people, the most immediate foreign threat might even live right next door. Perennial resentments against newcomers often centred on their perceived impact on employment and wages, an issue which provoked hostile commentary in both earlier and later centuries.[61] Thus, when thousands of Huguenot refugees arrived in England after the Revocation of the Edict of Nantes in 1685, popular animosity quickly found expression in street balladry. In that very year, *The Valiant Weaver* declared that 'We scarcely can get us bread … / Because the French are grown so ill, / In selling their work at an under price', leading to a bitter refrain: 'weavers all may curse their fates / Because the French work under rates'.[62] Later, in the 1690s, *The Poor Man's Complaint* argued that 'sad Poverty's reigning' because 'Strangers from France' have 'run down all Labour, / which pinches the Poor'.[63] These unwelcoming verses not only reflected an attitude common among certain groups of irregularly employed urban workers but also intensified it by providing a concise explanation for those experiencing material hardship. And, as seen later in the chapter, broadsides like these might well be connected to the violent anti-immigrant unrest which occasionally struck England's urban centres.[64]

Interestingly, it was not just French craftsmen who faced accusations of this sort. Scottish peddlers endured similar denigration in another ballad published in the 1690s, which claimed that the Scots were a 'pilfering', 'beggerly', 'runagate Crew' who 'swarm from their nation' onto English soil.[65] Likewise, when traders and shopkeepers petitioned against 'Pedlers, Hawkers, and Petty-Chapmen' in 1675, they carefully noted 'That the greatest part of

---

[61] For anti-French and anti-Dutch protests in sixteenth century see Robin Gwynn, *Huguenot Heritage: The History and Contribution of the Huguenots in Britain* (London, 1985), ch. 7; Laura Yungblut, *Strangers are Settled Here Among Us: Policies, Perceptions and Presence of Aliens in Elizabethan England* (London, 1996), ch. 2, esp. pp. 40–44. For anti-Irish protests in eighteenth and nineteenth centuries see Snell, *Parish*, pp. 53–4; Colley, *Britons*, pp. 348–9; Daniel Statt, *Foreigners and Englishmen: The Controversy over Immigration and Population, 1660–1760* (Newark, 1995), pp. 184–5.

[62] E. Lipson, *History of the Woollen and Worsted Industries* (London, 1921), p. 26 (Crawford ballad no. 1438).

[63] *The Poor Man's Complaint* (c.1692–9), in PB, II, p. 88, 2nd edn in PB, IV, p. 300. Likewise, another attack on foreigners, who 'are like the Plague of Lice in Egypt', singled out the French because 'they destroy the Trade of our Natives like so many Locusts, our poor Weavers are almost Ruin'd by them': 3 June 1704, *Observator*, issue 22. Even a tract proclaiming the benefits of immigration admitted that 'the general cry is that they eat the bread out of our mouths, they sell their goods when we can't, they work cheaper than we, live in holes, pay neither scot nor lot; and if we should have many more of them, sure we should have nothing to do': Houghton, *England's Great Happiness*, p. 8. See also the tracts and printed petitions discussed in Statt, *Foreigners*, pp. 58–60, 95–7, 114–19.

[64] See below pp. 212–13.

[65] *The Crafty Scotch Pedler* (c.1692–9), in PB, IV, p. 326.

these People are no Real Natives, but most of another Nation; whose great Encouragements are such, that they daily Flock from their own Country into Ours, only to follow this Trade'. Whereas native citizens supported the polity through taxes, these foreign 'loose and vagrant sort of People' did not.[66] Such sentiments were not confined to mere rhetoric: official actions against unlawful trading often specifically targeted foreigners. In 1683, for example, the town of Hereford issued a presentment against

> all wandering persons, especially Scotchmen, who under pretence of trade go as spies about the country having no habitation, nor paying his Majesty any tribute, but subverting his Majesty's subjects by taking their trade out of their hands. And if a rebellion should happen, which may God forbid, they would prove very dangerous to this nation, as this city and county can affirm by woeful experience.[67]

So, although Nigel Goose and Joseph Ward have recently argued that we should not overestimate popular xenophobia in early modern England, it is clear that economic anxiety could easily combine with a more general fear of aliens to produce undeniably ugly results.[68] The national economic community remained, at least in the minds of many, a polity that ought to be exclusive.[69]

Sometimes, commodities themselves seemed to imperil the livelihoods of ordinary citizens. Foreign goods, claimed prolific pamphleteer Richard Haines in 1674, were 'the *grand Cause* of our *Miseries*', which 'hath brought the Body Politick into this pining Consumption, and makes us so loudly complain of bad Trade and empty Pockets'. Hence, the country must 'shut the door' to linen, brandy, bay salt, saltpetre, iron, and most French wines, because they were 'superfluous and injurious to the *well-being* of the

---

[66] *Reasons Humbly Offered to … Parliament by the Drapers … and other Trading House-keepers* (1675). Foreign merchants who traded in England were another source of nationalist complaints: John Blanch, *An Abstract of the Grievances of Trade* (1694), esp. pp. 3–4.

[67] HMC, *The Manuscripts of Rye and Hereford Corporations, Capt. Loder-Symonds, Mr. E. R. Wodehouse, M.P., and others: Thirteenth Report, Appendix VI* (no. 31, London, 1892), p. 350. For similar orders that specifically target Scotsmen see *Carlisle Muni. Recs*, pp. 112, 155, 214; *County of Buckingham Sessions Records*, I, p. 156.

[68] Nigel Goose, '"Xenophobia" in Elizabethan and Early Stuart England: An Epithet Too Far?' in Nigel Goose and Lien Luu (eds), *Immigrants in Tudor and Early Stuart England* (Brighton, 2005), pp. 110–35; Joseph Ward, 'Fictitious Shoemakers, Agitated Weavers and the Limits of Popular Xenophobia in Elizabethan England', in Randolph Vigne and Charles Littleton (eds), *From Strangers to Citizens: The Integration of Immigrant Communities in Britain, Ireland and Colonial America, 1550–1750* (Brighton, 2001), pp. 80–87.

[69] Indeed, recent events indicate that this attitude remains significant. For an example see below, p. 230.

Kingdom'.[70] During the reign of William III, a ballad expressed the same sentiment more simply when it declared that luxurious merchandise 'From Forreign-Lands' brought 'sorrow ... to the Nation', and *England's Almanack* described Indian imports as 'prejudicial to this Kingdom'.[71] By 1719, *The Just Complaint of the Poor Weavers* could draw on decades of hostile commentary to claim that the decay of trade was caused by an overseas enemy much worse than Spain. Instead, the culprit was 'an Invasion from India; the Plague of Callicoes over-spreading the Land, starving our Men out of their Looms, and taking the Bread out of their Mouths'.[72]

Depicting certain imports as inherently 'anti-English' was common enough, but protectionists often applied the same trope to the people who provided material support for this 'prejudicial' trade, especially those who appeared to betray their fellow subjects merely for the sake of vanity. A vicious doggerel produced in 1719, at the height of the anti-calico campaign, offers an illuminating example of the rhetoric employed against these consumers:

> [Calico wearers] neglect their own Works,
> Employ Pagans and Turks,
> And let foreign Trump'ry
>   o'er spread em:
> Shut up their own Door,
> And starve their own Poor,
> For a tawdery Callico Madam.
> O! this Tatterdemalion Madam.
> Were there ever such Fools!
> Who despising the Rules,
> For the common Improvement
>   of Nations:
> Tye up the Poor's Hands,
> And search foreign Lands,
> For their Magpie ridiculous Fashions.
> For their Magpie ridiculous Fashions.[73]

---

[70] Richard Haines, *The Prevention of Poverty* (1674), pp. 4–14, quotes at p. 4. See also Slingsby Bethel, *An Account of the French Usurpation upon the Trade of England* (1679), pp. 7–10. For a complaint from Jesey in 1714 about French textile imports, which is 'prejudicial to Great Britain' and violates the 'antient Right and Priviledge' of the island's inhabitants see TNA, SP 44/249, pp. 26–8.

[71] *The Troubles of this World* (1688–1702), in PB, II, p. 87; Capp, *Astrology*, p. 116.

[72] *The Just Complaint of the Poor Weavers* (1719), p. 31. See also Rey, *The Weavers True Case*, p. 14; Smith, 'Callico Madams', p. 32.

[73] Plummer, *London Weavers' Company*, p. 297. A different version of the same ballad was printed in *The Northern Cuckold, Or, The Garden House Intrigue ... With ... the Spitle-Fields Ballad on the Calicos* (1721).

Here, the evocations of alterity ('Pagans and Turks', 'foreign Trump'ry', 'foreign Lands') were sharpened by accusations of national betrayal ('neglect their own Works', 'starve their own Poor', 'despising ... common Improvement'), forging a potent weapon in the weavers' crusade against East Indian fabrics.[74] While this was neither the first nor the last time particular consumers were accused of disloyalty, its ferocity and intensity indicates how firmly this association had become embedded in the English consciousness.

As might be expected, the deepest animosity was often reserved for the wealthy men who directly managed trade of this kind. The merchants of the East India Company were obvious targets as they seemed to be 'very rich, and live like *Lords*', even though 'a whole *Million* of Souls must starve and perish, and the *Nation* be ruin'd, to satisfy [their] boundless Ambition'.[75] According to 'a Weaver of London', their practice of sending out a ship loaded with gold which then returned filled with Asian cloth was 'like drawing out the pure and spirituous Blood of a Man's Veins, and filling them with Hydropick Humours'.[76] The visceral language used to denounce these merchants emphasised their dubious function in the body-politic; indeed, it implied that they were more likely to contribute to its *dis*function than to provide useful nourishment, a claim inspired by both contemporary balance-of-trade theories and a traditional distrust of foreign extravagance.

Those involved in the East India trade probably faced more condemnation than most merchants, but others involved in importing overseas luxuries sometimes fared little better in the public eye. Commentators such as John Bellers and John Blanch, for example, argued that 'too many of our Subjects are at present engaged against the true Interest of their Native Mother', pursuing 'sinister and private Gain' by selling necessities like food and raw wool abroad 'to supply the Pride and Luxury of others by the returns'.[77] In the minds of contemporaries, the damage caused by such exchanges was inexcusable, for the needs of the national community should have ranked far higher than the trading privileges of individual merchants. In 1675, for instance, shoemakers complained that many leather merchants forced up the price while lowering the quality by

---

[74] For other references to calico-wearers and other 'traitorous' consumers as impoverishing 'the poor working People in this your own *dear Native Countrey*; when at the same time you encourage, enrich and advance the Well being and Prosperity of a *Heathenish, Barbarous, and Savage People*, who are many thousands of Miles distant from you', see Johnson, *The Weavers Case*, p. 12; *The Female Manufacturer's Complaint*, p. 10; Rey, *The Weavers True Case*, pp. 5–6, 9, 19; John Dunton, *The Parable of the Top-Knots* (1691). For similar complaints in the Elizabethan and early Stuart period see Hentschell, *Culture of Cloth*, ch. 4, esp. pp. 112–14, 124–5.
[75] Rey, *The Weavers True Case*, p. 33; *The Great Necessity and Advantage of Preserving Our Own Manufacturies* (1697), p. 5.
[76] *The Great Necessity and Advantage* (1697), p. 9. For a similar use of this analogy see Peacham, *The Worth of a Peny*, p. 4.
[77] Bellers, *Essays About the Poor*, pp. 10–12; Blanch, *The Naked Truth*, pp. 1–2; Culpeper, *Plain English*, pp. 13–14.

'Transporting, Fore-stalling and Ingrossing'. This apparently became a national concern because 'these Purse-proud people' were denying the 'many hundred of poore Shoe-makers all *England* over' of 'their proper Rights and freedome of buying Leather' while mocking the state by 'bragging and boasting the Law can take no hold on them'.[78] The problem seems to have persisted as the shoe-makers issued another printed plea more than a decade later. Here, they used the idioms of Englishness even more explicitly, declaring that a prohibition on 'transporting' leather overseas 'would greatly increase that Trade of the Nation', save thousands from impoverishment, and support 'many Jolly men ... who will be ready to serve the King and Country on all occasions'. In short, they sought only to promote the country's welfare and 'preserve our Native Right' from the perfidies of rich miscreants.[79]

That some subjects might have aims antithetical to 'the true Interest of their Native Mother' was a perception which pervaded the voluminous pamphlet literature on international trade. However, it was just one mani-festation of an oft-recurring trope: the enemy within. Any individual or group who seemed to oppress or exploit their fellow countrymen was likely to be attacked as a traitor to the commonweal, frequently in the provocative (and topical) language of conspiracy or usurpation. Hence, discussions of economic morality regularly incorporated national villains from the rogue's gallery of popular political culture – including long-established figures and recent additions, both official and oppositional.[80]

The idioms used were sometimes relatively generic, invoking basic notions of malevolence, criminality, and culpability. Profiteering grain merchants, for instance, appeared in cheap print as nefarious outlaws. A broadsheet claiming to be *The Poor Man's Complaint* cast 'Meal-men' as 'covetous Villains' who 'endeavor to starve up the poor' by carrying corn 'as March-andize / Across the wide ocean', and by hoarding, 'a crime which cannot be excus'd' through which 'the whole Kingdom was grossly abus'd'.[81] Likewise, almanac writers depicted exporters and engrossers as felonious at best, with one astrologer reporting that the 'most excellent justice done upon hoarders of corn (as I have read it in our English chronicles) [is] to hang them up as enemies to the country'.[82] Variations on this last phrase also appeared in the calico campaign. Here, self-described weavers denounced wearers of East India fabrics as 'Foes of their Country' and claimed that the merchants

---

[78] *A Remonstrance of all the Shoemakers ... against Transporting, Forestalling and Ingrossing of Leather* (1675).
[79] *The Humble Petition of the Poor Journymen Shooe-makers* (1691?).
[80] For medieval examples of particular economic malefactors being seen as a threat to the whole 'commonwealth' see Davis, *Market Morality*, pp. 107, 120, 130.
[81] *The Present State of England: Containing The Poor Man's Complaint* (c.1690–1703), in *PB*, II, p. 77. This notion of corn merchants as 'traitors' in times of war survived for centuries: Searle, *Morality*, p. 204.
[82] Capp, *Astrology*, pp. 104–5.

who taught Indians how to make English styles had engaged in 'a Practice so inconsistent with the Love, and contrary to the interest of their Native Country, that is reckoned in some Countries a capital Crime'.[83] Although complaints like these were hardly as elaborate as some, they still helped to mark the borders of the national community by employing imagery which turned unpopular economic behaviour into an offence against the English state and 'the whole Kingdom'.[84]

The more conspiratorially minded saw economic problems as the direct result of foreign influence or political plotting. In its most innocuous form, this might simply involve blaming the discredited previous regime for impoverishing the country through malicious taxation, injurious commercial policies, and the various other baleful instruments of tyranny. Two ballads published in 1689, for example, thanked William and Mary for the 'rooting out of popery, / that always spoyl'd our Trade'. Formerly, the husbandman had been so ruined 'by the Papists villany' that his 'Wife and Bearns were like to starve', and the hearth tax had sorely 'oppresst' poor people in every corner of England.[85] Such accusations might be entirely benign when offered retrospectively, but they took on a very different meaning in the context of the Exclusion Crisis of 1678–81. It is thus remarkable that two broadsheets of this sort appeared on the streets in the aftermath of the Popish Plot.[86] Perhaps sung by the same rowdy crowds of apprentices who fired squibs and burnt effigies of the pope on 5 November, these ballads brazenly declared that 'Papish Jesuits they have spoyl'd our trade: / Which makes the Nation for to suffer sore', because

> The Times are hard and Money scant,
> The Poor e're long will Pine for want,
>   unless they be Reliev'd;
> Whilst Children cry for lack of Bread,

---

[83] 'The Spittle-Fields Ballad: Or, The Weavers Complaint against the Callico Madams', in *The Northern Cuckold* (1721), p. 3; *The Great Necessity and Advantage* (1697), p. 8. See also Smith, 'Callico Madams', p. 32. In a rather different context, pamphleteers denounced any attempt to protect or expand the economic rights of resident aliens as 'the Contrivance of those within our own Bowels to Oppress our Poor', 'a Conspiracy to incite our Poor to a Levelling against their own Inclination', 'a Design against the Common Good of our Nation': Blanch, *An Abstract of the Grievances of Trade*, p. 17; Statt, *Foreigners*.

[84] Likewise, in many popular tales of highwayman, rich oppressors were portrayed as the 'Great Villains' while ordinary robbers were depicted as 'Robin Hoods': McKenzie, *Tyburn's Martyrs*, ch. 4.

[85] *Popery's Downfal, and the Protestants Uprising* (1689), in *PB*, II, p. 316; *England's Joy For the Taking off The Chimney-Money* (1689), in *PB*, IV, p. 308. For the violent opposition to the hearth tax see below p. 216.

[86] *A Looking-glass for all True Protestants* (c.1678–9), in *PB*, II, p. 68; *The Coblers New Prophesie* (c.1679–81), in *PB*, IV, p. 230.

> The Popish Crew are largely fed,
> which makes me much to grieve.

So, although they repeatedly declared their loyalty to 'our King and Parliament', the broadsides contained a deeply politicised message. They were, after all, circulating at a moment when mass protests inspired by the royal heir's Catholicism were sweeping through London. As such, only a provocative balladeer would sing that England must round up the 'Plotting' papists who sought 'to devour … The Nations Wealth' and 'send them packing to the Pope' – yet these basic sentiments were both very widely believed and superficially uncontroversial, so it would hardly be surprising if such verses reached an extremely broad audience. Indeed, householders concerned about their economic situation and the threat of international popery might have found this interpretation of recent events alluringly persuasive. The defence of English Protestantism seemed to align tidily with the defence of English trade.[87]

The Revolution of 1688 banished court Catholicism and many of the anxieties which had accompanied it, but virulent anti-popery remained common among the poorer sort. Groups seeking popular support for particular economic policies often incorporated these prejudices into their arguments. As usual, textile workers provided a number of examples of this tactic, including a printed petition from December 1689 in which the silk-weavers of London set out their opposition to a bill that would have required the wearing of wool or leather for five months of the year. They claimed that the proposed law would cause 'the great Depopulation, Dishonour, and Danger of the Nation' as these weavers would be forced to emigrate or 'take rude and desperate courses'. Since it would thus 'much depress the Protestant, and advance the Papal Interest', the petitioners suggested that it might be one of the many 'designs' by Jesuits to turn 'the People from the Love of Parliaments' and 'carry away the Trade of the Nation … to other parts of the World that are generally our Enemies'. As an alternative, they argued that if parliament instead prohibited the import of 'Foreign Manufactured' textiles such as calicoes, it would 'strengthen' both the nation and 'the Prot-

---

[87] For example, in many economic complaints, anti-popery was intertwined with francophobia, and some laments about French economic 'incroachments' indirectly blamed the English government: *The Case of the English Weavers and French Merchants truly Stated* (c.1670); JHC, IX, pp. 183–4 (15 Dec 1670); *A Scheme of the Trade …* *Between England and France* (1674); *An Account of the Proceedings at Guild-Hall, London, at the Tolke-moot, or Common-Hall, held 24th of June 1676* (1676), esp. pp. 2–3, 9; Bethel, *An Account of the French Usurpation*. For the context of these complaints about French imports and their restrictions on English exports see Margaret Priestley, 'Anglo-French Trade and the "Unfavourable Balance" Controversy, 1660–85', *Economic History Review*, 2nd ser., 4:1 (1951), pp. 37–40, 48.

estant Religion'.[88] Though there were presumably several reasons why this
bill failed to pass, this strikingly nationalist petition may well have contributed to its demise. This politicised paranoia returned in 1719, though by this
time the focus had narrowed exclusively to calicoes. Accordingly, Claudius
Rey argued that 'the *Disaffected Party* hath greatly *forwarded* and *incouraged*
this pernicious Fashion … as they knew must *necessarily* bring the utmost
Calamity and *Misery* upon the poorest sort of *working People*', and 'then
[they] tell 'em that it was the *King* and *Government's* Fault'.[89] Although the
blame seemed to shift from the Jesuits to the Jacobites over these decades,
both sets of conspirators shared an association with popish tyranny.

In contrast, the outsiders at the opposite end of the religious spectrum
had a much more ambiguous place in later Stuart political discourse. Variously labelled 'fanatics', 'sectaries', and 'dissenters', their relationship with
the regime changed frequently between the Restoration and the Hanoverian
Accession. However, for many conformists, they connoted both political
and economic deviance throughout this period. For instance, while parliament was erecting the pillars of the Clarendon Code, a rhyming pamphlet
entitled *The Citizens Complaint* declared that the 'want of Trading' was
caused by the 'Disloyalty' of those who claim to be 'Saints' even though
they show no charity, hurt the kingdom, ignore the law, and disregard the
king. Hence, 'the poor distressed Tradesman's Cry' was 'Down with all Sects;
but up with Loyalty':

> Were this but so, you need not then to fear
> But Trade would mend, and every thing appear
> In its full Lustre; Then the poor would cry,
> God blesses us because of Unity.'[90]

A ballad printed around three decades later, after the Act of Toleration had
begun the process of unravelling the penal laws against nonconformists, indicates that the popular stereotype of the seditious, avaricious dissenter had
lost little of its appeal. It attacked 'Presbyter Jack, / that zealous Professor',
whose fealty lasted only until the king asked for a share of his 'Mammon'
to defend the realm – then 'Covetousness' led to 'the Destruction of Reli-

[88] *The Weavers of London do humbly offer to … Parliament; That this Kingdom of England will Sustain Great Evils and Damage by Enjoyning the Wear of Woollen Manufactures and Leather* (1689). For the bill itself and petitions against it see JHC, X, pp. 298 (29 Nov. 1689), 302 (6 Dec.1689), 306 (12 Dec. 1689).
[89] Rey, *The Weavers True Case*, pp. 15–16. He also argued that the only workers in England whose sole livelihood was calico printing were 'those *French Roman Cathlicks*, who were forced to fly from their Country, after this *pernicious Trade* was totally forbidden in *France*': ibid., p. 23.
[90] *The Citizens Complaint*, pp. 1, 7. See also Schlatter, *Social Ideas*, p. 172.

gion and Loyalty'.[91] The omnipresence of the 'greedy puritan' as a stock figure made it easy for commentators to blame economic ills on religious and political nonconformity, thus reinforcing the equation of unity with prosperity and of disunity with distress.[92]

Few in William III's government would have objected to crude attacks on tax resisters as unpatriotic. Yet, they too could face opposition based on negative stereotypes of the Williamite state and the Whigs who ran it. Many of their subjects seem to have regarded the new regime as no less beholden to a foreign interest than its predecessor had been, though now influence appeared to come from Holland rather than from Paris or Rome. This suspicion had its roots in the image of Dutchmen as mercenary Mammonists and plundering 'leather-apron-lords', a stereotype promoted by English propagandists during the three wars fought against the United Provinces between 1652 and 1674.[93] One broadside published in 1665, for example, depicted them visually as spiders, rats, vipers, and many other 'Monstrous' creatures, while describing their 'foul Incroachments … Upon our English in their way of Trade' (Fig. 3.3). It did not take long for this prejudice to re-emerge after 1688 under the growing burden of high taxes, food scarcities, and currency shortages. Sometimes critics grafted xenophobic idioms on to very specific economic complaints, as in the ballad published in 1691 which claimed to speak for loyal sailors. The versifier asserted that the 'New Government' had refused to pay its 'poor Seamen' even after they protected the nation by fighting off the French. Instead, the 'Foreigners and Confederates' appointed by the regime stole these 'poor Men's Pay' and treated them 'like Slaves', forcing them 'to hang or starve', thus 'Brave England does to ruine run, / And Englishmen must be undone'.[94] Such writers, whether outright Jacobites or merely angry Tories, easily politicised the assumed binary opposition between English welfare and foreign interests. An even more explicit example can be found in a short tract printed only a few years after the seamen's ballad. The anonymous author claimed that William III and his foreign henchmen, 'whose Business and Interest it is to advance and secure the Trade of our Rivals the Dutch', had sent corn overseas and ensured that

91 *The Dissatisfied Subject* (c.1692–6), in *PB*, V, p. 136.
92 For denunciations of 'puritans' for oppression, mercilessness, inhospitality, hoarding, and sharp dealing see Wing, *Almanack* (1669), sig. C5r; *A Brief Survey of the Growth of Usury in England* (1673), pp. 2–4; Pittis, *A Spittle Sermon*, pp. 18–19; *Yea & Nay the Quaker, Deceiv'd* (1685–8), in *PB*, IV, p. 280; Dunton, *Englands Alarum*, pp. 11–12; 'Poor Robin', *An Almanack* (1697), sigs. B8r, C6r; Ward, *The Wealthy Shop-keeper*; Tawney, *Religion*, p. 250; Sommerville, *Popular Religion*, p. 102.
93 Pincus, 'From Holy Cause', pp. 288–90; idem, 'Popery, Trade and Universal Monarchy: The Ideological Context of the Outbreak of the Second Anglo-Dutch War', *English Historical Review*, 107 (1992), pp. 22–6; idem, 'From Butterboxes to Wooden Shoes: The Shift in English Popular Sentiment from anti-Dutch to anti-French in the 1670s', *Historical Journal*, 38:2 (1995), pp. 336–40.
94 *The Sea Martyrs* (1691), in *PB*, V, p. 375.

Figure 3.3. The central images in *The Dutch Boare Dissected* (1665) depicted Hollanders as, among other things, plotting 'Spider-Imps' (A), all-consuming rats (B), devious 'Vipers' (C), perjuring forgers (D), and croaking 'Frogs' (L).

'the Weavers Act hath been some time industriously baffled, and still meets with Demurs and Delays'. Their 'Design', apparently, was to cause mass unemployment and hunger because they 'think they shall want no Souldiers if they can make Beggars enough'.[95] Though few other ballads or pamphlets were as direct in alleging a foreign conspiracy, complaints about the expense of William III's wars often implied that 'We Bankrupt our Selves for Maintaining the Dutch'.[96]

[95] *The Present State of England* (1694), p. 4.
[96] John Vincent Beckett, 'Land Tax or Excise: The Levying of Taxation in Seventeenth- and Eighteenth-Century England', *English Historical Review*, 100 (1985), p. 290. For more

The ease with which the idioms of patriotism and nationality could be employed to discuss economic issues shows the prominence of the English polity (and its supposed enemies) in the popular psyche. Indeed, the moralised binary between nationality and foreignness apparently became stronger, rather than weaker, during this period.[97] Other historians have shown that the later Stuart era witnessed the expansion of 'protectionism', an increasing focus on the 'national interest', and, more broadly, a heightened public awareness of 'Englishness' (or, later, 'Britishness').[98] These changes gave national identity an unprecedented role in the economic culture of the era. Appeals to patriotism could turn a recommendation about trade policy into a call for civic solidarity and communal advancement. More negatively, this mentality could also stoke fears of foreign danger that might be projected onto immigrant workers, imported commodities, disloyal merchants, alien plotters, or even the government itself. More than ever before, the 'imagined community' shaped economic relations by influencing state policies, commercial practices, and everyday interaction in the marketplace.

3 Little Commonwealths[99]

Just as loyalty to the nation often cut through the ties which supposedly bound together all of humanity, localised identities could take precedence over a more general sense of 'Englishness'. People almost invariably prioritised the place they regarded as 'home' – whether a neighbourhood or village, or a more institutionalised entity such as a parish or borough. In part, this resulted from the many practical concerns and interests that neighbours tended to share, but these identities also drew much of their

complaints about the poor suffering 'to defend the Country of Strangers, not their own' see *The Poor Man's Petition to the Lords and Gentlemen of the Kingdom: or, Englands Cry for Peace* (c.1693), p. 7.

[97] Denunciations of insufficiently patriotic businessmen as 'war profiteers' or 'traitors' continued even when the political economy of free trade was at its height in the 1850s, and of course these tropes were extremely common during the world wars: Searle, *Morality*, pp. 205–12.

[98] For examples see Ormrod, *Rise of Commercial Empires*; Davis, 'Rise of Protection'; Pincus, 'From Holy Cause'; Colley, *Britons*, ch. 3; Knights, *Representation and Misrepresentation*, pp. 150–51, 286–7.

[99] For the use of terms like 'little commonwealth' to refer to parishes and towns see Hindle, *On the Parish?* p. 334; Withington, *Politics of Commonwealth*, esp. pp. 10–11. It should be noted that the word 'commonwealth' became much rarer after the Restoration, but this should not be equated with the decline of local 'community' itself: Withington, *Society*, ch. 5, esp. pp. 145–6; Early Modern Research Group, 'Commonwealth Contexts: The Social, Cultural, and Conceptual Contexts of an Early Modern Keyword', *Historical Journal*, 54:3 (2011), pp. 679–84.

strength from the fecund soil of a culture which promoted localised mutuality and solidarity against economic 'interlopers'.

In the case of London, the grandest of all these 'little commonwealths', this sense of economic community found expression in cheap broadsides. The city's printers produced several ballads extolling its wealth and prosperity, including one entitled *Londons Praise* which stands out thanks to its especially communalist tone. Like others of the genre, *Londons Praise* emphasised the strength of the urban economy and the virtues of its 'good substantial' citizens; yet it also repeatedly lauded civic unity and equality. For example, the balladeer specifically acknowledged the horizontal ties which bound together all the city's freemen by claiming that the magistrates defended 'their Neighbours' from malefactors and

> every year they change Lord Mayor,
> to shew their mutual Love,
> And that in power they equal are,
> and none the other above.[100]

So, while not neglecting to extol the stately grandeur of the mayor and aldermen, this panegyric simultaneously called attention to the presumed solidarity, perhaps even egalitarianism, inherent in urban citizenship.

This attitude also suffused the economic culture of England's other incorporated cities and towns. Jonathan Barry has provocatively described it as 'bourgeois collectivism', arguing that townspeople tirelessly promoted 'all those qualities, such as thrift, respectability, and industry, often labelled as the 'Protestant work ethic' and seen as the foundation of individualism', but 'their success was assumed to depend on *collective* rather than individual action' and 'they were matched by a set of overtly collective virtues, of sociability and good fellowship'.[101] The instruments used to propagate these ideals were manifold. Not only did freemen directly instruct their children and apprentices in the virtues of civic mutuality, they also attempted to give their imagined community physical form though elaborate pomp and circumstance on special occasions. Ritualised urban festivities – such as the Lord Mayor's Show in London and Guild Day in Norwich – revived markedly after 1660, and their undeniable elements of hierarchy should not blind us the fact that, at the same time, they clearly celebrated urban unity and local identity.[102] On a smaller scale, those who sought to trade in towns

---

100 *Londons Praise, or, The Glory of the City* (c.1666–89) in *PB*, IV, p. 339. For songs lauding the city in more general terms see *PB*, I, pp. 188–9; IV, p. 274. For a discussion of London as a 'moral community' see Ward, *Metropolitan Communities*, esp. pp. 11–26.
101 Barry, 'Bourgeois Collectivism', p. 98.
102 Hutton, *Rise and Fall*, p. 230; Joyce Ellis, 'A Dynamic Society: Social Relations in Newcastle-upon-Tyne, 1660–1760', in Peter Clark (ed.), *The Transformation of English Provincial Towns, 1600–1800* (London, 1984), pp. 200–201; Peter Burke, 'Popular

such as Sudbury and Dartmouth could only be granted their 'freedom' by 'performing those ceremonies which are requisite', which included publicly swearing an oath to defend 'the Commonweale and Honour of this Borough and Corporation, and the Liberties, Franchises, priviledges and Customs of the Same'.[103]

In many cases, the participants in these civic events reiterated their loyalty to such ideals by twinning their symbolic displays with practical expressions of mutuality. Corporate feasts, for example, often ended with a distribution to the town's poor, and Lammas Day celebrations in Coventry coincided with the regulation of common lands.[104] Moreover, these pragmatic adjuncts to urban festivity were only small parts of the extensive systems of material support and relief established by townsfolk to protect the welfare of fellow inhabitants. In addition to the well-established structures of parochial support, townspeople might have access to free schools, sponsored apprenticeships, charitable loans, short-term aid, and long-term pensions.[105] Here, 'belonging' was usually contingent on holding 'the freedom of the city', a privilege often assumed to be rather restricted. However, the proportion of freemen in the urban population actually expanded in the later Stuart period, and even in the notoriously oligarchic City of London about 75 per cent of male householders were freemen in 1675.[106] Moreover,

---

Culture in Seventeenth-Century London', *London Journal*, 3 (1977), pp. 151–2. Even Peter Borsay and John Miller, despite emphasising the social and political divisions found in some later Stuart urban festivity, have noted ways that it might also promote unity: Peter Borsay, '"All the town's a stage": Urban Ritual and Ceremony', in Clark (ed.), *Provincial Towns*, pp. 239–43; Miller, *Cities Divided*, ch. 4.

103   SRO–BSE, EE 501/2/8, p. 145; DRO, SM1990. See also the London Freeman's Oath, printed in Richard Garnet, *The Book of Oaths* (1649), pp. 22–4.

104   Ben-Amos, *Culture of Giving*, pp. 217–20; VCH: *Warwickshire*, VIII, p. 204. For examples of 'unusually inclusive' corporate feasting, which could include subsidies for freemen and 'the commons', see Miller, *Cities Divided*, p. 95.

105   Barry, 'Bourgeois Collectivism', pp. 95–6, 99; Withington, *Politics of Commonwealth*, pp. 180–86; Perry Gauci, *Politics and Society in Great Yarmouth, 1660–1722* (Oxford, 1996), p. 43. Also, many new inter-parochial 'Corporations for the Poor' were founded in the late seventeenth century, which strengthened city-wide economic ties: Slack, *From Reformation*, ch. 5; Miller, *Cities Divided*, pp. 71–3. For the increasing number of civic apprenticeship in York during this period see Withington, 'Citizens', pp. 141–3.

106   The proportion of male householders who were freemen in other towns in the late seventeenth century could also be substantial: more than two-thirds in York; over half in Newcastle; around one-third in Norwich and Great Yarmouth: Phil Withington, 'Public Discourse, Corporate Citizenship, and State Formation in Early Modern England', *American Historical Review*, 112:4 (2007), p. 1033; Jonathan Barry, 'Civility and Civic Culture in Early Modern England: The Meanings of Urban Freedom', in Peter Burke, Brian Harrison, and Paul Slack (eds), *Civil Histories: Essays presented to Sir Keith Thomas* (Oxford, 2000), p. 184; Ellis, 'Dynamic Society', pp. 201, 223 n. 31; Gauci, *Politics and Society*, p. 18. Over the early modern period as a whole, freemen may have been 'commonly between a quarter and a half of male householders in the larger

while access to subsidised education and pensions was usually limited to the families of freemen, other forms of civic support were offered to the town-dwellers more generally. In Northampton the corporation distributed about £100 annually in bread, clothes, and money to the local poor throughout this period, and in Bury St Edmunds a charity established in 1662 provided for six 'aged, poore & necessitous people' as long as they were also 'ancient Inhabitants borne within this Towne'.[107] So, poor relief and charitable loans certainly 'reified civil and communal boundaries', but the span of the urban community could often be very wide indeed and access to these resources could itself become a cultural signal, what Phil Withington has called 'a badge of communal belonging'.[108]

That said, this revival of urban communal culture was sometimes temporary. It might be gradually undermined by the social and political divisions which emerged in many towns, sometimes appearing as early as the 1670s. In Oxford, for example, the custom of ritually riding the bounds of the city led to openly partisan disputes that peaked during the reign of William III, and in Norwich the Guild Day celebrations became an occasion for party politics when the mayor decided to decorate his door with pictures linking the Whigs with Oliver Cromwell in 1715.[109] Similarly, Peter Borsay has shown that much of the culture of the post-Restoration 'urban Renaissance' was restricted to the elites.[110] This suggests that, by the eighteenth century, public expressions of civic mutuality were becoming increasingly unlikely to promote unity among townspeople, perhaps leading to an eventual weakening in the bonds of this particular form of economic community. Nonetheless, it would be misleading merely to dismiss this period as one of civic polarisation. In fact, the strength of 'bourgeois collectivism' seems to have been reinvigorated by the outburst of civic festivity after 1660, only starting to wane slowly in later decades.

This same mix of revelry, ritual, and commensality helped to define local communities in rural areas as well. Villagers developed much of their sense of locality from the many seasonal celebrations which filled the agricultural calendar, and this had tangible effects on the nature and dynamics of everyday social relations. According to Robert Malcolmson, 'popular recreations' of this sort 'celebrated those ideals which transcended self' and 'served to foster social cohesiveness and group unity' – they could even temporarily create 'a rough and ready social equality' which cut across differences in

English towns': Paul Slack, 'Great and Good Towns, 1540–1700', in Peter Clark (ed.), *The Cambridge Urban History of Britain, Vol. 2: 1540–1840* (Cambridge, 2000), p. 363.

107 *Northam. Boro. Recs*, II, p. 58; SRO–BSE, EE 500/D4/1/2, fol. 45.

108 Withington, *Politics of Commonwealth*, pp. 184–6.

109 Miller, *Cities Divided*, p. 104. In London, although procession continued long after, the last full Lord Mayor's Show was held in 1702.

110 Borsay, 'All the town's a stage'; idem, *The English Urban Renaissance: Culture and Society in the Provincial Town, 1660–1770* (Oxford, 1998), ch. 11.

wealth and status.[111] The particular form taken by such festivities varied considerably, though most seem to have included some type of feasting, gift-giving or charitable collection. Ronald Hutton, the pre-eminent historian of seasonal customs, has found evidence of these features in numerous cases from the late seventeenth and early eighteenth centuries, especially in the customs associated with Christmas, New Year, Plough Monday, May Day, sheep-shearing, and harvesting.[112] Even newly invented holidays sometimes included elements of mutuality. At Ashby Folville in Leicestershire, for example, the churchwardens feasted 'the neighbours' on Restoration Day.[113] Indeed, under the later Stuarts, the number of localities celebrating annual festivals reached proportions not seen since the sixteenth century, including a temporary revival of parish wakes.[114] So, despite suffering considerable attrition at the hands of would-be reformers under earlier regimes, villages continued to reinforce communal ties with revelry and generosity into the eighteenth century and beyond.

The parochial perambulations during Rogation week offer perhaps the quintessential example of this process of defining and promoting community through ritualised festivity. Historians have long emphasised the social, economic, and cultural importance of this yearly event, and recent research indicates that 'beating the bounds' became more elaborate and more widespread after the Restoration.[115] For instance, some perambulating parishioners carried banners, others wore coloured silk ribbons, and at least one group sang a brief rhyme describing their route.[116] Such visual and aural expressions of locality encouraged participants to focus on collective, rather than individual, concerns – a perspective suggested more explicitly in the 'Exhortation' appointed by the church for this exact purpose. As prepara-

---

[111] Robert Malcolmson, *Popular Recreations in English Society, 1700–1850* (Cambridge, 1973), ch. 5, esp. pp. 81, 84–5. Of course, like Malcolmson, I would note that they could also become focal points of social conflict; they were not inherently forces of cohesiveness.

[112] Hutton, *Stations of the Sun*, pp. 19–20, 61–5, 127, 229–33, 242, 322, 334.

[113] Hutton, *Rise and Fall*, p. 250.

[114] Ibid., ch. 7, esp. pp. 229–30, 238–9; Heal, *Hospitality*, pp. 358–65. For a more subversive, carnivaleque celebration of locality see the Hocktide mock-mayoral elections in the weaving village of Randwick (Glos.) discussed in David Rollison, *The Local Origins of Modern Society: Gloucestershire, 1500–1800* (London, 1992), pp. 211–18.

[115] Much of the inspiration for later work came from Thomas, *Religion*, pp. 71–4. For the importance of Rogation in the later Stuart period see Hindle, 'Beating the Bounds'; Hutton, *Rise and Fall*, pp. 247–8; Hutton, *Stations of the Sun*, ch. 26, esp. pp. 285–6; Snell, *Parish*, pp. 37–40; David Fletcher, 'The Parish Boundary: A Social Phenomenon in Hanoverian England', *Rural History*, 14:2 (2003), esp. pp. 183–6; Nichola Whyte, 'Landscape, Memory and Custom: Parish Identities, c. 1550–1700', *Social History*, 32:2 (2007), pp. 175–80. For urban examples from this period see HA, HBR 20&21, pp. 13, 439; LMA, GL MS01046/1; GL MS01453/3; VCH: *City of York*, pp. 315–18; HMC, *Portland*, II, p. 267 (Yarmouth).

[116] Hindle, 'Beating the Bounds', p. 223.

tion for the Rogation march, the clergyman would tell his flock that 'it is the part of every good Townsman, to preserve as much as lieth in him, the Liberties, Franchises, Bounds, and Limits of his Town and Country', though without causing a breach in 'Love and Charity' through thoughtless strife. The perambulation was, according to the 'Exhortation', an opportunity to discover and condemn those 'greedy men' who 'plough and grate upon their Neighbours Land' or who encroach on 'the common balkes and walkes'; they ought to be 'admonished, and charitably reformed, who be the doers of such private gaining, to the slander of the township, and the hindrance of the Poor'. In addition, the minister would remind parishioners of their collective duties, including mundane responsibilities such as maintaining the local highways and, of course, relieving the local poor.[117] Indeed, the events themselves often became occasions for communal feasting and hospitality, while younger participants sometimes received treats.[118] The economic welfare of the community and its members was thus central to the ritual, rhetoric, and reality of perambulation.

The enthusiasm with which parishioners expressed their collective identity through such festivals and ceremonies was doubtlessly linked to the growing economic importance of one particular institution: the parochial poor relief system. Whether urban or rural, almost every parish in the country collected funds for this purpose by the end of the seventeenth century, and the sums involved grew increasingly large.[119] Of course, under this system, only those regarded as full members of the community had access to communal resources. The first criterion was legal residence: one needed to have earned 'settlement' in the parish, usually through paternity, marriage, year-long employment or apprenticeship. This understanding of 'settlement' – codified in 1662 and reinforced thereafter – arose mostly from practical concerns, but it also helped to ensure that no one who claimed relief would be a stranger to other parishioners.[120] The second criterion was

---

[117] 'An Exhortation' in *Certain Sermons or Homilies*, II, pp. 303–7.

[118] Hindle, 'Beating the Bounds', pp. 213–16, 218; Fletcher, 'Parish Boundary', pp. 185–6. It must be noted, however, that Hindle has argued that both the participation and the accompanying charity became more restricted over the course of the seventeenth century. Moreover, the gradual spread of enclosure may have made perambulations less common.

[119] Hindle, *On the Parish?* pp. 255–6, 262–82; Slack, *Poverty and Policy*, pp. 169–82; Boulton, 'Going On the Parish?', pp. 22–5; Joan Kent and Steve King, 'Changing Patterns of Poor Relief in some English Rural Parishes, circa 1650–1750', *Rural History*, 14:2 (2003), pp. 119–56. As Hindle has shown, the range of support funded by parish rates was extensive. It included not only long-term pensions and short-term relief but also housing, stocks of raw materials, medical care, etc.

[120] One could also earn 'settlement' by renting at £10 per annum or more, serving in a parish office, paying local taxes, owning immoveable property, or simply by birth in the case of illegitimacy. For post-1662 'settlement' more generally see Snell, *Parish*, ch. 3; Snell, *Annals*, pp. 71–3, 99–100; Hindle, *On the Parish?* pp. 304–5; Slack, *Poverty*

moral rather than legal: one had to display the requisite virtues of piety, industry, thrift, sobriety, respectfulness, honesty, and so forth. Only by living within the bounds of the 'moral community' could the poor hope to receive relief from their fellow parishioners.[121] These two preconditions imposed obvious limits on the provision of communal aid, blocking access for those regarded as outsiders or deviants.

The poor themselves were well aware of these limits. When seeking help from magistrates they emphasised the length of their residency and their good standing among their neighbours, sometimes including testimonials to their honest reputations. Typical were the labourer who claimed to have been 'an Inhabitant and resident within the townshipe … all his life time' and the widow who described 'beinge Borne in Yeadon & haivinge lived in a good Condition & was never as yet troblesom to any nor ever had any thinge but through my owne hard Labor'.[122] They clearly understood that support would be provided only to worthy members of the parish community. But if they met these criteria – if, in other words, they could prove that they 'belonged' – many of the poorer sort appear to have expected relief forthwith. Of course very few claimants actually used the language of 'rights' – after all, membership in the 'moral community' of the parish was predicated on a humble, respectful attitude.[123] Still, as the system of local welfare expanded, the poor may have increasingly felt a sense of 'entitlement' and begun to see the parochial relief less as a gift from 'superiors' and more as a resource shared among notional equals.[124] Perhaps this is why, from the 1670s onward, villagers could be heard singing about time spent 'on the parish' as a normal part of growing old and dying:

> A Fig for care, why should we spare
> The Parish is bound to find us,

---

and Policy, pp. 194–5. For a particularly detailed set of examples of the importance of 'settlement' in the late seventeenth century see Gough, History of Myddle, pp. 251–64. This issue was complicated by non-resident relief for certificate holders, but this became common only in the later eighteenth century.

[121] For the virtues expected of the poor see Hindle, On the Parish? pp. 379–98. For the 'moral community' see Wrightson, English Society, pp. 61–2.

[122] WYAS–W, QS 1/25/5/6 (petition of Richard Greenbank, 1686), QS 1/20/6/6/14. See also WYAS–W, QS 1/25/5/6 (petition of Elizabeth Lister, 1686); QS 1/40/1/6 (petition of Francis Walker on behalf of Susan Batley, 1701); NYCRO, QSB 1696/151; Hindle, On the Parish? p. 410; Snell, Parish, pp. 87–9.

[123] For exceptions see Hindle, On the Parish? pp. 416–17.

[124] For growing 'assumptions about entitlement' and 'the right to relief' see Slack, Poverty and Policy, pp. 190–92; Snell, Annals, pp. 72–3, 112; Tim Hitchcock, Peter King, and Pamela Sharpe, 'Introduction', in Tim Hitchcock, Peter King, and Pamela Sharpe (eds), Chronicling Poverty: The Voices and Strategies of the English Poor, 1640–1840 (Basingstoke, 1997), pp. 10–12. For a critique of this historiographical 'consensus' see Hindle, On the Parish? pp. 398–405, 446.

> For thou and I and all must dye,
>   And leave the world behind us.
> The Clark shall Sing, the Bells shall Ring
>   And the Old Wives wind us;
> Sir John shall lay our Bones in Clay,
>   Where no body means to find us.[125]

No ratepayer or overseer would have smiled on such a presumptuous (if fatalistic) attitude towards institutionalised relief, but it may have been a commonplace among many potential paupers.

The destitute were not the only ones to benefit locally managed resources, as can be seen in the case of common rights.[126] A wide range of people – from chief inhabitants to humble cottagers – might enjoy lawful access to pasture, firewood, timber, turf, braken, reeds, sedge, wild fruit and nuts, fish, wildfowl, and even gleaned corn. Restrictions on these rights varied considerably from place to place: occasionally they were monopolised by a resident lord or substantial farmers, but more often 'commoners' included all manorial tenants or urban freemen, and sometimes the inhabitants as whole. In the small Cambridgeshire market town of Whittlesey, tenants who held only a cottage were still entitled to graze several cows on the commons throughout this period.[127] Similarly, while a new agreement for Wigston Magna (Leics.) in 1707 limited communal grazing, it also granted poor men

---

[125] *Merry Drollery, Compleat* (1670; reprinted 1691), p. 217. These verses (or at least the opening couplet) were regarded as a 'famous Song' by the eighteenth century and were still irritating the elite in the mid-nineteenth century: 26 Nov. 1711, *Spectator*, no. 232; J. S. Mill, *Principles of Political Economy* (2 vols, London, 1848), I, p. 331. See also Hindle, *On the Parish?* p. 416.

[126] There is an abundant literature on common rights, but for examples that engage directly with the issues discussed here see Thompson, *Customs in Common*, ch. 3; Hindle, *On the Parish?* pp. 27–48; Neeson, *Commoners*, ch. 2, 6; Withington, *Politics of Commonwealth*, pp. 180–81; Barry, 'Bourgeois Collectivism', pp. 95–6, 99; Sara Birtles, 'Common Land, Poor Relief and Enclosure: The Use of Manorial Resources in Fulfilling Parish Obligations, 1601–1834', *Past and Present*, 165 (1999), pp. 74–106; Peter King, 'Customary Rights and Women's Earnings: The Importance of Gleaning to the Rural Labouring Poor, 1750–1850', *Economic History Review*, 44:3 (1991), pp. 462–6, 469–70; Angus Winchester, *The Harvest of the Hills: Rural Life in Northern England and the Scottish Borders, 1400–1700* (Edinburgh, 2000); Henry French, 'Urban Agriculture, Commons and Commoners in the Seventeenth and Eighteenth Centuries: The Case of Sudbury, Suffolk', *Agricultural History Review*, 48:2 (2000), pp. 171–99; Brodie Waddell, 'Governing England through the Manor Courts, 1550–1850', *Historical Journal*, 55:2 (2012), pp. 279–315.

[127] CA, 126/M72 (Easter 1678; Easter 1718). However, in much of the south-east it appears that most agricultural labourers lacked common rights by the mid-eighteenth century: Leigh Shaw-Taylor, 'Labourers, Cows, Common Rights and Parliamentary Enclosure: The Evidence of Contemporary Comment, c.1760–1810', *Past and Present*, 171 (2001), pp. 95–126.

the right to rent a 'stint' in the pasture at low rate, and cottagers could freely use the shared 'town plow'.[128] In some cases, even the most pitiable of residents had a legally enforceable stake in a village's shared resources. For example, the officers of Acaster Selby, a rural township near York, were told that they would be required to maintain a needy woman living there if they continued to 'deny her pasture on the Comon for a Cow'.[129] In addition, the strength of custom ensured that many of the landless poor came to believe that the access to commons 'was a right equal in rank and value to the property rights so assiduously defended by the gentry', even when they had no legal claim.[130] So, although commentary on commons and enclosure was comparatively rare in the later Stuart period, these rights remained a vital part of the economy of makeshifts in many areas. Even in the early eighteenth century, around 90 per cent of the population of Northamptonshire lived in unenclosed parishes, and at least 180 English towns had commons or common rights at that time.[131] This meant that vast numbers of labouring families had access to land and resources through their status as local commoners.

In contrast to legally defined concepts such as 'parishioner', 'freeman', and 'commoner', the notion of 'neighbour' was entirely subjective. As such, the interaction between the rhetoric and practice of 'neighbourhood' is an especially revealing example of the influence of local 'imagined communities' on everyday life. Thanks to a repeated mistranslation of the Hebrew Bible, the idiom of 'neighbours' and 'neighbourliness' became central to seventeenth-century thinking about social relations, especially in the context of charity. According to Naomi Tadmor, the reworking of ancient scriptural injunctions to fit the social world of early modern England 'helped to underpin contemporary norms of Christian neighbourliness and endow them with fresh significance'.[132] Moreover, the 'language of neighbourly love' was constantly re-interpreted and continually communicated through media such as catechism, sermons, cheap print, and proverbial wisdom – as a result, it infused everyday interactions in both towns and villages.[133]

Yet, one should not assume that the connection between this abstract concept and the neighbourhood economy was unambiguous. In fact, minis-

128 W. G. Hoskins, *The Midland Peasant: The Economic and Social History of a Leicester-shire Village* (London, 1957), pp. 238–9, 241.
129 YCA, F.8, p. 90.
130 Birtles, 'Common Land', p. 96.
131 Neeson, *Commoners*, pp. 58–9; French, 'Urban Agriculture', p. 172.
132 Tadmor, *Social Universe*, p. 26. This terminology appeared in a variety of biblical passages, but probably the most important phrase was: 'Thou shalt love thy neighbour as thy self' (Mark 12:31, Rom. 13:9, Lev. 19:18). This fruitful mistranslation was essentially canonized in the Authorized Version of 1611.
133 Tadmor, *Social Universe*, ch. 1; Green, *Christian's ABC*, pp. 451, 460–66; Wrightson, 'Decline', pp. 22, 25, 30; Tilley, *Proverbs*, pp. 494–6.

ters usually tried to dissuade their audiences from reading the idiom too literally. For example, Isaac Barrow, like most preachers, reflexively used the phrase 'poor neighbour' to refer to *any* suitable objects of charity, irrespective of locality. In his sermon on the subject, published in 1680, he argued that neighbourly love and charity were 'duties of common humanity', because Christ's blood had 'demolished' the 'wall of partition' which had separated the 'holy neighbourhood' of Jews from the gentile 'strangers and foreiners', thus ensuring that 'neighbourhood is universal and unlimited'.[134] In other words, a poor family on the other side of the country had no less a claim to neighbourly benevolence than one living next door. This was the interpretation offered by most later Stuart preachers, but not all were quite so unequivocally anti-literal. White Kennett's sermon at the London mayoral election of 1711, for instance, must have left a slightly different impression. Although he denounced men who used the notion of 'neighbour' to act uncharitably towards those outside the nation or neighbourhood, he also acknowledged that some people were 'our more especial Neighbours, [which] do entitle them to our more peculiar Care and Love'. More specifically, he prioritised Londoners, then Britons, and lastly Protestants in general.[135] So, despite his protestations, Kennett ultimately condoned a more exclusive conception of 'neighbourhood', one that would have been much more comprehensible to those already inclined to prioritise the local poor over distant 'strangers'.

After all, it would have seemed obvious to most people that members of one's own community should be privileged – both formally and informally – in day-to-day economic dealings. While the institutions of parish relief served as a useful means for the localised redistribution of wealth, more casual acts of neighbourliness also had a significant place in the lives of the poor, even in highly developed environments such as London. Historians have uncovered innumerable examples of poor men and women relying on these localised networks of charity for both minor favours and major help in times of hardship. Many paupers, for example, reported surviving only through 'what good people are pleased to bestow ... for their relief', and when the Bingley family lost their farm in Adwick-le-Street (Yorks.) to a fire in 1700, their sole means of subsistence was 'such as their kind neighbours are pleased to afford them'.[136] This sort of consideration for one's fellow

---

[134] Barrow, *Of the Love of God and Our Neighbour*, pp. 79–83 (on Matt. 22:39). See also idem, *The Duty and Reward of Bounty*; Thomas Manton, *A Fifth Volume of Sermons* (1701), pp. 699–700; Anthony Horneck, *Several Sermons on the Fifth of St. Matthew, Being part of Christ's Sermon on the Mount* (2 vols, 1698), II, pp. 420–21, 426–7, 432.

[135] White Kennett, *A Sermon Preach'd in the Church of St. Lawrence-Jewry* (1711), pp. 17–23.

[136] WYAS–W, QS 1/5/1/6/2; QS 1/39/10/6 (petition of John Bingley, 1700). See also NYCRO, QSB 1696/152; *Leic. Boro. Recs*, VII, pp. 24–5; Hindle, *On the Parish?* pp. 58–81; Ben-Amos, *Culture of Giving*, pp. 64–9; Capp, *When Gossips Meet*, pp. 55–7;

villagers probably underlay some of John Crakanthorp's petty disbursements in the early eighteenth century, such as the shilling he gave 'to one or two of my neighbours being hard put to it' in June 1708.[137] Such practices were encouraged by sympathetic portrayals in cheap printed literature. Thus, one ballad told of a poor man from Somerset who became unable to pay his rent after the death of his wife and a sudden rise in the price of corn. His merciless landlord imprisoned him, but his neighbours heard of his suffering and took pity. They raised money amongst themselves and 'quickly releas'd their poor Neighbour from thrall'. Unsurprisingly, the ballad reported that God rewarded the virtuous husbandman and his supporters while punishing the 'cruel Oppressor' with madness.[138] So, although Keith Wrightson has recently argued that 'obligations of neighbourliness perhaps became more narrowly defined and ... more restricted in their accessibility' over the early modern period, both the culture and the customs of the time indicate that this avenue for redress remained open for many people in later Stuart England.[139]

However, the stream of favours shared among locals had a sinister undercurrent, for it emerged not only from mutuality between insiders but also from hostility to outsiders. In the ballad first discussed at the beginning of this section, for example, London was depicted as praiseworthy in part because of its unapologetically exclusionary economic policies:

> No forraigner can set up there,
> the orders are so strong,
> In Shop they must not sell no ware,
> least they the Free-men wrong.[140]

Thanks to the 'constitutions' granted to England's cities and towns, urban freemen enjoyed considerable practical advantages over the non-freemen who lived in suburban areas or in rural hinterlands. Those who had not acquired the 'freedom of the corporation' were officially prohibited from exercising most trades, limited to buying and selling only on market days,

---

Wrightson, 'Decline', pp. 24–5. Although focused on the early seventeenth century, an excellent study of 'neighbourly' economics in London can be found in Jeremy Boulton, *Neighbourhood and Society: A London Suburb in the Seventeenth Century* (Cambridge, 1987), ch. 9–10, esp. pp. 236–47. Perhaps the most pervasive form of neighbourly help was the extension of credit within 'the moral community' of the locality: Muldrew, *Economy of Obligation*, p. 298.

137 Crakanthorp, *Accounts*, pp. 248, 266 and passim.
138 *The Cruel Land-Lord: Or, The Fortunate Husband-man* (1685?), in *RB*, II, p. 186.
139 Wrightson, 'Decline', p. 38.
140 *Londons Praise, or, The Glory of the City* (c.1666–89) in *PB*, IV, p. 339. Similarly, those taking the London freeman's oath swore to 'cullour no Foraigne Goods under or in your name' and 'know no Forraigner to buy or sell any Merchandise with any other Forraigner': Garnet, *The Book of Oaths*, pp. 22–4.

and liable to various tolls or duties.[141] By the late seventeenth century the enforcement of exclusivity had long ago become routine and rarely provoked comment. Thus, in 1662, the corporation of Bury St Edmunds issued warrants against three men 'for using severall trades within this Burghe being not infranchised or made freemen' and, in 1704, St Albans seized and sold the goods of one Mr Lockerby because 'he had traded, not being free'.[142] To this one might add many more examples. Dozens of towns both large and small – ranging from London and Norwich to Wallingford and Wootton Bassett – sought to prevent 'foreigners' from encroaching on the crafts and trades of freemen.[143]

The power to exclude individuals could also, more rarely, be employed against 'insiders'. Urban freemen risked civic expulsion if they betrayed the economic well-being of their town. This was the fate inflicted upon John Walter of Bristol in 1667, when he was caught colouring strangers' goods 'contrary to the oath of a free burgesse'. As a result, he was 'disenfranchised' and lost his freedom; henceforth he was 'taken and reputed to all intents and purposes as a foreigner, and in all respects to be dealt withal accordingly'. The corporation 'shutt downe his shop windowes' and had his offence cried 'up and downe the citty and particularly att [his] doore'.[144] Similar cases of towns disenfranchising traders who broke the freeman's oath by abetting 'strangers' or launching vexatious suits occurred in Carlisle in 1673, Totnes in 1675, and Exeter in 1699.[145] These sanctions were an essential tool for

---

[141] Withington, *Politics of Commonwealth*, ch. 6; Barry, 'Civility and Civic Culture', pp. 186, 190.

[142] SRO–BSE, EE 500/D4/1/2, fol. 42; *St Albans Corp. Recs*, p. 102.

[143] For cases from London, Hertford, Sudbury, Saffron Walden, Great Dunmow, Cambridge, Exeter, Totnes, York, Carlisle, Leicester, Nottingham, Northampton, Beverley, Chester, Wallingford, Warwick, Norwich, Oxford, Penrith, Wootton Bassett, Tiverton, Wilton, Maidstone, Yarmouth, Bristol, and Lincoln see LMA, COL/CC/01/01/050, COL/CA/01/01/107, pp. 86–7; HA, HBR 20&21, p. 223, HBR 9/420; SRO–BSE, EE 501/2/8, pp. 145, 156, 208, 265; ERO, D/B 2/BRE1/28, fols 5–6; ERO, D/B 1/2, p. 85; CUA, V.C.Ct/III/45/209; DRO, ECA B 1/13, pp. 41–5; DRO, 1579A/9/35, pp. 47–8 and passim; YCA, F.9, fols 83–8; *Carlisle Muni. Recs*, pp. 31–4; *Leic. Boro. Recs*, V, pp. 59–61, 82–3; VII, pp. 23–4; *Nott. Boro. Recs*, V, pp. 330–31, 340, 384, 397, 399; *Northam. Boro. Recs*, II, pp. 53, 316; *Beverley Borough Records, 1575–1821*, J. Dennett ed. (Yorks. Arch. Soc. Rec. Series, vol. 84; York, 1933), pp. 90–93, 128; *VCH: Cheshire*, V, pt. 1, pp. 140–41; *VCH: Berkshire*, III, pp. 538–9; *VCH: Warwickshire*, VIII, pp. 506–7; Miller, *Cities Divided*, pp. 82–6; Gauci, *Politics and Society*, pp. 40–48, 194–8, 218–21; Carl Estabrook, *Urbane and Rustic England: Cultural Ties and Social Spheres in the Provinces* (Manchester, 1998), p. 121; J. W. F. Hill, *Tudor and Stuart Lincoln* (Cambridge, 1956), pp. 205–6.

[144] James Lee, '"Ye shall disturbe noe man's right": Oath-Taking and Oath-Breaking in Late Medieval and Early Modern Bristol', *Urban History*, 34:1 (2007), p. 37. For more on disenfranchisement in Bristol, which in some cases was reversed after the payment of a fine, see Miller, *Cities Divided*, p. 85.

[145] *Carlisle Muni. Recs*, p. 305; DRO, 1579A/9/35, p. 42; DRO, ECA B 1/13, p. 241.

imposing communal standards, forcibly uniting the group against members who undermined the common good.

However, to focus exclusively on evidence confirming the exclusionary power of these local bodies would leave a misleadingly static impression of their fortunes over the course of the late seventeenth and early eighteenth centuries. The economic regulations of towns seem to have been least effective during the turmoil and disarray of the Interregnum.[146] In the 1660s, however, they vigorously re-established their economic authority and, as indicated in the examples outlined above, they generally maintained it for decades thereafter. Yet, in the years that followed, these bold efforts to shut out outsiders sometimes began to falter. Because their prohibitions on non-freemen were only rarely buttressed by acts of parliament, they could face an increasing number of challenges to their authority. Norwich, Oxford, and other towns discovered that legal ambiguity made fining and suing interlopers ever more difficult. Although they responded by passing by-laws to strengthen their position, lawyers continued to undermine the effectiveness of civic attempts to prevent non-free trading by emphasising the uncertain legal status of such prohibitions.[147] Increasingly frequent partisan electoral conflict could also undermine the economic strength of established freemen. In some parliamentary boroughs, politicised town councils freed large groups of party loyalists in order to expand their voting base, though these 'mushroom freemen' were sometimes later purged and lost 'their pretended right' because they were 'strangers or foreigners'.[148] Elsewhere, enforcing exclusionary policies proved less problematic. Successful defences of freemen's privileges were not uncommon under William III and sometimes these continued into the eighteenth century.[149] In York, for instance, the community's relentless defence of its economic monopoly lasted long after the later Stuart period and, in 1736, an observer complained that freemen 'have for many years last past, by virtue of their charters, as it were locked themselves

---

[146] Margaret James, *Social Problems and Policy During the Puritan Revolution* (London, 1930), pp. 172–4, 193–223; M. J. Walker, 'The Extent of Guild Control of Trades in England, c.1660–1820: A Study Based on a Sample of Provincial Towns and London Companies' (Ph.D. thesis, University of Cambridge, 1986), pp. 55–6; Roger Howell, *Newcastle Upon Tyne and the Puritan Revolution: A Study of the Civil War in North England* (Oxford, 1967), pp. 277–80; VCH: *Cheshire*, V, pt. 2, p. 122; Hill, *Tudor and Stuart Lincoln*, p. 204. But for countervailing evidence see G. D. Ramsey, 'Industrial Laisser-Faire and the Policy of Cromwell', *Economic History Review*, 16:2 (1946), pp. 93–110; Ben Coates, *The Impact of the English Civil War on the Economy of London, 1642–50* (Aldershot, 2004), pp. 216–17.

[147] Miller, *Cities Divided*, pp. 82–5.

[148] *Carlisle Muni. Recs.*, pp. 31–4. From the late 1690s, Hertford seems to have experienced a pattern of mass enfranchisement and subsequent purges presumably due to electioneering: HA, HBR 20&21, pp. 257ff.

[149] For cases after 1688 see those of London, Hertford, Carlisle, Leicester, Nottingham, Northampton, St Albans, Wallingford, and Yarmouth cited above p. 188 n. 143.

up from the world, and wholly prevented any foreigner from settling any manufacture amongst them'.[150] So, most later Stuart towns probably experienced a revival of concerted action against 'foreigners' in the 1660s and 1670s, followed by declining strength by the beginning of the eighteenth century in some and continued resiliency in others.

Economic exclusivity also exerted a powerful force at the parochial level, where long-standing cultural traditions emphasised the division between 'settled' inhabitants and 'foreigners'. The 'impermeability' of village dialect and proverbs, the ubiquity of colourful localised insults, the violence of inter-parish football matches – all of these contributed to the strength of 'local xenophobia' in the seventeenth and eighteenth centuries.[151] A variety of local by-laws formalised these distinctions. All villages sought to prevent outsiders from using their common lands and to punish those who infringed, whereby the 'communal economy' was kept 'parochial and exclusive' rather than 'generous and universalistic'.[152] In 1687, for example, the tenantry of Sessay (Yorks.) imposed a fine of nearly £2 on William Kitchingman, a resident of the neighbouring manor of Birdforth, 'for puting goods & Cattle upon Seazey Comon not haveing Antient Messuage or Cottage'.[153] Other shared resources also had to be guarded against the encroachments of outsiders, even when the threat might appear rather pathetic in retrospect. This can be seen in the sad case of Edward Shynke, a poor man living in Bury St Edmunds who was nominated to receive 12s from the annual town charity in 1667 but soon after had this offer revoked because it was discovered that he was 'nott borne within this Towne'.[154]

These sorts of efforts were almost always accompanied by the routine rejection or expulsion of 'poor strangers'. Towns and villages throughout England sought to protect themselves from an influx of potential 'charges' to the poor rate and competitors in the labour market. This often involved punishing anyone who attempted to build a cottage on marginal land at the edge of the parish and prohibiting residents from lodging poor subtenants as 'inmates'. The jurors of the manor court of Whixley (Yorks.) were typical – in the 1670s they fined those caught 'erecting a Cottage upon the Lords wast' and ordered that 'none shall entertaine any vagrants or wandring persons in harvest or at any other time'.[155] In urban areas, locals made and

---

150 VCH: City of York, p. 215. Moreover, this level of enforcement continued throughout the century: ibid., pp. 215–18. For earlier cases see YCA, F.9, fols 83–8.

151 Rollison, Local Origins, ch. 3, esp. pp. 68–9; Snell, Parish, ch. 2.

152 Thompson, Customs in Common, p. 179. See also Estabrook, Urbane and Rustic, pp. 31–5.

153 NYCRO, ZDS III/11 (MIC 259). For more examples see DA, DD/DC/A2/2; Waddell, 'Governing'. Towns were equally protective of their commons: HA, HBR 9/351; Nott. Boro. Recs, V, p. 342; Carlisle Muni. Recs, p. 296.

154 SRO–BSE, EE 500/D4/1/2, fol. 72.

155 TNA, ASSI 47/20/9. See also Waddell, 'Governing'.

enforced similar rules. For instance, the 'Constitutions' promulgated by the borough of Great Dunmow (Essex) in 1671 demanded that no inhabitants harbour any 'inmates' and that parish officers report 'the names of all serv-ants as others that come in to Inhabite within the Burrough', because 'divers Forrein poore people whoe bee likely to bee a charge to the Inhabitants of the Corporacion doe frequently resort theither, and there endeavour to settle themselves'.[156] This was just a small part of the widespread customary exclusion of poor outsiders carried out through the poor laws. Steve Hindle and Keith Snell have shown how parishes systematically 'removed' relief claimants who lacked legal 'settlement', a process which became increasingly pervasive in the late seventeenth century.[157] Indeed, at the beginning of the eighteenth century, when the yeoman Richard Gough wrote his history of the parish of Myddle in Shropshire, he devoted a lengthy appendix to docu-menting the many attempts by local communities to exclude paupers who they regarded as 'foreign'.[158]

A stranger from another village could face exclusion from the local economic community, but the situation was worse still for someone who appeared to lack a 'home' entirely. A dark cloud of suspicion had hung over poor itinerants since at least the Reformation and, despite lightening some-what over the course of the seventeenth century, it continued to follow this sort of traveller in the later Stuart period.[159] For example, some clergymen preaching on charity showed a decidedly uncharitable attitude toward such people, calling them 'constant Wanderers from Place to Place, [who] can never settle themselves to any Trade or Labour, but love to live idly, and to do nothing'.[160] They saw this seemingly nomadic existence as a threat to good order and government, a danger that could only be countered with the whip and the stocks. They were not alone. Other learned commentators did their best to convince their audiences that there were 'some thousands of wandring persons that go from door to door, to the great dishonour & disadvantage of the Nation'; thus necessitating 'publick Work-houses ... for Vagrants, and sturdy Beggars, who have no habitation, and must be held

---

[156] ERO, D/B 1/2, pp. 85–6. For presentments against those accused of lodging poor strangers or not preventing their arrival see YCA, F.9, fols 14, 17; HA, HBR 9/404; *Nott. Boro. Recs*, V, pp. 327, 330, 351; *St Albans Corp. Recs*, pp. 86–7, 91, 97.
[157] Hindle, *On the Parish?* ch. 5; Snell, *Parish and Belonging*, ch. 3, esp. 139–43.
[158] Gough, *History of Myddle*, pp. 251–64.
[159] For the perception of vagrancy prior to 1660 see Slack, *Poverty and Policy*, pp. 22–7, 98–9; A. L. Beier, *Masterless Men: The Vagrancy Problem in England 1560–1640* (London, 1985), ch. 1; Fumerton, *Unsettled*, ch. 3; Hindle, *On the Parish?* pp. 73–5, 104, 107. For later Stuart vagrancy see David Hitchcock, 'A Typology of Travellers: Migration, Justice, and Vagrancy in Warwickshire, 1670–1730', *Rural History*, 23:1 (2012), pp. 21–39.
[160] Thomas Lynford, *Charity-schools Recommended: A Sermon* (1712), p. 8; William Stainforth, *The Duty of Doing Good Recommended and Press'd In a Sermon* (York, 1711), p. 9; Nourse, *Practical Discourses*, I, p. 121.

to their Labour, as Gally-slaves are tied to their Oars'.[161] The image that emerges is one of ceaseless transience, of shadowy figures moving at the edge of the community 'from Place to Place' and 'from door to door'.

A slightly less threatening portrayal can be found in contemporary ballads, perhaps because their buyers had more in common with vagrants than did most ministers and pamphleteers. Yet, despite their comedic style and upbeat mood, these songs show a similar antipathy to wandering mendicants. Taking on the voice of 'a jovial Beggar bold', the balladeer invariably described a life which mixed rambling around the country with innumerable petty crimes and deceits.[162] His constant mobility means spending nights in barns, under hedges or even inside 'a Hollow Tree'; and, in turn, this lack of a fixed locale ensured that he would 'pay no rent', guaranteed a fresh supply of gullible benefactors, offered new targets for theft, and helped him to avoid hostile officials. For instance, one band of 'Merry' beggars reported that

> we do pass from Town to Town;
> but for a time we stay,
> Least the Magistrates hear of us,
> and Whip us thence away.[163]

According to the stereotype presented in these ballads, the vagrant's irregular movement 'from Place to Place' indicated that he actually belonged to *no place* at all: he was not merely excluded from a particular local community, but lacked both locality and community entirely. Although in practice this strict dichotomy between the 'placed' and the 'displaced' rarely withstood close examination, its presence in sermons, pamphlets, and ballads framed many people's perceptions of poor travellers.

This rhetoric was often accompanied by very tangible efforts to forcibly suppress these outsiders. Local authorities in this period frequently issued public orders demanding harsh measures and justified themselves by portraying needy wanderers as threat to collective order and stability. In London, several proclamations condemned the 'Rogues, Vagabonds, Beggars, and other idle Persons', who took 'inordinate liberty' in 'pester[ing] the streets' and 'begging from doore to doore' – such interlopers should not be

---

161 Haines, *The Prevention of Poverty*, pp. 5–6; Firmin, *Some Proposals*, p. 5.
162 This paragraph is based on a group of ballads which shared similar themes (and sometimes whole verses): *The Beggars Song, Both in City and Country* (1685–8), in *PB*, IV, p. 250; *The Beggers Chorus, In the Jovial Crew* (c.1684–96), in *PB*, IV, p. 251; *The Merry Beggars of Lincolns-Inn-Fields* (1685–8), in *PB*, IV, p. 252; *The Beggars Delight* (n.d.), in *PB*, IV, p. 253; *The Jovial Beggars Merry Crew* (1684), in *RB*, IV, p. 51.
163 *The Beggars Song, Both in City and Country* (1685–8), in *PB*, IV, p. 250. Interestingly, in one verse of this particular ballad, the beggars admit that they 'come home at night' to see their families, yet the rest of the song focuses on their mobility.

relieved 'to the wrong of the native poor' but rather 'openly whipped, and sent away'.[164] These sorts of extraordinary measures merely augmented the standing policy of having such people whipped and sometimes imprisoned 'at hard labour' for several days before being sent back to their last place of 'settlement'.[165] Alongside the ceaseless grind of the machinery of the poor law, this ensured that the needy suffered a constant risk of expulsion if they dared to cross into the civic or parochial space reserved for local paupers.

The imagined rift between settled householders and incorrigible vaga-bonds was merely the most visible part of a much longer and deeper fissure, one which split the economic landscape of early modern England into two supposedly distinct territories. Ultimately, in the minds of many, one either belonged to a particular locality or one did not. The shared sense of place which bound together fellow 'citizens', 'inhabitants', 'parishioners' or 'neighbours' necessarily involved excluding those regarded as outsiders, and this process of unifying the community while defining its limits was clearly visible in the many expressions of solidarity discussed above. Moreover, such sentiments were not moribund relics of a bygone age. The later Stuart period actually witnessed a heightened awareness of locality in some impor-tant respects. Communal festivities, including Rogation processions, revived markedly in many villages, and this coincided with the expansion of paro-chial poor relief and disputes about 'settlement'. Likewise, contemporary religious idioms continued to promote an 'ethos of communalism' among neighbours, leading Keith Wrightson to note that 'reports of the death of neighbourliness in early modern England would appear to have been greatly exaggerated'.[166] Hence, the influence of local identity on economic behav-iour may have increased at the very moment when the practical business of determining 'belonging' was becoming ever more important. Despite the often pressing claims of country and craft, this geographically circumscribed conception of community lost little of its appeal.

4 Tradesmen's Fraternities

Work-based communities, perhaps even more than other forms of collective identity, had direct and unmistakable implications for later Stuart economic

---

164 Charles II, A Proclamation for ... the Suppressing of Rogues (1661); Corporation of London, By the Mayor ... [Against] Vagrants and Common Beggars (1676); LMA, COL/CC/01/01/050, fol. 273. For a similar demand issued in 1691 by the grand jury of Here-ford see HMC, Manuscripts of Rye and Hereford Corporations, p. 351.

165 Nicholas Rogers, 'Policing the Poor in Eighteenth-century London: the Vagrancy Laws and Their Administration', Histoire sociale/Social History, 24 (1991), esp. pp. 131–2, 139–41; Hitchcock, 'Typology'.

166 Wrightson, 'Decline', p. 21; Tadmor, Social Universe, ch. 1.

life. Indeed, attempting to understand the economic culture of this period without considering the customs associated with tradesmen's associations and other clusters of workers would be absurd.[167] For many labouring people, the rituals and rhetoric of 'the trade' reinforced bonds of solidarity which often became crucial in times of hardship.

In many cases, these bonds enjoyed considerable institutional support. England's urban economies had long been dominated by a plethora of occupational 'companies' and similar organisations sometimes emerged beyond the large incorporated cities that formed their traditional base, springing up in small market towns and rural manufacturing districts. These various organisations could not have endured without the vibrant communal culture which flourished in their midst, and their fraternal ideals influenced the lives of both members and outsiders. Early modern vocabulary offers a convenient introduction for this analysis, as its tone is startlingly clear. The words used by craftsmen and tradesmen to describe their organisations were diverse, but they all carried connotations of harmony and mutuality. Each group saw itself as a 'fellowship', 'society', 'company', 'corporation', 'body', 'fraternity' or 'brotherhood' – in fact, metalworkers of Bridgnorth in Shropshire used these highly charged terms interchangeably, thus re-imagining a mere legal entity as a paragon of communal strength.[168] In addition to pursuing unity through amicable language, these institutions also tried to protect themselves from verbal divisiveness by punishing members who insulted either their 'brethren' or (still worse) the company itself. The Barbers of Newcastle-upon-Tyne, for example, fined Robert Lampton in 1664 for his 'unbrotherly speeches' in which he claimed that Richard Potts 'was not worthy to trim any man because where he took one hair off he left three on'.[169] The appearance of fraternal amity had to be carefully cultivated

---

[167]   Here the focus is on formal and semi-formal tradesmen's groups, as they are the best-documented of early modern occupational communities, but female workers, agricultural workers, and others must also be acknowledged and their communal bonds deserve closer study. For examples see Pamela Sharp, 'Lace and Place: Women's Business in Occupational Communities in England, 1550–1950', *Women's History Review*, 19:2 (2010), pp. 283–306; Thomas, *Ends of Life*, pp. 106–7.

[168]   BL, Add. MS 38834 (where 'company', 'society', 'fraternity', brotherhood', and 'fellowship' are all used in the late seventeenth century); Malcolm Chase, *Early Trade Unionism: Fraternity, Skill and the Politics of Labour* (Aldershot, 2000), p. 4; Griffiths, *Youth and Authority*, p. 302. I have used these terms (especially 'company') as they were frequently used by contemporaries, whereas 'guild' or 'gild' was rarely used after the Reformation, so it has been avoided. For the many meanings of the word 'company' (almost all of which centred on commonality and mutuality) see Withington, *Politics of Commonwealth*, pp. 129–37; idem, 'Company and Sociability in Early Modern England', *Social History*, 32:3 (2007), esp. pp. 297–303. For 'fellowship' and 'society' see Hailwood, 'Sociability', pp. 15–17; Withington, *Society*, ch. 4.

[169]   Withington, *Politics of Commonwealth*, p. 177. For many more examples of fines for 'unbrotherly' or 'uncivill' words, including a Carlisle glover fined 13s 4d 'for scan-

and guarded, otherwise innumerable minor disagreements might well over-whelm the practical and emotional ties of 'brotherhood'.

The solemn oaths sworn upon admission to one of these companies provide another example of craftsmen and tradesmen publicly affirming their economic solidarity. These initiation ceremonies saw men proudly declaring their loyalty to each other and, just as importantly, ritually subor-dinating themselves 'to the will of the company'.[170] They also emphasised secrecy, as in the oath of the London Leather-Sellers of this period, which bound new members to 'conceal and keep' all of 'the lawful councils and secrets' of the trade.[171] Of course, the membership restrictions inherent in craft companies ensured that their oaths excluded far more people than they included. Yet even workers without access to such select institutions could find ways to signal their communal strength. An observer of the keelmen of Newcastle in the early eighteenth century, for example, remarked that they 'have a particular manner of giving a pledge for their standing by one another on any occasion, which is spitting on a stone.'[172] Doubtless the keelmen employed this phlegmatic avowal of unity many times during their frequent disputes with their employers during this same period.[173]

In much the same way, participation in feasts and ceremonies could instil a palpable sense of occupational identity. Long after the Reforma-tion, many trades and crafts retained their attachment to a patron saint and this resulted in often raucous festivities on particular 'holy days'. In late seventeenth-century Staffordshire, for example, ironworkers celebrated St Clement's Day (23 November) by 'going about that night, to beg drink to make merry with'; and wool-workers in Oxfordshire 'made good cheer' on St Blaise's Day (2 February), but 'if they found any of their neighbour-women a-spinning, set their distaff on fire'.[174] This combination of merri-ment and menace established very clear boundaries between full members of 'the trade' and those on the outside or at the margins. Urban craftsmen took part in similar festivities, though they took advantage of their more durable organisational structures to express their 'fellowship' more elaborately than

---

daleous words speaking against the trade', see NRO, NCR Case 17d, fol. 5; *Carlisle Muni. Recs*, pp. 127, 156–8, 214, 233; Walker, 'Guild Control', p. 236.

170 Withington, *Politics of Commonwealth*, p. 174. Journeymen's associations, which could include both local and 'stranger' craftsmen, also demanded an oath from entrants: Walker, 'Guild Control', p. 89. For the importance of oaths of office as a tool for binding together civic elites see Lee, 'Oath-Taking and Oath-Breaking'.

171 'Leather-Seller's Oath, London' (temp. William III): CHC, PA 219/9/4.

172 Levine and Wrightson, *Industrial Society*, p. 392. Aggrieved pitmen used the same ritual expression of solidarity in 1738.

173 For examples of the keelmen protests see below pp. 200, 207.

174 Hutton, *Stations of the Sun*, pp. 54–5, 144. Perhaps this sense of occupational commu-nity also played a role in the Plough Monday custom wherein 'plough boys dragged a plough around their neighbourhood, collecting money from homes and passers-by to be spent on a feast for themselves': ibid., p. 127.

their rural counterparts. Civic events thus became opportunities for them to publicise their strength while enhancing fraternal ties. The London Livery Companies, for instance, ensured occupational visibility through ostentatious participation in the Lord Mayor's Show.[175] At the mayoral celebrations of 1672, for example, the Coopers provided nearly two thousand cakes and eighteen gallons of wine for their members, in addition to decorating their barge as was customary.[176] Likewise, the craftsmen of Coventry appear to have spent significant sums parading in finery at the yearly 'Great Fair'. In the late seventeenth century the procession included 'Armour Bearers' from the Carpenters, 'a boy to ride' and 'streamers' from the Weavers, and a growing ceremonial contingent from the Cappers and Feltmakers.[177] Even the Braintree wool-combers – whose institutional 'fraternity' was hardly venerable – organised parades and public dinners for themselves.[178]

Company ordinances and account books from the later Stuart era indicate that these groups were well aware of the importance of sociability in promoting occupational solidarity. In many cases, for example, members were required to attend the weddings and funerals of their fellows, and thus partook in the accompanying eating and drinking.[179] Moreover, at some funerals, the mourning feast was served on company plate, while the corpse was often borne to the church by company brethren, sometimes draped in a company pall.[180] More common religious occasions could also become opportunities for fraternal unity. The Carpenters of Coventry, for example, gathered together in 'the Company Seats' at church every Sunday in the late seventeenth century.[181] Most gatherings, however, emphasised conviviality rather than solemnity. Communal feasts, normally including the consumption of considerable quantities of alcohol, marked the admission of new members, the election of officers, and the seasonal meetings

---

[175] George Unwin, *The Gilds and Companies of London* (London, 1908), pp. 271–2, 289–92; Plummer, *London Weavers' Company*, pp. 222–32; Burke, 'Popular Culture', pp. 151–2; Earle, *Making*, pp. 255, 260.

[176] *Coopers' Company, London: Historical Memoranda, Charters, Documents and Extracts from the Records of the Corporation and the Books of the Company, 1396–1848*, James Francis Firth ed. (London, 1848), pp. 59–60.

[177] CHC, PA 3/3, unfol.; CHC, PA 34/3, pp. 29, 44; CHC, PA 1494/5/1, p. 5.

[178] A. F. J. Brown, *Essex at Work, 1700–1815* (Chelmsford, 1969), p. 24. This appears to have been an example of the 'convivial gatherings' hosted by journeymen's associations mentioned in Walker, 'Guild Control', p. 89.

[179] CHC, PA 8, no. 2; CHC, PA 100/5, no. 24; *Carlisle Muni. Recs*, pp. 127, 160, 196, 217; Rebecca King, 'The Sociability of the Trade Guilds of Newcastle and Durham, 1660–1750: The Urban Renaissance Revisited', in Helen Berry and Jeremy Gregory (eds), *Creating and Consuming Culture in North-East England, 1660–1830* (Aldershot, 2004), pp. 57–71. For a vivid example of a printed summons to a company funeral in London from 1716 see Unwin, *Gilds and Companies*, p. 349.

[180] King, 'Sociability', pp. 60–61.

[181] CHC, PA 3/3. For Edinburgh examples see Houston, *Social Change*, pp. 66–7, 69.

held to conduct company affairs.[182] Here, the multiple meanings of 'fellow-ship' and 'company' became explicit, denoting not a just particular type of economic institution but also the modes of sociability that held these bodies together. By encouraging participants to collectively enjoy the fruits of their co-operation, these events promoted camaraderie and 'good cheer' while also reminding each 'fellow' of the need to share the bounty of the trade among the fellowship as a whole.

The revellers at these sorts of festivities often engaged in boisterous singing which, in a few cases, can still be heard thanks to the survival of printed broadside versions. Shoemakers and cobblers, for example, could have drawn inspiration from at least five different ballads reciting the 'Glory of the Gentle-Craft', including *The Shooe-maker's Triumph* 'as it was sung at a General Assembly of Shooe-makers, on the 25th of October 1695, being St. Crispin [Day]'.[183] Similarly, weavers and sailors surely enjoyed singing the verses praising them for their contributions to the economic welfare and defence of the nation.[184] In a rather different tone, the weavers were also honoured by a Scottish poetaster who extolled 'the gallant Weavers' and threatened to 'beat ... with a Rung' anyone who 'discommends' their craft.[185] Perhaps this militant occupational pride accounts for the bloody inter-trade battles which annually took place at London's Moorefields, such

[182] Feasting is recorded in company books in every part of the country throughout this period: YMA, Hailstone QQ80/3/2, fols 17–18; BL, Add. MS 38834, fol. 98; CHC, PA 3/3; Northants. RO, D3382, fol. 86; *Carlisle Muni. Recs*, pp. 184–5, 218–19, 221, 223, 225; Plummer, *London Weavers' Company*, ch. 11; Ben-Amos, *Culture of Giving*, pp. 170–76; Earle, *Making*, pp. 254–60; King, 'Sociability'. For the importance of social drinking in the maintenance of occupational identities see Hailwood, 'Sociability'. For one particularly good example see *The Jolly Porters* (1693), in PB, IV, p. 292.

[183] *The Glory of the Gentle-Craft* (1690), in PB, IV, p. 318; Richard Rigby, *The Cobler's Corrant* (c.1683–1703), in PB, IV, p. 231; idem, *A New Song in Praise of the Gentle-Craft* (c.1682–95), in PB, IV, p. 233; idem, *The Shooe-makers Delight* (n.d.), in PB, V, p. 392; idem, *The Shooe-maker's Triumph* (1695), in PB, V, p. 427. For other St Crispin Day songs intermixed with stories about the mythical origins and early history of shoemaking see the chapbooks based on Thomas Deloney, *The Gentle Craft* (orig. c.1597–8; repr. 1660, 1674, 1675, 1678, 1685, 1690, 1696, 1700, 1720).

[184] *A New Coppy of Verses of The Weavers Loyal Resolution* (1689) in PB, V, p. 138; Fumerton, *Unsettled*, p. 147. For chapbooks in which clothworkers featured as heroes see Thomas Deloney, *Jack of Newbery* (orig. c.1597; repr. 1672, 1680, 1684, 1700); idem, *Thomas of Reading* (orig. 1612; repr. 1672, 1680, 1715). For a discussion of Deloney and occupational identity see David Rollison, 'Discourse and Class Struggle: The Politics of Industry in Early Modern England', *Social History*, 26:2 (2001), pp. 182–5. For other trade ballads see *The Bonny Black-smiths Delight: A Noble Song in Praise of Black-smiths* (c.1663–74) in PB, IV, p. 264; 'The Brewers Praise', in *Merry Drollery, Compleat: or, A Collection of Jovial Poems, Merry Songs, Witty Drolleries, Inxtermixed with Pleasant Catches* (1691), pp. 221–5.

[185] *Proper New Ballad in Praise of the Gallant Weavers* (Edinburgh, c.1700) in RyB, Ry.III.10(023).

as the one in 1664 at which the butchers 'were soundly beaten out of the field, and some deeply wounded and bruised'.[186] Many other examples of craft loyalty – whether violent or merely rhetorical – must have gone unrecorded, though the curiosity of a travelling gentlemen preserved evidence of the song of the weavers of Randwick in Gloucestershire. This festive 'Psalm' emphasised the antiquity of 'Our Trade' – supposedly born 'When Archelus began to spin, / and 'Pollo wrought upon a loom' – while also lauding 'the bonds of amity' that held the weavers together.[187]

However, perhaps the best illustration of the complex culture of work-based communities in later Stuart England can be seen in the notes that Joseph Bufton, a Coggeshall journeyman wool-comber, jotted down on the blank pages of his printed almanacs.[188] Here, he not only transcribed the official ordinances of his company but also a remarkable collection of laudatory verses and short rhymes about his trade. He began, as one might expect, with a simple poem ('from Colchester') about 'Blase, the founder of our art', emphasising the saintly origin of 'our mystery' and representing it as 'a wheel [that] set all trades going'.[189] Moreover, these lengthy 'Verses' inspired Bufton to write his own series of poetic tributes to 'our trade'. One, written 'for the Guild day morning' and probably read aloud at the event, exclaimed

> This day Here will a noble feast be made
> For all among us of the fullers trade
> This ancient custome they do still uphold
> Which hath been used from the days of old
> There Wardens for next year will chosen be
> By voice of those that of the Trade are free.[190]

In another, he spoke to more practical concerns, urging his fellow combers to 'relieve' each other if ever any of them fell into poverty. This intra-company 'charity' would, he argued, allow them to live 'Without assistance from another hand', so 'Let's bravely act our parts' and 'play the men' by supporting any fellows who 'grow poor and low'. As an added incentive, the money raised could also contribute to 'keeping out intruders from our

---

[186] Pepys, *Diary*, V, pp. 222–3 (26 July 1664). See also *CSPD, Charles II,1663–4*, p. 664.
[187] Rollison, *Local Origins*, pp. 213–18. Although the song was recorded only in 1784, the festival at which it was sung was first noted in 1703.
[188] For previous discussions of the Coggeshall combers see Chase, *Early Trade Unionism*, pp. 28–31; Thompson, *Customs in Common*, pp. 62–3. For Bufton himself see French, *Middle Sort*, pp. 245–50.
[189] ERO, T/A 156/1, vol. 3 (1686). I am grateful to Malcolm Chase for a digital copy of this volume, which is also transcribed as the 'Diary of Joseph Bufton' in HMC, *Various Collections*, VIII, pp. 573–92.
[190] ERO, T/A 156/1, vol. 2 (1680).

trade'.[191] Together, the ideals which Bufton inscribed in his notebook formed the foundation upon which a great many groups of later Stuart tradesmen built their communities: ancient lineage, festive sociability, mutual support, collective autonomy, selfless bravery, fraternal masculinity, and defensive exclusivity. The presence of all of these values in the ill-formed verses of a journeyman from a minor Essex market town demonstrates both the strength and the breadth of their influence.

Bufton's emphasis on brotherly charity reflects the importance of this aspect of occupational culture at the time. Individual craftsmen – or their widows – could often draw on the large sums which their fellowships devoted to relieving poor members. The Blacksmiths of Bridgnorth, for example, offered aid to unfortunate members of their 'brotherwhod', such as the 10s given to William Richards 'toward the repayre of the loose he hath sustayned by feir' after his house and shop burned down in 1665.[192] Even companies such as the London Fishmongers, which had lost many of its regulatory powers by the end of the seventeenth century, still spent considerable amounts on fraternal welfare. For instance, a typical entry in their accounts from this period recorded that they paid 40s 'for coles and faggotts distributed to poore and needy fishmongers in St Michael Crooked Lane and elsewhere'.[193] Indeed, using a sample of five London companies, Ilana Ben-Amos has shown that the amount of resources that these organisations devoted to the poor 'grew immensely' in the seventeenth century and remained important 'well beyond 1700'.[194] Even members of relatively humble companies might, by pooling their resources, undertake remarkably ambitious charitable projects. In 1709, one such group, the Watermen of London, passed an order on their own initiative for every member to pay a shilling 'towards Endowing a Free School for the Poor Children of their Community, Especially those Whoose Fathers have been or shall be kill'd or maimed in the [naval] service'.[195] By acting collectively, as a self-declared 'Community', these labouring men created an opportunity to ensure that their children would receive an education irrespective of lowly status or ill fortune.

One of the most striking forms of fraternal assistance was the support offered to needy 'brethren' passing through town in search of work. The Smiths' Company of Lichfield, for example, regularly helped fellow craftsmen who had been forced to take to the road, and the Silkweavers of Coventry relieved more than fifty travelling journeymen in the 1670s alone, including a shilling to 'a silk weaver, his wife and four children come out

191 ERO, T/A 156/1, vol. 3 (1686).
192 BL, Add. MS 38834, fol. 78.
193 Earle, *Making*, p. 259.
194 Ben-Amos, *Culture of Giving*, pp. 95–106; Ward, *Metropolitan Communities*, pp. 57–72; Walker, 'Guild Control', pp. 102–5; Hey, *Fiery Blades*, p. 143.
195 LMA, COL/CA/05/01/0010 (petition of Watermen, 1709).

of Ireland' in 1678.[196] It seems that the informal bonds which held together members of 'the trade' might temporarily bridge the sharp division between inhabitants and strangers. Indeed, some companies established auxiliary organisations specifically for 'foreign' journeymen residing within their towns. These societies – recorded in Exeter, Salisbury, Beverley, Worcester, and Coventry – collected funds and disbursed relief on a quarterly basis, thus providing a simple form of social insurance for workers who might be otherwise excluded from local relief schemes.[197]

The principle of communal risk-pooling was equally widespread amongst the many unofficial fellowships which began to spring up around this time. The popularity of benefit clubs as a potential remedy for personal economic calamity was obvious by the end of the seventeenth century, when they could be found among coal-heavers, printers, and coachmakers in London, wool-combers in Tiverton, and keelmen in Newcastle.[198] As noted above, the wool-combers of Coggeshall offer one of the earliest and best-documented examples. Joseph Bufton recounted that informal 'gatherings' had long been 'common amongst us in case of affliction'.[199] In 1688, however, 'in imitation of their brethren at Colchester', they set about 'raising & maintaining a purse for the help of such of us as may by sickness, lameness or the want of work fall into decay'.[200] According to the articles drawn up at this time, the 'purse' established by these 'poor labouring men' did not admit any members who had not served a full apprenticeship, but they did allow combers who left the town to maintain their membership and even ordered that any 'stranger' who duly observed the rules of the purse 'shall injoy equall priveledges with the Townesman in every particular.'[201] In other

---

196 VCH: Staffordshire, XIV, p. 134; Walker, 'Guild Control', pp. 148, 333. For examples from the Mercers of Sandwich from the 1660s to the 1710s see BL, Add. MS 27462, fols 24–83. For examples from northern companies in the 1670s and 1680s see Donald Woodward, Men at Work: Labourers and Building Craftsmen in the Towns of Northern England, 1450–1750 (Cambridge, 1995), p. 71.

197 Walker, 'Guild Control', pp. 88–91. This may have been the purpose of the 'Stock' reportedly used for maintaining journeymen weavers at Norwich: NRO, NCR Case 20a/16, 16 July 1698.

198 LMA, COL/CA/05/01/0002/1689 (petition of Coalheavers, 1689), COL/CA/01/01/104, f. 141; Peter Clark, British Clubs and Societies c. 1580–1800: The Origins of An Associational World (Oxford, 2000), pp. 353–4; Martin Dunsford, Historical Memoirs of the Town and Parish of Tiverton (Exeter, 1790), p. 205; Extracts from the Hostmen, pp. 154–5. Similarly, the families of dead seamen were supported by auctioning off the seaman's possessions to his comrades at voluntarily inflated prices in a 'ritual of redistribution': Rediker, Between, pp. 197–8.

199 ERO, T/A 156/1, vol. 3 (1686), fol. 18r.

200 Ibid., fol. 12r–v.

201 Ibid., fols 18r, 22v, 24r–v. In addition to the combers of Colchester and Coggeshall, the weavers of Bocking also seem to have begun raising a 'stock' amongst themselves by 1629 which was still running sixty years later, and the journeyman weavers of Norwich had 'a Stock' by 1698: ERO, Q/SR 462/92, 93; NRO, NCR, Case 20a/16, 16 July 1698.

words, much like an official craft company, the 'purse' offered relief to individuals based on occupational solidarity rather than on residency.

The Coggeshall combers also gathered funds for less amicable purposes. Two years before founding their 'purse', they held a meeting and 'freely contributed 6 pence a man' towards the 'prosecuting of all Intruders into their trade', which resulted in a warrant from the Justices of the Peace authorising the combers themselves to search out and apprehend such offenders.[202] Other groups of Essex textile workers pursued similar strategies at around this time. In 1674 'the whole company of the occupacion of the Weavers inhabiting in the Towne of Braintree' successfully sought to have their 'goode Orders and Ordinances' against outsiders ratified by the county magistrates, because they found themselves 'to be very much wronged by such as have intruded themselves into the Art and mistery of weaving'.[203] Their example was followed in later decades by 'companies' of fullers, tuckers, weavers, and clothiers in Bocking, Witham, Great Dunmow, and Coggeshall.[204] Even craftsmen who seem to have lacked any official recognition might act collectively to protect themselves from 'Intruders'. In Cambridge, a town without any formal companies, thirty men calling themselves 'the Society of Taylors' demanded the prosecution of Lancelot Hooper because he

> contrairy to all Justice Equity and good Conscience hath and daily doth practice the Trade of a Taylor which he ... never serv'd a tyme to [as an apprentice] and in the said Trade doth act very fraudulently and unjustly to the great abuse of such as deal with him and to the hinderance of those ... whose right it is to follow the said Trade only and likewise to the enevitable ruine of many a poor family if not suddenly prevented.[205]

Indeed, such hostility seems to have been the chief motive for many tradesmen who sought to be legally chartered in the later Stuart period. This was what drove the sawyers of London to seek formal incorporation in 1671, apparently hoping to bring about 'an utter exclusion of all those sort of Laborers who dayly resort to the Citty of London', because these casual workers 'keepe the wages & prizes ... att an equal and indifferent rate'.[206] In other cases, craftsmen argued that giving them the power to

---

[202] ERO, T/A 156/1, vol. 3 (1686), fols 7r–8r, 10r–12r.

[203] ERO, Q/SO 2, fol. 87.

[204] ERO, Q/SO 3, pp. 76, 91, 147, 439; Q/SO, p. 66. Specifically, the Fullers and Tuckers of Bocking (1700), Woollen Cloth Weavers of Witham (1700), Fullers and Tuckers of Great Dunmow (1703), Clothiers, Fullers, Baymakers and Drapers of Coggeshall (1710), and Weavers of Braintree (1719).

[205] CUA, V.C.Ct/III/45/48.

[206] E. B. Jupp, *An Historical Account of the Worshipful Company of Carpenters of the City of London* (London, 1848), p. 308. See also the sawyers' successful complaint against carpenters who employ 'Forrigners' in 1693: LMA, COL/CA/01/01/02, pp. 19–20. For

exclude outsiders would benefit the kingdom as a whole. This was the rationale offered in the petitions of shipwrights and woollen workers in the final decades of the seventeenth century. According to their complaints, the right of occupational communities to exclude 'Uncapable Persons' from the craft aligned closely with the needs of the larger 'Comon Wealth'.[207]

For fraternities that were already officially incorporated, prosecuting 'interlopers' who attempted to practise a trade without having served an apprenticeship was habitual rather than extraordinary. The right to search out and punish outsiders was, of course, routinely included in the ordinances granted to craft companies by royal charters and civic bylaws. The trades of Norwich, Coventry, York, Lancaster, Chester, Lichfield, Durham, Carlisle, Sandwich, Lincoln, London, and elsewhere had rules designed to restrain 'outmen' and 'unlawful' workers in this period.[208] And they did not hesitate to use these powers to target anyone who threatened their monopoly, especially woman and migrants. To take just one instance, the Exeter Tailors fined or prosecuted 'foreigners' more than 130 times in the first half of the eighteenth century.[209] Moreover, the efforts of fraternities and urban corporations often coincided. Hence, in July 1712, the Corporation of London ordered the prosecution of non-freemen who 'use any manual occupation or handicraft or to sell or put to sale any Wares or Merchandizes by Retail in any Shop inward or outward' which led many companies to enforce their regulations concerning foreigners 'with renewed vigour', though some faced resistance from their targets.[210] Here, as elsewhere, the defensive mentality fostered by urban citizenship strengthened the ability of workers to police the boundaries of their trade.

'Intruders' were not the only ones to find themselves aggressively pursued by assertive occupational communities. Also punished were wayward brethren deemed to have betrayed their fellows for personal gain. The Bakers of Coventry, for example, fined any members who disclosed the company's

---

the petition of the Shipwrights to the Navy Commissioners regarding the same see *CSPD: Charles II, Addenda*, p. 325 (13 Feb. 1671).

[207] *Reasons for the Regular Re-Establishment of the Corporation of Shipwrights* (c.1696), p. 4; CHC, PA 100/16/8. For more on these petitions see above p. 166.

[208] NRO, NCR Case 17d, fols 3–4, and passim; CHC, PA 8, nos. 11, 19; YMA, Hailstone QQ80/4/1, n.p. (4 Jun 1662, 15 Jan 1669); Stout, *Autobiography*, pp. 100–102; *VCH: Cheshire*, V, pt. 2, p. 117; *VCH: Staffordshire*, IVX, p. 133; *VCH: Durham*, III, pp. 42–4; *Carlisle Muni. Recs*, pp. 105, 128, 151–2, 244; BL, Add. MS 27462, fols 1, 10 and passim; Walker, 'Guild Control', ch. 4; Ward, *Metropolitan Communities*, pp. 134–42; Hill, *Tudor and Stuart Lincoln*, p. 204; Hey, *Fiery Blades*, pp. 140–43.

[209] Walker, 'Guild Control', p. 229.

[210] John R. Kellet, 'The Breakdown of Gild and Corporation Control over the Handicraft and Retail Trade in London', *Economic History Review*, 2nd ser., 10 (1958), pp. 386–8. For other examples of urban corporations such as Bristol, Coventry, Oxford, and Newcastle reinforcing regulations against 'strangers' in the eighteenth century see Walker, 'Guild Control', p. 124.

secrets, and the city's Weavers imposed a heavy penalty of £5 on those who taught the mysteries of the craft to anyone who did not belong to the company.[211] In some cases, such groups inflicted even harsher punishments. Hence, although the Exeter Tailors directed most of their regulative energy at harassing 'foreigners', they also disenfranchised five members 'for offences against the trade' in the first two decades of the eighteenth century.[212] In their attempts to ensure that every 'brother' supported the common interests of the fraternity as a whole, English craftsmen showed a real willingness to discipline deviant members through financial sanctions or, when pressed, forcible expulsion and the denial of the right to practice the trade.

Clearly, then, the values and practices described by the Essex woolcomber, Joseph Bufton, were neither waning nor obsolete when he sat down to record them in the 1680s. But neither were they permanent and immutable. As with urban corporations, many venerable fraternities probably suffered a weakening of their regulatory powers during the Civil Wars and Interregnum.[213] After 1660, however, they enjoyed a burst of strength. Although a few of these organisations – principally the Twelve Great Livery Companies in London and their 'entrepreneurial' counterparts in the provinces – continued to lose economic relevance, most fraternities were reinvigorated by the Restoration. Membership, recruitment, and regulation recovered rapidly, and often underwent several decades of growth, not peaking until sometime in the early decades of the eighteenth century.[214] Moreover, some metropolitan companies extended their authority beyond its previous limits by reaching into the burgeoning suburban neighbourhoods where much production now took place.[215] Others adapted to growing numbers of wage-earning journeymen by allowing these workers to form their own sub-fraternities within the larger corporate structure. Indeed, one prominent sign of the continued importance of these organisations is the fact that many

[211] CHC, PA 8, no. 5; PA 100/5, no. 28. See also *Carlisle Muni. Recs*, pp. 127–9, 214–18, 245–6, 248.

[212] Walker, 'Guild Control', p. 229.

[213] See above p. 189.

[214] Walker, 'Guild Control', esp. ch. 4; Michael Berlin, 'Guilds in Decline? London Livery Companies and the Rise of a Liberal Economy, 1600–1800', in Stephan Epstein and Maarten Prak (eds), *Guilds, Innovation, and the European Economy, 1400–1800* (Cambridge, 2008), pp. 325–38; Snell, *Annals*, ch. 5, esp. pp. 235–6; Ward, *Metropolitan Communities*, ch. 2, 6. One should also note that, in the 1680s, probably in response to the political struggle over town charters, many companies successfully had their 'constitutions' renewed or amended, giving themselves a firmer legal foundation. Thus, in Norwich eight trades had their by-laws ratified by the city in 1683–84, with another five trades doing so between 1690 and 1719, and in Exeter seven trades renewed their charters in 1685–87, and again in 1690–92: NRO, NCR Case 17d; DRO, ECA B 1/13.

[215] Ward, *Metropolitan Communities*, ch. 2; Ian Gadd and Patrick Wallis, 'Reaching Beyond the City Wall: London Guilds and National Regulation, 1500–1700', in Epstein and Prak (eds), *Guilds*, pp. 288–315.

groups of craftsmen that had lacked formal status as self-regulating trades sought and received recognition for the first time under the later Stuarts. These included not only the textile workers of several Essex towns, but also London groups such as Tinplate-workers, who, after being incorporated in 1670, regulated apprenticeship, prosecuted 'foreigners', priced piece-work, and carried out searches as late as 1773.[216] Such vigorous expressions of communal strength suggest that fraternal organisations had a powerful role in the economic lives of England's tradesmen and artisans in the late seventeenth century.

By the early eighteenth century, however, a less robust approach seems to have become more common. In Coventry, for example, the Weavers' Company launched vigorous efforts against non-freemen in 1663 and passed supplementary orders on this issue in 1686 and 1690, but authorised only a single prosecution of a non-freeman weaver thereafter.[217] The Crown, despite authorising several new companies, may have contributed to this shift by refusing to grant charters to some growing London trades, including sawyers, paviors, basket-makers, and others.[218] The tendency of some tradesmen to invest less energy in the regulation of their 'mystery' after the surge of concern that followed the Restoration was mirrored in a gradual loss of some of the fraternal customs and rituals that supported more practical aspects of these occupational communities. Eventually, companies began to lose their hold on the cultural world of middling townspeople, even if the precise chronology varied considerably between different crafts and different locales. The Coventry Carpenters' Company recorded payments 'for the Company Seates in the Church', 'for the Armour Bearers at the faire', and for a variety of seasonal feasting continued long into the eighteenth century, whereas the city's Weavers' Company cut their participation in the Great Fair owing to expense in 1685 and it was only briefly revived in the 1668 and 1694.[219] Among fellowships in north-eastern England, Rebecca King has found that some forms of sociability had 'eroded by the mid-eighteenth century' as company funerals were shortened and initiation celebrations were curtailed – yet, she also has noted the 'resilience' of this culture in spite of institutional changes.[220] In other words, the resurgent fraternal spirit that emerged from the dislocations of the mid-seventeenth century began to

---

[216] For the textile workers see above p. 201. For the Tinplate-workers see Unwin, *Gilds and Companies*, p. 348. Others in London that were incorporated during this period include the Glass-sellers (1664), the Patternmakers (1670), the Wheelwrights (1670), the Coachmakers (1677), and the Fan-makers (1709).

[217] CHC, PA 34/3, pp. 8, 30, 47, 73. The final suit came in 1707.

[218] George Unwin, *Industrial Organization in the Sixteenth and Seventeenth Centuries* (Oxford, 1904), pp. 212–13; Berlin, 'Guilds', p. 329.

[219] CHC, PA 3/3, pp. 8–175; CHC, PA 34/3/1, pp. 29, 44, 57.

[220] King, 'Sociability', pp. 62–5, 70. For the decline (but not disappearance) of large-scale feasting in London companies see Ben-Amos, *Culture of Giving*, pp. 170–76.

falter in subsequent years in some communities while in others it remained a potent force well into the next century. Overall, irrespective of this variability, it would be difficult to find many later Stuart craftsmen who were not influenced by the powerful appeal of 'the trade' and its norms.

As this section has shown, tradesmen's associations instilled these beliefs in their members through a diverse range of media: oaths, festivals, meals, processions, collective worship, songs, and rhymes. Almost any occasion, whether jubilant or mournful, could become an instrument for promoting 'fellowship' and shared identity. But this thicket of customs and idioms was also inherently exclusionary, for it encouraged craftsmen to define themselves against the 'intruders' who constantly seemed to threaten the unity of their trade. While wives and widows of company members could be incorporated, the vast majority of tradeswomen were regarded as troublesome outsiders. Likewise, the boundaries of fellowship might be stretched to include some 'foreign journeymen' who had served their apprenticeships elsewhere, but most 'strangers' could expect only hostility and persecution. Hence, these restrictive communities deepened some economic divisions while bridging others. They built walls between workers in different callings, making inter-occupational solidarity more difficult, and they heightened the partition separating unskilled labourers from those who had trained in an 'art' or 'mystery'. Their patriarchal conception of 'the trade' also accentuated the segregation of male and female labour. But these same ideals – and the customs that perpetuated them – created a culture which transcended the all-too-obvious economic rifts between apprentices, journeymen, and masters. A sense of fraternal unity could eclipse differences in wealth or age, at least for a time. As such, the continued resilience of craft culture disrupted the appeal of 'class' identity in the later Stuart period. Yet, it also instilled a somewhat egalitarian mentality and provided an unmatched environment for organising collective action.

5 Redress: Collective Action

The bonds of community – forged through shared identities and cultures – provided an invaluable defence against economic threats for many people in later Stuart England. As this chapter has shown, individual members often had direct access to a variety of common resources and material support from their fellows. These 'imagined communities' could also allow members to peacefully promote their shared interests, while isolating or excluding opponents and competitors. England's rulers generally regarded these various manifestations of community as harmless at worst and useful at best. In some cases, the authorities clearly welcomed these activities because they seemed to contribute to the maintenance of social stability and order. Yet, many other collective efforts received a much less favourable reception.

Some were simply legally dubious, but others directly targeted representatives of the state or involved riotous violence. Over the course of the later Stuart period, many groups showed a growing willingness to seek remedies using methods that put them in direct opposition to legal authority, even when they continued to deploy the idiom of 'law' to justify their actions.

One of the most common of these methods was illicit collective bargaining. Although the 'strike' is a tactic normally associated with the labour unions of the nineteenth and twentieth centuries, some of the earliest examples of this expression of worker solidarity can be found among the men of the naval dockyards in the 1660s. At Woolwich, for example, an official reported 'the great discontent among our workmen' that arose when they were banned from collecting scrap wood – a customary perquisite known as 'chips' – in the spring of 1665. It began on 3 April when 'about fifty of them, all strangers, refused to come this morning to work', and the next day it had spread to 'a great number of our townsmen [who] exempted themselves from their work ... so that 139 in all stand out on their privilege of chips', leaving very few in the yard. The official recommended granting them 'the liberty ... of carrying off lawful chips twice a day'.[221] Around three months later, the ropemakers at Portsmouth undertook a similar 'mutiny' and 'desertion', apparently protesting against the long arrears in overdue wages. Although the manager of the yard wanted to 'punish' them, he reported that completely stopping their pay would 'bring the works to a standstill'. Money for wages soon arrived.[222] Over the following years, the Navy Commissioners received many more reports of this sort: 'Very many absent themselves' at Harwich in 1667; 'the able calkers ... utterly refuse to come to their duty' at Woolwich in 1668; 'the workmen ... left off work' at Chatham in 1671; and so forth.[223] In fact, sometimes these strikes spread from one yard to another, as in June 1668, when William Bodham, clerk of the ropeyard at Woolwich, reported that 'On news from Chatham [of a strike], most of our men have absented themselves from work, and I hear they do the like at the dock and at Deptford'.[224] Such remarkable examples of communal solidarity seem to have arisen from very specific circumstances. For instance, the workmen drew considerable strength from the sheer size of

---

[221] *CSPD: Charles II, Addenda*, p. 135 (3–4 Apr. 1665). For a discussion of the long-term struggle over 'chips' see Linebaugh, *London Hanged*, ch. 11.

[222] *CSPD, Charles II, 1664–5*, pp. 463–5 (4–6 Jul. 1665), p. 480 (17 Jul. 1665). Two years earlier, there was a seemly less successful 'mutiny among the spinners' in the Portsmouth ropeyard: *CSPD: Charles II, 1663–4*, p. 276 (21 Sep. 1663).

[223] *CSPD: Charles II, Addenda*, p. 175 (11 Apr. 1667); *CSPD, Charles II, 1667–8*, p. 226 (12 Feb. 1668); *CSPD, Charles II, 1671*, p. 578 (20 Nov. 1671). It is highly likely that much of the unspecified 'clamour', 'tumult', and 'discontent' reported in the naval yards during these years was also accompanied by work stoppages. For examples see *CSPD, 1665–6*, p. 12 (11 Oct. 1665); *CSPD: Charles II, Addenda*, pp. 193–4 (15 Jun. 1667); *CSPD, 1671*, pp. 127–8 (11 Mar. 1671).

[224] *CSPD, 1667–8*, pp. 455–6 (23 Jun. 1668).

labour force employed at each of the naval yards and the unusual amount of organisation required to build and repair these ships.[225] Moreover, the concentration of strikes between 1665 and 1671 indicates that they probably emerged from the unique conjunction of rapidly heightened demand and a deeply dysfunctional system of payment, both of which were linked to the Dutch Wars of these decades.

Strikes of this kind may have been exceptional but they were not unique. From the late 1690s onward, other tradesmen resorted to this tactic with increasing frequency. The London Company of Feltmakers and Hatmakers, for example, split into two antagonistic groups in November 1696 when the masters attempted to lower the wages of their employees. The journeymen, who had organised themselves into 'Clubs', responded by refusing to work at the new rates and allegedly 'raised several sums of money for the abetting and supporting such of them who should desert their masters' service'. Though the dispute dragged on for several years, they seem eventually to have won.[226] Other groups of metropolitan workers – including coal-heavers, wheelwrights, and tailors – engaged in collective work stoppages as well.[227] Unsurprisingly, labour conflict of this type also erupted in the rapidly changing Tyneside region amongst ironworkers, keelmen, and shipwrights.[228] Indeed, the workmen involved in the Newcastle coal trade quickly became notorious for their assertiveness. English sea captains faced similar tactics as crews of sailors employed strikes and mass desertion to remedy harsh conditions or raise wages.[229] In each case, workers sought redress for their grievances by forging their solidarity into an economic weapon. An individual withholding his or her labour would have little impact, but 'combinations' could achieve measurable successes if the bonds of fraternity were strong enough to hold them together.

Employers were not the only 'superiors' to encounter concerted non-cooperation from their 'inferiors'. In the 1670s, for example, some land-owners faced tenants who formed 'combinations' to resist rising rents or

---

[225] D. C. Coleman, 'Naval Dockyards under the Later Stuarts', *Economic History Review*, 2nd ser., 6 (1953), pp. 134–55.

[226] Unwin, *Industrial Organization*, pp. 220–21, 248–52.

[227] For the coal-heavers, who struck in 1696, see *CSPD, William III, 1696*, pp. 338 (11 Aug. 1696), 343 (13 Aug. 1696); LMA, COL/CA/01/01/104, fols 129–30, 135–44. For the wheelwrights, who struck three times between 1718 and 1734 after establishing a 'club' in 1714, see Unwin, *Gilds and Companies*, p. 351. For the journeymen tailors, who had by 1721 established a large and sophisticated 'combination' to raise their wages and shorten their workday, see 'The Case of the Master Taylors' (1721), in *Select Documents Illustrating the History of Trade Unionism: I. The Tailoring Trade in London (1721–1866)*, Frank Wallis Galton ed. (London, 1923), pp. 2–3.

[228] For a strike by the hammermen of Winlaton in 1700 see Levine and Wrightson, *Industrial Society*, p. 382. For strikes by the Newcastle shipwrights in 1705 and 1718, and by Newcastle keelmen in 1707, see *Extracts from Hostmen*, pp. 167–9, 177, 184–6.

[229] Rediker, *Between*, pp. 97–106, 109–11.

even to lower them, a strategy made possible by the decline in land value and the resultant shift in power towards renters.[230] Likewise, the threat to large estates posed by organised poaching was heightened by the silent solidarity shown by most commoners when landowners tried to have them inform on their fellows – the 'simples' usually presented a united front against the 'gentles' in such cases.[231] Even the central government could find their economic policies foiled by collective defiance. Attempts to ban domestic tobacco-growing, for example, met passive resistance from people at all levels of the local community until William III reversed the policy in 1689. Poor planters, tenant farmers, and estate owners all shared a stake in the survival of the crop, so Privy Council orders often remained unenforced by county officials and local officers alike.[232] Likewise, when parliament sought to impose a new leather duty in 1697, those involved in the leather trades resisted by systematically withholding information essential to the process of taxation and when a London leather dealer co-operated with the excise office he 'was blackballed by his fellow tradesmen and driven out of business'.[233]

This latter example serves as a reminder of the other side of communal solidarity: expulsion and exclusion. After all, deviants and outsiders could create disunity and undermine the strength of the group, so they became immediate targets for collective action. Hence, just as leather traders punished a collaborator by ostracising him, the journeymen feltworkers disciplined a strikebreaker who had agreed to work at the rates demanded by the masters by seizing him, tying him in a wheelbarrow, and then proceeding 'in a tumultuous and riotous manner to drive him therein through all the considerable places in London and Southwark'.[234] Despite their illegality, such rough tactics fulfilled much the same function as the fines and disenfranchisement authorised by the official charters of self-governing boroughs and craft fellowships. Sometimes, in fact, crowd violence was used to enforce

---

[230] Hainsworth, *Stewards*, pp. 57–8.

[231] Douglas Hay, 'Poaching and the Game Laws on Cannock Chase', in Douglas Hay et al. (eds), *Albion's Fatal Tree: Crime and Society in Eighteenth Century England* (New York, 1975), pp. 189–253; Hainsworth, *Stewards*, pp. 211–21; E. P. Thompson, *Whigs and Hunters: The Origin of the Black Act* (London, 1990). The key legislation that solidified the division between gentlemen hunters and common poachers was the Game Law of 1671: P. B. Mucsche, *Gentlemen and Poachers: The English Game Laws, 1671–1831* (Cambridge, 1981), esp. ch. 3.

[232] Joan Thirsk, 'New Crops and their Diffusion: Tobacco-Growing in 17th-Century England', in C. W. Chalklin and M. A. Havinden (eds), *Rural Change and Urban Growth, 1500–1800: Essays in English Regional History in Honour of W. G. Hoskins* (London, 1974), pp. 76–103.

[233] Brewer, *Sinews*, pp. 232–3.

[234] Unwin, *Industrial Organization*, p. 221. For an example of a group who (like the leather traders) boycotted a perceived collaborator see the discussion of the Southwark Minters below pp. 217–18.

exclusionary company by-laws when formal mechanisms proved insufficient. For instance, according to their order book, the Framework Knitters of London forbid masters from taking more than three apprentices for every journeyman, but this restriction was being flouted with impunity by around 1710. In response, the knitters decided to make an example out of a master named Nicholson who had taken twelve apprentices. They began by beating him and his apprentices and breaking his frames, but they then continued on to the shops of other unpopular masters, breaking nearly a hundred frames in all. This seems to have led the rest of the masters to more assiduously obey company rules. Although some masters soon fled to Nottingham to avoid these restrictions, the knitters certainly succeeded in demonstrating the strength of concerted action against uncooperative individuals.[235]

Urban freemen could band together against their superiors as well. When local governors undermined the economic exclusivity of the community, collective opposition might quickly emerge. At Totnes (Devon) it was the tenant-burgesses of the town's manor court who, in 1676, presented the mayor for permitting two 'Strangers' to sell cloth 'from house to house', allowing them 'to Infringe the Ancient liberties of the Inhabitants'. Such a bold flouting of their 'Priveledges' could not be tolerated.[236] About two decades later the 'Tradesmen and Freemen' of Hertford offered several equally assertive complaints against the heads of their corporation, demanding an immediate end to the injurious practice of granting freedoms to 'Straingers' who had not served an apprenticeship. According to them, it

> doth Impoverish the trade of this Towne; And a greater detriment may follow for that therby Our Poore are much increased, Our Rights and priveliges greatly Obstructed, Our Commons eaten up and distroyed by them whoe have noe Right, All which mischeifes have falne upon us by reason those Orders and Constitucions our forefathers have sett us have not beine followed and pursued by you, which by your oaths you are bound to mainteyne.[237]

Even townspeople without any formal corporate structure sometimes demonstrated a degree of collective strength. In 1693, for example, the residents of Whitehaven frustrated the lord of the manor by resisting his attempts to bring in new craftsmen from outside the community. The inhabitants, he complained, 'treat [the newcomers] as interlopers, and endeavour to lay them under all the discouragments they can', which succeeded in dissuading at least one stranger from settling there.[238]

---

[235] Gravenor Henson, *The Civil, Political, and Mechanical History of the Framework-Knitters in Europe and America* (Nottingham, 1831), pp. 94–6.

[236] DRO, 1579A/9/35, p. 62.

[237] HA, HBR 25/37, 25/40, 25/43.

[238] *The Correspondence of Sir John Lowther of Whitehaven, 1693–1698: A Provincial*

This defensive attitude also manifested itself in illicit attempts to maintain a 'closed shop' within particular trades. The textile industry in south-western England produced the most widespread and long-standing examples of such organisations, and a brief examination of their growth under the later Stuarts seems worthwhile. It may have begun on 15 June 1700, when the wool-combers of Tiverton formed a 'society' for mutual support.[239] The 'society' appears to have rapidly evolved and multiplied, because the employers in Taunton reported that, beginning in 1702 or 1703, the weavers in most of the region's woollen towns had 'formed themselves into Clubs … and by their arbitrary Proceedings they hinder many honest Labourers, who refuse to join in their Club, from using their lawful Employments'.[240] The exact terms imposed by the Bristol journeymen were described in 1707:

> That no Master Weavers shall take a Prentice, without Leave of the Confederacy, and the Apprentice to be inrolled in their Books; and a Master shall not employ a Journeyman, before he become one of the Bristol Confederacy, or brings a Certificate, that he is confederated at some other Place.[241]

The journeymen accompanied these 'unreasonable Demands' with coordinated direct action. According to their masters, the 'Confederates' at Bristol, Taunton and Tiverton 'committed many Outrages and Riots' including strike threats, vandalism, violence, and gaol-breaking.[242] By 1718, these 'Clubs' had spread to Exeter and Bradninch, and the authorities of both towns complained that 'Thousands' of their workers 'have made it their frequent Practice to cut and break the Chains, Serges, and Looms of several Masters who opposed their Laws', while threatening to pull down the houses of others.[243] Likewise, the officials at Tiverton reported that a group of workers gathered and angrily 'carried several of the Masters on

---

Community in Wartime, D. R. Hainsworth ed. (British Academy Records of Social and Economic History, n.s., vol. 7, London, 1983), pp. 11–12.

[239] Dunsford, *Historical Memoirs*, p. 205. There are obviously similarities with the societies which spread throughout Essex, perhaps beginning in Colchester in the 1680s, which were discussed above p. 201. However, the Essex societies seem to have had the support of local officials, whereas the organisations in the South West quickly came to be regarded as 'unlawful'.

[240] 'A Petition of the Drugget-makers, Serge-makers, Fullers, Dyers, and other principal Inhabitants of the Town of Taunton', in *JHC*, XV, p. 312 (25 Feb. 1707). Although the petition dates from 1707, the authors claimed to describe events 'within four or five Years last'.

[241] 'A Petition of the Clothiers, Serge-makers, and Stuff-makers, in and near the City of Bristol', in *JHC*, XV, pp. 312–13 (25 Feb. 1707).

[242] Taunton and Bristol petitions in *JHC*, XV, pp. 312–13 (25 Feb. 1707); Dunsford, *Historical Memoirs*, p. 206.

[243] Bradninch and Exeter petitions in *JHC*, XVIII, p. 715 (5 Feb. 1718).

Poles, in a sort of mock Triumph'.[244] In response to these aggressive demonstrations of associational strength, the government issued a royal proclamation against 'unlawful Clubs, Combinations, etc.' in February of 1718, but this failed to stop the workers for imposing their own 'Laws' on the entire workforce as the clothiers of Exeter, Taunton, Tiverton, Bristol, and other towns were making many of the same complaints in the mid-1720s.[245] Even after parliament officially outlawed these organisations in 1726, they continued to assert control over many aspects of their trade throughout the eighteenth century.[246]

This first generation of woollen workers' 'Clubs' – from their emergence in 1700 to their criminalisation in 1726 – reveals much about the radical potential of later Stuart occupational communities. Although they may have begun merely as benefit societies, they quickly became 'pseudo-companies', fulfilling the same functions as their lawful counterparts. Perhaps the transition came in response to the events of late 1702, when the weavers of Taunton were rebuffed after petitioning the House of Commons against employers who 'take Five, Six, or Seven Apprentices at one time, and many intrude into that Trade, who never served their Apprenticeships thereto'.[247] After all, according to the later reports from this same town, it was around this time that the workers formed 'Clubs' and began to regulate the labour market independently.[248] The features that they shared with authorised companies were manifold. Rather than simply pushing up wages through sudden strikes, they sought control over 'the trade' itself by monopolising access to employment, appointing supervisors, keeping membership books, collecting dues, ratifying 'By-Laws and Orders', setting prices, determining 'the manner and materials' of production, supporting persecuted members,

[244] 'A Petition of the Mayor and Burgesses of ... Tiverton', in *JHC*, XVIII, p. 715 (5 Feb. 1718); Robert Malcolmson, 'Workers' Combinations in Eighteenth-Century England', in Margaret Jacob and James Jacob (eds), *The Origins of Anglo-American Radicalism* (London, 1984), p. 154.

[245] *The Historical Register* (1718), III, pp. 6–7 (in separately paginated 'Chronological Register'). For Dartmouth and Exeter in 1724 see *JHC*, XX, pp. 268–9 (24 Feb. 1724); for Tiverton, Exeter, Bristol, Taunton, Crediton, and Callington in 1726 see ibid., pp. 598–9 (3 Mar. 1726), 602 (7 Mar. 1726), 648 (31 Mar. 1726).

[246] For the law see *Statutes at Large*, V, pp. 605–6 (12 Geo. I, c. 34). For examples of vigorous collective action by south-western woollen workers in the late 1720s and beyond see Malcolmson, 'Combinations', pp. 152, 154–5; Rollison, *Origins*, ch. 9; and the work cited there.

[247] The petition was referred to committee and, although the committee agreed with the petitioners about apprenticeship, the House voted down their resolution: *JHC*, XIV, pp. 31–2 (14 Nov. 1702), 67–8 (4 Dec. 1702). Interestingly, the petitioners also complained that 'many Persons come into the said Town, with Discharges, who cannot be removed by Law, until they become chargeable to the Parish, although the Townsmen, upon Heat of Elections to Parliament, are turned out of Work, and others employed in their room'.

[248] 'A Petition of the Drugget-makers, Serge-makers, Fullers, Dyers, and other principal Inhabitants of the Town of Taunton', in *JHC*, XV, p. 312 (25 Feb. 1707).

and generally presuming 'to act as Bodies Corporate' in their relations with outsiders.[249] Their reach even extended beyond particular localities, accepting 'foreign' workers as long as they could certify being 'confederated' elsewhere. Most revealingly of all, members of these fellowships also shared a fraternal culture. By 1708, one 'Club' had 'a common Seal, Tipstaffs, and Colours, which they display at Pleasure, and meet, as often as they think fit, at their Club-house, being an Inn at Taunton', and in 1726 Mr William Pike, an employer, reported having 'seen the Weavers at their Clubs, where none but Weavers are admitted; and that they have their Ensigns and Flags hung out at the Door of their Meetings'.[250] These workers expressed their collective identity unapologetically, and their economic communities were no doubt stronger for it.

Despite the violence which accompanied these attempts at collective redress, one might be tempted to lionise these 'Clubs' as admirable responses to employment practices that relied on exploitation and immiseration. Yet, not all such actions are as amenable to glorification. In some cases the defence of 'community' was simply a matter of a local group of poor people attacking a 'foreign' pauper. In 1664, for example, women at Thorpe Market in Norfolk beat a woman who tried to glean even after 'Thorpe had refused' to give her permission.[251] Likewise, England's textile workers did not always direct their ire at targets consistent with modern conceptions of 'social justice' – sometimes they defined their 'enemies' by nationality rather than by economic position. This was especially true at the height of anti-French paranoia under Charles II.[252] As early as 1670, poor Londoners could read a libel from 'your brethren Apprentices and Journimen' calling on them to take up arms against the aliens in their midst 'on Mayday next'. Although this squib argued that 'wee are impoverished by them tradinge within our Nation espeatially by the French', it also stressed that 'we may be fearfull of our lives first by theyr Rebellion in their owne land [and] secondly by the fire'.[253] The threat of direct action became a reality five years later when thousands of weavers took to the streets in a violent attempt to remedy various grievances. Not all of their victims were immigrants, but more than one observer believed that the riots in London resulted from 'the dangerous

---

[249] These features are all mentioned in the various petitions and mostly summarised in the proclamation of 1718.

[250] JHC, XV, p. 312 (25 Feb. 1707); XX, p. 648 (31 Mar. 1726). For insightful discussions of these sorts of expressions of fraternal culture among eighteenth-century workmen see Malcolmson, 'Combinations'; Chase, Early Trade Unionism.

[251] Hindle, On the Parish? p. 38. For later cases of often violent 'collective sanctions' against gleaning interlopers or those who ignored local customs about timing see King, 'Gleaners', pp. 132–3.

[252] The examples below focus on the 1670s and 1680s, but for economically inspired violence against the 'poor Palatines' who arrived in 1709 see Statt, Foreigners, pp. 150–52.

[253] Gwynn, Huguenot Heritage, p. 110.

discontent that the silk weavers and other have taken up against the French inhabitants in the city and suburbs, robbing them as they conceive of their trade and livelihood', and similar riots in Exeter and Topsham at this time were clearly directed against aliens.[254] In 1683, the workers of Norwich launched several attacks on the Huguenot weavers who had recently arrived in the city:

> the Mob brake open one of their Houses, and misused a Women so, that she died in 2 or 3 Days after; the Pretence was, that these People would under-work them; however, the French that dwelt there were forced to quit the Street that Night.... The Poor being still discontented at the French which were left in the City, ... and coming in a large Body into the Market Place, declared that the French came to under-work them, and accordingly going to Mr Barnham's in St. Andrew's Parish, they pulled them and their Goods out of their Houses, abused their Person &c.[255]

Soon after, one Frenchman reported to a compatriot that the townspeople of Norwich believed the settlers to be 'only a troop of Papists masquerading as Protestants and would ruin their trade'.[256] These examples indicate that English workers readily conflated economic threats with religio-political ones.[257] Despite their impeccable Protestantism, Huguenot immigrants could be imagined as crypto-papists whose willingness to 'under-work' loyal citizens was simply part of a larger conspiracy to weaken the national interest.

When frustrated textile workers illicitly targeted 'outsiders' in an attempt to redress various economic complaints, their blows often landed

---

[254] HMC, *Sixth Report of the Royal Commission on Historical Manuscripts* (no. 5, London, 1877), p. 372. For another observer who described the riots as 'against the French' see Gwynn, *Huguenot Heritage*, pp. 116–17. 'The English hatters', according to the Venetian ambassador, 'have also made a move against the French ones, as well as some other artisans in order to drive away from London all the workmen who are not natives or subjects of these realms. One day there was a rumour that they were going to massacre all the French, who have introduced various manufactures and who work for less than the English': *CSPV, 1673–5*, p. 449 (30 Aug. 1675). For more evidence of anti-alien sentiment and for the contemporaneous riots in Devon see Harris, *London Crowds*, pp. 138, 201.

[255] Francis Blomefield, *An Essay Towards a Topographical History ... of Norfolk* (5 vols, Fersfield, 1739–75), II, p. 294. Although he dates these events to 1682, this appears to be incorrect based on the sources cited in the note below and in Miller, *Cities Divided*, pp. 45–6.

[256] *CSPD, Charles II, January to June, 1683*, p. 363 (4 Sep. 1683). Journeymen and apprentice weavers in London also hatched a 'design' in 'their clubs' in August of this year. They planned to seek the support of their Company or the king 'in opposition to the French weavers in their neighbourhood', but also agreed that 'if they can get a sufficient number together, they will rise and knock them on the head': ibid., p. 330 (27 Aug. 1683).

[257] For other cases of such conflation see Statt, *Foreigners*, pp. 19–20, 168–72.

on employers of 'foreigners' or the 'foreigners' themselves, with bloody or even fatal results. But not every target had blood that could be spilled or flesh that could be bruised. Sometimes, the external threat was an object rather than a person. In the London riots of 1675, for example, 'engine looms' rather than immigrants bore the brunt of the attacks. The large crowds of men and women directed most of their rage at these labour-saving looms, systemically dragging at least eighty-five of them into the streets and setting them alight over the course of five days.[258] Participants in this ritual of destruction had considerable support from their communities. The Company of Weavers had tried to legally suppress the engine looms in the late 1660s and tried again in the aftermath of the riots, as well as giving money to some of those who had been arrested.[259] Moreover, many constables and militiamen refused to stop the attacks because they too 'sought to see the French inventions (as they called them) burnt'.[260] It seems that there was widespread opposition to the 'French' (or, as it was sometimes called, 'Dutch') loom, so when ten of the weavers were sentenced to stand in the pillory 'not a single [outrage] was seen against them but there was rather a sentiment of universal sympathy'.[261] Clearly, many English people regarded these machines as foreign impositions which threatened the weaving trade, the urban economy, and even the whole 'common weal'.

In the decades that followed, many of these same connotations of alterity came to be attached to another economically threatening object: imported calico. As shown earlier in the chapter, this commodity provoked intense hostility among the country's textile workers, which was expressed in print and in petitions from the 1690s onward.[262] However, weavers also sought redress for their grievances against calicoes through less peaceable methods. In 1696–7 they launched repeated assaults on the symbols of this notorious trade, including both the East India House and city shops selling the commodities.[263] This direct action, in combination with an extensive

[258] For substantial discussions of the riot see Dunn, 'Weavers' Riot'; Harris, *London Crowds*, pp. 191–201.

[259] Harris, *London Crowds*, pp. 195–6.

[260] HMC, *Seventh Report of the Royal Commission on Historical Manuscripts* (no. 6, London, 1879), p. 466. For examples of officers and soldiers 'countenancing the weavers', 'refusing to assist in the suppression of the rabble', 'letting one of the rabble committed to them escape', and even 'inviting some of the weavers to burn an engine' see *CSPD, Charles II, 1675–6*, pp. 257–9.

[261] *CSPV, 1673–5*, p. 466 (25 Oct. 1675). For the tendency to occasionally describe the looms as 'Dutch' see Plummer, *London Weavers' Company*, p. 163.

[262] For the nationalist idioms of complaint see Chapter 3.2 above. Some of the protests analysed below have been noted in P. J. Thomas, *Mercantilism and the East India Trade* (London, 1963) and elsewhere.

[263] Vernon, *Letters*, I, pp. 76–7; 21 January 1697, *Post Boy*, issue 268; 21 January 1697, 20 March 1697, *Post Man and the Historical Account*, issues 267, 295; Luttrell, *Brief Historical Relation*, IV, pp. 172, 174, 198–9.

petitioning campaign, encouraged the passage of an act against importing printed calicoes in 1700.[264] But a loophole in the act allowed for unprinted calicoes and soon enough the complaints resumed, culminating in violent campaign which began in 1719. As with the earlier riots, this was preceded by numerous attempts to gain redress through entirely lawful means. For instance, a ballad from this period only hinted at the possibility of illicit action by noting that 'if Steps be not made / To recover our Trade, / It will wear out each Sufferer's Patience'.[265] Over the next two years, however, weavers in London and elsewhere set out to destroy the calico trade with their own hands. It began with small groups – usually of journeymen, but sometimes including women or children – insulting and harassing women caught wearing the despised fabric, but the attacks soon became more vicious.[266] In June 1719 they began attacking every 'Callico Madam' they encountered, ripping the dresses from their backs or splashing them with ink or acid.[267] By the start of July Londoners found 'the Gibbet on Stone-bridge was hung from top to bottom with fragments of Callicoe, stuff torn or rather stolen from Women by Journey Men Weavers', and many more tales appeared in the newspapers of women roughly stripped of their gowns in the streets, both in London and in Norwich.[268] Yet they did not just attack calico-wearers. Initially led by a weaver calling himself 'Commodore Shuttle', one group boarded East India ships and damaged their rigging, while another attempted to march to Lewisham and 'destroy the Callico-Printers

---

[264] *Statutes of the Realm*, VII, pp. 598–9 (11 & 12 Will. III, c. 10).

[265] 'The Spittle-Fields Ballad: Or, The Weavers Complaint against the Callico Madams', in *The Northern Cuckold*, p. 4. By 1721, various versions of this ballad had been circulating for at least two years. For a reprint of a 1715 petition against calicoes, full of nationalist idioms, see 4 July 1719, *Weekly Journal or British Gazetteer*.

[266] As early as 1701, the Weavers' Company had to issue a disavowal of 'their Journeymen [who] abuse Gentlewomen and others that shall wear East India Silks': 4 October 1701, *Post Man and the Historical Account*, issue 883.

[267] 13 June 1719, *Weekly Journal or Saturday's Post*; 13 June 1719, *Weekly Journal or British Gazetteer*. The attacks 'frighted some [women] into fits, and it is said others into Miscarriages': 20 June 1719, *Weekly Journal or British Gazetteer*.

[268] 4 July 1719, *Weekly Journal or British Gazetteer*; 11 July 1719, *Weekly Journal or Saturday Post*; Blomefield, *Topographical History*, II, p. 309. For other calico-related disorders in Norwich (and Pockthorpe) see Miller, *Cities Divided*, p. 52. I have focused on the summer of 1719, but attacks continued in 1720–21. Interestingly, this practice of seizing and displaying threatening imports also took place in Tiverton sometime around 1720. Here, the wool-combers 'attacked the houses of those merchants who had introduced the greatest quantity of Irish worsted; dragged it out into the streets, tore it in pieces, and rendered useless all that they could find: large quantities they hung on sign posts (Some of which hung there more than twelve months afterwards), as trophies of their victory': Dunsford, *Historical Memoirs*, p. 208. Another economic dispute, this time between the glovemakers and the stocking weavers, resulted in cotton gloves being 'hanged' at Tyburn in 1739: McKenzie, *Tyburn's Martyrs*, p. 256.

there'.[269] Then, around a year later, a great crowd of weavers 'threatened to demolish the House of a French weaver and rifle that of the East-India Company'.[270] In other words, these were primarily regarded as assaults on those 'Foes of their Country' who dared to undermine the nation's staple industry, rather than mere attempts to despoil a particular commodity. Ultimately, the weavers achieved their goal in 1721, when parliament passed a bill that comprehensively forbade the buying, selling or wearing of calicoes.[271] Many of the supporters of the anti-calico cause justified themselves by appealing to English nationhood and stressing communal improvement, but they could not have succeeded without the savage assaults on those regarded as the enemy.

Several themes have emerged from the investigation so far: the strength of unanimous non-cooperation, the hostility to collaborators and outsiders, the links between legal and illegal tactics. Yet most of the analysis has focused on manufacture and trade, so it would be useful to compare this with other types of collective mobilisation. After all, occupational communities were not the only group to aggressively seek redress for economic grievances in the later Stuart period. Hence, the remainder of this section focuses briefly on four other sorts of communal action: those based on taxation, debt, land, and food.

Despite both the ever-increasing levels of revenue collected by the national government and endemic rates of individual tax evasion, organised resistance to state impositions was decidedly rare. When it did occur, local solidarity appears to have been perhaps the most important factor. It seems likely, for example, that resistance to the hearth tax resulted as much from animosity towards the intrusions of non-local collectors as from opposition to Charles II's government. If so, these crowds – sometimes supported by magistrates – believed that they were defending their whole community when they drove off and stoned 'Chimney-men' in St Neots, Newcastle, the North Riding, Hexham, Hereford, Banbury, Pewsey, Winchcombe, Weymouth, Bridport, Marlborough, and Taunton in the late 1660s.[272] Likewise, opposition to the excise – which 'threw into stark relief the potential conflict between centre and locality' – and to the destruction of illegal

---

[269] 6 June 1719, *Weekly Packet*, issue 362; 11 June 1719, *Post Boy*, issue 4662.

[270] Maitland, *The History and Survey of London*, I, p. 530.

[271] *Statutes at Large*, V, pp. 338–40 (7 Geo. I, c. 7). Even this did not resolve the problem entirely, but both calico wearing and anti-calico attacks decreased substantially: Plummer, *London Weavers' Company*, pp. 304–11.

[272] *CSPD, Charles II, 1666–7*, pp. 327, 330–31, 336; *CSPD, Charles II, 1667–8*, pp. 222, 224; *CTB*, II, pp. 69, 79, 81; III, pp. 71, 406; V, 318–19; HMC, *Le Fleming*, p. 47; Harris, *London Crowds*, pp. 205–6; L. M. Marshall, 'The Levying of the Hearth Tax, 1662–1688', *English Historical Review*, 51 (1936), pp. 632, 635–6; Michael Braddick, *Parliamentary Taxation in Seventeenth-Century England: Local Administration and Response* (London, 1994), pp. 252–66. For negative representations of hearth tax collectors in ballads see *PB*, IV, pp. 308–9.

tobacco crops spurred violent rioting in the mid-seventeenth century, and resentment continued to simmer in the decades after the Restoration.[273] This hostility to state intrusion also partly explains the 'communal solidarity' found in some coastal villages confronted by officials seeking to suppress smuggling.[274] Although violent reactions to centralised taxation undoubtedly stemmed from a variety of different causes, the bonds of locality may well have been the determining factor in many of these incidents.

Insolvent debtors normally relied on support from their friends and neighbours to make ends meet, but sometimes they actually banded together with other debtors to form permanent territorial communities in the 'liberties' of London.[275] One such organisation emerged in the district of Southwark known as 'The Mint', which seems to have become formalised in the late seventeenth century.[276] According to a series of complaints to parliament in 1706, 'the said Minters have several Clubs, and a Chairman presiding amongst them, being attended by Beadles and Constables of their own making, by whom they send for the Offenders of their Laws', for which they even established their own 'Gaol'. They tenaciously defended each other from outsiders by regularly fighting off groups of invading constables, rescuing captured Minters, and subjecting many hostile intruders to extremely unpleasant punishments. Specifically, they ritually 'pumped' outsiders under taps ('the Law of the Mint') or threw them into sewage ditches ('the Law of the Black Ditch'), and in one case they made an enemy solemnly swear never to return using an excrement-covered brick as a Bible. In addition to violently excluding outsiders, they also targeted any member of their self-declared 'honourable Society' who dared to collaborate with external authorities. When a local brewer and tavern-keeper aided some constables, they 'voted him out of their pretended Society; and such of them as were his Debtors ... bound themselves under an Oath, that they would never

---

[273] Braddick, *Parliamentary Taxation*, pp. 285–6; Thirsk, 'New Crops', pp. 95–7. For excise riots in Somerset (1675), Shropshire (1699), and various places in Wales (1699, 1704, 1712) see P. J. Norrey, 'The Restoration Regime in Action: The Relationship between Central and Local Government in Dorset, Somerset & Wiltshire, 1660–1678', *Historical Journal*, 31:4 (1988), p. 801; Beloff, *Public Order*, pp. 94–5.

[274] Paul Monod, 'Dangerous Merchandise: Smuggling, Jacobitism, and Commercial Culture in Southeast England, 1690–1760', *Journal of British Studies*, 30 (1991), p. 181. For violent clashes between smugglers and government officers see Beloff, *Public Order*, pp. 95–8.

[275] These 'places of pretended privilege' are listed in *Statutes of the Realm*, VII, pp. 271–5 (8 & 9 Will. III, c. 27). For more on arrest and imprisonment for debt see Muldrew, *Economy of Obligation*, pp. 276–90.

[276] Unless otherwise noted, all information and quotations in this paragraph are from the committee report in *JHC*, XV, pp. 169–70 (23 Feb. 1706). See also *CSPD: Anne*, IV, pp. 85, 92, 103. For more on the context of these incidents see Nigel Stirk, 'Arresting Ambiguity: The Shifting Geographies of a London Debtors' Sanctuary in the Eighteenth Century', *Social History*, 25:3 (2000), pp. 316–29.

pay him one Farthing of their Debts; which will prove his Ruin'. It was only in 1722 that an act of parliament effectively disbanded this unlawful community.[277] A combination of desperate individuals and legal ambiguity made the creation of these 'Clubs' possible, but they were maintained by much more than mere practicality. Here, solidarity required both a shared commitment to violent mutual defence and an alternative understanding of 'law' and 'honour'.

The defence of 'The Mint' as a particular territorial unit mirrored, in some ways, the collective actions undertaken to defend other types of land. Just as with debtors' sanctuaries, intruders were expelled and local people protected from outside prosecution. However, the central object in these conflicts was the preservation of a common resource, so the participants could usually appropriate existing organisational structures rather than building entirely new ones. Urban common lands, for example, were often managed coopera-tively using civic ordinances and customs. Hence, when Charles II tried to give a loyalist named Robert Townsend control over Cheylesmore Park in 1661, the citizens of Coventry – who had long managed the land themselves – responded with a series of acts of collective resistance.[278] They destroyed 'new inclosures' several times in the 1660s and then, in January 1689, they marched in 'a great rabble' led by burgesses to drive the encloser from his house and destroy his fences and ditches. More 'Ryots & Tumults' followed in the 1690s, and by 1705 Coventry's citizens had regained legal control over the park. Perhaps unsurprisingly, these protests not only sometimes involved burgesses – a group of men who supposedly represented the community as a whole – but also seem to have occasionally coincided with the Lammas Day ceremonies that customarily signalled the opening of the commons for grazing. Both the participants and timing of these actions thus implied a conflict between a defensive local citizenry and an encroaching outsider.

In contrast to these 'civic' protests, the defence of commons in fens and forests was often more violent. Riots at the Hatfield Level, which lay at the borders of Yorkshire, Lincolnshire, and Nottinghamshire, typify the sort of direct action that some fen-dwellers employed to defend their territory from intruders. Although the first protests began in the 1620s, unrest continued on a regular basis into the eighteenth century. On several occasions after the Restoration groups of commoners – sometimes led by local gentlemen and supported by a 'common purse' – showed their collective strength and determination through a variety of tough tactics: they assaulted the drainer

[277] *Statutes at Large*, V, pp. 470–72 (9 Geo. I, c. 28). However, even then resistance continued in some liberties. In 1724, for example, the inhabitants of the Wapping Mint sanctuary organised resistance to intrusion with such violence that one Minter was tried and executed: Linebaugh, *London Hanged*, pp. 56–8.
[278] For the Cheylesmore enclosure riots see *CSPD, Charles II, 1667–8*, p. 435; *CSPD, Charles II, 1668–9*, p. 438; CHC, BA/H/C/17/3, p. 55 (Sep. 1699); VCH: *Warwickshire*, VIII, p. 204.

and his agents; seized livestock and crops; burnt building supplies; levelled fences and ditches; destroyed a windmill and houses. Indeed, they conveyed their message especially clearly in the summer of 1660 when they targeted the church of recent settlers by smashing the windows, destroying the furnishings, and driving a flock of maggoty sheep into the nave. It was not until the 1710s that the commoners were finally quieted using a combination of concessions, judicial settlement, and military force.[279] Likewise, in the Forest of Dean, long-running disputes over land use resulted in several violent protests in the decades that followed the new Reforestation Act of 1668. Here, too, the commoners repeatedly destroyed enclosures, felled trees, and broke into the pound. In 1688 they chose more prominent targets when they attacked the site of the Verderer's Court and pulled down two forest keepers' lodges – thus directing their collective ire at the bridgeheads of outside authority.[280] The objects targeted by these various groups of commoners – the encloser's fence, the settlers' church, the keeper's lodge – clearly embodied the very essence of 'alterity', a symbol of foreign encroachment erected within the bounds of the local community. By levelling or desecrating these physical emblems of intrusion, those who 'belonged' collectively reasserted their claims over the land.

Like the battles over land use, communal responses to dearth often hinged on the division between insiders and outsiders. Indeed, widespread assumptions about local entitlement ensured that, in times of sudden distress, the needs of each 'little commonwealth' could take precedence over the supposedly universal reach of the law of property. When examining grain riots, it is usually impossible to disentangle the influence of this logic from that of simple necessity; however, many incidents in the later Stuart period demonstrate the strength of these assumptions. Just before Christmas in 1662, for example, five hundred women raised 'a tumult at Weymouth, because a quantity of corn was bought for transportation; the people seized it, and kept guard that it should not be shipped in the night'.[281] Their willingness to set guards rather than merely pillaging the captured grain indicates that the primary objective of 'the people' was to keep the grain within the

---

[279] In the later Stuart period there were incidents in 1660–61, 1664, 1668, 1682, 1684, 1691, 1697, and 1712. All the information on the Hatfield Level has been drawn from Keith Lindley, *Fenland Riots and the English Revolution* (London, 1982), pp. 233–52.

[280] For the various protests in the Forest of Dean during this period see *CTB*, III, p. 457; IX, pp. 586–7, 1495; *CSPD, Anne*, III, p. 59; Cyril Hart, *The Commoners of Dean Forest* (Gloucester, 1951), pp. 72–7; idem, *The Free Miners of the Royal Forest of Dean and Hundred of St. Briavels* (Gloucester, 1953), pp. 171, 184–6, 189, 192–3. 'Tacit support for the rioters came from some local gentry': *VCH: Gloucestershire*, V, p. 368. See also Simon Sandall, 'Custom, Memory and the Operations of Power in Seventeenth-Century Forest of Dean', in Fiona Williamson (ed.), *Locating Agency: Space, Power and Popular Politics* (Newcastle, 2009), pp. 133–60.

[281] *CSPD, Charles II, 1661–1662*, p. 602 (25 Dec. 1662). For more examples of anti-exportation riots between c.1650 and c.1740 see Bohstedt, *Politics of Provisions*, ch. 3.

locality, rather than to satisfy the immediate hunger of the rioters themselves. Several similar events occurred in early 1674 when 'the poorer sort of people' in Stratford-upon-Avon prevented the departure of corn barges and crowds in Colchester seized grain being shipped from the port.[282]

Many more townspeople adopted these sorts of tactics when confronted with the dearths of the 1690s and 1709–10. The patterns revealed by the events of these years indicate that the strength of community was closely linked to the threat of alterity. Complaints often began with the arrival of outsiders and, as one would expect, foreign corn factors frequently met hostility from hungry locals when prices were high. This led to riots against Dutch merchants buying up grain in Colchester in 1692 and against Bristolian dealers doing the same in Worcester in 1693.[283] Yet, the intended destination of exports was also important, especially if the beneficiary was France. The prospect of sending corn overseas during a dearth was offensive enough, but for an exporter to feed the nation's arch-enemy while England went hungry instilled outrage, and this prompted 'Insurrections' in at least nine places in 1693–4.[284] Attitudes were little changed when the spectre of dearth returned during yet another conflict with the French fifteen years later. Thus, in May 1709, there were death threats and 'great disturbance in all the markets' around Wrexham after it was 'said that the Corne bought in our country was bought for Lord Powis and Lord Molyneux who they say have transported it all to France', and during this same month hundreds of colliers from Kingswood near Bristol launched 'an insurrection' in response to the 'scarcity of corn, and it being brought up by the merchants to send abroad'.[285] Around the same time, an armed crowd in Suffolk barred a dealer from entering their town, threatening to stone him and crying 'that he was a Rogue & was going to carry the corn into France'.[286] The constant references to this national rival in the context of these events indicates that many rioters may have imagined themselves as patriotic citizens seeking to

[282] Nicholas Fogg, *Stratford-upon-Avon: Portrait of a Town* (Chichester, 1986), p. 76; Walter, 'Faces', p. 116.
[283] For Colchester see Luttrell, *Brief Historical Relation*, II, p. 629 (1 Dec. 1692); ibid., III, p. 29 (4 Feb. 1693). For other reports about the arrival of factors (including Dutch, Quakers, and unspecified 'foreigners') see ibid., III, pp. 20, 32; VI, p. 494.
[284] *The Price of the Abdication* (1693), p. 9; Wanklyn, 'Bridgnorth Food Riots', p. 100.
[285] William Barrett, *History and Antiquities of the City of Bristol* (1789), p. 696. They were 'appeased by reducing the price of wheat to 6s 8d per bushel'. See also HMC, *Eighth Report of the Royal Commission on Historical Manuscripts: Appendix I (Marlborough)* (no. 7, London, 1882), p. 46.
[286] Thompson, *Customs in Common*, p. 213. Likewise, towards the end of November, 'a corn factor, employed in buying up wheat at Kingston market for exportation, had like to have been mobb'd, with some foreigners who were with him': Luttrell, *Brief Historical Relation*, VI, p. 494.

foil a plot to aid the enemy.[287] Of course, 'exportation' in this period some-times just meant shipping grain to the next county, but this could provoke almost as much outrage as sending it overseas. This, too, was a betrayal of one's 'home'. The anger created by such behaviour was exemplified in the hundred armed women of Coggeshall who, in 1709, threatened to shoot several men and burn down their houses 'by reason they have been dealers in corn to London'.[288]

The relationship between the crowd and the community as a whole was not always entirely clear. Sometimes, observers attributed the action to specific subsections of the local population, such as 'the poorer sort of people' or 'the rabble'. In these cases, it is unlikely that contemporaries would have deemed the crowd to be a suitable 'representative' of communal sentiment. Yet, in contrast, other observers described these events as the actions of 'the people' of a town or village, which indicates that crowd and community were regarded as one and the same. The men and women who actually seized corn or stopped wagons could often count on widespread support from their neighbours and compatriots, a support which resulted from a shared set of assumptions of the sort found in the ballads, alma-nacs, and other cheap print discussed above. Moreover, the crowd could also emphasise these common values while obscuring their own legal culpa-bility by projecting accusations of treachery onto their opponents. In the spring of 1693, for example, 300 of the townspeople of Shrewsbury 'went to the [market]place and made proclamation against carrying corn out of the nation, which might occasion a famine'.[289] They thus presented them-selves as quasi-official tribunes of the English people and, at the same time, transformed the exporter into one of the Four Horsemen. Not every action against exporters earned the blessing of the community, but the ability to define oneself in opposition to men who – according to one newspaper account – 'care not for a Farthing for what becomes of the Nation' made the task much easier.[290]

Indeed, this tendency can be seen in practically every attempt at redress which built on the logic of communal solidarity. Each of these cases – from parochial poor relief and local common land to labour strikes and anti-immi-grant riots – emerged from a division between insiders and outsiders. Hence,

---

[287] It should also be noted that worries about exportation were not confined to England and Wales. There were also threats and riots about this issue in Scotland and Ireland: Christopher Whatley, 'The Union of 1707, Integration and the Scottish Burghs: The Case of the 1720 Food Riots', *Scottish Historical Review*, 78:2 (1999), pp. 192–218; *A Further and More Perticular Account of the Cruel Desperate and Bloody Fight and Uproar* (1700).

[288] Nicholas Corsellis to Lord Rivers, 16 May 1709, in HMC, *Eighth Report: Appendix I (Marlborough)*, p. 46.

[289] Luttrell, *Brief Historical Relation*, III, p. 88; Wood, *Life and Times*, III, p. 421.

[290] 16 November 1709, *Observator*, issue 84.

resolving the grievance apparently necessitated supporting or defending insiders while excluding or expelling outsiders. More importantly, participants imagined that the 'agent' in these actions was the community itself, rather than some external power such as God or the monarch. This was obviously a fiction – after all, it was usually a tiny minority of the whole that actually made key decisions or engaged in agitation – but it was a vitally important one, as it vested these attempts at redress with the legitimacy they needed if they were to have any hope of succeeding. The fiction of unanimity also empowered ordinary people to take the law into their own hands or even create their own pseudo-laws.[291] Following the model of self-government set out in the charters of incorporated towns and craft companies, these men and women collectively asserted their right 'to act as Bodies Corporate' by demanding the enforcement of rules such as the 'Law of the Mint', the 'By-Laws and Orders' of the woollen workers, and the 'proclamation' of the Shrewsbury townspeople. This meant protecting common resources while punishing trespassers and traitors according to standards adjudged by the community. In short, ordinary people used these concerted actions to leap onto the public stage with a confidence that their superiors must have found frightening.

6 Conclusions

The dissolution of community has long been considered to be self-evident. Thus, when Ferdinand Tönnies wrote his powerful elucidation of *Community and Society* in 1887, he assumed that the former inevitably lost ground to the latter. The decaying culture of *Gemeinschaft* – i.e. co-operation, commonweal, concord, and rural folkways – was gradually subsumed by the developing culture of *Gesellschaft* – i.e. contracts, calculation, competition, and urban cosmopolitanism.[292] This simple notion of 'development' offered an endlessly flexible explanatory model and, in turn, it influenced the work of practically every historian of early modern society.

In many ways, the story of the shift from *Gemeinschaft* to *Gesellschaft* mirrors the declension narratives discussed in previous chapters, yet it differs in one important respect. Whereas these other theories have implicitly continued to govern much contemporary scholarship, assumptions about the 'decline' of community have faced sustained criticism. Historians have now shown that the teleology inherited from nineteenth-century thinkers is woefully inadequate, as the entities normally associated with

---

[291] This probably accounts for the prevalence of violence in these types of protests when compared to petitionary ones.
[292] Tönnies, *Community and Society*, esp. pp. 231–5.

'pre-modern' community – such as kinship, friendship, parishes, guilds, and especially neighbourliness – did not simply wither away.[293] This scepticism has pushed aside older claims; yet, as Keith Wrightson has recently argued, 'we have stumbled over the question of change'.[294] In response, Wrightson has suggested that there was no inevitable movement from selfless communalism to self-centred individualism, but there was a shift in the balance between differing types of social institutions and identities. According to him, two interlocking trends emerge: first, the erosion of the most broad and inclusive forms of 'mutuality'; second, the tightening of collective bonds of social class and religious denomination. Ultimately, social solidarities became more 'selective'.[295] Tönnies and Wrightson obviously offer very different narratives. Nonetheless, neither version accords completely with the arguments presented so far in this chapter. The ignominious decay of *Gemeinschaft* is notably absent in the preceding pages, while the narrowing of communal boundaries is belied by the revival of many corporate bonds and the strengthening of national solidarities. So, this chapter concludes with an attempt to sketch the decidedly non-linear history of economic communities in the late seventeenth and early eighteenth centuries.

In at least one respect, the inherited metanarrative seems plausible. The sacramental communities that had once been found in every parish church no longer had a firm hold over the economic lives of their members. Of course, clergymen and tract-writers did not cease to forcefully proclaim the social implications of 'spiritual consanguinity'. Isaac Barrow's magnificent sermons on charity showed the continuing vigour of these idioms, and these beliefs appear to have been shared by many in his audiences, as evidenced by the considerable sums of money for poor relief which continued to be raised at informal Sunday collections.[296] But the central manifestation of Christian fellowship – the act of communion – lost much of its power as a result of the expansion of toleration during this period, a trend which began long before 1660 and continued long after 1720.[297] Religious pluralism meant that, despite all the frightening images of uncharitable 'fiends' and oppressive 'cormorants' found in contemporary religious culture, parochial communities normally lacked the ability to effectively punish 'unchristian'

---

[293] Both the previous historiography and its critics are ably surveyed in Smith, '"Modernization"'; Wrightson, 'Mutualities and Obligations'; idem, 'Decline'; Shepard and Withington, 'Introduction'; Walker, 'Modernization'. For the most direct and theoretically informed critique see Muldrew, '"Light Cloak"'.

[294] Wrightson, 'Mutualities and Obligations', p. 161.

[295] Ibid., pp. 176–89; Wrightson, 'Decline', pp. 38–40. This is of course a simplification, but I hope not a straw-man.

[296] Barrow, *The Duty and Reward of Bounty*; idem, *Of the Love of God and Our Neighbour*; Ben-Amos, *Culture of Giving*, pp. 84–95.

[297] Hunt, 'The Lord's Supper', pp. 81–3; John Addy, *Sin and Society in the Seventeenth Century* (London, 1989), ch. 14.

economic conduct. The only exceptions to this pattern of attenuation were the committed nonconformist congregations, especially highly disciplined groups such as the Quakers, who apparently had more success policing the commercial conduct of their co-worshippers.[298] Still, for the vast majority of English Protestants, the bonds of Christian fellowship were significantly and irreversibility weakened.

In contrast to the waning powers of spiritual communion, other types of economic community experienced a reinvigoration in the late seventeenth century. For most urban corporations and craft fellowships, the Restoration was just that. They eagerly reasserted their rights after years, sometimes decades, of disorder and neglect. Towns established inter-parochial 'corporations for the poor', punished 'unfree' tradespeople, and celebrated the values of 'bourgeois collectivism' through a variety of texts, rituals, and festivities. Companies did likewise. In the years following 1660 they enrolled increasing numbers of apprentices, sought new charters (or renewed old ones), launched actions against 'foreigners', reinforced a shared culture of fellowship, and generally succeeded in making their voices heard. The Worshipful Company of Weavers in London provides a telling example of a fraternity that showed its health through spirited debate amongst its members, significant control over the production process, and real impact on public discussion right into the 1720s. However, neither towns nor companies maintained this upward trajectory through this whole period. Increasing legal uncertainty made prosecuting 'foreigners' more difficult, while partisan divisions began to handicap urban 'corporations for the poor' and become embedded in festivities that had previously emphasised civic unity. Craft fellowships followed a similar trajectory. Membership numbers appear to have peaked near the beginning the eighteenth century, after which many companies started to lose their regulatory powers while suffering slow declines in enrolments and fraternal sociability. Generalising about such a diverse set of institutions is difficult, but it would certainly be more accurate to depict their trajectory in the later Stuart period as something akin to a bell-curve rather than a simple downward slope of unmitigated decline.

For some people, the weakening of one type of economic community was offset by the emergence or strengthening of others. The social power of communion, for example, may have decreased in the later Stuart period, but the economic influence of the civil parish grew immensely. Indeed, the expansion of the parochial poor relief system made 'belonging' to a particular locality much more important for many people. While parish vestries undoubtedly became more selective, this push for exclusivity may have been outweighed by the system's new-found egalitarian elements, such as a deepening sense of entitlement and the revival of communal festivals.

---

[298] Bebb, *Nonconformity*, ch. 4; Ashby, 'Religion', pp. 66–85, esp. 74–6; William Charles Braithwaite, *The Second Period of Quakerism* (2nd edn, Cambridge, 1961), pp. 560–64.

Similarly, handicraft workers who became frustrated with the ineffective-ness and employer-orientation of some eighteenth-century companies could find new forms of fellowship and collective power in the trade-based socie-ties that sprang up in several parts of the country. Whether an innocuous benefit club, a semi-formal journeyman's association or a violently assertive 'confederacy', each of these organisations served as self-governing economic communities supported by a shared fraternal culture. Most importantly, they multiplied at an astounding rate in the early eighteenth century, so despite the eventual weakness of established companies there is no evidence of a declining commitment to occupational fellowship. Declension narratives also fail to account for the swift rise of another type of community: the nation. A heady mixture of patriotic and xenophobic idioms percolated into numerous commentaries on commercial affairs, rendering claims of 'English-ness' and charges of 'treason' commonplace. Explaining this shift is not easy, but it appears to be linked to the expanding role of parliament, increasing involvement in international warfare, heightened economic competition over colonial markets, and the development of networks for rapidly circu-lating cheap print which stretched to every corner of the country. As a result, people at every level of society became more and more aware of their collective national identity, an awareness that they expressed in agita-tion for protectionism and direct action against foreigners. Moreover, this faith in the English polity did not result in an especially socially 'selective' mentality. Patriotism rather than wealth was the criterion for inclusion.

So, some economic communities became increasingly debilitated, others revived and strengthened only to begin ailing several decades later, and several emerged from infancy filled with newfound vigour. This hardly seems amenable to any unilinear narrative of change. But perhaps something may nonetheless be revealed through the manifold stories that one can tell about this particular habit of mind in the later Stuart period. As the conclusion demonstrates, its very untidiness helps to illuminate the history of economic cultures.

Conclusion:
Rethinking Economic Culture

This book is intended to contribute to the process of reconfiguring the way we think about early modern economic relations. As I have shown, the most popular of our current methods are deeply flawed and the conclusions that they have produced are often unsustainable. Much of the existing historiography has failed to adequately acknowledge the importance of cultural norms. Specifically, profound problems have arisen from methodologies that assume the primacy of material concerns in economic relations and the tendency of previous scholars to reduce the history of this issue to a conflict between 'the moral economy' and 'the market economy'. The preceding chapters have thus documented the ways in which this dualism elides the complexity and diversity of social and economic behaviour. Some previous historians have already remarked on these weaknesses, a few even offering potential alternatives – yet, this process of questioning, criticising, and superseding has rarely been sustained, especially in the historiography of the later Stuart period. I conclude, therefore, with an explanation of the implications of this historiographical argument and the evidence presented in the book as a whole, emphasising the fruitful possibilities it opens up for future research.

Any prospective synthesis must begin with an earnest recognition of the importance of morality in economic culture, both in the seventeenth and eighteenth centuries and more generally. This means abandoning methodologies that neglect moral norms or that reduce them to mere 'tricks' and 'tactics'. Moreover, it also requires challenging the many narratives that supposedly show (or, more commonly, just assume) the 'de-moralising' of economic relations during this period.[1] These economistic, instrumentalist, and declensionist approaches all prove unable to explain the influence exerted by 'irrational' beliefs in the later Stuart economy. As the preceding chapters have shown, this was an England wherein God regularly asserted his power over worldly affairs, wherein social 'superiors' had both patriarchal authority and paternal duties, wherein rights and privileges depended on belonging to a community. How else can one explain, for example, the many cases of poor people invoking (sometimes successfully) supernatural

---

[1] For 'de-moralising', see Thompson, *Customs in Common*, p. 201.

sanctions when requesting aid from potential benefactors? If their neighbours were rational utility-maximising agents, they would simply ignore such pleas rather than giving alms 'for fear of their curses' or accusing the beggars of witchcraft.[2] In other words, teachings about Christian charity and tales of providential intervention were not only extremely popular but also directly affected people's material lives. Examples like these were innumerable in early modern England and collectively they show that moralised conceptions of economic relations were ubiquitous, accepted, and often efficacious. By examining these as engrained parts of everyday behaviour, rather than regarding them as mere tools or ignoring them altogether, we can learn much more about the value-laden economic cultures of our predecessors.

A revised methodological approach offers a foundation for building towards the main purpose of this book, namely the construction of a new way of conceiving the history of economic culture. After all, even scholars who have accepted the existence and influence of these ideals have usually produced narratives which still imply 'a succession of confrontations between an innovative market economy and the customary moral economy of the plebs'.[3] This book has demonstrated the inadequacy of this dichotomous, teleological paradigm, but providing a replacement is hardly easy. Keith Wrightson recently offered a useful prototype. Rather than employing a bipolar model with only two possible ideals, he recognised the diversity of 'social bonds', 'identities', and 'values'. His approach also allowed for the possibility that these different 'solidarities' were not all simply fading away: 'Some were eroded. Some were redefined. Some developed greater strength and centrality, albeit within different social boundaries.'[4] Yet, as I noted earlier, Wrightson still insisted that there were 'dominant patterns' giving a unity to this 'connected process', trends that seemed ultimately to tend in the same direction as if pulled by some elementary magnetic force.[5] Perhaps unsurprisingly, the underlying image of social change implied in his conclusions bore a more than passing resemblance to the one depicted by so many previous historians.

The vision of economic culture that emerges from this book thus has several prominent features that it shares with other recent scholarship, but its implications are ultimately quite different. At the very least, it necessitates making explicit the message implied in some previous work: we must pluralise 'the moral economy'. There was neither a singular 'legitimising notion' nor a unified 'popular consensus' that 'can be said to constitute the moral economy of the poor'.[6] Instead, there were a host of different ideals, different 'moral economies', in the early modern period. By illuminating the

2   See Chapter 1.5–6 above.
3   Thompson, *Customs in Common*, p. 12.
4   Wrightson, 'Mutualities and Obligations', p. 188.
5   Ibid., pp. 189, 193. See above pp. 144–5.
6   Thompson, *Customs in Common*, p. 188.

unique attributes of each of the three broad groups of ideas discussed above, this book proves the necessity of attempting to distinguish between these various ways of thinking. Plainly, a multitude of conceptions co-existed in English culture – sometimes supporting one another, sometimes contradicting one another. One can, for instance, find inequality endorsed both in doctrines of divine omnipotence and in analogies of familial interdependence. However, this emphasis on hierarchy stood in contrast to the elements of egalitarian logic that can be seen in notions of Christian community, civic unity, and occupational solidarity. In addition, the potential agency of most men and women differed significantly in each case, with some ideals emphasising passive contentment while others promoted collective action. This meant that people in later Stuart England did not adhere to a single, monolithic morality when considering or conducting economic affairs, or simply switch back and forth between 'moral' and 'market' beliefs. Rather, their actions were informed by a blend of innumerable different cultural streams – including ideals based on theology, family, and community, as well those based on custom, honour, friendship, and so on.

This list of concepts must also include what is often called 'possessive individualism'. Indeed, doing so is a crucial part of process of dismantling the 'moral'/'market' binary, because we must not only disaggregate 'the moral economy' but also demote 'the market economy'. As this study demonstrates, the mentality normally labelled 'market' (or perhaps 'capitalist') was not one half of a zero-sum equation – rather, it was merely one impulse among many, a single component in an array of different 'moral economies'. The profit-motive obviously had an important role in early modern economic culture and it cannot be ignored, but many of the other ideals of the period had much stronger rhetorical force. Social sanction pulled the less-individualist moralities into central positions in this era's culture, whereas this same logic pushed 'self-interest' towards the margins. When this situation is taken into account, it becomes clear that we must stop using 'possessive individualism' as a ruler against which all other behaviours are measured.

Furthermore, evidence from the later Stuart period indicates that the same logic applies to narratives of change. By revealing the multiplicity of early modern economic culture, this book also shows its multilinearity: there was no consistent movement from 'morality' to 'the market'. Some of the strands in this tangle of 'moral economies' appear to have tugged in approximately the same direction, but many others did not. Finding a single, comprehensive pattern is thus impossible. Still, the lack of a metanarrative does not exclude the possibility of narration altogether. At the risk of replacing one unhelpful schematic with another, it seems that the many changes examined in the preceding chapters might be represented as effectively following four different trajectories: rising, declining, enduring, and arching.

First, some ideals grew significantly stronger, especially those associated with the increasing administrative power of the nation and the parish.

Parliamentary authority, patriotism, xenophobia, and parochialism had more economic impact than ever before. It seems likely that certain forms of 'worker identity' and 'contractual equality' also gained adherents, though I would hasten to add that this cannot be naively equated with evidence of the rise of 'class' or 'property'.

Second, several institutions, including the monarchy and the episcopacy, lost some of their influence over English economic life.[7] Royal proclamations mostly gave way to legislative initiatives and threats of excommunication stultified owing to religious toleration. Neither of these forces of moral authority ceased to have a role in the economy, but they both appear to have become gradually weaker, just as 'custom' may have suffered a diminution over the same period.

Third, the economic influence of some beliefs probably remained largely stable over the course of the period. This appears to have been in the case with popular religiosity, as there is little evidence that the social impact of faith in providence and the afterlife underwent any noticeable decline, despite many previous claims about 'secularisation' and the supposed growth of 'the Protestant ethic'. Continuity, rather than change, characterised these sorts of ideals – a group that may have also included conceptions of 'credit' and 'repute', which remained important to English economic culture throughout the seventeenth and eighteenth centuries.

Fourth, a number of social bonds experienced a revitalisation at around the time of the Restoration, only to begin to attenuate at some point in the century that followed. Paternalism among landed elites, for example, seems to have temporarily revived, perhaps partly as a response to the unfavourable agricultural situation and partly as a reassertion of hierarchical values after the 'levelling' of the previous decades. Similarly, the communal solidarities of urban corporations and craft fellowships were almost certainly stronger under the later Stuarts than they were during the Interregnum or under the Hanoverians. The prominence of this arcing trajectory, while not unique to the late seventeenth and early eighteenth centuries, was perhaps the most distinctive feature of this period of English economic culture, setting it apart from many other eras.

This quadripartite typology is far from exact and no doubt deserves to be challenged by scholars who have studied particular aspects of these issues in more depth; however, it certainly represents the history of these attitudes more accurately than the conventional notion of a binary transition. In fact, by emphasising the diverse and variable nature of 'moral economies' in the past, the approach taken in this book may even provide a useful perspective for those who seek to understand economic culture in the present.

[7] The 'episcopacy' here denotes only the institutional power of the Church of England manifested in, for example, the ecclesiastical courts. This is quite distinct from the cultural influence of Anglican and Dissenting clergy, and of religious ideals more generally, both of which followed a different trajectory.

Once we accept that 'amorality' and 'capitalist modernity' cannot be taken as the inevitable end-point towards which all these changes have tended, it becomes clear that our own world is perhaps more complex than often assumed. Notwithstanding the practical and intellectual impact of 'neo-liberalism' (including the Chicago School, Thatcherism, Reaganomics, and the Washington Consensus), it is not difficult to find many other ideals affecting today's economic culture. To cite just a few obvious examples, explicitly 'moral' concerns have inspired participation in 'fair trade', vegetarianism, 'ethical investment', and cooperative businesses. On a larger scale, the movements of vast amounts of resources are determined by public policy decisions on matters ranging from healthcare to labour law to foreign aid; by various forms of formal and informal philanthropy; and by the familial and gender norms associated with housework, childrearing, and other aspects of 'home economics'. Moreover, these values and assumptions permeate our culture, disseminated through media such as television, books, newspapers, blogs, and even music. There has, if anything, been a resurgence of 'moralised' perceptions of economics since the summer of 2008 when the financial crisis created a wave of fear and misery. One need only glance through a copy of a typical British newspaper to see the nation's current social and economic problems attributed to traditional bogeymen such as greedy financiers, tyrannical officials, scrounging idlers, and parasitical immigrants.[8] The revitalisation of such sentiments has also been accompanied by mobilisations of groups of ordinary people under slogans such as 'British Jobs for British Workers' and 'People Before Profits'.[9] These attitudes – which can be found across the whole political spectrum – are built on ways of thinking that often bear more than a passing resemblance to those of the seventeenth and eighteenth centuries.

So, even today the logic of 'free market capitalism' is only one of the many 'moral economies' that inform our thinking and behaviour, just as it was 300 years ago. We, like our predecessors in early modern England, have an economic culture that is irreducibly plural and infinitely changeable. To assume that ideals of 'stewardship', 'paternalism' or 'parochialism' were inevitably gasping their last breath by the end of the seventeenth century does not do justice to the contingent nature of history. 'After all, we are not

---

8 Sam Fleming and Benedict Brogan, 'Greed that fuelled the crash', *Daily Mail*, 14 Oct. 2008; Polly Toynbee, 'Bankers caused the crash and now they strangle recovery', *The Guardian*, 28 May 2011; Tim Shipman, 'EU ups the ante with plan to squander £30m on quangos', *Daily Mail*, 24 Oct. 2010; Ryan Sabey, '10 kids with 4 different men, £30k benefits: now she's demanding handouts from charity', *The Sun*, 13 Aug. 2011; Anon., 'Each illegal immigrant costs us £1m, says study as Government faces calls for amnesty', *Daily Mail*, 4 May 2009.

9 Andrew Gillan and Andrew Sparrow, 'Strikes spread across Britain as oil refinery protest escalates', *guardian.co.uk*, 30 Jan. 2009; Anon., 'Uncut protesters target Barclays bank', *Telegraph*, 19 Feb. 2011.

at the end of social evolution ourselves', and apparent 'lost causes' may 'yet be won'.[10] Even the supposed victory of 'possessive individualism' has been so far from total that it hardly merits the laurels that many scholars think it now wears. While it has won many skirmishes, it has also lost many. And other 'moral economies' may prove more persuasive in the future.

[10] Thompson, *Making of the English Working Class*, p. 12.

Bibliography

Manuscript Sources

British Library

Add. MS 27462 Register of the Company of Mercers, etc., of Sandwich
Add. MS 38834 Guild book of the Company of Smiths, etc., of Bridgnorth

Cambridgeshire Archives

126/M72 St Mary Whittlesey Manor Court, Verdicts
Q/SO Cambridgeshire Quarter Sessions, Order Books

Cambridge University Archives

T/VII/2 Assize of bread, declarations
V.C.Ct/I Vice-Chancellor's Court, Act Book
V.C.Ct/III Vice-Chancellor's Court, Exhibita Files and Index

Coventry History Centre

BA/H/C/17 Coventry City Council Books
PA 3 Carpenters' Company, Accounts and Memoranda
PA 8 Bakers' Company, Ordinances
PA 34 Weavers' Company, Order Book
PA 100 Weavers' Company, Records
PA 219/9 Awson Family Papers
PA 1494 Cappers' and Feltmakers' Company, Records

Devon Record Office

1579A/9/35 Totnes Town Courts Proceedings
ECA B 1/13 Exeter City Act Book of the Chamber
QS/4 Devon Quarter Sessions, Bundles
SM1990 Dartmouth Borough Court Book

Doncaster Archives

AB/5/2 Doncaster Apprenticeship Indentures
DD/DC/A2 Thorpe in Balne Court Leet, Papers

Essex Record Office

D/B 1/2 Great Dunmow Borough Court Book

D/B 2/BRE1/28 Saffron Walden Borough Order Book
D/DBm Z7–Z14 Notebooks of Joseph Bufton of Coggeshall
Q/SBb Essex Quarter Sessions, Bundles, Later Series
Q/SO Essex Quarter Sessions, Order Books
Q/SR Essex Quarter Sessions, Rolls
T/A 156/1 Notebooks of Joseph Bufton of Coggeshall

Hertfordshire Archives

HBR 9 Hertford Borough Sessions of the Peace, Book of Orders
HBR 20&21 Hertford Borough Months Court, Book of Proceedings
QSR Hertfordshire Quarter Sessions, Rolls

London Metropolitan Archives

COL/CA/01 London Court of Aldermen, Repertories
COL/CA/05 London Court of Aldermen, Papers
COL/CC/01 London Court of Common Council, Journals
GL MS01046/1 St Antholin Budge Row, Churchwardens' Accounts
GL MS01453/3 St Botolph Aldgate, Vestry Minutes
X015/198 St Olaves Southwark, Parish Register

The National Archives

ADM Navy Board
ASSI 47/20/9 Whixley (Yorks.) Manor Court Papers
SP State Papers
T Treasury Board

Norfolk Record Office

NCR Case 12b Norwich Quarter Sessions, Informations and Examinations
NCR Case 17d Norwich By-laws of Trades
NCR Case 20a Norwich Quarter Sessions, Minute Books

Northamptonshire Record Office

D3382 Company of Masons [et al.] of Daventry, Order Book
Misc. Q.S. Recs, I Northamptonshire Quarter Sessions, Presentments Book
QSR 1 Northamptonshire Quarter Sessions, Rolls

North Yorkshire County Record Office

QSB North Riding of Yorkshire Quarter Sessions, Bundles
ZDS III/11 Sessay Manor Court Book

Suffolk Record Office at Bury St Edmunds

EE 500/D4/1 Bury St Edmunds Corporation, Court Minutes
EE 501/2/8 Sudbury Borough, Order Book

Suffolk Record Office at Ipswich

B/105/2 Suffolk Quarter Sessions Books
EE 1/H2/1 Aldeburgh Borough Sessions Minute Books

West Yorkshire Archive Service at Wakefield

QS 1 West Riding of Yorkshire Quarter Sessions, Rolls

York City Archives

F Series York Quarter Sessions, Minute Books

York Minster Archives

Hailstone QQ80/3 York Carpenters' Company, Ordinances
Hailstone QQ80/4 York Cordwainers' Company, Ordinances

Manuscript Sources: Transcriptions and Calendars

Beverley Borough Records, 1575–1821, J. Dennett ed. (Yorks. Arch. Soc. Rec. Series, vol. 84, York, 1933).
Calendar of State Papers, Domestic: Anne (4 vols, London, 1916–2006).
Calendar of State Papers, Domestic: Charles II (28 vols, London, 1860–1947).
Calendar of State Papers, Domestic: William III (11 vols, London, 1896–1937).
Calendar of State Papers, Venice (39 vols, London, 1864–1939).
Calendar of Treasury Books (28 vols, London, 1865–1943).
Coopers' Company, London: Historical Memoranda, Charters, Documents and Extracts from the Records of the Corporation and the Books of the Company, 1396–1848, James Francis Firth ed. (London, 1848).
The Corporation Records of St Albans, A. E. Gibbs ed. (St Albans, 1890).
Correspondence of the Family of Hatton, Edward Maunde ed. (2 vols, Camden Society, n.s., 22–23, London, 1878).
The Correspondence of Sir John Lowther of Whitehaven, 1693–1698: A Provincial Community in Wartime, D. R. Hainsworth ed. (British Academy Records of Social and Economic History, n.s., vol. 7, London, 1983).
County of Buckingham: Calendar of the Sessions Records, William Le Hardy et al. eds (7 vols, Aylesbury, 1933–80).
Crakanthorp, John, *Accounts of the Reverend John Crakanthorp of Fowlmere, 1682–1710*, Lambert Brassley and Philip Saunders eds (Cambridgeshire Record Society, vol. 8, Cambridge, 1988).
de la Pryme, Abraham, *The Diary of Abraham de la Pryme, the Yorkshire Antiquary*, Charles Jackson ed. (Surtees Society, vol. 54, Durham, 1870).
Evelyn, John, *The Diary of John Evelyn*, E. S. de Beer ed. (6 vols, Oxford, 1955).
Extracts from the Records of the Company of Hostmen of Newcastle-upon-Tyne (Surtees Society, vol. 105, Durham, 1901).
Gough, Richard, *TheHistory of Myddle*, David Hey ed. (Harmondsworth, 1981).
Hertford County Records, William Le Hardy and G. L. Reckitt eds (10 vols, Hertford, 1905–57).

HMC, *Eighth Report of the Royal Commission on Historical Manuscripts* (no. 7, London, 1882).

HMC, *The Manuscripts of Rye and Hereford Corporations, Capt. Loder-Symonds, Mr. E. R. Wodehouse, M.P., and others: Thirteenth Report, Appendix VI* (no. 31, London, 1892).

HMC, *The Manuscripts of S. H. Le Fleming, esq., of Rydal Hall: Twelfth Report, Appendix VII* (no. 25, London, 1890).

HMC, *Report on the Manuscripts of His Grace the Duke of Portland, Preserved at Welbeck Abbey* (no. 29, 8 vols, London, 1891–1931).

HMC, *Reports on Manuscripts in Various Collections* (8 vols, no. 55, London, 1901–13).

HMC, *Seventh Report of the Royal Commission on Historical Manuscripts* (no. 6, London, 1879).

HMC, *Sixth Report of the Royal Commission on Historical Manuscripts* (no. 5, London, 1877).

Jeake, Samuel, *An Astrological Diary of the Seventeenth Century: Samuel Jeake of Rye, 1652–1699*, Michael Hunter and Annabel Gregory eds (Oxford, 1988).

Josselin, Ralph, *The Diary of Ralph Josselin, 1616–1683*, Alan Macfarlane ed. (London, 1976).

Journals of the House of Commons (London, 1742–).

Journals of the House of Lords (London, 1767–).

The Law Book of the Crowley Ironworks, M. W. Flinn ed. (Surtees Society, vol. 167, Durham, 1957).

The Liverpool Town Books, 1649–71, Michael Power ed. (Record Society of Lancashire and Cheshire, no. 136, Chester, 1999).

Luttrell, Narcissus, *A Brief Historical Relation of State Affairs, from September 1678 to April 1714* (6 vols, Oxford, 1857).

Middlesex County Records: Calendar of the Sessions Books, 1689 to 1709, W. J. Hardy ed. (London, 1905).

Minutes of Proceedings in Quarter Sessions Held for the Parts of Kesteven in the County of Lincoln, 1674–1695, S. A. Peyton ed. (Lincoln Record Society, nos. 25–26, 2 vols, Lincoln, 1931).

Moore, Edward, *The Moore Rental*, Thomas Heywood ed. (Chetham Society, Manchester, 1847).

Moore, Giles, 'Day Book, 1655–1680', in F. Stenton Eardley, *Horsted Keynes, Sussex: The Church and the Parish of St. Giles* (London, 1939).

Pepys, Samuel, *The Diary of Samuel Pepys: A New and Complete Transcription*, Robert Latham and William Matthews eds (11 vols, London, 1970–83).

Records of the Borough of Leicester, M. Bateson et al. eds (7 vols, Leicester, 1899–1974).

Records of the Borough of Northampton, C. A. Markham and J. C. Cox eds (2 vols, Northampton, 1898).

Records of the Borough of Nottingham, W. H. Stevenson et al. eds (9 vols, London, 1882–1951).

Records of the County of Wilts., Being Extracts from the Quarter Sessions Great Rolls of the Seventeenth Century, B. H. Cunnington ed. (Devizes, 1932).

Select Documents Illustrating the History of Trade Unionism: 1. The Tailoring Trade in London (1721–1866), Frank Wallis Galton ed. (London, 1923).

Some Municipal Records of the City of Carlisle, R. S. Ferguson and W. Nanson eds (Carlisle and London, 1887).

Stout, William, *The Autobiography of William Stout of Lancaster, 1665–1752*, J. D. Marshall ed. (Manchester, 1967).

Thomlinson, John, 'Diary [1717–1722]', in *Six North Country Diaries*, John Crawford Hodgson ed. (Surtees Society, vol. 118, Durham, 1911), pp. 64–167.

Two East Anglian Diaries: 1641–1729: Isaac Archer and William Coe, Matthew Storey ed. (Suffolk Records Society, 38, Woodbridge, 1994).

Vernon, James, *Letters Illustrative of the Reign of William III from 1696 to 1708 Addressed to the Duke of Shrewsbury by James Vernon*, G. P. R. James ed. (3 vols, London, 1841).

Whitley, Roger, *Roger Whitley's Diary 1684–1697: Bodleian Library, MS Eng. Hist. c. 711*, Michael Stevens transcriber (British History Online, 2004). Available at: <www.british-history.ac.uk/source.aspx?pubid=121>.

Wood, Anthony, *The Life and Times of Anthony Wood, Antiquary, of Oxford, 1632–95*, A. Clark ed. (Oxford Historical Society, 5 vols, Oxford, 1881–1900).

Historical Newspapers and Periodicals

Historical Register (1714–38).
Observator (1702–12).
Post Boy (1695–1728).
Post Man and the Historical Account (1695–1729).
Spectator (1711–12).
Weekly Journal or British Gazetteer (1715–1730).
Weekly Journal or Saturday Post (1717–1725).
Weekly Packet (1714–1721).

Printed Primary Sources

Note that the printed ballads in the Euing, Pepys, Roxburghe, Rosebery and Wood collections have been examined in the facsimile editions listed below, and their individual titles are therefore not included here.

An Account of the Proceedings at Guild-Hall, London, at the Tolke-moot, or Common-Hall, held 24th of June 1676 (1676).

Act of the General Assembly, anent a Solemn National Fast and Humiliation (Edinburgh, 1700).

Archer, Edmund, *A Sermon Preach'd at the Parish Church of St Martin … for the Charity Schools of the City of Oxford* (Oxford, 1713).

Aristotle, *Politics: Books I and II*, Trevor J. Saunders ed. (Oxford, 1995).

Aristotles Politiques, or Discourses of Government (1598).

Avaritia Coram Tribunali: Or, the Miser Arraign'd at the Bar of Scripture and Reason; for his Sinful Neglect of Charity (1666).

Barrett, William, *History and Antiquities of the City of Bristol* (1789).

Barrow, Isaac, *The Duty and Reward of Bounty to the Poor: In a Sermon Preached at the Spittal upon Wednesday in Easter Week* (1671).

Barrow, Isaac, *Of the Love of God and Our Neighbour, In Several Sermons* (1680).
Baxter, Richard, *A Christian Directory: or, A Summ of Practical Theologie, and Cases of Conscience* (1673).
Mr Baxters Rules & Directions for Family Duties (1681).
Beaulieu, Luke, *The Reciprocal Duty Betwixt Kings and Subjects, Impartially Stated, in a Sermon … in the Cathedral Church of Gloucester at the Assizes* (1706).
Becon, Thomas, *The Fortresse of the Faythfull* (1550).
Bellers, John, *Essays About the Poor, Manufactures, Trade, Plantations, & Immorality* (1699).
Bethel, Slingsby, *An Account of the French Usurpation upon the Trade of England* (1679).
Blanch, John, *An Abstract of the Grievances of Trade* (1694).
Blanch, John, *The Naked Truth in an Essay upon Trade* (1696).
Blomefield, Francis, *An Essay Towards a Topographical History … of Norfolk* (5 vols, Fersfield, 1739–75).
Bodin, Jean, *Six Bookes of a Common-weale* (1606).
The Book of Common Prayer and the Administration of the Sacraments (1662, 1700, etc.).
Boughen, Edward, *A Short Exposition of the Catechism of the Church of England* (1662).
Bowker, James, *An Almanack* (1679).
Braddon, Laurence, *An Abstract of the Draught of a Bill for Relieving, Reforming, and Employing the Poor* (1717?).
Bralesford, Humphrey, *The Poor Man's Help: Being, I. An Abridgement of Bishop Pearson on the Creed … II. A Short Exposition of the Lord's Prayer … III. The Ten Commandments Explain'd* (1689).
Brent, Charles, *Persuasions to a Publick Spirit: A Sermon Preach'd Before the Court of Guardians of the Poor in the City of Bristol, at St. Peter's Church* (1704).
A Brief Survey of the Growth of Usury in England (1673).
Bucknall, John, *Ro'eh, or, The Shepherds Almanack* (1676).
Bunyan, John, *The Life and Death of Mr. Badman* (1680).
Bunyan, John, *The Pilgrim's Progress*, Roger Sharrock ed. (1678; Harmondsworth, 1965).
Cartwright, Thomas, *The Danger of Riches, Discovered in a Sermon Preach'd at St. Pauls … before the Right Honorable the Lord Mayor* (1662).
The Case of the English Weavers and French Merchants truly Stated (c.1670).
Causes of a Solemn National Fast and Humiliation, Agreed upon by the Commissioners of the late General Assembly (Edinburgh, 1696).
Certain Sermons or Homilies, Appointed to be Read in Churches (2 vols, 1673).
Charles II, *A Proclamation for a General Fast* (1674).
Charles II, *A Proclamation for … the Suppressing of Rogues* (1661).
Child, Josiah, *Sir Josiah Child's Proposals for the Relief and Employment of the Poor* (c.1670).
The Choice: A Poem (1700).
The Citizens Complaint for Want of Trade (1663).
Clarkson, David, *Sermons and Discourses on Several Divine Subjects* (1696).
Cobbett, William, *Rural Rides* (2 vols, 1830).
Conant, John, *Sermons Preach'd on Several Occasions* (3 vols, 1693–98).
Constitutions and Canons Ecclesiastical (1660).

Cooke, Thomas, *Workhouses the Best Charity: A Sermon Preacht at the Cathedral Church of Worcester* (1702).

Cornwallis, Henry, *Set on the Great Pot: A Sermon upon Hospitality, Preach'd at a Late Visitation at Tunbridge in Kent* (1703).

Corporation of London, *By the Mayor ... [Against] Vagrants and Common Beggars* (1676).

The Countrey-Miser or the Unhappy Farmers Dear Market (1693).

Croft, Richard, *The Wise Steward: Being a Sermon Preached the Thursday in Whitson-week, 1696: In the Parish Church of Feckenham, in the County of Worcester* (1697).

Cruso, Timothy, *Discourses upon the Rich Man and Lazarus* (1697).

Culpeper, Thomas, *Plain English, in a Familiar Conference* (1673).

Curteis, Thomas, *Religious Princes the Greatest Blessing and Safety to the Church and State: A Sermon Preach'd in the Parish Church of Wrotham in Kent* (1716).

Dade, William, *A New [Almanack] and [Prognostication]* (1666).

Dawes, William, *Wor[l]dly Men Wiser, in Their Way than Christians, in Theirs: A Sermon Preach'd at Saint James's in Lent, 1698* (1707).

The Death and Burial of Mistress Money (1678).

Defoe, Daniel, *A Journal of the Plague Year: ... During the last Great Visitation In 1665* (1722).

Deloney, Thomas, *The Gentle Craft* (1597).

Deloney, Thomas, *Jack of Newbery* (c.1597).

Deloney, Thomas, *Thomas of Reading* (1612).

Dod, John, and Cleaver, Robert, *A Godlie Forme of Household Gouernment for the Ordering of Priuate Families, according to the Direction of Gods Word* (1621).

Dove, Jonathan, *Dove Speculum Anni à Partu Virginis MDCLXXII, or, An Almanack* (1672).

Dunning, Richard, *Bread for the Poor* (Exeter, 1698).

Dunsford, Martin, *Historical Memoirs of the Town and Parish of Tiverton* (Exeter, 1790).

Dunton, John, *Englands Alarum, or Warning-piece: Declaring by Ten Infallible Evidences, that Her Ruine and Destruction is at Hand* (1693).

Dunton, John, *Life and Errors* (1705).

Dunton, John, *The Parable of the Top-Knots* (1691).

Durham, William, *Encouragement to Charity: A Sermon Preached at the Charter-House Chapel ... at an Anniversary Meeting in Commemoration of the Founder* (1679).

The Dutch Boare Dissected, or a Description of Hogg-land (1665).

Dyalogue of Diues [and] Paup[er] (1493).

Edwards, John, *Sermons On Special Occasions and Subjects* (1698).

An Elegy, From the Mercers, Lacemen, Milliners, Weavers and Wyerdrawers (1702).

England's Great Joy and Gratitude, F. H. Van Hove engraver (c.1700).

The English and Scottish Popular Ballads, Francis James Child ed. (5 vols, New York, 1965).

Erasmus, Desiderius, *The Education of a Christian Prince*, Lester Born ed. and trans. (1516; New York, 1963).

'The Euing Ballads', held at the University of Glasgow Library. Facsimile edition published online at <http://ebba.english.ucsb.edu/> (English Broadside Ballad Archive, University of California – Santa Barbara).

The Female Manufacturer's Complaint (1719).

Firmin, Thomas, *Some Proposals For the Imployment of the Poor, and for the Prevention of Idleness and the Consequence thereof, Begging* (1681).

Fleetwood, William, *The Justice of Paying Debts: A Sermon Preach'd in the City* (1718).

Fleetwood, William, *The Relative Duties ... in Sixteen Sermons* (1705).

A Form of Prayer, To be Used Upon ... the Several Days appointed for a General Fast (1662).

Fox, George, *Christs Parable of Dives and Lazarus* (1677).

Fox, George, *This is a Warning to All that Profess Christianity and Others: To Beware of Covetousness, which is Idolatry* (1679).

A Further and More Perticular Account of the Cruel Desperate and Bloody Fight and Uproar (1700).

Gale, Theophilus, *The Life and Death of Thomas Tregosse* (1671).

Garnet, Richard, *The Book of Oaths* (1649).

God's Great and Wonderful Work in Somerset-shire: Or the Charitable Farmer Miraculously Rewarded (1674).

Gouge, Thomas, *The Principles of Christian Religion Explained to the Capacity of the Meanest* (1675).

Gouge, William, *Of Domesticall Duties* (1622).

The Great Necessity and Advantage of Preserving Our Own Manufacturies (1697).

Haines, Richard, *The Prevention of Poverty* (1674).

Hale, Matthew, *Some Necessary and Important Considerations ... taken out of (that late Worthy and Renowed Judge) Sir Matthew Hale's Writings* (9th edn, 1697).

Hammond, Henry, *A Practical Catechism: Whereunto is Added The Reasonableness of Christian Religion* (7th edn, 1662).

Hart, John, *The Charitable Christian: or, A Word of Comfort ... to such as are Truly Poor And a Word of Christian Counsel and Advice to such as are Worldly Rich* (8th edn, 1662).

Hart, John, *Heavens Glory And Hells Horror: or, the Parable of Dives and Lazarus Opened and Applied* (1662).

Hickes, George, *A Sermon Preached at the Church of St. Bridget on Easter-Tuesday ... Upon the Subject of Alms-Giving* (1684).

Horneck, Anthony, *Several Sermons on the Fifth of St. Matthew, Being part of Christ's Sermon on the Mount* (2 vols, 1698).

Houghton, John, *England's Great Happiness: Or, A Dialogue Between Content and Complaint* (1677).

Housewifery and Family Government, queen of hearts in untitled playing cards (c.1700).

Howe, John, *A Sermon Preach'd ... at the Request of the Societies for Reformation of Manners* (1698).

The Humble Petition of the Poor Journymen Shooe-makers of the City of London, Westminster and Southwark, and their Brethern of the Countrey (1691?).

Izacke, Samuel, *Remarkable Antiquities of the City of Exeter* (1722).

James II, *A Proclamation ... for the Preventing the Exportation of Sheep, Wooll, ... and Fulling-Clay* (1688).

Jeffery, John, *The Duty and Encouragement of Religious Artificers Described in a Sermon* (1693).

Jesserson, Susanna, *A Bargain for Bachelors* (1675).

Johnson, Edward, *The Weavers Case* (1719).

Johnson, Robert, *Dives and Lazarus, Or Rather Devilish Dives: Delivered in a Sermon at Paul's Cross* (22nd edn, 1684).

Johnson, Thomas, *A General Proposal for the building of Granaries* (1696).

Jones, Andrew, *The Black Book of Conscience, or, Gods High Court of Justice in the Soul* (36th edn, 1679).

Jones, Andrew, *Morbus Satanicus, The Devils Disease: Or The Sin of Pride Arraigned and Condemned* (27th edn, 1677).

Jones, David, *A Farewel-Sermon Preached to the United Parishes of St. Mary Woolnoth, & St. Mary Woolchurch-Haw in Lombard-Street* (1692).

Jones, David, *A Sermon Preached at Christ-Church, London, November the 2nd* (1690).

The Just Complaint of the Poor Weavers Truly Represented (1719).

Kennett, White, *A Sermon Preach'd in the Church of St. Lawrence-Jewry* (1711).

Lamentable News From Southwark: Or the Cruel Landlord (1675).

Letsome, Sampson, *The Preacher's Assistant* (1753).

Littleton, Adam, *Solomons Gate, or, An Entrance into the Church being a Familiar Explanation of the Grounds of Religion Conteined in the Four Heads of Catechism* (1662).

Lynford, Thomas, *Charity-schools Recommended: A Sermon* (1712).

Maitland, William, *History and Survey of London* (3rd edn, 2 vols, 1760).

Manton, Thomas, *A Fifth Volume of Sermons* (1701).

Mayo, Richard, *A Present for Servants* (1693).

Merry Drollery, Compleat: or, A Collection of Jovial Poems, Merry Songs, Witty Drolleries, Inxtermixed with Pleasant Catches (1691).

Milbourne, Luke, *Debtor and Creditor Made Easy: or, The Judgment of the Unmerciful Demonstrated, in a Sermon* (1709).

Miseries of the Miserable: or, An Essay Towards Laying Open the Decay of the Fine Wollen Trade (1739).

A Modest Proposal for the More Certain and yet more Easie Provision for the Poor (1696).

Moss, Robert, *The Providential Division of Men into Rich and Poor, and the Respective Duties thence Arising, Briefly Consider'd in a Sermon* (1708).

The Mowing-Devil: Or, Strange News out of Hartford-shire (1678).

The Nature, Nobility, Character and Complement of Money (1684).

The New Art of Thriving: Or, The Way to Get and Keep Money (c.1685).

Newnam, Richard, *The Complaint of English Subjects, Delivered in Two Parts* (1700).

The Northern Cuckold, Or, The Garden House Intrigue ... With ... the Spitle-Fields Ballad on the Calicos (1721).

Nourse, Peter, *Practical Discourses on Several Subjects being Some Select Homilies of the Church of England, Put into a New Method and Modern Style* (2nd edn, 2 vols, 1708).

The Oppressions of the Market-people: or, The Extortions of the Farmers of the City-Markets (1720).

Pargiter, Thomas, *A Sermon Preached before ... the Lord Mayor* (1682).

Peacham, Henry, *The Worth of a Peny* (1664).

Pead, Deuel, *The Wicked Man's Misery, and the Poor Man's Hope and Comfort: Being a Sermon upon the Parable of Dives and Lazarus* (1699).

The Pepys Ballads, W. G. Gay ed. (5 vols, Cambridge, 1987). Facsimile edition published online at <http://ebba.english.ucsb.edu/> (English Broadside Ballad Archive, University of California – Santa Barbara).

The Petition of the Oppressed Market People, Humbly offer'd to the Consideration of the Lord Mayor, Aldermen, and Common Council of the City of London (1699).

Pittis, Thomas, *A Spittle Sermon Preach'd in St Brides Parish-Church, on Wednesday in Easter Week* (1684).

The Poor Man's Petition to the Lords and Gentlemen of the Kingdom: or, Englands Cry for Peace (c.1693).

The Poor Man's Plea against the Extravagant Price of Corn (1699).

'Poor Robin', *An Almanack* (1690).

'Poor Robin', *An Almanack* (1697).

'Poor Robin', *Four for a Penny* (1678).

'Poor Robin', *A Hue and Cry after Money* (1689).

Poor Robins Hue and Cry After Good House-Keeping: Or, A Dialogue betwixt Good House-Keeping, Christmas, and Pride (1687).

Powel, John, *The Assize of Bread* (1671).

The Present State of England (1694).

The Price of the Abdication (1693).

The Profit and Loss of the East-India-Trade, Stated, and Humbly Offer'd to the Consideration of the Present Parliament (1700).

Puckle, James, *England's Way to Wealth and Honour* (1699).

Rawlet, John, *The Christian Monitor, Containing an Earnest Exhortation to an Holy Life, with some Directions in order Thereto: Written in a Plain and Easie Style* (2nd edn, 1686).

Reasons for the Regular Re-Establishment of the Corporation of Shipwrights of England (c.1696).

Reasons Humbly Offered to … Parliament by the Drapers, Mercers, Haberdashers, Grocers, Hosiers, and other Trading House-keepers (1675).

Reasons Humbly offer'd to … Parliament assembled, for … the Assize of Bread (1710).

Reflexions upon the Moral State of the Nation: With an Offer at some Amendments Therein (1701).

A Remonstrance of all the Shoemakers … against Transporting, Forestalling and Ingrossing of Leather (1675).

Rey, Claudius, *The Weavers True Case* (1719).

'The Rosebery Ballads', held at the National Library of Scotland. Facsimiles published online at <http://digital.nls.uk/broadsides/> (The Word on the Street, NLS).

'The Roxburghe Ballads' (5 vols), held at the British Library. Facsimile edition published online at <http://ebba.english.ucsb.edu/> (English Broadside Ballad Archive, University of California – Santa Barbara).

Ruskin, John, *The King of the Golden River, or the Black Brothers* (1851).

A Sad, Amazing and Dreadful Relation of a Farmer's Wife, near Wallingford in Barkshire (1697).

Sad News from the Countrey, or A True and Full Relation of the Late Wonderful Floods in Divers Parts of England (1674).

Saunder, Richard, *Apollo Anglicanus, The English Apollo* (1698).

A Scheme of the Trade … Between England and France (1674).

The Servants Calling; With Some Advice to the Apprentice (1725).

Sharp, John, *A Sermon Preach'd at the Coronation of Queen Anne* (1702).

Sheppard, Robert, *By His Majesty's Permission ... a Play call'd, Dives and Lazarus* (1720?).

Sherlock, Richard, *The Charity of Lending without Usury ... In a Sermon Preach'd before the Right Honourable the Lord Mayor, at St. Bridget's Church* (2nd edn, 1692).

Sherlock, Richard, *The Principles of Holy Christian Religion* (1663).

Stainforth, William, *The Duty of Doing Good Recommended and Press'd In a Sermon* (York, 1711).

Stanhope, George, *The Danger of Hard-heartedness to the Poor: A Sermon Preach'd in the Parish-Church of St. Sepulchers, May 31, 1705, Being Thursday in Whitson Week* (1705).

The Statutes of the Realm, John Raithby et al. eds (9 vols, London, 1816–28)

Steele, Richard, *The Husbandmans Calling: Shewing the Excellencies, Temptations, Graces, Duties, &c. of the Christian Husbandman Being the Substance of XII Sermons* (1668).

Stephens, Edward, *An Admonition Concerning a Publick Fast, the Just Causes we have for It, from the Full Growth of Sin, and the Near Approaches of God's Judgments* (1691).

Stephens, Edward, *Relief of Apprentices Wronged by their Masters* (1687).

Stephens, Richard, *The Queen a Nursing Mother: A Sermon Preach'd on ... the Anniversary Day of Her Majesty's Happy Accession to the Throne* (1705).

Stevens, John, *The Whole Parable of Dives and Lazarus, Explain'd and Apply'd: being Several Sermons Preached in Cripplegate and Lothbury Churches* (1697).

Stevenson, Matthew, *Norfolk Drollery: Or, a Compleat Collection of the Newest Songs, Jovial Poems, and Catches, &c.* (1673).

Stillingfleet, Edward, *Protestant Charity: A Sermon Preached at S. Sepulchres Church, on Tuesday in Easter Week* (1681).

Stillingfleet, Edward, *A Sermon Preached before the Honourable House of Commons ... Being the Fast-day Appointed for the Late Dreadfull Fire in the City of London* (4th edn, 1666).

Strange, Dreadful, and Amazing News from York: Giving a Sad and Terrible Account of God's Fearful Judgment on one Winam Tendin, near Rippon (1697).

Talbot, William, *The Foolish Abuse and Wise Use of Riches: A Sermon Preach'd in the Parish-Church of Bromsgrove in Worcester-shire* (1695).

Theed, Richard, *Admonition from the Other World: Or, The Story of Dives and Lazarus Practically Improv'd, in Two Sermons, Preach'd at Sutton-Cofield, in Warwickshire, on Sunday, October the 22d MDCCX* (1711).

Thomas, William, *The Mammon of Unrighteousness Detected and Purified in a Sermon Preached at the Cathedral Church of Worcester* (1688).

A Threefold Alphabet of Rules, Concerning Christian-Practice (1681).

Tillotson, John, *Sixteen Sermons, Preached on Several Subjects ... Being the third volume* (1696).

Varlo, Charles, *The Modern Farmers Guide* (2 vols, Edinburgh, 1768).

Vincent, Thomas, *An Explicatory Catechism* (1673).

A Voice from Heaven To the Youth of Great Britain: Containing, A Dialogue Between Christ, Youth, and the Devil (c.1714).

Wake, William, *The Principles of the Christian Religion Explained: In a Brief Commentary upon the Church Catechism* (1699).

Ward, Edward, *The Wealthy Shop-keeper, or, The Charitable Citizen: A Poem* (1700).

Watson, Thomas, *A Body of Practical Divinity Consisting of … Sermons* (1692).

Waugh, John, *The Duty of Apprentices* (1713).

The Weavers of London do Humbly Offer to … Parliament; That this Kingdom of England will Sustain Great Evils and Damage by Enjoyning the Wear of Woollen Manufactures and Leather (1689).

Welchman, Edward, *The Duty and Reward of Charity, Especially as it Regardeth the Education of Poor Children: A Sermon Preach'd at Banbury in Oxfordshire* (1707).

White, Lawrence, *The Charitable Farmer of Somersetshire: or, God's Great and Wonderful Work* (1674?).

Williams, John, *A Brief Exposition of the Church Catechism, with Proofs from Scripture* (3rd edn, 1691).

Wing, John, *Olympia Domata, or, An Almanack* (Cambridge, 1685).

Wing, Vincent, *Olympia Domata, or, An Almanack* (1668).

Wing, Vincent, *Olympia Domata, or, An Almanack* (1669).

'The Wood Ballads' (6 vols), held at the Bodleian Library. Facsimiles published online at <http://www.bodley.ox.ac.uk/ballads/> (Bodleian Library Broadside Ballads database, University of Oxford).

The Workhouse Cruelty, Being a Full and True Account of one Mrs. Mary Whistle, a Poor Woman (c.1731).

Xenophons Treatise of House-hold (1573).

Younge, Richard, *The Poors Advocate Epitomized: Or, Christ's call To Rich Men, in Behalf of his Poor Members* (1665).

Younge, Richard, *A Precious Mithridate for the Soule made up of those Two Poysons, Covetousness and Prodigality* (1661).

The Young-mans Victory Over the Power of the Devil: Or, Strange and Wonderful News from the City of London (c.1693).

Youths Divine Pastime: Containing Forty Remarkable Scripture Histories (1691).

Secondary Sources

Addy, John, *Sin and Society in the Seventeenth Century* (London and New York, 1989).

Akerlof, George A., and, Shiller, Robert J., *Animal Spirits: How Human Psychology Drives the Economy, and Why It Matters for Global Capitalism* (Princeton, 2009).

Almond, Philip, *Heaven and Hell in Enlightenment England* (Cambridge, 1994).

Amussen, Susan, *An Ordered Society: Gender and Class in Early Modern England* (New York, 1993).

Amussen, Susan, 'Punishment, Discipline, and Power: The Social Meanings of Violence in Early Modern England', *Journal of British Studies*, 34:1 (1995), pp. 1–34.

Anderson, Benedict, *Imagined Communities: Reflections on the Origin and Spread of Nationalism* (London, 1983).

Appleby, Joyce, *Economic Thought and Ideology in Seventeenth-Century England* (Princeton, 1978).

Ariely, Dan, *Predictably Irrational: The Hidden Forces that Shape Our Decisions* (New York, 2008).

Aston, Margaret, *England's Iconoclasts* (Oxford, 1988).

Aylmer, G. E., 'The Meaning and Definition of "Property" in Seventeenth-Century England', *Past & Present*, 86 (1980), pp. 87–97.

Baehr, Peter, and Wells, Gordon C., 'Introduction', in Weber, *Protestant Ethic*, pp. xi–xxxii.

Bailey, Joanne, 'Reassessing Parenting in Eighteenth-Century England', in Berry and Foyster (eds), *Family*, pp. 209–32.

Barry, Jonathan, 'Bourgeois Collectivism? Urban Association and the Middling Sort', in Jonathan Barry and Christopher Brooks (eds), *The Middling Sort of People: Culture, Society and Politics in England, 1550–1800* (Basingstoke, 1994), pp. 84–112.

Barry, Jonathan, 'Civility and Civic Culture in Early Modern England: The Meanings of Urban Freedom', in Peter Burke, Brian Harrison, and Paul Slack (eds), *Civil Histories: Essays presented to Sir Keith Thomas* (Oxford, 2000), pp. 181–96.

Baugh, Daniel, 'Poverty, Protestantism and Political Economy: English Attitudes towards the Poor 1660–1800', in S. B. Baxter (ed.), *England's Rise to Greatness, 1660–1763* (Berkeley, 1983), pp. 63–108.

Bebb, E. D., *Nonconformity and Social and Economic Life: Some Problems of the Present as They Appeared in the Past* (Philadelphia, 1980).

Beckett, John Vincent, 'Land Tax or Excise: The Levying of Taxation in Seventeenth- and Eighteenth-Century England', *English Historical Review*, 100 (1985), pp. 285–308.

Beier, A. L., *Masterless Men: The Vagrancy Problem in England 1560–1640* (London, 1985).

Beloff, Max, *Public Order and Popular Disturbances, 1660–1714* (London, 1938).

Ben-Amos, Ilana Krausman, *Adolescence and Youth in Early Modern England* (London, 1994).

Ben-Amos, Ilana Krausman, *The Culture of Giving: Informal Support and Gift-Exchange in Early Modern England* (Cambridge, 2008).

Berg, Maxine, *The Age of Manufactures, 1700–1820: Industry, Innovation and Work in Britain* (2nd edn, London, 1996).

Berg, Maxine, *Luxury and Pleasure in Eighteenth-Century Britain* (Oxford, 2005).

Berlin, Michael, 'Guilds in Decline? London Livery Companies and the Rise of a Liberal Economy, 1600–1800', in Epstein and Prak (eds), *Guilds*, pp. 316–42.

Berry, Helen, and Foyster, Elizabeth (eds), *The Family in Early Modern England* (Cambridge, 2007).

Birtles, Sara, 'Common Land, Poor Relief and Enclosure: The Use of Manorial Resources in Fulfilling Parish Obligations, 1601–1834', *Past & Present*, 165 (1999), pp. 74–106.

Bohstedt, John, 'The Moral Economy and the Discipline of Historical Context', *Journal of Social History*, 26 (1992), pp. 265–84.

Bohstedt, John, *The Politics of Provisions: Food Riots, Moral Economy, and Market Transition in England, c.1550–1850* (Farnham, 2010).

Booth, William James, 'Household and Market: On the Origins of Moral Economic Philosophy', *Review of Politics*, 56:2 (1994), pp. 207–35.

Booth, William James, *Households: On the Moral Architecture of the Economy* (Ithaca, 1993).

Borsay, Peter, '"All the town's a stage": Urban Ritual and Ceremony', in Clark (ed.), *Provincial Towns*, pp. 228–58.

Borsay, Peter, *The English Urban Renaissance: Culture and Society in the Provincial Town, 1660–1770* (Oxford, 1998).

Bossy, John, 'Moral Arithmetic: Seven Sins into Ten Commandments', in Edmund Leites, *Conscience and Casuistry in Early Modern Europe* (Cambridge, 1988), pp. 214–34.

Boulton, Jeremy, 'Going on the Parish: The Parish Pension and its Meaning in the London Suburbs, 1640–1724', in Tim Hitchcock, Peter King, and Pamela Sharpe (eds), *Chronicling Poverty: The Voices and Strategies of the English Poor, 1640–1840* (London, 1997), pp. 19–46.

Boulton, Jeremy, *Neighbourhood and Society: A London Suburb in the Seventeenth Century* (Cambridge, 1987).

Bowden, P. J., 'Agricultural Prices, Wages, Farm Profits, and Rents', in Joan Thirsk (ed.), *The Agrarian History of England and Wales, Vol. V: 1640–1750* (2 parts, Cambridge, 1985), pt. 2, pp. 1–118.

Braddick, Michael, *Parliamentary Taxation in Seventeenth-Century England: Local Administration and Response* (London, 1994).

Braddick, Michael, *State Formation in Early Modern England, c.1550–1700* (Cambridge, 2000).

Braddick, Michael, and Walter, John, 'Grids of Power: Order, Hierarchy and Subordination in Early Modern Society', in Braddick and Walter (eds), *Negotiating Power*, pp. 1–42.

Braddick, Michael, and Walter, John (eds), *Negotiating Power in Early Modern Society: Order, Hierarchy and Subordination in Britain and Ireland* (Cambridge, 2001).

Braithwaite, William Charles, *The Second Period of Quakerism* (2nd edn, Cambridge, 1961).

Brewer, John, *The Sinews of Power: War, Money and the English State, 1688–1783* (London, 1989).

Brewer, John, and Porter, Roy (eds), *Consumption and the World of Goods* (London, 1993).

Brewer, John, and Styles, John (eds), *An Ungovernable People? The English and Their Law in the Seventeenth and Eighteenth Centuries* (London, 1980).

Broad, John, *Transforming English Rural Society: The Verneys and the Claydons, 1600–1820* (Cambridge, 2004).

Brown, A. F. J., *Essex at Work, 1700–1815* (Chelmsford, 1969).

Burke, Peter, 'Popular Culture in Seventeenth-Century London', *London Journal*, 3 (1977), pp. 143–62.

Burley, Kevin, 'A Note on a Labour Dispute in Early Eighteenth-Century Colchester', *Bulletin of the Institute of Historical Research*, 29 (1956), pp. 220–30.

Burns, William, *An Age of Wonders: Prodigies, Politics and Providence in England, 1657–1727* (Manchester, 2002).

Capp, Bernard, *Astrology and the Popular Press: English Almanacs, 1500–1800* (London, 1979).

Capp, Bernard, *When Gossips Meet: Women, Family and Neighbourhood in Early Modern England* (Oxford, 2003).

Charlesworth, Andrew (ed.), *An Atlas of Rural Protest in Britain, 1548–1900* (London, 1983).

Chase, Malcolm, *Early Trade Unionism: Fraternity, Skill and the Politics of Labour* (Aldershot, 2000).

Clark, J. C. D., *English Society, 1660–1832: Religion, Ideology and Politics during the Ancien Regime* (2nd edn, Cambridge, 2000).

Clark, J. C. D., 'Providence, Predestination and Progress: or, Did the Enlightenment Fail?' *Albion*, 35:4 (2004), pp. 559–89.

Clark, Peter, *British Clubs and Societies c.1580–1800: The Origins of An Associational World* (Oxford, 2000).

Clark, Peter (ed.), *The Transformation of English Provincial Towns, 1600–1800* (London, 1984).

Coates, Ben, *The Impact of the English Civil War on the Economy of London, 1642–50* (Aldershot, 2004).

Coleman, D. C., 'Naval Dockyards under the Later Stuarts', *Economic History Review*, 2nd ser., 6 (1953), pp. 134–55.

Colley, Linda, *Britons: Forging the Nation, 1707–1837* (London, 1992).

Collinson, Patrick, 'Christian Socialism in Elizabethan Suffolk: Thomas Carew and his Caveat for Clothiers', in Carole Rawcliffe, Roger Virgoe, and Richard G. Wilson (eds), *Counties and Communities: Essays on East Anglian History presented to Hassell Smith* (Norwich, 1996), pp. 161–78.

Collinson, Patrick, 'Puritanism and the Poor', in Rosemary Horrox and Sarah Rees Jones (eds), *Pragmatic Utopias: Ideals and Communities, 1200–1630* (Cambridge, 2001), pp. 242–58.

Crawford, Patricia, *Parents of Poor Children in England, 1580–1800* (Oxford, 2010).

Cressy, David, *Literacy and the Social Order: Reading and Writing in Tudor and Stuart England* (Cambridge, 1980).

Crick, Julia, and Alexandra Walsham (eds), *The Uses of Script and Print, 1300–1700* (Cambridge, 2004).

Cullen, Karen, *Famine in Scotland: The 'Ill Years' of the 1690s* (Edinburgh, 2010).

Davidson, Lee, Hitchcock, Tim, Keirn, Tim, and Shoemaker, Robert (eds), *Stilling the Grumbling Hive: The Response to Social and Economic Problems in England, 1689–1750* (Stroud, 1992).

Davis, James, *Medieval Market Morality: Life, Law and Ethics in the English Market-place, 1200–1500* (Cambridge, 2011).

Davis, Ralph, 'The Rise of Protection in England, 1689–1786', *Economic History Review*, New Series, 19:2 (1966), pp. 306–17.

De Kray, Gary, *Restoration and Revolution in Britain: A Political History of the Era of Charles II and the Glorious Revolution* (Basingstoke, 2007).

Desmedt, Ludovic, 'Money in the "Body Politick": The Analysis of Trade and Circulation in the Writings of Seventeenth-Century Political Arithmeticians', *History of Political Economy*, 37:1 (2005), pp. 79–101.

Dickinson, H. T., *The Politics of the People in Eighteenth-Century Britain* (Basingstoke, 1995).

Dickson, P. G. M., *The Financial Revolution in England: A Study in the Development of Public Credit, 1688–1756* (London, 1967).

Dunn, R. M., 'The London Weavers' Riot of 1675', *Guildhall Studies in London History*, 1:1 (1973), pp. 13–23.

Earle, Peter, *The Making of the English Middle Class: Business, Society and Family Life in London, 1660–1730* (Berkeley, 1989).

Early Modern Research Group, 'Commonwealth Contexts: The Social, Cultural, and Conceptual Contexts of an Early Modern Keyword', *Historical Journal*, 54:3 (2011), pp. 659–87.

Ellis, Joyce, 'A Dynamic Society: Social Relations in Newcastle-upon-Tyne, 1660–1760', in Clark (ed.), *Provincial Towns*, pp. 190–227.

Epstein, Stephan, and Prak, Maarten (eds), *Guilds, Innovation, and the European Economy, 1400–1800* (Cambridge, 2008).

Erickson, Amy Louise, 'Married Women's Occupations in Eighteenth-century London', *Continuity & Change*, 23:2 (2008), pp. 267–307.

Erickson, Amy Louise, *Women and Property in Early Modern England* (London, 1993).

Estabrook, Carl, *Urbane and Rustic England: Cultural Ties and Social Spheres in the Provinces* (Manchester, 1998).

Ewen, C. L'Estrange, *Witchcraft and Demonianism: A Concise Account Derived from Sworn Depositions and Confessions Obtained in the Courts of England and Wales* (London, 1933).

Ferrell, Lori Anne, and McCullough, Peter (eds), *The English Sermon Revised: Religion, Literature and History, 1600–1750* (Manchester, 2001).

Finkelstein, Andrea, *The Grammar of Profit: The Price Revolution in Intellectual Context* (Leiden, 2006).

Finkelstein, Andrea, *Harmony and the Balance: An Intellectual History of Seventeenth-Century English Economic Thought* (Ann Arbor, 2000).

Finkelstein, Andrea, 'Nicholas Barbon and the Quality of Infinity', *History of Political Economy*, 32:1 (2000), pp. 83–102.

Flather, Amanda, *Gender and Space in Early Modern England* (Woodbridge, 2006).

Fletcher, Anthony, *Gender, Sex and Subordination in England, 1500–1800* (New Haven and London, 1995).

Fletcher, Anthony, *Reform in the Provinces: The Government of Stuart England* (New Haven, 1986).

Fletcher, David, 'The Parish Boundary: A Social Phenomenon in Hanoverian England', *Rural History*, 14:2 (2003), pp. 177–96.

Fogg, Nicholas, *Stratford-upon-Avon: Portrait of a Town* (Chichester, 1986).

Fox, Adam, *Oral and Literate Culture in England, 1500–1700* (Oxford, 2000).

Fox, Adam, and Woolf, Daniel (eds), *The Spoken Word: Oral Culture in Britain, 1500–1850* (Manchester, 2002).

Foyster, Elizabeth, *Manhood in Early Modern England: Honour, Sex and Marriage* (London, 1999).

French, Henry, *The Middle Sort of People in Provincial England, 1600–1750* (Oxford, 2007).

French, Henry, 'Social Status, Localism and the "Middle Sort of People" in England 1620–1750', *Past & Present*, 166 (2000), pp. 66–99.

French, Henry, 'Urban Agriculture, Commons and Commoners in the Seventeenth and Eighteenth Centuries: The Case of Sudbury, Suffolk', *Agricultural History Review*, 48:2 (2000), pp. 171–99.

Friedman, Jerome, *Miracles and the Pulp Press during the English Revolution: The Battle of the Frogs and Fairford's Flies* (London, 1993).

Froide, Amy M., *Never Married: Singlewomen in Early Modern England* (Oxford, 2005).

Fumerton, Patricia, Guerrini, Anita, and McAbee, Kris (eds), *Ballads and Broadsides in Britain, 1500–1800* (Farnham, 2010).

Fumerton, Patricia, *Unsettled: The Culture of Mobility and the Working Poor in Early Modern England* (Chicago, 2006).

Gadd, Ian, and Wallis, Patrick, 'Reaching Beyond the City Wall: London Guilds and National Regulation, 1500–1700', in Epstein and Prak (eds), *Guilds*, pp. 288–315.

Gaskill, Malcolm, *Crime and Mentalities in Early Modern England* (Cambridge, 2000).

Gaskill, Malcolm, 'Witchcraft and Evidence in Early Modern England', *Past & Present*, 198 (2008), pp. 33–70.

Gauci, Perry, *Politics and Society in Great Yarmouth, 1660–1722* (Oxford, 1996).

Gauci, Perry, *The Politics of Trade: The Overseas Merchant in State and Society, 1660–1720* (Oxford, 2001).

Gilmour, Ian, *Riot, Rising and Revolution: Governance and Violence in Eighteenth Century England* (London, 1992).

Glaisyer, Natasha, *The Culture of Commerce in England, 1660–1720* (Woodbridge, 2006).

Glaisyer, Natasha, '"A due circulation in the veins of the publick": Imagining Credit in Late Seventeenth and Early Eighteenth-Century England', *Eighteenth Century: Theory and Interpretation*, 46:3 (2005), pp. 277–97.

Goose, Nigel, '"Xenophobia" in Elizabethan and Early Stuart England: An Epithet Too Far?' in Nigel Goose and Lien Luu (eds), *Immigrants in Tudor and early Stuart England* (Brighton, 2005), pp. 110–35.

Goux, Jean-Joseph, *Symbolic Economies: After Marx and Freud* (Ithaca, 1990).

Gowing, Laura, *Domestic Dangers: Women, Words and Sex in Early Modern London* (Oxford, 1996).

Green, Ian, *The Christian's ABC: Catechism and Catechizing in England, c.1530–1740* (Oxford, 1996).

Green, Ian, *Print and Protestantism in Early Modern England* (Oxford, 2000).

Gregory, Jeremy, '"For all sorts and conditions of men": The Social Life of the Book of Common Prayer during the Long Eighteenth Century: or, Bringing the History of Religion and Social History Together', *Social History*, 34:1 (2009), pp. 29–54.

Griffiths, Paul, *Youth and Authority: Formative Experiences in England, 1560–1640* (Oxford, 1996).

Griffiths, Paul, Fox, Adam, and Hindle, Steve (eds), *The Experience of Authority in Early Modern England* (Basingstoke, 1996).

Gritt, A. J., 'The "Survival" of Service in the English Agricultural Labour Force: Lessons from Lancashire, c.1650–1851', *Agricultural History Review*, 50:1 (2002), pp. 25–50.

Gwynn, Robin, *Huguenot Heritage: The History and Contribution of the Huguenots in Britain* (London, 1985).

Hailwood, Mark, 'Sociability, Work and Labouring Identity in Seventeenth-Century England', *Cultural and Social History*, 8:1 (2011), pp. 9–29.

Hainsworth, D. R., *Stewards, Lords and People: The Estate Steward and his World in Later Stuart England* (Cambridge, 1992).

Harris, Tim, *London Crowds in the Reign of Charles II: Propaganda and Politics from the Restoration until the Exclusion Crisis* (Cambridge, 1987).

Harris, Tim (ed.), *Popular Culture in England, c.1500–1850* (Houndmills, 1995).

Harris, Tim, *Restoration: Charles II and His Kingdoms, 1660–1685* (London and New York, 2005).

Harris, Tim, *Revolution: The Great Crisis of the British Monarchy, 1685–1720* (London and New York, 2006).

Harris, Tim, Seaward, Paul, and Goldie, Mark (eds), *The Politics of Religion in Restoration England* (Oxford, 1990).

Hart, Cyril, *The Commoners of Dean Forest* (Gloucester, 1951).

Hart, Cyril, *The Free Miners of the Royal Forest of Dean and Hundred of St. Briavels* (Gloucester, 1953).

Hatcher, John, *The History of the British Coal Industry, Vol. I: Before 1700* (Oxford, 1993).

Hawkes, David, 'Commodification and Subjectivity in John Bunyan's Fiction', *Eighteenth Century: Theory and Interpretation*, 41:1 (2000), pp. 37–55.

Hawkes, David, *Idols of the Marketplace: Idolatry and Commodity Fetishism in English Literature, 1580–1680* (New York, 2001).

Hay, Douglas, 'England, 1562–1875: The Law and Its Uses', in Douglas Hay and Paul Craven (eds), *Masters, Servants, and Magistrates in Britain and the Empire, 1562–1955* (Chapel Hill, 2004), pp. 59–116.

Hay, Douglas, 'Poaching and the Game Laws on Cannock Chase', in Douglas Hay et al. (eds), *Albion's Fatal Tree: Crime and Society in Eighteenth Century England* (New York, 1975), pp. 189–253.

Heal, Felicity, 'Food Gifts, the Household and the Politics of Exchange in Early Modern England', *Past & Present*, 199 (2008), pp. 41–70.

Heal, Felicity, *Hospitality in Early Modern England* (Oxford, 1990).

Heal, Felicity, and Holmes, Clive, *The Gentry in England and Wales, 1500–1700* (Basingstoke, 1994).

Henderson, Lizanne, 'The Survival of Witchcraft Prosecutions and Witch Belief in South-West Scotland', *Scottish Historical Review*, 85:1 (2006), pp. 52–74.

Henson, Gravenor, *The Civil, Political, and Mechanical History of the Framework-Knitters in Europe and America* (Nottingham, 1831).

Hentschell, Roze, *The Culture of Cloth in Early Modern England* (Aldershot, 2008).

Hey, David, *The Fiery Blades of Hallamshire: Sheffield and its Neighbourhood, 1660–1740* (Leicester, 1991).

Hill, Bridget, *Servants: English Domestics in the Eighteenth Century* (Oxford, 1996).

Hill, Christopher, *Change and Continuity in Seventeenth-Century England* (London, 1974).

Hill, Christopher, *Puritanism and Revolution: Studies in Interpretation of the English Revolution of the Seventeenth Century* (London, 1958).

Hill, Christopher, 'Puritans and the Poor', *Past & Present*, 2 (1952), pp. 32–50.

Hill, Christopher, *Reformation to Industrial Revolution: A Social and Economic History of Britain, 1530–1780* (London, 1967).

Hill, Christopher, *Society and Puritanism in Pre-Revolutionary England* (London, 1964).

Hill, Christopher, *Some Intellectual Consequences of the English Revolution* (London, 1980).

Hill, Christopher, *A Turbulent, Seditious, and Factious People: John Bunyan and His Church, 1628–1688* (Oxford, 1988).

Hill, Christopher, *The World Turned Upside Down: Radical Ideas During the English Revolution* (1972; London and New York, 1991).

Hill, J. W. F., *Tudor and Stuart Lincoln* (Cambridge, 1956).

Hindle, Steve, 'Beating the Bounds of the Parish: Order, Memory, and Identity in the English Local Community, c.1500–1700', in Michael Halvorson and Karen Spierling (eds), *Defining Community in Early Modern Europe* (Aldershot, 2008), pp. 205–28.

Hindle, Steve, 'Civility, Honesty and the Identification of the Deserving Poor in Seventeenth-Century England', in Henry French and Jonathan Barry (eds), *Identity and Agency in England, 1500–1800* (Basingstoke, 2004), pp. 38–59.

Hindle, Steve, 'Dearth, Fasting and Alms: The Campaign for General Hospitality in Late Elizabethan England', *Past & Present*, 172 (2001), pp. 44–86.

Hindle, Steve, 'Dependency, Shame and Belonging: Badging the Deserving Poor, c.1550–1750', *Cultural and Social History*, 1:1 (2004), pp. 6–35.

Hindle, Steve, 'The Growth of Social Stability in Restoration England', *European Legacy*, 5:4 (2000), pp. 563–76.

Hindle, Steve, 'Imagining Insurrection in Seventeenth-Century England: Representations of the Midland Rising of 1607', *History Workshop Journal*, 66 (2008), pp. 21–61.

Hindle, Steve, 'Labour Discipline, Agricultural Service and the Households of the Poor in England, c.1640–1730', in Joanne McEwan and Pamela Sharpe (eds), *Accommodating Poverty: The Housing and Living Arrangements of the English Poor, c.1600–1850* (Houndmills, 2011), pp. 169–90.

Hindle, Steve, *On the Parish? The Micro-Politics of Poor Relief in Rural England, c.1550–1750* (Oxford, 2004).

Hindle, Steve, 'Persuasion and Protest in the Caddington Common Enclosure Dispute, 1635–1639', *Past & Present*, 158 (1998), pp. 37–78.

Hirschman, Albert O., *The Passions and the Interests: Political Arguments for Capitalism Before Its Triumph* (Princeton, 1977).

Hitchcock, David, 'A Typology of Travellers: Migration, Justice, and Vagrancy in Warwickshire, 1670–1730', *Rural History*, 23:1 (2012), pp. 21–39.

Hitchcock, Tim, 'The Publicity of Poverty in Early Eighteenth-century London', in Julia F. Merritt (ed.), *Imagining Early Modern London: Perceptions and Portrayals of the City from Stow to Strype, 1598–1720* (Cambridge, 2001), pp. 166–84.

Hitchcock, Tim, King, Peter, and Sharpe, Pamela (eds), *Chronicling Poverty: The Voices and Strategies of the English Poor, 1640–1840* (Basingstoke, 1997).

Hitchcock, Tim, King, Peter, and Sharpe, Pamela, 'Introduction', in idem (eds), *Chronicling Poverty*, pp. 1–18.

Hont, Istvan, and Ignatieff, Michael, 'Needs and Justice in the *Wealth of Nations*: An Introductory Essay', in idem (eds), *Wealth and Virtue: The Shaping of Political Economy in the Scottish Enlightenment* (Cambridge, 1983), pp. 1–44.

Hoppit, Julian, 'The Contexts and Contours of British Economic Literature, 1660–1760', *Historical Journal*, 49:1 (2006), pp. 79–110.

Horne, Thomas, *Property Rights and Poverty: Political Argument in Britain, 1605–1834* (Chapel Hill, 1990).

Hoskins, W. G. *The Midland Peasant: The Economic and Social History of a Leicestershire Village* (London, 1957).

Houston, Alan, and Pincus, Steve (eds), *A Nation Transformed: England after the Restoration* (Cambridge, 2001).

Houston, Robert, *Social Change in the Age of the Enlightenment: Edinburgh, 1660–1760* (Oxford, 1994).

Howell, Roger, *Newcastle Upon Tyne and the Puritan Revolution: A Study of the Civil War in North England* (Oxford, 1967).

Humphries, Jane, *Childhood and Child Labour in the British Industrial Revolution* (Cambridge, 2010).

Hunt, Arnold, 'The Lord's Supper in Early Modern England', *Past & Present*, 161 (1998), pp. 39–83.

Hunt, Margaret, *The Middling Sort: Commerce, Gender, and the Family in England, 1680–1780* (Berkeley, 1996).

Hunt, William, *The Puritan Moment: The Coming of Revolution in an English County* (Cambridge, MA, 1983).

Hutchison, Terrence, *Before Adam Smith: The Emergence of Political Economy, 1662–1776* (Oxford, 1988).

Hutton, Ronald, *The Rise and Fall of Merry England: The Ritual Year, 1400–1700* (Oxford, 1994).

Hutton, Ronald, *Stations of the Sun: A History of the Ritual Year in Britain* (Oxford and New York, 2001).

Innes, Joanna, 'Prisons for the Poor: English Bridewells, 1555–1800', in Francis Snyder and Douglas Hay (eds), *Labour, Law and Crime: An Historical Perspective* (London, 1987), pp. 42–122.

Jacob, Margaret, and Kadane, Matthew, 'Missing, Now Found in the Eighteenth Century: Weber's Protestant Ethic', *American Historical Review*, 108:1 (2003), pp. 20–49.

James, Margaret, *Social Problems and Policy During the Puritan Revolution* (London, 1930).

Jones, Norman, *God and the Moneylenders: Usury and Law in Early Modern England* (Oxford, 1989).

Jones, Whitney R. D., *The Tree of Commonwealth, 1450–1793* (Cranbury, 2000).

Joyce, Patrick, *Work, Society and Politics: Culture of the Factory in Later Victorian England* (London, 1980).

Jupp, E. B., *An Historical Account of the Worshipful Company of Carpenters of the City of London* (London, 1848).

Kellett, John R. 'The Breakdown of Gild and Corporation Control over the Handicraft and Retail Trade in London', *Economic History Review*, 2nd ser., 10 (1958), pp. 381–94.

Kent, Joan, and King, Steve, 'Changing Patterns of Poor Relief in some English Rural Parishes, circa 1650–1750', *Rural History*, 14:2 (2003), pp. 119–56.

King, Peter, 'Customary Rights and Women's Earnings: The Importance of Gleaning to the Rural Labouring Poor, 1750–1850', *Economic History Review*, 44:3 (1991), 461–76.

King, Peter, 'Gleaners, Farmers, and the Failure of Legal Sanctions in England, 1750–1850', *Past & Present*, 125 (1989), pp. 116–50.

King, Rebecca, 'The Sociability of the Trade Guilds of Newcastle and Durham, 1660–1750: The Urban Renaissance Revisited', in Helen Berry and Jeremy Gregory (eds), *Creating and Consuming Culture in North-East England, 1660–1830* (Aldershot, 2004), pp. 57–71.

Klamer, Arjo, McCloskey, Donald, and Solow, Robert (eds), *The Consequences of Economic Rhetoric* (Cambridge, 1988).

Knights, Mark, 'Participation and Representation before Democracy: Petitions and Addresses in Pre-Modern Britain', in Ian Shapiro, Susan C. Stokes, Elizabeth Jean Wood, and Alexander S. Kirshner (eds), *Political Representation* (Cambridge, 2009), pp. 35–60.

Knights, Mark, *Representation and Misrepresentation in Later Stuart Britain: Partisanship and Political Culture* (Oxford, 2005).

Kussmaul, Ann, *Servants in Husbandry in Early Modern England* (Cambridge, 1981).

Lake, Peter, and Pincus, Steven (eds), *The Politics of the Public Sphere in Early Modern England* (Manchester, 2007).

Lamont, William, *Puritanism and Historical Controversy* (London, 1996).

Landau, Norma, *The Justices of the Peace, 1679–1760* (Berkeley, 1984).

Laslett, Peter, *The World We Have Lost: Further Explored* (3rd edn, London, 1983).

Lee, James, '"Ye shall disturbe noe man's right": Oath-Taking and Oath-Breaking in Late Medieval and Early Modern Bristol', *Urban History*, 34:1 (2007), pp. 27–38.

Lehmann, Hartmut, and Roth, Guenther (eds), *Weber's Protestant Ethic: Origins, Evidence, Contexts* (Cambridge, 1993).

Lemire, Beverly, *Fashion's Favourite: The Cotton Trade and the Consumer in Britain, 1660–1800* (Oxford, 1991).

Lessnoff, Michael H., *The Spirit of Capitalism and the Protestant Ethic: An Enquiry into the Weber Thesis* (Aldershot, 1994).

Levine, David, *Reproducing Families: The Political Economy of English Population History* (Cambridge, 1987).

Levine, David, and Wrightson, Keith, *The Making of an Industrial Society: Whickham, 1560–1765* (Oxford, 1991).

Lindley, Keith, *Fenland Riots and the English Revolution* (London, 1982).

Linebaugh, Peter, *The London Hanged: Crime and Civil Society in the Eighteenth Century* (London, 1991).

Lipson, E., *The History of the Woollen and Worsted Industries* (London, 1921).

McClain, Molly, 'The Wentwood Forest Riot: Property Rights and Political Culture in Restoration England', in Susan Amussen and Mark Kishlansky (eds), *Political Culture and Cultural Politics in Early Modern England* (Manchester, 1995), pp. 112–32.

McCloskey, Donald, *The Rhetoric of Economics* (Brighton, 1985).

Macfarlane, Alan, *The Family Life of Ralph Josselin: A Seventeenth-Century Clergyman. An Essay in Historical Anthropology* (London, 1970).

Macfarlane, Alan, *The Origins of English Individualism: The Family, Property and Social Transition* (Oxford, 1978).

Macfarlane, Alan, *Witchcraft in Tudor and Stuart England: A Regional and Comparative Study* (London, 1970).

McKenzie, Andrea, *Tyburn's Martyrs: Execution in England, 1675–1775* (London, 2007).

Macpherson, C. B., *The Political Theory of Possessive Individualism: Hobbes to Locke* (Oxford, 1962).

McRae, Andrew, *God Speed the Plough: The Representation of Agrarian England, 1500–1660* (Cambridge, 1996).

McShane, Angela, *Political Broadside Ballads of Seventeenth-Century England: A Critical Bibliography* (London, 2011).

Malcolmson, Robert, *Life and Labour in England, 1700–1780* (London, 1981).

Malcolmson, Robert, *Popular Recreations in English Society, 1700–1850* (Cambridge, 1973).

Malcolmson, Robert, '"A set of ungovernable people": The Kingswood Colliers in the Eighteenth Century', in Brewer and Styles (eds), *Ungovernable People*, pp. 85–127.

Malcolmson, Robert, 'Workers' Combinations in Eighteenth-Century England', in

Margaret Jacob and James Jacob (eds), *The Origins of Anglo-American Radicalism* (London, 1984), pp. 149–61.

Marsh, Christopher, *Music and Society in Early Modern England* (Cambridge, 2010).

Marshall, Gordon, *Presbyteries and Profits: Calvinism and the Development of Capitalism in Scotland, 1560–1707* (Edinburgh, 1992).

Marshall, Gordon, *In Search of the Spirit of Capitalism: An Essay on Max Weber's Protestant Ethic Thesis* (London, 1982).

Marshall, L. M., 'The Levying of the Hearth Tax, 1662–1688', *English Historical Review*, 51 (1936), pp. 628–46.

Marx, Karl, *The German Ideology*, C. J. Arthur ed. (London, 1974).

Marx, Karl, *Selected Writings in Sociology and Social Philosophy*, T. B. Bottomore and Maximilien Rubel eds (2nd edn, Harmondsworth and Ringwood, 1970).

Marx, Karl, and Engels, Fredrick, *The Communist Manifesto* (Harmondsworth, 1967).

Mendelson, Sara Heller, and Crawford, Patricia, *Women in Early Modern England, 1550–1720* (Oxford, 1998).

Mill, J. S., *Essays on Some Unsettled Questions of Political Economy* (London, 1844).

Mill, J. S., *Principles of Political Economy* (2 vols, London, 1848).

Miller, John, *Cities Divided: Politics and Religion in English Provincial Towns, 1660–1722* (Oxford, 2007).

Minchinton, W. E. (ed.), *Wage Regulation in Pre-Industrial England* (Newton Abbot, 1972).

Monod, Paul, 'Dangerous Merchandise: Smuggling, Jacobitism, and Commercial Culture in Southeast England, 1690–1760', *Journal of British Studies*, 30 (1991), pp. 150–82.

Morgan, Mary S., 'Economic Man as Model Man: Ideal Types, Idealization and Caricatures', *Journal of the History of Economic Thought*, 28:1 (2006), pp. 1–27.

Mucsche, P. B., *Gentlemen and Poachers: The English Game Laws, 1671–1831* (Cambridge, 1981).

Muldrew, Craig, *The Economy of Obligation: The Culture of Credit and Social Relation in Early Modern England* (Basingstoke, 1998).

Muldrew, Craig, *Food, Energy and the Creation of Industriousness: Work and Material Culture in Agrarian England, 1550–1780* (Cambridge, 2011).

Muldrew, Craig, 'From a "Light Cloak" to an "Iron Cage": Historical Changes in the Relations between Community and Individualism', in Shepard and Withington (eds), *Communities*, pp. 156–77.

Muldrew, Craig, '"Hard Food for Midas': Cash and Its Social Value in Early Modern England', *Past & Present*, 170 (2001), pp. 78–120.

Muldrew, Craig, 'Interpreting the Market: The Ethics of Credit and Community Relations in Early Modern England', *Social History*, 18:2 (1993), pp. 163–83.

Nash, David, 'Reconnecting Religion with Social and Cultural History: Secularization's Failure as a Master Narrative', *Cultural and Social History*, 1:3 (2004), pp. 302–22.

Neeson, Jeanette, *Commoners: Common Right, Enclosure and Social Change in England, 1700–1820* (Cambridge, 1993).

Newby, Howard, *The Deferential Worker: A Study of Farm Workers in East Anglia* (London, 1977).

Nicholls, David, 'Addressing God as Ruler: Prayer and Petition', *British Journal of Sociology*, 44:1 (1993), pp. 125–41.

Norrey, P. J., 'The Restoration Regime in Action: The Relationship between Central and Local Government in Dorset, Somerset & Wiltshire, 1660–1678', *Historical Journal*, 31:4 (1988), pp. 789–812.

O'Brien, Patrick, Griffiths, Trevor, and Hunt, Philip, 'Political Components of the Industrial Revolution: Parliament and the English Cotton Textile Industry, 1660–1774', *Economic History Review*, 2nd ser., 44 (1991), pp. 395–423.

Ormrod, David, *The Rise of Commercial Empires: England and the Netherlands in the Age of Mercantilism, 1650–1770* (Cambridge, 2003).

Outhwaite, R. B., *Dearth, Public Policy and Social Disturbance in England, 1550–1800* (Houndmills, 1991).

Overton, Mark, Whittle, Jane, Dean, Darron, and Hann, Andrew, *Production and Consumption in English Households, 1600–1750* (London, 2004).

Oxford Dictionary of National Biography (online edn, last revised in 2004).

Oxford English Dictionary (online edn, last revised in 2007).

Peck, Linda, *Consuming Splendor: Society and Culture in Seventeenth-Century England* (Cambridge, 2005).

Pennell, Sara, 'Consumption and Consumerism in Early Modern England', *Historical Journal*, 42 (1999), pp. 549–64.

Persky, Joseph, 'Retrospectives: The Ethology of Homo Economicus', *Journal of Economic Perspectives*, 9:2 (1995), pp. 221–31.

Pincus, Steven, *1688: The First Modern Revolution* (Newhaven, 2009).

Pincus, Steven, 'From Butterboxes to Wooden Shoes: The Shift in English Popular Sentiment from anti-Dutch to anti-French in the 1670s', *Historical Journal*, 38:2 (1995), pp. 333–61.

Pincus, Steven, 'From Holy Cause to Economic Interest: The Study of Population and the Intervention of the State', in Houston and Pincus (eds), *Nation Transformed*, pp. 272–98.

Pincus, Steven, 'Popery, Trade and Universal Monarchy: The Ideological Context of the Outbreak of the Second Anglo-Dutch War', *English Historical Review*, 107 (1992), pp. 1–29.

Plummer, Alfred, *The London Weavers' Company, 1600–1970* (London, 1972).

Pocock, J. G. A., *The Machiavellian Moment: Florentine Political Thought and the Atlantic Republican Tradition* (Princeton, 1975).

Polanyi, Karl, *The Great Transformation* (Boston, 1957).

Price, Richard, *British Society, 1680–1880* (Cambridge, 1999).

Price, Richard, *Labour in British Society: An Interpretive History* (London, 1990).

Priestley, Margaret, 'Anglo-French Trade and the "Unfavourable Balance" Controversy, 1660–85', *Economic History Review*, 2nd ser., 4:1 (1951), pp. 37–52.

Poole, Steve, 'Scarcity and the Civic Tradition: Market Management in Bristol, 1709–1815', in Randall and Charlesworth (eds), *Markets*, pp. 91–114.

Ramsey, G. D., 'Industrial Laisser-Faire and the Policy of Cromwell', *Economic History Review*, 16:2 (1946), pp. 93–110.

Randall, Adrian, and Charlesworth, Andrew (eds), *Markets, Market Culture and Popular Protest in Eighteenth-Century Britain and Ireland* (Liverpool, 1996).

Randall, Adrian, and Charlesworth, Andrew (eds), *Moral Economy and Popular Protest: Crowds, Conflict and Authority* (London, 2000).

Randall, Adrian, and Charlesworth, Andrew, 'The Moral Economy: Riots, Markets and Social Conflict', in idem (eds), *Moral Economy*, pp. 1–32.

Randall, Adrian, Charlesworth, Andrew, Sheldon, Richard, and Walsh, David, 'Introduction', in Randall and Charlesworth, *Markets*, pp. 1–24.

Reay, Barry (ed.), *Popular Culture in Seventeenth-Century England* (London, 1985).

Reay, Barry, *Popular Cultures in England, 1550–1750* (London, 1998).

Rediker, Marcus, *Between the Devil and the Deep Blue Sea: Merchant Seamen, Pirates, and the Anglo-American Maritime World, 1700–1750* (Cambridge, 1987).

Renton, Simon, 'The Moral Economy of the English Middling Sort in the Eighteenth Century: The Case of Norwich in 1766 and 1767', in Randall and Charlesworth (eds), *Markets*, pp. 115–36.

Richardson, R. C., *Household Servants in Early Modern England* (Manchester, 2010).

Rogers, Nicholas, 'Policing the Poor in Eighteenth-century London: the Vagrancy Laws and Their Administration', *Histoire sociale/Social History*, 24 (1991), pp. 127–47.

Rollison, David, 'Discourse and Class Struggle: The Politics of Industry in Early Modern England', *Social History*, 26:2 (2001), pp. 166–89.

Rollison, David, *The Local Origins of Modern Society: Gloucestershire, 1500–1800* (London, 1992).

Rose, Craig, *England in the 1690s: Revolution, Religion and War* (Oxford and Malden, 1999).

Rosenheim, James, 'Landownership, the Aristocracy and the Country Gentry', in Lionel Glassey (ed.), *The Reigns of Charles II and James VII & II* (Houndmills, 1997), pp. 152–70.

Rule, John, 'Employment and Authority: Masters and Men in Eighteenth-Century Manufacturing', in Griffiths, Fox, and Hindle (eds), *Experience of Authority*, pp. 286–317.

Rule, John, 'The Property of Skill in the Period of Manufacture', in Patrick Joyce (ed.), *The Historical Meaning of Work* (Cambridge, 1987), pp. 99–118.

Ruskin, John, *Unto This Last, and Other Writings*, Clive Wilmer ed. (Harmondsworth, 1985).

Ryan, John, 'Were the Church Fathers Communists?' *International Journal of Ethics*, 14:1 (1903), pp. 26–39.

Sandall, Simon, 'Custom, Memory and the Operations of Power in Seventeenth-Century Forest of Dean', in Fiona Williamson (ed.), *Locating Agency: Space, Power and Popular Politics* (Newcastle, 2009), pp. 133–60.

Schlatter, Richard, *The Social Ideas of Religious Leaders, 1660–1688* (New York, 1971).

Schochet, Gordon, *Patriarchalism in Political Thought: The Authoritarian Family and Political Speculation and Attitudes especially in Seventeenth-century England* (Oxford, 1975).

Scott, James C., *Domination and the Arts of Resistance: Hidden Transcripts* (New Haven, 1990).

Scott, James C., *The Moral Economy of the Peasant: Rebellion and Subsistence in Southeast Asia* (New Haven, 1977).

Scott, James C., *Weapons of the Weak: Everyday Forms of Peasant Resistance* (New Haven, 1985).

Scribner, Robert, 'Is a History of Popular Culture Possible?' *History of European Ideas*, 10:2 (1989), pp. 174–91.

Searle, G. R., *Morality and the Market in Victorian Britain* (Oxford, 1998).

Seaver, Paul, *Wallington's World: A Puritan Artisan in Seventeenth-Century London* (London, 1985).

Sen, Amartya, *On Ethics and Economics* (Oxford, 1987).

Shammas, Carole, *The Pre-Industrial Consumer in England and America* (Oxford, 1990).

Shapiro, Ian, 'Resources, Capacities, and Ownership: The Workmanship Ideal and Distributive Justice', in John Brewer and Susan Staves (eds), *Early Modern Conceptions of Property* (London, 1995), pp. 21–42.

Sharp, Pamela, 'Lace and Place: Women's Business in Occupational Communities in England, 1550–1950', *Women's History Review*, 19:2 (2010), pp. 283–306.

Sharpe, J. A., *Crime in Seventeenth-Century England: A County Study* (Cambridge, 1983).

Shaw, Jane, *Miracles in Englightenment England* (New Haven, 2006).

Shaw-Taylor, Leigh, 'Labourers, Cows, Common Rights and Parliamentary Enclosure: The Evidence of Contemporary Comment, c.1760–1810', *Past & Present*, 171 (2001), pp. 95–126.

Shepard, Alexandra, 'Manhood, Credit and Patriarchy in Early Modern England c.1580–1640', *Past & Present*, 167 (2000), pp. 75–106.

Shepard, Alexandra, *Meanings of Manhood in Early Modern England* (Oxford, 2003).

Shepard, Alexandra, and Withington, Phil (eds), *Communities in Early Modern England: Networks, Place, Rhetoric* (Manchester and New York, 2000).

Shepard, Alexandra, and Withington, Phil, 'Introduction: Communities in Early Modern England', in idem (eds), *Communities*, pp. 1–15.

Slack, Paul, *From Reformation to Improvement: Public Welfare in Early Modern England: The Ford Lectures* (Oxford, 1999).

Slack, Paul, 'Great and Good Towns, 1540–1700', in Peter Clark (ed.), *The Cambridge Urban History of Britain, Vol. 2: 1540–1840* (Cambridge, 2000), pp. 347–76.

Slack, Paul, 'Material Progress and the Challenge of Affluence in Seventeenth-Century England', *Economic History Review*, 62:3 (2009), pp. 576–603.

Slack, Paul, 'The Politics of Consumption and England's Happiness in the Later Seventeenth Century', *English Historical Review*, 122:497 (2007), pp. 609–31.

Slack, Paul, *Poverty and Policy in Tudor and Stuart England* (London, 1988).

Smith, Adam, *An Inquiry into the Nature and Causes of the Wealth of Nations* (London, 1776).

Smith, Chloe Wigston, '"Callico Madams": Servants, Consumption, and the Calico Crisis', *Eighteenth Century Life*, 31:2 (2007), pp. 29–55.

Smith, Richard, '"Modernization" and the Corporate Village Community in England: Some Sceptical Reflections', in Alan R. H. Baker and Derek Gregory (eds), *Explorations in Historical Geography: Interpretative Essays* (Cambridge, 1984), pp. 140–79.

Smith, S. R., 'The Ideal and Reality: Apprentice–Master Relationships in Seventeeth-Century London', *History of Education Quarterly*, 21 (1981), pp. 449–59.

Smith, S. R., 'The London Apprentices as 17th Century Adolescents', *Past & Present*, 61 (1973), pp. 149–61.

Snell, K. D. M., *Annals of the Labouring Poor: Social Change and Agrarian England, 1660–1900* (Cambridge, 1985).

Snell, K. D. M., *Parish and Belonging: Community, Identity, and Welfare in England and Wales, 1700–1950* (Cambridge, 2006).

Sommerville, C. J., *Popular Religion in Restoration England* (Gainesville, 1977).

Sommerville, C. J., *The Secularization of Early Modern England: From Religious Culture to Religious Faith* (Oxford and New York, 1992).

Spaeth, Donald, *The Church in an Age of Danger: Parson and Parishioners, 1660–1740* (Cambridge, 2000).

Spufford, Margaret, *Small Books and Pleasant Histories: Popular Fiction and Its Readership in Seventeenth-Century England* (London, 1981).

Spurr, John, '"Rational religion" in Restoration England', *Journal of the History of Ideas*, 49:4 (1988), pp. 563–85.

Spurr, John, *The Restoration Church of England, 1646–1689* (New Haven, 1991).

Statt, Daniel, *Foreigners and Englishmen: The Controversy over Immigration and Population, 1660–1760* (Newark, 1995).

Stevenson, John, *Popular Disturbances in England, 1700–1832* (2nd edn, London, 1992).

Stevenson, Laura Caroline, *Praise and Paradox: Merchants and Craftsmen in Elizabethan Literature* (Cambridge, 1984).

Stirk, Nigel, 'Arresting Ambiguity: The Shifting Geographies of a London Debtors' Sanctuary in the Eighteenth Century', *Social History*, 25:3 (2000), pp. 316–29.

Swanson, Scott, 'The Medieval Foundations of John Locke's Theory of Natural Rights: Rights of Subsistence and the Principle of Extreme Necessity', *History of Political Thought*, 18:3 (1997), pp. 399–459.

Swedberg, Richard, *Max Weber and the Idea of Economic Sociology* (Princeton, 1998).

Tadmor, Naomi, *Family and Friends in Eighteenth-Century England: Household, Kinship, and Patronage* (Cambridge and New York, 2001).

Tadmor, Naomi, *The Social Universe of the English Bible: Scripture, Society, and Culture in Early Modern England* (Cambridge, 2010).

Tawney, R. H., *The Agrarian Problem in the Sixteenth Century* (London, 1912).

Tawney, R. H., *Religion and the Rise of Capitalism* (1926; London, 1948).

Thirsk, Joan, 'New Crops and their Diffusion: Tobacco-Growing in 17th-Century England', in C. W. Chalklin and M. A. Havinden (eds), *Rural Change and Urban Growth, 1500–1800: Essays in English Regional History in Honour of W. G. Hoskins* (London, 1974), pp. 76–103.

Thomas, Keith, *The Ends of Life: Roads to Fulfilment in Early Modern England* (Oxford and New York, 2009).

Thomas, Keith, *Religion and the Decline of Magic* (Harmondsworth, 1973).

Thomas, P. J., *Mercantilism and the East India Trade* (London, 1963).

Thompson, E. P., *Customs in Common: Studies in Traditional Popular Culture* (New York, 1993).

Thompson, E. P., *The Making of the English Working Class* (1963; London, 1991).

Thompson, E. P., 'The Moral Economy of the English Crowd in the Eighteenth Century', *Past & Present*, 50 (1971), pp. 76–136.

Thompson, E. P., *The Poverty of Theory and Other Essays* (London, 1978).

Thompson, E. P., *Whigs and Hunters: The Origin of the Black Act* (London, 1990).

Thwaites, Wendy, 'The Assize of Bread in Eighteenth-Century Oxford', *Oxoniensia*, 51 (1986), pp. 171–81.

Thwaites, Wendy, 'The Corn Market and Economic Change: Oxford in the Eighteenth Century', *Midland History*, 16 (1991), pp. 103–25.

Tilley, Morris, *A Dictionary of Proverbs in England in the Sixteenth and Seventeenth Centuries* (Ann Arbor, 1950).

Tönnies, Ferdinand, *Community and Society*, Charles P. Loomis ed. and trans. (Mineola, 2002).

Tubach, Frederic, *Index Exemplorum: A Handbook of Medieval Religious Tales* (Helsinki, 1969).

Underdown, David, *Revel, Riot and Rebellion: Popular Politics and Culture in England, 1603–1660* (Oxford, 1985).

Unwin, George, *The Gilds and Companies of London* (London, 1908).

Unwin, George, *Industrial Organization in the Sixteenth and Seventeenth Centuries* (Oxford, 1904).

The Victoria Histories of the Counties of England (c.240 vols, 1899–).

Viner, Jacob, *The Role of Providence in the Social Order: An Essay in Intellectual History* (Philadelphia, 1972).

Waddell, Brodie, 'Economic Immorality and Social Reformation in English Popular Preaching, 1585–1625', *Cultural and Social History*, 5:2 (2008), pp. 165–82.

Waddell, Brodie, 'Governing England through the Manor Courts, 1550–1850', *Historical Journal*, 55:2 (2012), pp. 279–315.

Walker, D. P., *The Decline of Hell: Seventeenth-Century Discussions of Eternal Torment* (London, 1964).

Walker, Garthine, 'Expanding the Boundaries of Female Honour in Early Modern England', *Transactions of the Royal Historical Society*, 6th ser., 6 (1996), pp. 235–45.

Walker, Garthine, 'Keeping it in the Family: Crime and the Early Modern Household', in Berry and Foyster (ed.), *Family*, pp. 67–95.

Walker, Garthine, 'Modernization', in eadam (ed.), *Writing Early Modern History* (London, 2005), pp. 25–48.

Walsham, Alexandra, 'Miracles in Post-Reformation England', *Studies in Church History*, 41 (2005), pp. 273–306.

Walsham, Alexandra, *Providence in Early Modern England* (Oxford, 1999).

Walsham, Alexandra, 'The Reformation and "the Disenchantment of the World" Reassessed', *Historical Journal*, 51:2 (2008), pp. 497–528.

Walter, John, '"Abolishing Superstition with Sedition"? The Politics of Popular Iconoclasm in England, 1640–1642', *Past & Present*, 183 (2004), pp. 79–123.

Walter, John, *Crowds and Popular Politics in Early Modern England* (Manchester, 2006).

Walter, John, 'Faces in the Crowd: Gender and Age in the Early Modern Crowd', in Berry and Foyster (eds), *Family*, pp. 96–125.

Walter, John, 'Grain Riots and Popular Attitudes to the Law: Maldon and the Crisis of 1629', in Brewer and Styles (eds), *Ungovernable People*, pp. 47–84.

Walter, John, 'Public Transcripts, Popular Agency and the Politics of Subsistence in Early Modern England', in Braddick and Walter (eds), *Negotiating Power*, pp. 123–48.

Walter, John, 'A "rising of the people"? The Oxfordshire Rising of 1596', *Past & Present*, 107 (1985), pp. 90–143.

Walter, John, 'The Social Economy of Dearth in Early Modern England', in John Walter and Roger Schofield (eds), *Famine, Disease and the Social Order in Early Modern Society* (Cambridge, 1989), pp. 75–128.

Walter, John, and Wrightson, Keith, 'Dearth and the Social Order in Early Modern England', *Past & Present*, 71 (1976), pp. 22–42.

Wanklyn, Malcolm, 'The Bridgnorth Food Riots of 1693/4', *Transactions of the Shropshire Archaeological and Historical Society*, 68 (1993), pp. 99–102.

Ward, Joseph, 'Fictitious Shoemakers, Agitated Weavers and the Limits of Popular Xenophobia in Elizabethan England', in Charles Vigne and Randolph Littleton (eds), *From Strangers to Citizens: The Integration of Immigrant Communities in Britain, Ireland and Colonial America, 1550–1750* (Brighton, 2001), pp. 80–87.

Ward, Joseph, *Metropolitan Communities: Trade Guilds, Identity and Change in Early Modern London* (Stanford, CA, 1997).

Watt, Tessa, *Cheap Print and Popular Piety, 1550–1640* (Cambridge, 1991).

Weatherill, Lorna, *Consumer Behaviour and Material Culture in Britain, 1660–1760* (2nd edn, London, 1996).

Weber, Max, *Economy and Society: An Outline of Interpretative Sociology*, Guenther Roth and Claus Wittich eds (3 vols, New York, 1968).

Weber, Max, *The Protestant Ethic and the 'Spirit' of Capitalism, and Other Writings*, T. B. Bottomore and Maxilien Rubel eds (New York, 2002).

Whatley, Christopher, 'Scotland, England and "the Golden Ball": Putting Economics in the Union of 1707', *The Historian*, 51 (1996), pp. 9–13.

Whatley, Christopher, 'The Union of 1707, Integration and the Scottish Burghs: The Case of the 1720 Food Riots', *Scottish Historical Review*, 78:2 (1999), pp. 192–218.

Whyman, Susan, *Sociability and Power in Late-Stuart England: The Cultural Worlds of the Verneys, 1660–1720* (Oxford, 1999).

Whyte, Nicola, 'Landscape, Memory and Custom: Parish Identities, c.1550–1700', *Social History*, 32:2 (2007), pp. 166–86.

Williams, Dale, 'Morals, Markets and the English Crowd in 1766', *Past & Present*, 104 (1984), pp. 56–73.

Williams, Reymond, *The Country and the City* (Oxford, 1975).

Winchester, Angus, *The Harvest of the Hills: Rural Life in Northern England and the Scottish Borders, 1400–1700* (Edinburgh, 2000).

Withington, Phil, 'Citizens, Community and Political Culture in Restoration England', in Shepard and Withington (eds), *Communities*, pp. 134–55.

Withington, Phil, 'Company and Sociability in Early Modern England', *Social History*, 32:3 (2007), pp. 291–307.

Withington, Phil, *The Politics of Commonwealth: Citizens and Freemen in Early Modern England* (Cambridge, 2005).

Withington, Phil, 'Public Discourse, Corporate Citizenship, and State Formation in Early Modern England', *American Historical Review*, 112:4 (2007), pp. 1016–38.

Withington, Phil, *Society in Early Modern England: The Vernacular Origins of Some Powerful Ideas* (Cambridge, 2010).

Wood, Andy, 'Custom, Identity and Resistance: English Free Miners and their Law, c.1550–1800', in Griffiths, Fox, and Hindle (eds), *Experience of Authority* (Basingstoke, 1996), pp. 249–85.

Wood, Andy, 'Fear, Hatred and the Hidden Injuries of Class in Early Modern England', *Journal of Social History*, 39:3 (2006), pp. 803–26.

Wood, Andy, *The Politics of Social Conflict: The Peak Country, 1520–1770* (Cambridge, 1999).

Wood, Andy, *Riot, Rebellion and Popular Politics in Early Modern England* (Houndsmills, 2002).

Wood, Andy, 'Subordination, Solidarity and the Limits of Popular Agency in a Yorkshire Valley c.1596–1615', *Past & Present*, 193 (2006), pp. 41–72.

Woodward, Donald, 'The Determination of Wage Rates in the Early Modern North of England', *Economic History Review*, New Series, 47:1 (1994), pp. 22–43.

Woodward, Donald, 'Early Modern Servants in Husbandry Revisited', *Agricultural History Review*, 48:2 (2000), pp. 141–50.

Woodward, Donald, *Men at Work: Labourers and Building Craftsmen in the Towns of Northern England, 1450–1750* (Cambridge, 1995).

Woolf, Daniel, *The Social Circulation of the Past: English Historical Culture, 1500–1730* (Oxford, 2003).

Worden, Blair, 'The Question of Secularization', in Houston and Pincus (eds), *Nation Transformed*, pp. 20–40.

Wrightson, Keith, 'The "Decline of Neighbourliness" Revisited', in Norman Jones and Daniel Woolf (eds), *Local Identities in Late Medieval and Early Modern England* (Basingstoke, 2007), pp. 19–49.

Wrightson, Keith, *Earthly Necessities: Economic Lives in Early Modern Britain, 1470–1750* (London, 2002).

Wrightson, Keith, 'The Enclosure of English Social History', in Adrian Wilson (ed.), *Rethinking Social History: English Society, 1570–1920 and Its Interpretation* (Manchester, 1993), pp. 59–77.

Wrightson, Keith, *English Society, 1580–1680* (2nd edn, London, 2003).

Wrightson, Keith, 'Estates, Degrees, and Sorts: Changing Perceptions of Society in Tudor and Stuart England', in Penelope Corfield (ed.), *Language, History and Class* (Oxford, 1991), pp. 30–52.

Wrightson, Keith, 'Mutualities and Obligations: Changing Social Relationships in Early Modern England', *Proceedings of the British Academy*, 139 (2006), pp. 157–94.

Wrightson, Keith, and Levine, David, *Poverty and Piety in an English Village: Terling, 1525–1700* (2nd edn, Oxford, 1995).

Wrigley, E. A., and Schofield, R. S., *The Population History of England, 1541–1871* (2nd edn, Cambridge, 1989).

Young, Brian William, 'Religious History and the Eighteenth-Century Historian', *Historical Journal*, 43:3 (2000), pp. 849–68.

Yungblut, Laura, *Strangers are Settled Here Among Us: Policies, Perceptions and Presence of Aliens in Elizabethan England* (London, 1996).

Zaret, David, *Origins of Democratic Culture: Printing, Petitions and the Public Sphere in Early-Modern England* (Princeton, 2000).

Unpublished Secondary Sources

Ashby, Michael, 'Religion and the Governance of Consumption, 1675–1725' (M.A. thesis, University of Cambridge, 2011).

Walker, M. J., 'The Extent of Guild Control of Trades in England, c.1660–1820: A Study Based on a Sample of Provincial Towns and London Companies' (Ph.D. thesis, University of Cambridge, 1986).

Index

STUDIES IN EARLY MODERN CULTURAL,
POLITICAL AND SOCIAL HISTORY

XII

London's News Press and the Thirty Years War
Jayne E. E. Boys

Printed and bound by CPI Group (UK) Ltd, Croydon, CR0 4YY

23/04/2025

14661041-0003